Children and Youth in the Labour Process in Africa

Edited by

Osita Agbu

Council for the Development of Social Science Research in Africa

Council for the Development of Social Science Research in Africa
Avenue Cheikh Anta Diop, Angle Canal IV
BP 3304 Dakar, 18524, Senegal
Website: www.codesria.org

ISBN: 978-2-86978-251-8

Typesetter: Sériane Camara Ajavon

Cover Designer: Florent Loso Tonadio

Printed by Graphiplus, Dakar, Senegal

Distributed in Africa by CODESRIA

Distributed elsewhere by African Books Collective, Oxford, UK.
Website: www.africanbookscollective.com

The Council for the Development of Social Science Research in Africa (CODESRIA) is an independent organisation whose principal objectives are to facilitate research, promote research-based publishing and create multiple forums geared towards the exchange of views and information among African researchers. All these are aimed at reducing the fragmentation of research in the continent through the creation of thematic research networks that cut across linguistic and regional boundaries.

CODESRIA publishes a quarterly journal, *Africa Development*, the longest standing Africa-based social science journal; *Afrika Zamani*, a journal of history; the *African Sociological Review*; the *African Journal of International Affairs*; *Africa Review of Books* and the *Journal of Higher Education in Africa*. The Council also co-publishes the *Africa Media Review*; *Identity, Culture and Politics: An Afro-Asian Dialogue*; *The African Anthropologist* and the *Afro-Arab Selections for Social Sciences*. The results of its research and other activities are also disseminated through its Working Paper Series, Green Book Series, Monograph Series, Book Series, Policy Briefs and the CODESRIA Bulletin. Select CODESRIA publications are also accessible online at www.codesria.org.

CODESRIA would like to express its gratitude to the Swedish International Development Cooperation Agency (SIDA/SAREC), the International Development Research Centre (IDRC), the Ford Foundation, the MacArthur Foundation, the Carnegie Corporation, the Norwegian Agency for Development Cooperation (NORAD), the Danish Agency for International Development (DANIDA), the French Ministry of Cooperation, the United Nations Development Programme (UNDP), the Netherlands Ministry of Foreign Affairs, the Rockefeller Foundation, FINIDA, the Canadian International Development Agency (CIDA), IIEP/ADEA, OECD, IFS, OXFAM America, UN/UNICEF and the Government of Senegal for supporting its research, training and publication programmes.

Contents

Contributors iv

1. Introduction: Children and Youth in the Labour Process
Osita Agbu 1

2. Child Labour in Contemporary Africa: Issues and Challenges
Osita Agbu 11

3. Getting Them Young: Child Labour in Ikot Ekpene from a Historical Perspective
Mfom Umoren Ekpo-Otu 21

4. Economic Crises and Child Trafficking in Nigeria: A Comparative Analysis of the 1930s and 1990s
Rasheed Olaniyi 35

5. Children Exploitation in the Labour Process: Empirical Exposition from Ile-Ife, Nigeria
Olu Torimiro 63

6. Internal Child Trafficking in Nigeria: Transcending Legal Borders
Oluwatoyin O. Oluwaniyi 81

7. Le Phénomène 'Vidomégon': une autre forme de Traffic d'Enfant dans la ville de Cotonou
A. Ludovic Couao-Zotti 111

8. Problématique du Travail des Enfants et les Stratégies de Survie au Congo Brazzaville
Ngodi Etanislas 133

9. Étude sur le Travail des Enfants dans L'Agriculture: Région de Meknès – Tafilalet, Maroc
Hassan Khalouki 151

10. Problématique de la Prostitution Infanto-Juvénile à Kinshasa: Cas des 'Tshel'
Jose Mvuezolo Bazonzi 175

11. Enfants et jeunes dans le métier de la danse au sein des groupes musicaux modernes à Kinshasa
Leon Tsambu Bulu 197

12. Conclusion
Osita Agbu 225

Contributors

A. Ludovic Couao-Zotti is a researcher based in Cotonou, Republic of Benin.

Etanislas Ngodi est Doctorant en Histoire et Civilisations Africaines, Faculté des Lettres et des Sciences Humaines, Université Marien Ngouabi, Brazzaville, Congo.

Hassan Khalouki est Professeur à la Faculté des Sciences Juridiques, Economiques et Sociales, Université Moulay Ismail, Meknès.

José Mvuelo Bazonzi est Chercheur en Economie et Développment, Centre d'Etudes Politiques (CEP), Université de Kinshasa, Kinshasa, R.D. Congo.

Leon Tsambu Bulu est Chercheur au Centre d'Etudes Politiques, Chef de Travaux au Département de Sociologie & Anthropologie, Faculté des Sciences, Administratives et Politiques, Université de Kinshasa, R.D. Congo.

Mfon Umoren Ekpo-Otu is a Lecturer at the Department of Political Science, University of Port Harcourt, Port Harcourt, Nigeria.

Olu Torimiro is a Senior Lecturer in the Department of Agricultural Extension and Rural Sociology, Obafemi Awolowo University, Ile-Ife, Nigeria.

Oluwatoyin O. Oluwaniyi is an Assistant Lecturer in the Department of Policy and Strategic Studies, College of Business and Social Sciences, Covenant University, Sango-Ota, Ogun State, Nigeria.

Osita Agbu is an Associate Research Professor at the Nigerian Institute of International Affairs, Lagos, Nigeria. He co-directed the CODESRIA Child and Youth Studies Institute, 2004.

Rasheed Olaniyi is a researcher based at the Centre for Research and Documentation, Kano, Nigeria.

1

Introduction: Children and Youth in the Labour Process

Osita Agbu

Among the many problems facing the African continent is that of ensuring that the African child has a meaningful future. But for us to even begin to imagine this future implies the necessity of understanding the plight of children and the youth in Africa today – in particular, in the labour process. Africa is a youthful continent, but so far occupies little policy environment. On the subject matter of children and youth, it is very important to examine the issues from the perspective of the African environment, and in particular, the existential conditions of the children. The social and economic environment of an African child is completely different from that of an European child, for example. In general terms, whereas children are supposed to be sheltered, protected or be in school, in many countries in Africa they are rather exposed to the vagaries of eking out a living in a largely adult world. This is not, however, to say that children do not naturally assist with work or understudy their parents in the process of work in the various societies. An observation is that there have been studies about young people, but not what the young people think of themselves and their role in the labour process. The expectation is that some of the case studies in this volume will bring this into sharp relief.

The International Labour Organization (ILO) estimates that around the world, some 250 million children between the ages of 5 and 14 work for a living. Almost half, some 120 million, work full time, every day, all year round. African children constitute 32 per cent of this number, about 80 million, and there could be a surge to over 100 million by the year 2015 as a result of the increasing number of impoverished people and inadequate economic growth in the continent. Also, as many as 70 per cent toil in dangerous environments unsuitable for children. Of the 250 million children concerned, some 50–60 million are between 5 and 11 years old and work, by definition, in hazardous circumstances, considering their age and vulnerability. Many more are hidden from view, exploited in virtual slavery.

Increased awareness of these facts has prompted a global mobilization unlike any seen in recent memory. Many governments, workers, enterprises, religious bodies, non-governmental organizations (NGOs) and individuals the world over have recognized the need to seek new, more effective ways to combat child labour and to eliminate its most unacceptable manifestations. This is a worldwide phenomenon, but with serious and troubling manifestations in Africa and Asia. It has been shown that child labour occurs mainly in the semi-formal and informal sectors of the economy. Most instances of child labour in Africa are found in the informal sector. Often, children could be observed on the streets as vendors, car washers, touts, scavengers, beggars, head-load carriers, feet-washers and bus conductors. In cottage industries and mechanical workshops, children also work as apprentices in various crafts or as traders such as in weaving, tailoring, catering, hairdressing, vulcanizing and auto repair (Oloko 1997:48).

It is increasingly clear that children and the youth today play significant roles in the labour process in Africa. However, what have not been well interrogated are the theoretical moorings and the dynamic nature of the roles they play, which oftentimes are inhumane, exploitative and degrading for the victims. Generally, it appears that children are forced by the economic needs of their parents to engage in different modes of child labour. The crises associated with economic depression and the character of the capitalist mode of reproduction such as increasing unemployment, rural–urban migration, lack of access to education, poverty and the erosion of the extended family system have singly and collectively made children, who ordinarily should be engaged in learning and/or apprenticeship within family limits, become instruments and commodities in the labour process. Our perspective in this volume draws from both historical and economic analyses in explaining the problem, which in this case points to the fact that children and the youth in Africa are increasingly being forced by economic and other unpleasant circumstances, including political adversities, into becoming human cargo. Indeed, there is a sense in which war could be seen as a continuation of the labour process. When war goes on for a long time, it becomes normal, and children and youth are central to understanding wars in Africa.

The mainstream literature mostly published by international organizations and NGOs, though relevant, needs to be approached with detachment in order to better understand the African situation. The situation of children and the youth in Africa cannot be separated from the poverty and wars that becloud Africa, which create not only refugees but also economic migrants. Often economic migrants including children become part and parcel of a labour process predicated on devising 'coping mechanisms' in an era of harsh economic downturns occasioned by the negative dynamics of the global economy. It is therefore important for us to understand the relationship between the youth segment of African societies and the social relations existing at both national and continental levels. This is because existing social relations in society often determine what is produced or trafficked (the commodity), and where, when and how. Note that this process is replicated at two levels: first is at the level of social relations within individual African countries, and second at the level of global relations of production and exchange between the rich and poor countries of the world. Often the rich or dominant elite, together with the ruling class, determine what is produced or what serves as a commodity, where and when. Of course, they can not do this on their own, but are influenced or forced to act in a particular manner as a result of their linkages to the global capitalist system. It is therefore not surprising that it is the youth from the poor regions of the world that are trafficked to the richer regions for forced or child prostitution, sex tourism and entertainment, pornography and organ harvesting as the case may be. Organ harvesting, sometimes referred to as organ laundering, involves the trafficking of humans for the purpose of selling their organs for money. This shows the barbaric dimension that unbridled globalization and consumerism have attained.

For many African countries, it is a situation in which the ruling elite knowingly or unknowingly falls into the trap of the global dictates of consumerism. State policies that do not recognize or articulate the interests of the youth are usually designed and implemented, with dire consequences for all. It is therefore important that we understand the present character of the political elite in Africa, especially in the context of globalization. Their policy prescriptions under the guise of privatization and deregulation, with embargos on employment and so on, have served to undermine whatever welfarist measures could have modulated youth restiveness, unemployment and exploitation, and therefore the recourse to their becoming global commodities.

It appears that for the elite and supposed elders in the society to create and recreate their material needs, they inadvertently embrace the mantra of globalization without designing innovative ways of ameliorating its negative tendencies. This then creates not just a conducive environment, but equally justifies the exploitation of children and youth in the labour process as indicated in the scope of trafficking of women and children in Africa. The International Labour Organization (ILO) estimates that of the 246 million children presently engaged as child labourers worldwide, about 179 million of these are exposed to the worst forms of exploitation (*CODESRIA Bulletin*, 1&2, 2004). Suffice it to note that public policy also reflects the social relations of production in a particular society. And in a situation in which these policies are neither pro-poor nor do they address the problems of the youth, the result is usually a rise in youth restiveness, social delinquency and outright criminality either as agents or victims. Therefore, in addition to re-examining the post-colonial character of the state in Africa, and the social and psychological dimensions, the fact of globalization should as of necessity be factored into any effort at understanding the contemporary problem of child and youth exploitation in the labour process. It is a labour process largely influenced by the dynamics of the global economy that cares very little for the disadvantaged countries, and hence the disadvantaged masses of Africa, including its children.

Overall, it is our expectation that this volume will contribute to creating more awareness about the problem of children and youth in the labour process, and contribute also to the richness of the discourse concerning the development problems of children and the youth in Africa. Even the concept of the labour process is contestable, especially in view of the fact that the labour process has undergone transformation. Questions have arisen concerning our understanding of the 'site of labour', because new sites of labour are emerging. We should be able to interrogate inherited conceptual instruments – what, for instance, is the heuristic value of 'child labour' as conceptualized and used by the international organizations? We need to keep an open mind, for us to be able to proffer reasonable suggestions for addressing the problem of children in the labour process. There is an international geo-strategic conception of child labour, of which we must be careful, as social order is constantly in transformation.

The labour process in a sense could be understood as the sum of relationships and activities aimed directly or indirectly at earning a living. This could be at the domestic, community or national level. However, does this mean that activities not involving payment are not child labour? To what extent can children be allowed independence of action? Let us also note that the category of children is not necessarily a homogeneous group. Hence, child labour should be approached from a multi-pronged perspective. One way to intervene should be to enlighten and educate our political elite and decision-makers as to the deficiencies of their economic and social policies, which often do not incorporate the interests of the youths, mainly owing to the fact that they are seldom consulted. Sometimes it is also the case that governments lack the capacity to address the problems of the young. This lack of capacity provides a fertile ground for the proliferation of all sorts of informalization for survival. Again, deference to the dictates of global institutions like the World Bank, the IMF and the World Trade Organization (WTO) on privatization, deregulation and downsizing of the workforce should ideally be given with caution as they often project the interests of the powerful, whose interests may not necessarily coincide with those of the weaker countries. Though sometimes ignorant of the uses to which they have been put, these organizations are by design and ownership fundamentally agents of unbridled globalization whose prescriptions have in the main only contributed to the impoverishment of the African masses and the alienation of African youths. The necessity for innovative state–society partnerships through conscious intervention at ensuring youth empowerment and welfare in Africa cannot therefore be overemphasized.

Generally, there is some theoretical confusion about how to understand and explain the problem of child labour (*CODESRIA Bulletin* 2004:53). It is, however, our expectation that by the time one goes through this book, one would have been able to make some sense out of this from the very many predicaments of children in the labour market and their various implications. While children have always worked in African societies, the increasing poverty in sub-Saharan Africa since the 1970s and the various wars have driven millions of children into types of labour that are exploitative, hazardous and prejudicial to their welfare and development. Poverty, along with certain cultural traits, has resulted in the exploitation of child labour, while middlemen have exploited the desperation and ignorance of parents, particularly in the rural areas, to procure children for commercial trafficking.

Theoretically speaking, no single general picture of child labour can be based on its practice in one particular form alone. It necessarily has to be related to those shifts or changes in local context and to change over time – technological (how far child labour was useful to the employers); ideological (the rise of domestic ideology and its impact on both ruling and working classes); economic (the organization of labour markets and the need of the family for the child's economic contribution; whether that contribution was in cash, kind or labour); and political (the role of the state intervention through protective legislation and the introduction of compulsory schooling) (Devin 1982:650).

In terms of legislation, the ILO since its inception in 1909 has been in the forefront of designing and encouraging legislation that will help protect children and the youth in the labour process, both globally and nationally. The minimum Age (Industry) Convention (No. 5) and the Night Work of Young Persons (Industry) Convention (No. 6) were the first in a series of what would soon become a substantial list of conventions and resolutions aimed at abolishing child labour and establishing safe working conditions for young workers (Elder & Schmidt 2004:23). Other general legislation includes the Declaration of the Rights of the Child, adopted by the General Assembly on 20 November 1989; the Declaration on the Protection of Women and Children in Emergency and Armed Conflict and ILO Convention 182; the Convention Concerning the Prohibition and Immediate Action for the Elimination of the Worst Forms of Child Labour, Adopted by the Conference at the 87th Session in Geneva on 17 June 1999. For instance, the Convention on the Rights of the Child, Article 32, recognizes 'the right of the child to be protected from economic exploitation and from performing any work that is likely to be hazardous or to interfere with the child's health or physical, mental, spiritual, moral or social development'. States parties to the convention are required to take legislative, administrative, social and educational measures to ensure the implementation of this right, including enacting provisions for minimum ages for admission to employment, regulation of hours of work and conditions of employment, and penalties and other sanctions to ensure effective enforcement. Also, Article 35, of this convention stated: 'States parties shall take all appropriate national, bilateral and multilateral measures to prevent the abduction of, the sale of or traffic in children for any purpose or in any form'. In short, efforts at curbing child labour and its related dimensions through legislation are not in short supply; the problem has been the tendency for national governments to remain aloof in the implementation of this legislation.

We should note that ILO's prescriptions on child rights have come under criticism, especially from the developing world. Its prescriptions are perceived as embodying the standardization of western notions of childhood and have led to attempts at distinguishing child work from child labour. In spite of the 1999 Convention No. 182 on the Elimination of the Worst Aspects of Child Labour, this problem continue to pose fundamental challenges of definition and distinction. Take, for example, the criticisms relating to the call for a re-examination of the role of children as consumers of economic value and identifying who the beneficiaries of child labour are.

The generally common conclusion that child labour is contextual requires an analytical framework that recognizes specific contexts including the socio-cultural political contexts. Since socio-cultural environments differ, we should be careful to avoid unnecessary labelling of all children engaged in the labour process as doing 'exploitative work', at least within the African context. Therefore, understanding the social construction of child labour is imperative in responding to the real cases of children involved in an exploitative labour setting. Indeed, the recognition of the contextuality of child labour aids the assessor in distinguishing between the acceptable work that children ordinarily perform and child labour. Perhaps, a strict regime or categorization based on the African experience of what we understand as the exploitation of children in the labour process or of deprived children will help clarify the conceptual quagmire in which we find ourselves. While attention should be paid to the pull factors that give rise to child labour, like the economic benefits derivable from it, the nature and depth of the existing institutional framework also deserves a revisit. In perusing the substantial body of information on this subject, it is important that our definition of the working child in Africa is understood, not necessarily from preconceived notions and experiences of other peoples, but also from the African world-view and the lived experiences of the African child in a globalizing century.

This book therefore aims at understanding the sources, dynamics and consequences of the exploitation of the labour power of children and the youth in contemporary Africa. Participants at the Child and Youth Studies Institute 2004, organized by CODESRIA, which resulted in this book, were encouraged to undertake a critical revisit of the literature that had been produced on children and the youth in the labour process and contribute, in a substantial way, to questioning existing knowledge, creating new knowledge and proffering solutions to the manifestations of child labour based largely on case studies. Since child labour is a universal problem, the solutions will necessarily have some commonalities, but still there will be peculiarities in terms of the understanding and prioritization of the various types of child labour and the possible solutions.

The Institute, directed by myself and Pamela Reynolds of Michigan State University, was indeed able to dissect and expose the grave dimensions of child labour practices in contemporary Africa. Others who contributed to the very lively discussions on the subject included Ibrahim Abdullah, Evariste Tshishimbi and Ijeoma Nwachukwu. The Executive Secretary of CODESRIA, Adebayo Olukoshi, at the inception of the Institute, presented broad, but at the same time incisive, views on the question of children and youth in the labour process in Africa. He highlighted issues of how the labour process has undergone transformation in Africa and its diverse implications for the children and the youth, the site of labour and the transition taking place in Africa, the inherited conceptual instruments that have been popularized by international organizations, the broad socio-cultural contexts in which the labour process takes place and the international geo-strategic dimension of children in the labour process. His views were well received and thus set the tone for the gruelling days ahead that focused on these matters. Within the first two weeks, critical aspects of the subject matter were put under the microscope, namely: the meaning of the labour process, and who is a child and who is a youth? Child trafficking and women trafficking, child work as against child labour, types of child labour in contemporary Africa, the anthropology of labour/children/youth, conceptual and methodological issues and conflict, and the labour process itself.

The Organisation of the Book

This book is basically designed around identified issues of importance concerning children and youth in the labour process in Africa, beginning with methodological concerns and ending with case studies from different parts of Africa. The case studies come mainly from West, Central and North Africa.

In this first chapter, we review the theme and seek answers concerning the increase in the number of children in the labour process in Africa and why the enacted legislation has not been effective in checking the abusive tendencies inherent in the labour process.

In Chapter 2, the dichotomy between child labour as against domestic work in Africa is discussed and the various types and hazards of child labour outlined, observing that though child labour is global in its manifestation, it is however of serious concern in Africa owing to the kinds of labour that African children engage in, which largely occurs in and around family households, and in informal arrangements.

Mfom Umoren Ekpo-Otu in Chapter 3 carries out a study of child labour in Ikot Ekpene, Nigeria and takes as her point of intervention a historical excursion into the world of child labour in time and space. The study traces the dynamics of child labour and culture in the exploitation of the labour process of children in Ikot Ekpene. Against the background of colonial exploitation, the author posits that the complex social and economic relations occasioned by colonial imperialism effected a systematic exploitation of children's labour power in Nigeria. Not surprisingly, she is interested in knowing what feeds child labour at Ikot Ekpene, a community long associated with giving out children to third parties, and also in tracing the evolution of this phenomenon from colonial to contemporary times.

In examining economic crises and child trafficking in Nigeria, Rasheed Olaniyi in Chapter 4 embarks on a comparative analysis of the child trafficking in Nigeria in the 1930s and 1990s as a way of determining the underlying factors. He argues that the history of child trafficking in Nigeria was intertwined with social insecurity that followed colonial conquest and attained its apogee in the depression of the 1930s. His study interrogates the historical trajectory of child trafficking, and the interface between economic crises and child trafficking within which the economic exploitation of children and the youth occurs. He does this through a comparative historical interrogation of the economic regimes of the 1930s and 1990s.

In Chapter 5, Olu Torimiro offers an empirical exposition on child exploitation in the labour process, using a Nigerian case study. Utilizing various empirical variables in his analysis, he came to the conclusion that almost all the children studied were engaged and exploited in hazardous economic activities in the town of Ile-Ife. He notes that the situation is not likely to stop if the current household economic condition persists. He believes that the types of exploitation witnessed have implications for the welfare of the children and human capacity-building in that community.

In Chapter 6, Oluwatoyin Oluwaniyi examines internal child trafficking in Nigeria from the perspective of transcending the international legal framework of understanding. Noting that though the problem arose out of the larger context of cultural, political, social and economic conditions, these are problems predominantly caused by adults but disproportionately borne by children. Oluwatoyin focuses her study on internal trafficking of children for domestic work by adults. Based on fieldwork in Nigeria, the author explores the dynamics of international trafficking and puts forward recommendations for the eradication of the problem.

Ludovic Couao-Zotti in his study in Chapter 7 entitled, 'Le Phénomene "Vidomegon": une autre forme de Traffic d'enfants dans la ville de Cotonou', discusses the phenomenon of 'Vidomégon' in Cotonou, Republic of Benin. He studies the characteristics of children who are put under placement in third families, the mechanisms for the placement and the various legislation against child trafficking. He observes that the problem of 'Vi-domégon' (child living with someone else) had for long been ignored in the Benoinoise society, whereas the practice is characterized by transitional tendencies towards international child trafficking. From his study, it is necessary to determine at what point the placement of children in third families as practised in Benin become child exploitation and child trafficking.

Other contributions in this volume come from the Francophone African countries of Congo Brazzaville, Morocco and Democratic Republic of Congo (DRC). Ngodi Etanislas' study in Chapter 8 entitled 'Problématique du Travail des Enfants et les Stratégies de Survie au Congo Brazzaville', examines the problem of child labour and survival strategies in Congo Brazzaville. Hassan Khalouki, in his contribution in Chapter 9, is concerned with child labour in agriculture in the region of Meknes in Morocco. His work is entitled 'Etude sur le Travail des Enfants dans l'Agriculture: Region de Meknès – Tafilalet, Maroc'. Jose Bazonzi's interesting study in Chapter 10, entitled 'Problematique de la Prostitution Infanto-Juvenile á Kinshasa: Cas des "Tshel"', focuses on the problem of child/adolescent prostitution in Kinshasa, popularly referred to as 'Tshel'. It is a phenomenon that is closely associated with poverty in a post-conflict environment. In his contribution in Chapter 11 entitled, 'Enfants et Jeunes dans le Metier de la Danse et du Spectacle Populaires à Kinshasa', another interesting study from a post-conflict situation, Leon Tsambu Bulu examines the increasingly troublesome phenomenon of children and youth being exploited in the music industry in D.R. Congo. The last two studies from D.R. Congo indicate that post-conflict environments often throw up challenging problems of survival for children, the youth and women. New social issues arise that require not only proper identification and understanding by governments, social scientists and civil society including NGOs, but also innovative ways of seeking solutions.

The last chapter is the conclusion, which attempts to make some sense out of the findings from the case studies, firstly, in terms of understanding the underlying factors and dimensions of the problem and, secondly, in presenting possible ways, depending on circumstances, of addressing some of the problems associated with children and youth in the labour process in Africa.

By and large, the expectation from the presentation of this volume is that by the time readers go through some of these case studies, the situation of children and the youth in the labour process in Africa will become clearer, thereby paving the way for more effective national and global policies aimed at addressing the problem. The findings from the case studies taken from various parts of Africa are the strongest statement being made by this book, and attest to the commonality of the problems facing the African child in the labour process in the twenty-first century.

References

CODESRIA, 2004, 'Children and Youth in the Labour Process', *CODESRIA Bulletin*, Nos 1 & 2.

Devin, A., 1982, 'Child Labour, the Working-Class Family and Domestic Ideology in 19th Century Britain', *Development and Change* 13:633–652.

Elder, S. and Schmidt, D., 2004, *Global Employment Trends for Youth: An Analysis of Current Labour Trends of Young People*, Geneva: International Labour Organization.

ILO Convention 182 – *Convention Concerning the Prohibition and Immediate Action for the Elimination of the Worst Forms of Child Labour Adopted by the Conference at the 87th Session*, Geneva, 17 June 1999.

International Labour Organization, 1999, *A New Tool to Combat, the Worst Forms of Child Labour*, ILO Convention 182, Geneva: ILO.

Oloko, S. B. A., 1997, *The Hidden Work Force – Child Domestic Labour: A New Tool to Combat the Worst Forms of Child Labour*, Geneva: International Labour Organization.

UNICEF/FOS, 1997, *The Progress of Nigerian Children*, Lagos: African Book Builders Ltd.

2

Child Labour in Contemporary Africa: Issues and Challenges

Osita Agbu

Introduction

In Africa, children have always been involved in one form of domestic work or the other, oftentimes not necessarily exploitative and therefore not worrisome. However, in the Africa of today, it appears that children and the youth generally have been sucked into a world of exploitative labour, which in an extreme way creates a vicious cycle of poverty, generating hopelessness and reproducing poverty in a systemic manner. Indeed, the long-term implication of this phenomenon is frightful. Perhaps this is why many have expressed fears about the kind of future that awaits the African child.

In the Africa of the past, it used to be that work was a way of life, and not a means only of earning wages. Children were often involved in the work of their parents, and usually inherited the work. Even now, it is still common in many parts of Africa even for children who go to school to be involved in some form of work activity. This may be keeping shop for father or mother, hawking goods, working on the farm or similar occupations. In the eastern part of Nigeria, for instance, it is a common practice for male children to be apprenticed to traders from an early age, in preference to going to school. The child usually works for a 'master', learning the details of the business over a number of years. When the young man is ready for 'freedom', the 'master' is obliged to 'settle' him by providing the capital for him to set up his own business. In fact, some of the most prominent names in commerce from this part of Nigeria today came through this system (Olugbile 1998:29). This is not, however, to say that this is a good practice, especially when the child or youth is denied formal education and the joy of being a child. Indeed, sometimes the 'master' fails to 'settle' the apprentice, offering some reason(s) why this is not possible.

In terms of historical progression of the legislation on labour based on experience, Europe happens to be the initial theatre. In Europe, labour was initially not seen as a threat to child welfare, but rather a means of learning and socialization, as also existed in Africa. However, the rampant use of under-aged children sometimes as young as three or four years, and following the Reformation of the seventeenth century and the Industrial Revolution of the eighteenth and nineteenth centuries, attitudes were forced to change. The result is today articulated in the United Nations Conventions on the Rights of the Child (CRC). However, the legal definition of the child as seen from the legal documents is not wholly acceptable in the African context, even in today's world. This is because the environment and lived experiences of the African child are different from those of the European child. African children are required to perform adult roles even at tender ages as a result of increasing threats to survival arising from the negative aspects of liberalization and economic globalization.

The point that stares us in the face in Africa is that child labour has become neither a cultural nor a socio-economic phenomenon, but a contemporary problem of grave dimensions, in which the long-term effect is simply scary. This chapter intends to examine the various dimensions of this situation, with emphasis on the types and hazards of child labour. At the same time, it notes the various legislation put in place at the global and national levels towards addressing this universal problem, and the challenges it poses.

Child Labour and Domestic Work in Africa: Conceptual Clarification

It is important for us *ab initio* to clarify the meanings of whom and what we think a child is, who a youth is, and the distinction between child labour and domestic work or child work as the case may be. According to Oloko (1997:4), the definition of a child in the term 'child labour' made by the International Labour Organization (ILO), especially in Convention 138 of 1976, is 'persons below 15 years'. Subsequently, the United Nations Convention on the Rights of the Child (CRC) and the OAU Charter on the Rights of the Child in Articles 1 and 2 respectively, define a child as 'a person below 18 years old, unless, under the applicable law, maturity is attained earlier'. For our purposes in this volume, we should consider a child to be someone below the age of 18 years. This is also the universally acceptable age at which an individual is allowed the franchise. Again, it could be said that a child is someone who is not an adult, and inversely, an adult is someone who is not a child. But, the above perspective is only one side of the coin; the other side draws its view from the premise that being a child is socially constructed. From this angle, being a child is not necessarily biological. So, the issue is not necessarily about distinguishing who is or who is not a child, but rather should be the criminalization of the use of children in the labour process. Child labour can only be meaningfully understood in relation to exploitation. Therefore, definitions of the child could be socio-economic, biological, cultural or even functional. The functional perspective is in terms of the types of jobs that children do. Again, children not being in school is a form of exploitation, and as far as a child is under protection, the person is still a child. The category of a child begins to make more sense in relation to functions and in relation to adults.

On the other hand, the term child labour refers to any type of paid, unpaid or exploitative work that places the interests of the beneficiary above those of the child, and is detrimental to the physical, mental, social, educational or moral development of the child (Oloko 1997:48). To be precise, this means that child labour is the engagement on a regular basis of children in some productive or income-yielding activities to which the primary beneficiaries are persons other than themselves. Child labour basically connotes any physical or mental exertion undertaken wholly or in part by any person below the age of 18 years with a view to some reward, which could be in cash or in kind for the person, or any other person. Further, it embraces any work carried out by children that endangers their health or safety and which meddles with, prevents or slows down the child's education and development.

However, we do know that in Africa, children have always worked as part of their socialization process, often assuming adult roles through imitating, copying or some sort of apprenticeship. This socialization was not considered child labour. In Africa, the socialization of work is important and is normal. The socialization process usually takes place within the extended family, underpinned by the basic philosophy that a child belongs to the whole community and not just to the nuclear family. It is this communal world-view and ownership of the child that justifies the placement of children in third families within the extended family. But while this worked relatively well in the past, at present, with the increasing transformation from communal living in Africa to an individualistic capitalist survivalist orientation for many an African, the child has also become a commodity, and survival invariably has become a greater objective than that of enhancing the welfare of children within the society. Perhaps, this condition gave rise to the abundant literature on the notion of agency. The agency literature is more dominant in the discourse encapsulated in the writings and releases of international organizations such as the ILO and UNICEF. The literature is beginning to shape conceptions of the world of youth, and needs to be deconstructed. The approach is guided by the need to protect children. The dominant paradigms are not surprisingly Euro-centric, whereas the experiences of children differ around the world. However, the fact remains that the child is involved in a relationship that contributes substantially to shaping his or her world-view. A common conception of childhood is that it is a period of irresponsibility, but this is not really true. As earlier mentioned, childhood is socially constructed, and should be viewed from the perspective of the child. It is a transitory stage to adulthood. Youth-hood is a transition to adulthood. However, for the purposes of analysis, youth implies a person that is supposedly independent, and preferably between the ages of 18 to 35 years. This, however, should be against the understanding that contexts differ.

Understanding child labour should also imply understanding the sociology of work as it manifests in a particular context. While adulthood can be described as a period of responsibility and of control, childhood may not necessarily be a period of dependency, and some children may actually make up their minds not to be dependent on people, and therefore do not see what they do as being exploited.

Often in our study of the complexities of child studies we fail to capture and appreciate the transition from childhood to youth and to adulthood.

The literature indeed indicates that it is possible to draw a distinction between 'child labour' and 'domestic work' (Verlet 2000, Oloko 1997). According to Verlet (2000:69), 'domestic work' refers to the everyday tasks children have always done for the general maintenance of the family unit and as part of the normal run of socialization. 'Child labour', on the other hand, differs in that it oversteps the bounds of socially acceptable norms and uses. Furthermore, the end purpose of child labour is monetary gain. Between these two poles, children are exposed to a wide range of varying degrees and conditions of domestic work or exploitation, which to all intents and purposes leads to pauperization. This is not a case of gradation but degradation; domestic work very easily progressively slips into tougher forms of exploitation that tend to remove children from their family milieu, from the lands and life paths of childhood, and cast them on the labour market. Usually culture and/or domestic ideology tend to disguise and legitimate such changes. Some of the criteria for determining when child work becomes child labour include the following: full-time work at an early age, working for long hours, severe and stressful working conditions, deprivation, working under physical strain, lack of access to education and inadequate remuneration. Quite often, a child's access to the labour market is brokered by a family friend, parent, relation or a middleman. Channels of recruitment and exploitation techniques all capitalize on bonds of kinship and friendship, even if the former are often fictitious and the latter dubious (Schlemmer 2000).

Oloko (1997), also distinguishes between child labour and child work. From her perspective, child labour, as we saw earlier, is work that is essentially exploitative and injurious to the physical, social, cognitive and moral development of the child. And this occurs when children, especially young ones, are exposed to long hours of work in a dangerous or unhealthy environment, with too much responsibility for their age and at the expense of their schooling. Child work, on the other hand, is work in which the primary emphasis is on learning, training and socialization. As such, the work schedule is flexible, tends to be responsive to the developing capacity of the child and encourages his or her participation in appropriate aspects of the decision-making process.

But, why do children work at all? Children work for various reasons, but more so for survival and as a way of assisting their parents and family economically. This is especially so against the backdrop of crisis in the educational system, in the national economies of African countries, and increasing rate of divorce in the continent, all of which were not present some fifty years ago. It suffices to add that globalization has led to the increase in poverty in Africa, especially poverty of the family, with negative implications for children. It is therefore important to observe that African countries are now looking around for a credible philosophy of development, one that should not get lost in the globalization *tsunami* sweeping away most ideologies in the world.

Child labour is therefore exploitative, oftentimes for economic benefits to the older party, and basically plays on the naivety and powerlessness of the child. It is universally unacceptable, and global action is necessary to pressure national governments into taking action against this inhumane practice. The experience in Africa is that child work is often transformed into child labour, especially in the urban centres, with servant children populating many households. The notion of abuse is still important in addressing child labour. The kind of work the child does is important in identifying child labour. On the other hand, attempts to define abuse or exploitation should be socially determined and relevant to the particular society. Hence, there is the need to revisit the international conventions on children and the labour process with a view to capturing the different experiences of the children. There is a need to contextualize the instruments. In addition, there is undue emphasis on child labour to the detriment of the attention that should have been paid to the youth. There appears to be a contested space between childhood and adulthood, called adolescence in western societies, that should be further interrogated in Africa of the twenty-first century.

Types and Hazards of Child Labour

Generally, in terms of empirical information on the nature of child labour in Africa, the data is quite limited in respect of the nature of work environment, length and timing of work, allocation of workloads between children of different ages and gender. Indeed, there is no agreement on how many hours of work denote 'child labour'. Preliminary observations based on national-level data show that child labour rates in various African countries have no systematic correlation with the level of poverty. In fact, child labour rates positively correlate with the proportion of people who live and work in rural areas. As variously observed, child labour occurs mainly in the informal and semi-formal sector, where children are found working at construction sites, on streets as vendors, car washers, touts, scavengers, beggars, head-load carriers, bus conductors, prostitutes, child soldiers and domestic helps. They also work as apprentices in various crafts or trades like weaving, tailoring, catering, hairdressing, mechanics, in model and fashion houses, and as dancers in troupes and musical groups.

However, observations show that child labour arrangements vary greatly in Africa. According to World Bank findings, the more common types include:

- Domestic child labour performed in one's own household, or the household of relatives of other families;
- Farm work on the family farm or at commercial plantations; and
- Begging, petty sales and services performed by urban children, managed by their own household.

The most important divide is between child labour performed within the context of one's own close family and child labour performed away from home. In terms of child labour at home, given a broad definition of child labour, most African children work – rural children more than their urban peers. Studies in West Africa indicate that even though some children attend formal school, they still perform a considerable amount of work within the home. In Ethiopia, for instance, it was discovered that domestic labour is a major reason for school dropout. Usually, girls are needed for housework, while boys are needed on the family farm. This invariably means that the decision to send a child to school is not only a matter of expense, but also substantial in direct costs in terms of unused child labour. However, studies from Zimbabwe, Kenya and Benin indicate that girls work more than boys, and this raises a serious concern for their welfare (World Bank findings, *Daily Times* (Nigeria) 2002:16).

Quite interesting is the fact that findings of various studies challenge the claim that poverty and child labour are linked. While some studies see poverty as a major cause of child labour, as in the production of street children (Kilbride et al., 2000:60), others, reporting from Kenya, indicate that child labour increases with the size of the family land holding. Also, in Ghana, the correlation between poverty and child labour is weak (Verlet 2000). Observation shows that most rural children are involved in work activities, some of which are hazardous and strenuous. On the other hand, the share of working children in the more formal labour market is low, even though the working conditions are often extremely harmful. The reasons why these children leave home vary from household poverty to a search for better opportunities; and while the former are often 'pushed' out, the latter often depart voluntarily.

It is estimated that around five million children are engaged in paid work in commercial agriculture in Africa. The situation is particularly severe during harvest seasons. In Kenya, 30 percent of coffee pickers are children, while 25,000 school children work under hazardous conditions in Tanzanian plantations and mines. Large numbers of boys from Mali, Burkina Faso, Nigeria, Ghana, Togo and Benin migrate to work in plantations in Cote d'Ivoire (during peacetime), Gabon and Nigeria. Included in this group are refugee children from Liberia and Sierra Leone, who perhaps really do not have any work to do.

It is also important to observe that the contracting out of children only is fairly common in several countries, with the number of those contracted out being relatively large. These mainly work in agriculture or as domestic servants. They can also be found in mining and organized begging activities. Domestic service is probably the largest child labour market outside the agricultural sector. While an estimated 85 percent of child domestic servants in Africa are girls, boy servants are also common in many countries. These child servants are usually poorly paid, work long hours, are maltreated, discriminated against and abused while only a few go to school.

Street children and trafficked children are perhaps are most serious cases of child labour. Many urban children work in streets and public places, while a significant number actually live on the streets. Though child prostitution is less common in Africa than in Asia and Latin America, it is becoming an increasingly worrisome development. Usually, children working in the streets and as domestic servants are particularly defenceless to sexual harassment and abuse. Child and women trafficking in general also constitutes a more modern form of child abuse, verging on human slavery. Sometimes, these children are trafficked from one country to the other or from one part of the world to the other by organized criminal gangs to become victims of prostitution, and sexual objects.

However, we conclude this section by noting that child labour in Africa is not a homogeneous occurrence. The work activities that children engage in, and their social and economic contexts, differ significantly between ethnic groups, and not all forms of child labour are necessarily harmful. The concern should really be on how to ensure children's welfare, rather than children's work in itself (*Daily Times* 2002:16).

Legislation against Child Labour

Child labour is a very serious global social problem, and legislation both international and national has been put in place to attempt to regulate and control it. Although the internationally recommended age for admission into employment is 15 years, most countries around the world, especially the developing ones who have even ratified the International Labour Organization (ILO) Convention 138 of 1973, ignore the convention. ILO Convention 138 stipulates the minimum age for admission into full employment. It defines childhood as a period of life that should be devoted to education and training, and not work. Child labour is on the increase because of poor implementation of this convention: for example, at 31 December 2000, only 105 countries out of some 173 ILO members had ratified the convention.

To address child labour practices, the General Assembly of the United Nations adopted the 'Declaration of the Rights of the Child' in 1959, but the global response to minimize child labour actually came to force in 1979, the 'International Year of the Child'. The ILO in collaboration with other agencies such as the Human Rights Committee of the United Nations is working hard to eliminate child labour. With the adoption of legislation by ILO member countries, the problem of child labour can be minimized or curbed, as this is a highly concerted approach.

Generally, the minimum age for admission into full employment varies between countries. In some countries, it is 12 while in others it is between 14 and 18. The adoption of legislation specifying a minimum age of entry to employment and to curb or eliminate child labour can help establish labour norms and standards. The society concerned can aspire to use these norms and standards as a framework for policy and a yardstick for evaluation of performance. By so doing, the rights of children would be observed and respected. However, in practice there is no strict enforcement of child labour legislation, especially in Africa and Asia, as poverty, low levels of education, ignorance and lack of effective enforcement machinery act to undermine good legislation.

There is little doubt that the ILO set the pace for the eradication of child labour by the adoption of conventions like Convention 138 of 1973 and the accompanying Recommendation 146 of 1973 (minimum age for admission to employment recommendation) and sectoral conventions on the minimum age of admission to employment in industry, agriculture, trimmers and stokers, maritime work, non-industrial employment, fishing and underground work. ILO Convention 138 and its accompanying Recommendation 146 have set out the provision for a comprehensive guide to drafting national legislation.

Further, to complement the above convention and recommendation, the ILO, at its eighty-seventh session in 1999, adopted Convention 182 and Recommendation 190, concerning the prohibition and immediate action for elimination of the worst forms of child labour. With these comprehensive standards member countries of the ILO have available the yardstick to frame their legislation on child labour towards ensuring its minimization or total eradication (Hashim 2002:23).

In brief, the following constitute some of the legislative instruments for addressing the problem of child labour globally:

- General Declaration of the Rights of the Child of 1924;
- Universal Declaration of Human Rights, 1948;
- Declaration of the Rights of the Child, adopted by the General Assembly, 20 November 1959;
- International Convention on Civil and Political Rights (Articles 23 & 24);
- International Convention on Economic, Social and Cultural Rights (Article 10);
- ILO Convention 138 of 1973;
- ILO Convention 146 of 1973;
- ILO Convention 182 of 17 June 1999;
- ILO Recommendation 190 of 17 June 1999; and
- Declaration on the Protection of Women and Children in Emergency and Armed Conflict.

However, it suffices to note that many countries, especially in Africa and Asia, lack the political will to enforce such conventions and declarations, which would have gone a long way in ending child labour. This notwithstanding, the newer forms of child labour, involving child trafficking and the use of children in pornography, make it imperative for countries to begin to take more seriously the matter of enforcing these instruments.

The Challenges of Child Labour

The challenges of child labour in Africa critically revolve around the need to devise economic measures that can free up time for the child to engage in those things that children need to do as children. In Africa, the link between household poverty and child labour is still not quite clear. While poverty reduction remains a general long-term objective, it may not be an effective way to reduce child labour in the short and medium term. Measures such as finding ways to improve the organization and mechanization of labour-intensive domestic chores and farm work, reducing the cost of schooling, and ensuring access to supporting credits need to be addressed. Bank-assisted projects and programmes that improve access to schools and delivery of education, and accommodate flexible school hours, as well as school vouchers, are important. Special assistance and school feeding programmes may result in increased school enrolment and reduced child labour. Evidence indicates the important linkages between infrastructure and child labour. Therefore, improving rural roads and water supply, providing easy access to schools, and reducing the reliance of parents on children to ferry goods to the market may collectively result in the reduction of child labour side by side with legislation.

However, the challenge remains for national governments to muster the political will to address either the medium- to long-term objectives of eliminating child labour in Africa.

Conclusion

Though global in nature as a problem, child labour in Africa is fundamentally an African problem and should be seen as part and parcel of the African development crisis. Just as in the efforts that led to the abolition of the slave trade, African governments need to morally reject child labour, legally prohibit the practice and, thirdly, enforce the legislation protecting children from economic exploitation and securing their right to education. In fact, Article 7 of ILO Convention 182 enjoins each member state to take into account the importance of education in eliminating child labour.

Since child labour mostly takes place in and around family households, there is the need to enhance poverty alleviation schemes as a way of stopping parents from pushing their children into child labour. Civil society, through NGOs, should partner with national governments in mobilizing public opinion against the economic exploitation of children. In short, there can be no greater evidence of poor governance than the sight of children engaging in work meant for adults for a fee, and at the expense of their education and wellbeing. Finally, let us realize that is important to approach solutions to the problem of children and youth in Africa, as indeed in other societies, in a dynamic way.

References

Daily Times, 2004, Child Labour in Africa: Issues and Challenges, 7 January.

Hashim, T., 2002, 'Child Labour as Global Menace', *Daily Champion* (Nigeria), 10 June.

ILO, 1999, *Convention 182*, Convention Concerning the Prohibition and Immediate Action for the Elimination of the Worst Forms of Labour, Adopted by the Conference at its 87th Session, Geneva, 17 June.

ILO, 1999, *Recommendation 190*, Recommendation Concerning the Prohibition and Immediate Action for the Elimination of the Worst Forms of Child Labour, Adopted by the Conference at its 87th Session, Geneva, 17 June.

Kilbride, P. et al., 2000, *Street Children in Kenya*, Westprint: Bergin & Garvey.

Olugbile, F., 1998, 'Child Labour and the Nigerian Child', *The Guardian* (Nigeria), 24 July.

Oloko, A. B. S., 1997, *The Hidden Work Force – Child Domestic Labour: The Progress of Nigerian Children*, Lagos: UNICEF/FOS, African Book Builders Limited.

Schlemmer, B., ed., 2000, *The Exploited Child*, London: Zed Books.

Verlet, M., 2000, 'Growing up in Ghana: Deregulation and the Employment of Children', in Bernard Schlemmer, ed., *The Exploited Child*, London: Zed Books.

United Nations, 1999, 'Convention on the Rights of the Child', Adopted by the General Assembly of the United Nations, 20 November.

3

Getting Them Young: Child Labour in Ikot Ekpene from a Historical Perspective

Ufom Umoren Ekpe-Otu

Introduction

Much has been written about child labour from various parts of the world, so, it is not a new area of study. However, despite the proliferation of scholarly and non-scholarly work on the subject, the phenomenon still remains to be fully grasped, a clear indication of its complexity. The estimates of child labour remain a contested terrain induced in the main from definitional fuzziness. There still remains a lack of theoretical consensus on the question, who are the child labourers? Child labour has been variously defined in terms of occupational types and age, with the International Labour Organisation's (ILO) prescription often taken as a working criterion. ILO Convention No. 138 (1973) pegs the minimum age of employment at 15 years for different countries or the minimum age of completion of compulsory education. In recognition of the variation across different societies, this is lowered in cases of light work to 13 years for developed countries and 12 years for developing nations. In the case of hazardous work deemed harmful to the safety, health and morals of children, the legal age is unilaterally fixed at 18 years.

The premise for the evolution of child rights, upon which the ILO's prescriptions are fixed, has come in for considerable criticism, especially from Third World scholars. It has been derided as the standardization of western notions of childhood and has contributed to the attempt to distinguish between child work and child labour. The 1999 Convention No. 182, on the abolition of the worst aspects of child labour, is indicative of a greater awareness of the complexity and variation of child labour in different cultural contexts. In spite of these attempts by the international agencies, the study of child labour continues to be fraught with problems and contradictions. This is visible in unanswered questions relating to beneficiaries of child labour, and the call for a re-evaluation of the role of the child as a consumer of economic value.

The commonly acknowledged conclusion that child labour is contextual necessitates an analytical framework deriving from specific contexts and existent politico-economic and socio-cultural milieus. There is need for a perspective of child labour that draws its basic premise from the social construction of child labour in the country. The notion of children working is not perceived as an anathema in Nigerian society, but is regarded as a natural and legitimate practice entrenched in the local custom and tradition. At the same time, cultural practices could, and do indeed, facilitate the exploitation of children in the labour market. For instance, the practice of fostering has been utilized in the trafficking of children into forced labour. The cultural toleration of children working therefore plays an important part in any analysis of child labour issues in the country.

This study takes, as its point of departure, the historical interrogation of children in the labour process during the colonial era. It is posited here that the complex social and economic relations occasioned by colonial imperialism effected a systematic exploitation of children's labour power. It is not intended here to deny the existence of child labour in pre-colonial Nigeria. There are many instances in the rural areas where recalcitrant children were sold as slaves, as would be shown in the study. This notwithstanding, there is the need to interrogate the societal perception of such practices in pre-colonial Nigeria. Is it a question of a wrongful and alien deconstruction of the African child by the West? Selling undesirable children to slavery was not seen as the perpetration of child labour, but rather as a way of correcting societal ills. The practice of fostering may have led to undue hardship for certain children but, by and large, kinship ties, the communal ownership of children, which underpinned fostering, inhibited exploitation of children. The point being made here is that despite the existence of certain practices now termed child labour, traditional practices were inimical to its institutionalization, until the imposition of colonial rule.

In examining child labour in Ikot Ekpene, a town in south-eastern Nigeria, this study raises several questions. What fed child labour in Ikot Ekpene? How has societal perception of child labour evolved from the colonial to the contemporary period? In what ways has the utilization of children's labour power changed from a benign act to one of systematic exploitation and how have global economic changes impacted on this? How does the issue of child labour in Ikot Ekpene and Nigeria in general fit into the dominant paradigms of childhood?

This study, as mentioned, will focus on Ikot Ekpene in the south-eastern part of Nigeria. It is one of the major cities in Akwa Ibom State, located at the southern tip of the country. The major ethnic groups are the Igbo and Ibibio. According to the 1998 National Human Development Report, the proportion of urban-dwellers in Akwa Ibom State was 12 per cent. Here, child labour is pervasive; indeed, it is a major source for child domestics in the country.

In line with the historical approach used in this study, child labour is situated within the context of time and space. The study traces the dynamics of child labour from the colonial period to contemporary times. An examination of the role of tradition and culture in the exploitation of the labour process of children in the region is also undertaken. The study evaluates the notion of child labour within existent childhood paradigms vis-à-vis work and the labour process in Nigeria. It is intended here to give a close and critical analysis of child labouring activities. There is a need to stand apart from the sensationalism and emotions of child labour issues and interrogate history for a more nuanced understanding of the phenomenon. Such gaps in the study of child labour in Nigeria and in particular the Cross River Basin is the driving force behind this research. The peculiarities of child labour needs to be analyzed to ascertain relevant policy intervention.

The data on child labour has often been misleading, owing to what Lieten (2002) calls the 'mixing of apples, oranges, and bananas'. This is the lumping together of all categories of out-of-school children as well as school children working part-time as child labourers. This, Lieten points out, inhibits the attempt to uncover determinants of child labour and likely solutions. Not only does it befuddle scholarly work, but also such a neat division of children at work or at school belies the reality of children's lives in most countries of the developing world, including Nigeria. It connotes the false construction of a childhood without work.

In Ikot Ekpene, there are working children who attend part-time schooling or are engaged in learning a trade. A lot of street vendors engage in hawking after school hours. At the same time, not all out-of-school children are employed in the labour market, for some engage in household activities such as looking after siblings and helping in domestic chores.

Deriving from the recognition of the contextuality of child labour, there has been the delineation between the work of children and child labour, which implies the banning of the latter. This, however, has not cleared the fog surrounding the phenomenon. It leads to the question, when does child work become child labour? It is the subject of heated debate among scholars.

Mishra (2000) reiterates that the distinction is more artificial than real, more of a degree than of kind, and should therefore be disregarded. Lange (2000), following this line of argument, states that the socialization work of children is a smokescreen, which belies the children's working condition and their economic role. In a similar vein, Nieuwenhuys (2000) kicks against the notion of familial control as inhibiting the exploitation of children's labour power. Basing his argument on studies conducted in a village in Kerala, India, largely dependent on the manufacture of coir yarn with manually operated wheels and fishing in country crafts, Nieuwenhuys questions the ability of kinship relations to protect children from excessive drudgery and provide a harmonious environment in which to grow. While the universal applicability of these arguments is debatable, it does point to the hazardous nature of certain activities of children deemed acceptable under the tag of child work. Work in the household often runs into multiple tasks stretching over long periods of time, especially in rural areas.

The literature on child labour is suffused with efforts to uncover its causal factors and proffer solutions to its control/elimination. The commonly advanced determinants are poverty and education. In spite of the identification of the poverty of the household in many case studies (Oloko 1992, Mishra 2000, Chander 2004), it is also acknowledged that poverty is not the only reason for child labour, and in some cases its impact is minimal. Indeed, there are countries with similar levels of gross domestic product per capita (PPP) that differ in their incidence of child labour (World Bank 2000). Kerala in India is an example of a poor region with a low level of child labour (Lietan 2002). However, Kerala's case also helps to support the claim of a correlation between literacy and reduction in child labour. In Africa, according to a 1993 survey, the incidence of child labour in various countries indicates no systematic link with the level of poverty (Findings 2001). Zambia, with a lower GDP than Côte d'Ivoire, recorded a lower rate of child labour. Likewise the incidence of child labour was greater in Ghana than Nigeria despite its higher GDP. In a recent UNICEF publication, Côte d'Ivoire, regarded as a comparatively prosperous and stable economy in West Africa, still continues to draw public ire because of its growing rate of child labour, fed primarily by plantation agriculture (UNICEF 2002).

As with poverty, the link between child labour and levels of literacy is not tenable in all situations. In societies where the educational system is dysfunctional, many parents can and do view child labour as a preferred option. Unlike the Kerala case, where high literacy mitigates against child labour, Akwa Ibom State, despite being regarded as an educationally advantaged state in Nigeria, has a high incidence of child labour. Poverty here acts as a significant variable as well as tradition and culture.

What the above shows is that determinants of child labour are varied across and within countries. As Lietan points out, there is the need for a strict categorization of deprived children, which will help to yield answers to the questions raised earlier. It is posited here that the different causal factors identified in case studies – poverty, poor educational system, adult underemployment, tradition and culture – should not be taken as 'either/or' groupings into which they can be neatly divided but rather as 'more or less' dimensions along which child labour can be more properly understood. Greater attention needs also to be paid to pull factors that give rise to child labour. This is often disregarded or paid scant attention to in the literature. As a pull factor, the economic benefits derivable play a leading role in creating a demand for child labour. The institutional framework existent in a society also impacts greatly on child labour, and could help to explain the paradox of disparate levels of child labour in countries with similar GDP per capita (PPP).

The paucity of a scholarly documentation of the labour process of children from a historical perspective in Ikot Ekpene, and Nigeria in general, inhibits a nuanced understanding of the phenomenon for an efficient and realistic intervention. In contrast to the vast scholarly work carried out on child labour in Asia and the West, in Nigeria, the literature is far less developed and cohesive. It is often analyzed as part of the discourse on the informal sector (Fapohunda et al., 1978). The studies that exist have largely been carried out by sociologists, who tend to focus on the broad area of child abuse, with the children portrayed as victims (Vinolia and Fubara 1986). Nonetheless, with the growing awareness of the hazardous nature of child labour, especially in such activities as child prostitution, there is a growing literature on the subject, mostly sponsored by international agencies, in particular United Nations. Notably among these studies are those carried out by Oloko (1986, 1990, 1997).

Although studies on child labour on specific issues remain inadequate, the literature on the Nigerian colonial context provides data on the activities of children as well as insight into the socio-cultural and politico-economic scenario that gave rise to child labour (Nadel 1961; Callaway 1965; Uchendu 1965; Basden 1966; Rodney 1972; Latham 1973; Iliffe 1987).

This is a qualitative study conducted with a focus on Ikot Ekpene. As a historical study, use is made of documented sources such as books, journals, newspapers and magazines. Government records such as labour statistics, as well as publications by non-governmental organizations, are used. In historical documents relating to the colonial period, the economic activities of children in the region are available, and this proved invaluable. The perusal of archival materials gave insights as to how labour was measured and by whom, and to what extent colonial economic politics impacted on child labour.

In addition, structured questionnaires were also administered in the field as well as the use of an interview schedule. Integrating the use of secondary sources, archival materials and structured questionnaires enables a confirmation and corroboration of results.

Child Labour in Ikot Ekpene

The Statistical Information and Monitoring Programme on Child Labour Survey (SIMPOC) of 2002 estimates the number of economically active children in Nigeria to be about 15 million, and almost half of this figure are females. Six million of these were categorized as child labourers on the basis of their not attending school. Two million children were exposed to over 15 hours of work daily, with 51 per cent of them female. In spite of the excessive working hours 56.4 per cent of them were found to be attending school (FOS/ILO/SIMPOC 2002). These figures should be treated with caution. It seems far-fetched for children working over 15 hours daily to have the time to attend school even if it was part-time. Nonetheless the findings do give an indication of the economically active children in Nigeria. A World Bank Report shows a decline in the number of children under the age of 14 years that were working: the ratio to the population age 10–14 was 30.8 per cent in 1970, 29.2 per cent in 1980, 27.6 per cent in 1990, and 23.5 per cent in 2001. Despite the decline, these figures still demonstrate a high incidence of child labour when one considers that a larger percentage of Nigeria's population is below 15 years.

In Ikot Ekpene, children's work is deeply entrenched in local custom and regarded as a natural and legitimate practice. Children in this society and most African societies have always worked as part of their socialization process, assuming adult roles through emulation. This induction process takes place within the parenting circle, underpinned by the communal ownership of the Nigerian child. Children are introduced to work at an early age. A girl child by the age of four is already assisting her mother in childcare and household chores. The boys learn to work alongside their father. Labour is defined along gender roles, and the girl's labour time tends to be more adjustable than the boys. While the boys have a more clearly defined role, which can be definite, as in helping to clear the farm, the girl's labour power is deeply controlled by her mother and is less restricted. This dependency of the women over the girl child's labour could and indeed does become exploitative.

The communal ownership of the child ensures that he/she is moved between family members and kin freely. During this time, the child's labour is also utilized. For instance, they are commonly sent to their grandparents for a certain period to help out in domestic chores and also be trained in moral and traditional obligations. The farming season provides a good time for this, when the children can assist in farm work. During the harvest, the relatives show their appreciation by presenting the child and his/her family with the bounties of the harvest. Where it can be afforded, the child is also given a token at the end of the stay. Children, mostly girls, are also sent to stay with their relatives as babysitters. Running through all these tasks is the cohesive force of family ties. It has been argued in the literature that child labour becomes exploitative outside familial control. This proposition has been challenged in recent studies. The transmission and acquisition of knowledge within familial settings is not always harmonious, for the familial relationship is based on paternalism, which may act as a framework for the exploitation of the very young when the family is engaged in the production of marketable produce (Nieuwenhuys 2001). Despite this, it is generally agreed that familial relations are non-monetized, based rather on kinship bonds (Meillassoux 2000).

The Colonial Factor

The colonial period, on the other hand, facilitated demographic and socio-economic changes that proved critical to the commoditization of child labour. The major impulse in colonial Nigeria for economic growth was (and continues to be) the foreign trade sector. Foreign investment in the country was directed towards extractive industries and cash crops. The imperial colonial flow of capital led to unequal accumulation. It stimulated a division of labour whereby industrialization and economic diversification were rooted in the imperial centres while it effected a reliance on raw materials in Nigeria and thus a vulnerability to market price fluctuations.

Production for the market became a major activity and gradually rendered the peasant farmer dependent on sales for his livelihood. The major export commodities were palm products and other goods like cocoa, groundnuts and rubber. In spite of the relative diversification of the agrarian sector, these products were still raw materials and hence subject to market fluctuations. The peasant farmer was not left unaffected. The deteriorating terms of trade flowing from this encouraged a pricing policy that saw less real income through the marketing boards. To maintain a good profit, the trading companies formed 'pools' and fixed prices to be paid to the local farmer. In 1929, prices of palm products were drastically reduced by UAC in the face of rising costs of imported goods. In 1924, oil palm was sold at 14/- per gallon. This went down to 7/- in 1928 and 1/2d in 1929 (Rodney, 1972). At the same time, the cost of living was rising owing to increased charges for imported goods. For instance, a yard of khaki, which sold for 3/- in pre-war years, went up to 16/-, and a bundle of sheet from 30/- to 100/- (Latham 1973). The emergence of cash crop farmers solely dependent on sales for their livelihood, and the wage-earner, separated from the land, made the people vulnerable to market fluctuations.

The introduction of the system of direct taxation in southern Nigeria extended the money economy to all corners of the society. It created an increasing participation in wage employment as a means of obtaining money income. Cash was needed for several reasons: for instance, taxes were paid in money, and European goods, the taste for which the local people had come to acquire, were bought with European currency.

Rising economic instability and accompanying household insecurity was accentuated by the widening gab between urban and rural centres as well as between regions with or without strategic relevance to the colonial economy. Colonialism, the growth of the cash economy and integration of the domestic economy into the market economy, the attendant development of towns and increase in the urbanized population led to growth in the informal sector. Separated from the land, newly urbanized households constituted a pool of human capital that was subject to the fluctuating labour market. A situation then arose whereby domestic work progressively slipped into tougher forms of exploitation that tended to remove children from their family milieu, from the lands and life paths of childhood and on to the labour market. Industrialization and urbanization encouraged the growing numbers of domestic servants, especially in the late colonial period. Jane L. Parpart (1990) alludes to the women's party in 1944 in Lagos lobbying for more female employment and better conditions for domestic servants and girl hawkers.

Another outcome of colonial policy was prostitution, as a commoditization of sexual services. The period from the late 1930s to the early 1940s marked the beginning of a surge of rural immigration to Lagos. This was a response to the massive influx of Europeans as well as Africans, soldiers, sailors and administrators to the wartime city. According to government reports, 'their spending power [sic] caused the rapid development of facilities for drinking, dancing, and other less responsible social amenities'.[1] An important feature of this process was the vast number of young girls who streamed out of the rural areas, in the Cross River Basin and other parts of Nigeria, for prostitution in Lagos. As asserted, 'these girls mostly about the ages of twelve years, are not Yorubas, but appear to be mainly Ibos, Efiks, and Sobos'.[2] Most were trafficked to Lagos by relatives or friends of the family, under the pretext of getting the girl employment in the city. At other times, the girls were taken under the auspices of marriage with the dowry paid by the procurer, who in most cases was a retired prostitute.

On arrival in Lagos, the girl was gradually introduced into prostitution. Virgins fetched very high prices, but this gradually diminished as the girl aged, and venereal disease took its toil. It became a vicious circle as the girl over time might take up as a madam who also recruited fresh girls from the rural areas into the trade. Prostitution perpetuated child stealing in Ikot Ekpene on several levels. In Ogoja province of Upper Cross River, located to the north-west of Ikot Ekpene, prostitution in the colonial era had become a social menace, drawing the attention of the colonial government. The effect of this was a depletion of the population as a result of decline in birth rate. This situation was utilized by individuals who procured children from the thickly populated areas of Bende, Ikot Ekpene, Okigwe and Afikpo divisions for sale.[3] In many cases, retired prostitutes sponsored cases of child stealing, and some of them, rendered infertile by diseases, acquired children through this means. More prevalent, however, were cases of children bought and trafficked to the Gold Coast for prostitution. In a letter to the District Officer, Obubra division, the members of the Egbisim Improvement Union of the Agwaguna town stated:

> They (the prostitutes) … marry Ibo, Ibibio, and other tribe in the [south] eastern provinces. After doing so, they will send these so-called wives to the Gold Coast and other places for harloting and thus increase the population of harlots.[4]

In Ikot Ekpene, Etok Akpan was and still is a red light district whose reputation transcended the province. The road served as a centre for prostitutes, with bars and nightclubs lining the street. Indeed, it became so notorious that in the surrounding villages a promiscuous girl was usually taunted as being more fit to reside at EtokAkpan.[5]

Presently, the area has been overtaken by private homes and some small business enterprises, which dot the streets, though vestiges of the old trade still remain. One can still see houses occupied by prostitutes. One such is a couple of single rooms clustered together in the Etokeren road, a spillover from Etokakpan, which it joins. The cluster of rooms now houses the older prostitutes past their prime, whose bargaining power as well as choice has been greatly reduced with age. The proximity of the road to the motor-park ensures that men of all types, drunks, dropouts and young boys number among their clients.

In the colonial era, a large number of young girls and women emigrated from the rural areas to Ikot Ekpene, lured by the bright lights. More importantly, Ikot Ekpene boasted of the presence of missionaries, and establishments symbolizing the colonial presence – native court, warrant chiefs, government offices and factories. The stringent execution of traditional practices was therefore diluted. For instance, the missionaries tried to abolish the killing of twins, and often rehabilitated mothers of such children in their centres. It was no wonder that women with twin children fled to Ikot Ekpene to escape the wrath of the gods. In the same vein, women caught in extramarital liaisons also made for Ikot Ekpene. For these people such acts as those undertaken by the missionaries, as well as the presence of a large number of 'strangers' in Ikot Ekpene, encouraged the perception of the place as a 'no man's land', and therefore liberal in its governing rules.

The colonialization process, as has been seen above, triggered off the institutionalization of child labour in Ikot Ekpene and set into motion certain factors that removed children's work from familial control and to the streets and industrial settings. Precipitated thus, child labour was reinforced by such socio-cultural factors as the social structure and nuptial and fertility patterns.

The patriarchal structure of social relations in the traditional Ikot Ekpene, as in many African societies, bred male domination and engendered the exploitation of women through denial of status. There existed gender disparity in access to economic opportunities, and women's economic activities were often undervalued because of the low monetary compensation they attracted comparatively. Colonialism, the integration into the market economy, the demographic imbalance arising out of sustained male immigration for employment and evasion of tax, created a large number of female-headed households and necessitated the utilization of child labour as a survival tactic.

The proliferation of child labour in Ikot Ekpene was further influenced by nuptial and fertility patterns. In the traditional society, numerous progeny is perceived as a blessing from God. Childlessness or limited fertility is an object of reproach. Indeed, there is a generally intense cultural emphasis on fertility. From field surveys, low-income earners have been observed to be less responsive to efforts to limit the size of their families. The economy of the peasant household simply requires a large number of unpaid workers and helpers to satisfy the demands of the markets and survive the expanding capitalism. Parents value their children not merely as objects of emotional satisfaction but because they represent real economic assets. The practice of polygamy heightened this problem.

Also prevalent was the practice of early marriage and child bearing, with its social and demographic consequences. With reference to the data from the 1990 Nigerian Demographic and Health Survey (NDHS), the median age of marriage for Nigeria as a whole was 17 years, for adolescent and young adults aged 15–24 years. In the urban area the age was 17 years, and 15 years in the rural areas.[6] In the colonial period, these figures were much lower, especially for the female population, at about 12 years (Isiugo-Abanike 1977). Early marriage increased population growth by shortening the time span between generations, thereby increasing the total number of children born in a given span. The large number of adolescents meant an increased dependency ratio and an intensification of the struggle for employment opportunities. The situation was especially aggravated in rural areas, with the low level of infrastructure. Peasant households were forced to rely more and more on the labour power of their children. The struggle for employment opportunities ignited a rural/urban migration and an escalation of entries into the informal sector. Emigration to an urban environment creates new demands, which leads to more spending. In the process of coping with these financial constraints, several options are considered. Income earners seek to augment their earnings through a second job, usually in the informal sector. Alternatively, the women and children are gradually pushed on to the labour market.

Contemporary Manifestations of Child Labour in Ikot Ekpene

Child labour is a phenomenon that is multifaceted, not always legal and difficult to measure. This renders it problematic to check the direction in which it is growing. Nonetheless, in Ikot Ekpene, field study has revealed discernible changes in activities of child labourers. This is most evident in female-dominated forms of employment.

Over the years there has been a tremendous demand for young girls as domestic servants, within and outside Ikot Ekpene. Indeed, as noted earlier, Akwa Ibom is a source of domestic servants for the country as a whole. This has created a market opportunity and led to the emergence of organized networks whose economic activities are geared towards exploiting this market. These syndicates send out agents into the rural areas to lure and when necessary forcefully abduct young girls. They capitalize on the children's need for cash to maximize the economic exploitation of their labour power. Domestic work is an indication of the multifaceted use of labour. It entails long working hours, up to 15–17 hours daily, performing a range of services. Interviews conducted showed that the children until very recently earned between N300 and N500. In the last couple of years the cost of procuring a domestic servant has escalated to N1,000 or more, and in cases where the children are to go to big cities like Port Harcourt, Lagos and Abuja, fees could be as high as N3,000. In most cases, the money is not paid to the child but appropriated by the parents. Remuneration is not always in cash. Frequently, employers are expected to 'settle' the domestic servants after a certain number of years as agreed upon by the parents or guardians and the employer.

Domestic work is a classic example of the exploitation of the traditional practice of fostering. The employers are regarded as guardians and mentors equipped to imbue their domestics with social skills and empower them to be better placed in society. It should be pointed out that the working conditions of these domestic servants are not always perceived as harmful by the children themselves, some of who see placement in city homes as an escape route from the excessive drudgery of work and poverty in their own homes. This is the case of families in Ikot Ekpene who have migrated to the farming settlements in Akpabuyo in Calabar. The hard toil of farm work bears heavily on the children who are subjected to long working hours with inadequate feeding. This buttresses the postulation by Nieuwenhuys of kinship ties being incapable of protecting children from exploitation (Nieuwenhuys 2000). It could be, as Seabrook notes, that the impact of child labour on a child is determined by his/her sensibilities (Seabrook 2001).

An important feature of child domestics is their invisibility. Until recent times engendered by the furore raised in international circles on child labour, young girls working as maids in private homes went about unnoticed and their activities accepted as normal. Maggie Black (1995) calls this 'attitudinal invisibility', noting that in many Third World environments child labourers on the street only attract attention insofar as they are causing a public nuisance. The 'work' culture also affect people's attitude towards domestic servants. The maid's work is viewed as the continuation of her training for a better life in the future. These attitudes are reinforced by positive representations of ex-domestic servants – a large number in Ikot Ekpene – who have come to attain some status and are now employers of domestic servants. A number of the civil servants and traders fall into this group.

The ideology of kinship/friendship is the ploy in the mobilization of child labour. The medium of entry into the labour market gives the children a false sense of security, with the broker as a surrogate parent. It is usual to hear phrases like 'we are doing this for your own good' or 'you have to suffer today to enjoy tomorrow'. This paternalistic concept in the labour process masks the exploitation of children.

In Ikot Ekpene and the surroundings area, the traffic continues to grow in children lured to other African countries like Gabon and Mali for domestic work. Journalistic reports attest to the increasing number of girls being trafficked to European countries for prostitution. For instance, the *Sunday Champion* of 18 July 1999 reported the interception of a slave boat by the Akwa Ibom state police off the fishing settlement of Ibeno. It was ferrying 33 children to Gabon for 'slave labour'. The girls' ages ranged from 9 to 16, and about 23 of them were Nigerians, mostly from the eastern part of the country. In another media report, in the *Sunday Vanguard* of 15 July 2001, Akwa Ibom, Imo, Abia and Rivers States were pinpointed as targets of child trafficking syndicates. Akwa Ibom was said to be the largest supplier in Nigeria. Common routes used by the traffickers were detailed as follows: children from Nigeria and Benin taken through Cameroon to Gabon, and children from Benin taken through Nigeria or Togo to Gabon, Burkina Faso and Cameroon. The north-west and south-west of Cameroon supplied children to be trafficked to Nigeria. In Nigeria, Calabar was a transit port for children en-route to Gabon/Cameroon as well as children entering Nigeria from Cameroon.[7] According to the report, in 1996, 4,000 children were trafficked from Cross River State to various parts of Nigeria and beyond.

Globalization and the development of labour market segmentation have resulted in an expansion of the informal sector and the demand for unskilled labour including that of children. In this new wave of globalization, fuelled by technological innovations, there has been an accelerated global transfer of capital, labour information and knowledge (Mittelman 1996). The inability of the free market to induce an equitable sharing of the benefits of globalization has effected an increase in the number of children assuming social and economic responsibilities. In Nigeria, given the lacklustre performance of the economy and inadequacy of the state to provide for its citizens, there are increasingly greater numbers of children without work experience. To survive in a non-welfarist state, the people try to carve a life for themselves and in the process get locked squarely in the informal sector. One can therefore say that in most of Africa, south of the Sahara, the informal sector is steadily becoming formal.

Child labour in Ikot Ekpene manifests primarily in the service sector – with children as domestic servants, street vendors, beggars, shop attendants. An important feature of child labour is its multifaceted nature. It is not confined to a single activity, thus an apprentice could also be called upon to perform domestic duties for his/her boss. Likewise the street vendor in the quest for her own income unaccountable to her mistress could easily be lured into prostitution. The globalization of consumer culture, with its proliferation of images and commodities, and its promise of happiness through the possession of products, only heightens this possibility.

Regardless of this, the modern informalization of work promoted by globalization could, as contended by Liebel (2004), symptomize a means whereby people can actualize their ideas and ambitions in the space open to them. It also affords them the opportunity to negotiate for the recognition of this space by the state. The case of Latin America readily comes to mind in this instance where children are getting organized and demanding fair treatment by the state. The ability of children to grapple positively with globalization depends also to a large extent on institutional arrangements existent in a particular country. In Nigeria, where the macro-economic policies, institutional and structural strategies fail to provide an enabling environment for growth, the question of child labour and policies for its eradication becomes very important and in need of careful examination devoid of sensationalism.

The issue of child labour can be brought home more clearly by the question, who is the Nigerian child? This brings to fore the issue of the sociology of work in Nigeria, which is still highly complex because of the complexity of the labour process. Adulthood can be described as a time one of responsibility, of control. On the other hand, childhood is not necessarily a time of dependency. Issues on child labour mostly fail to capture the transition from childhood to youth to adulthood. One cannot talk of the sociology of work without an analysis of the above. Looking at the apprentice tradition, for instance, a large number of the participants are children over the age of 18 years, or one should say youths. The pervasive poverty in the country ensures that the transition to adulthood is delayed and in some cases permanent. Hence you have a 22-year-old boy still dependent on his family, trying to develop alternative means of survival as an apprentice.

The discourse on child labour shows that the dominant paradigm is determined by western perspectives, in particular modelled on the children of middle-class western societies It is a concept that projects an innocent, work-free and protected childhood (White 1994; Nieuwenhuys 2000; Liebel 2004). This model creates contradictions between global conceptions and lived experiences of childhood (Sarr 2000).

The peculiarities of child labour in Africa rebel against Eurocentric constructs. The notion of an innocent, work-free, protected childhood neglects the interaction of the child with society. Recruitment of children into the labour market poses questions in the sphere of culture. Nonetheless, the above is not a vindication of child labour, but rather an attempt to demonstrate the fact that childhood is socially constructed, and thus any examination of the phenomenon has to take into consideration the cultural context. Cultural Nigeria is a given, therefore the situation of the child in Nigeria should be perceived likewise. The definition of the working child in Nigeria should be redefined, and should not be determined by western notions of childhood.

Notes

1. Obubdist 4/1/71 D. O. Obubra Division to Resident, Ogoja Province, 'Prostitutes in Obubra Division', despatch, 22 December 1937.
2. Ibid.
3. OB: 197/84 D.O. Obubra Division to Resident, Ogoja Province, 'Slave Dealing and Child Stealing', despatch, 14 April 1944.
4. Letter from the Egbism Quarter, Agwagwune Town to D.O. Obubra Division, 3 April 1948, despatch, 24 April 1948.
5. Regina Akpan Umoren, Ikot Ekpene, 2/01/2005.
6. Chief Dan Essien, Etor Ikot, Afanga, 13/06/99.
7. Calabar is the state capital of present-day Cross River State, bordering Akwa Ibom State to the west. Prior to 1983, the latter was merged with the former. Consequently within the country members of both states are usually identified as 'Calabar people'. This close relationship also accounted for the sustained movements across both states. Presently there are a large number of people from Ikot Ekpene who have migrated to Akpabuyo to engage in the cultivation of crops like cassava.

References

Basden, G. I., 1966, *Among the Ibos of Nigeria*, London: Frank Cass.

Black, M., 1995, *Street and Working Children: Summary Report of the Innocenti Global Seminar*, Florence: UNICEF, International Child Development Centre, 15–25 February.

Callaway, A. C., 1964, 'Nigeria Indigenous Education: The Apprentice System', *Odu* 1, July.

Chander, S., 2004, *Child Labour in Informal Sector: A sociological survey*, New Delhi: Sunrise Publications.

Fapohunda, O. J. and Lubell, H., 1978, *Lagos: Urban Development and Employment*, Geneva: ILO.

Iliffe, J., 1987, *The African Poor: A History*, Cambridge: Cambridge University Press.

Isiugo-Abanihe, U., 1977, 'Nuptiality and Fertility Patterns among Adolescent and Young Adults', *CHESTRAD Status of Adolescents and Young Adults in Nigeria.*

Lange, M., 2000, 'The Demand for Labour within the Household: Child Labour in Togo', in Bernard Schlemmer, ed., *The Exploited Child*, London: Zed Books.

Latham, A. J. H., 1973, *Old Calabar 1600–1891*, Oxford: Oxford University Press.

Liebel, M., 2004, *A Will of their Own: Cross-cultural Perspectives on Working Children*, London: Zed Books.

Lieten, G. K., 2002, 'Child Labour and Poverty: The Poverty of Analysis', *The Indian Journal of Labour Economics* 45(3).

Meillassoux, C., 2000, 'Looking Ahead: A General Conclusion', in Bernard Schlemmer, ed., *The Exploited Child*, London: Zed Books.

Mistra, L., 2000, *Child Labour in India*, New Delhi: Oxford University Press.

Mittelman, J., 1996, 'Dynamics of Globalisation', in James Mittelman, ed., *Critical Reflection*, London: Lynne Rienner.

Nadel, S. F., 1961, *Black Byzantium*, London: International African Institute.

Nieuwenhuys, O., 2000, 'The Household Economy and the Commercial Exploitation of Children's Work: The Case of Kerala', in Bernard Schlemmer, ed., *The Exploited Child*, London: Zed Books.

Oloko, B. A., 1986, 'Children's Domestic versus Work and Economic School Achievement in Nigeria', *Child Labour in Africa*, Selected Proceedings of the First International Workshop on Child Labour in Africa, UNICEF: ANPPCAN.

Oloko, B. A., 1990, *Situational Diagnosis of Street and Working Children in Kaduna and Calabar*, UNICEF Report.

Oloko, B. A., 1992, *Situation Analysis of Children in Especially Difficult Circumstances (CEDC)*, A UNICEF Report in collaboration with J. Shindu, A. Olowu, R. A. Mohammed, Ben Arikpo and O. Soyomo.

Oloko, B. A., 1997, *Child Labour in Urban Nigeria: Statistics 1984, 1986*, UNICEF Report.

Parpart, J., 1990, 'Wage Earning Women and the Double Day: the Nigerian case', in Shawn Stichtu and J. Parpart, eds., *Women, Employment and the Family in the International Division of Labour*, London: Macmillan.

Rodney, W., 1972, *How Europe Underdeveloped Africa*, London: Bogle-L'Overture.

Sall, E., 2002, 'Cultural Paradigms against the Backdrop of Poverty Situation in Developing Countries (Africa)', in Karin Holm and Uwe Schultz, eds, *Kindheit in Armut Weltweit*, Opladen: Leske & Budrich.

Schlemmer, B., ed., 2000, *The Exploited Child*, London: Zed Books.

Seabrook, J., 2001, *Children of Other Worlds*, London: Zed Books.

Uchendu, V., 1965, *The Igbo of Southeast Nigeria*, New York: Holt, Rinehart and Winston.

UNICEF, 2002, *Child Trafficking in West Africa: Policy Responses*, UNICEF Innocenti Research Centre.

Vinolia, N. S. and Fubara, M. S., 1986, 'Street Hawking as an Aspect of Child Abuse and Neglect', in P. Ebigbo et al., eds., *Child Labour in Africa*, Proceedings of the First International Workshop on Child Abuse in Africa, Enugu: Chuka Printing Co.

White, Ben, 1994, 'Children, Work, and Child Labor: Changing Response to the Employment of Children', *Development and Change* 25(4).

4

Economic Crises and Child Trafficking in Nigeria: A Comparative Analysis of the 1930s and 1990s

Rasheed Olaniyi

Introduction

Arising out of debates over child trafficking and economic crises, this study compares two experiences of child trafficking during economic crises in Nigeria in the 1930s and 1990s. Under pervasive economic regimes children of marginalized social groups became targets of traffickers. This study offers an empirical investigation and suggests that child trafficking was propelled by economic crises and poverty in historical periods and in different economic phases. In a depressed economy, child trafficking became crucial in the labour process because of the cheap nature and lack of negotiation potentials. This study concerns the comparative analysis of child trafficking in Nigeria during the 1930s and 1990s. In the context of the household economy, child trafficking and child labour became survival strategies in a depressed economy. During periods of economic crises, many people find it difficult to fulfil social obligations and sustain themselves and their families. Economic deterioration pushed children into the labour process as vulnerable groups struggled to survive. Child trafficking enjoys parental consent, which considerably contributed to the meagre income of the family. There existed huge a market for children in the labour process and an abundant supply was ensured by poor families who fell prey to traffickers seeking to make profit by exploiting their vulnerability.

How does economic crisis explain child trafficking? Are there differences or similarities in the pattern of child labour and trafficking in the 1930s and 1990s? What is the nature of the trafficking network? Are anti-trafficking and child labour laws sufficient to track the menace? This study aims to determine the linkage between economic crises and trafficking; ascertain if there are differences or similarities in the pattern of child trafficking in the 1930s and 1990s; examine the nature of trafficking network; and ascertain the relevance of the anti-trafficking and child labour laws. The significance of the study lies in its focus, which brings a historical perspective to bear on the role of children in the labour process in Nigeria, through a parallel study of the linkages between economic crises and child trafficking in the 1930s and the 1990s. It is therefore significant to the extent that it takes a retroactive look at the genesis of the phenomenon prior to the post-colonial era in Nigeria. Secondly, its critical examination of this issue in the 1990s, especially in terms of the nature of the networks and the possible roles played by official institutions, serves as a source of critical information for the NGOs engaged in advocacy and intervention as well as for the formulation of anti-trafficking and child labour policies.

In terms of existing knowledge, child trafficking has become a major concern of human rights organizations, feminist activists and scholars researching its effects on the lives of women and youths. Many scholarly works and policy papers exist on the rising incidence of child trafficking in Nigeria, but none consider it as a historical continuity of exploitation experienced by marginalized families or communities during economic crises engendered by the capitalist mode of production. Ubah (1991, 1992) discusses the efforts of the colonial government in tracking child trafficking and resettling the victims. Lovejoy and Hogendorn (1993), provide an historical analysis of child trafficking within the context of the colonial legislation against slavery and the slave trade in northern Nigeria. But these works discuss only the problems of child labour within the colonial context, whereas the present study intends to bridge the lacuna by studying the contemporary patterns in comparison with the 1930s.

Dottridge (2002) argues that poverty is a central factor in the decision of parents to send their children away to work. He contends that children fleeing poverty or seeking better prospects are manipulated, deceived and bullied into working conditions that they would not choose. However, the causes of child labour are more complex than just poverty. The causes of child labour can be studied within the economic structure and production relations in which it occurs.

From a political economy perspective, it can be concluded that the trajectory of capitalist development has pushed young men and women into slavery and bonded labour. The driving forces in the commodification of women, for instance, were the advance of capital over labour and nation states, economic recession, neo-liberal political transition and corruption (Olaniyi 2003). This work focuses mainly on sex work and trafficking in the 1990s. The hope is that the present research will bridge the lacuna that exists in the literature.

Methodology

For this study, interviews and observation methods were utilized. Archival documents and content analysis of newspapers as well as magazines constituted other sources of materials. In Kano, research visits and interviews were held at the Malam Aminu Kano International Airport, Kano; the Anti-Human Trafficking Unit of the Nigerian Immigration Service; and the Motherless Children Home, which served as a resettlement base for trafficked victims in order to decipher the magnitude of the trafficking and the statistics of deported victims. I interviewed officials of the Nigerian

Immigration Service, where I observed the handling of cases of child trafficking, deported children and young women and cases of missing children working as domestic servants or babysitters. I visited and interviewed NGOs that engaged in the campaign against child trafficking in Kano State, particularly the Kano State Branch of the Women Trafficking and Child Labour Eradication Foundation (WOTCLEF). Interviews were conducted, albeit through deception, with child trafficking agents in order to know the source areas, social conditions of the children and working conditions and profits of the traffickers. I also observed within my neighbourhood how children in the labour process ran errands from morning till dawn, often appearing unkempt and sustaining injuries from episodic battering (see my interview with Abdullahi Oseni, a 10-year-old domestic servant in note 30). I interviewed some employers of the trafficked girls who informed me that some of the girls were often withdrawn by their parents after having accumulated enough for the purpose of early marriages. Data for child trafficking in the 1930s were obtained from the National Archives, Kaduna (NAK) and in a couple of published works. For the 1990s, I relied on oral interviews, personal observations and content analysis of newspapers, magazines and reports.

Child Trafficking in the 1930s: When Children were Sold for Food

Globally, the 1930s was a period of depression. The Great Depression was triggered by fiscal crisis, structural disequilibria and the collapse of stock prices at the New York Stock Exchange (Abdulkadir 2004:1). In Nigeria, the 1930s was a devastating period for the colonized, which witnessed economic exploitation under British rule. The depression marked a significant decrease in government revenue, as expenditure diminished and capital projects were halted. Nigeria's gross income in 1928 was 198 per cent higher than that of 1929, plummeting from £74 million to £25 million; while gross expenditure in 1932–3 decreased by 28 per cent from £6.9 million to £5 million (Abdulkadir 2004:1). The fiscal crises were further complicated by the policy of 'lending' and 'exporting' money from the already depressed Nigerian economy to other British colonies. Between 1930 and 1934, out of the Northern Nigeria Native Administration's surplus of £5,589,270 5s. 2d., about 44.87 per cent, amounting to £2,508,354 1s. 9d., was invested in Crown Colonies, Ceylon, Singapore, Trinidad, New Zealand and Australia. Indeed, the drastic fall in structural saving and foreign investments systematically reduced the velocity of money and triggered social misery and widespread poverty.

Between 1929 and 1934, prices of agricultural products plummeted. The Lagos price of palm kernel dropped from £21 per ton in 1929 to £14 in 1930 (a fall of 33.33 per cent); it continued to drop, reaching £7 in 1934 (a fall of 66.66 per cent); cotton prices also declined by 66.66 per cent, from 2.25d. per 1b in the 1928/9 buying season to 0.75d. in 1930/1; and the average price of groundnuts fell by a comparable 62.4 per cent, from £12 18s. per ton in the 1927/8 buying season to £4 17s. in 1930/1, and by 1933/4 it was only 54.63 per cent of the 1927/8 price, decreasing to £2 13s. (Abdulkadir 2004:2).

During the Great Depression, the grave financial conditions lead to reduction of staff wages and salaries, and indeed massive unemployment. Certain allowances for bicycle and horses were reduced during the 1931–2 fiscal year. In the 1930s, forced labour was retained for the execution of public works. There was an imposition of additional taxation in the form of special 'fees', with the alternative of compulsory labour in default of payment. According to Shea and Abdulkadir,

> … (T)he real incomes of agricultural producers declined sharply both because their cash incomes from the sale of the produce declined and because the prices of any imported goods which they were able to consume became relatively more expensive… (Shea and Abdulkadir 1987: 6).

In the 1930s in Nigeria, there were tax deficiencies, overestimation, embezzlements and increases in taxation despite the economic difficulties. Children, old people, the destitute and sick people were all taxed. The burden of taxation led to massive migration to areas of economic opportunities. Economic disparities between regions and provinces further led to huge migration flows. The migration of adult males owing to taxation gave rise to child labour and trafficking in the farming areas of Bida and Lapai. During the 1935–6 fiscal year, there was high taxation imposed on the people while on the part of the Native Authorities and District Heads there was an increase in embezzlement.

Survival strategies became polarized along class categories. Among the impoverished masses, trading and trafficking in children became accelerated as economic crises intensified. Embezzlement of public funds among district heads and tax collectors became endemic on an unprecedented scale. For example, there were 30 districts in Kano Emirate with 1205 Village Heads. Tax deficiencies occurred in only three districts, caused by defalcations of five Village Heads, of whom three were brought to trial, convicted and given sentences of one or two months' imprisonment, and two absconded. In the period 1927–30, a total of over £441 was embezzled in the Kano Emirate.

In the 1930s, child trafficking was the direct by-product of economic crises and the British policy to abolish the legal status of slavery. The trade continued for at least three decades despite steady pressure from the colonial regime and the League of Nations to end it. Children became slaves as a result of pawnship (the pledging of a third person for debt), kidnapping and slave raiding – the very methods of enslavement that had operated before the imposition of British rule. Among the Yoruba in Western Nigeria, pawning was a credit as well as educational institution. Wealthy men pawned their unruly children for paltry sums of money in order that they might be properly trained on another man's farm and to give the impression that there was no money in their family. When a man was in dire need of money to defray the expenses of a funeral, marriage or chieftancy ceremony, he was customarily at liberty to pawn his son. Pawn children, *iwofa*, carried out domestic work such as tending horses, drawing water for housewives, chopping wood for cooking, but retained the liberty of sports and holidays like the children of their master.

Under British rule, more children were trafficked through pawnship than hitherto practised. Pawnship showed no signs of disappearing well into the depression of the 1930s. Children became slaves as a result of the debts of their parents or other kin, often during famines. Parents, and occasionally other kin when children were orphaned, used the children as pawns to secure food or money to buy food. The famines of 1903–4, 1907–8 and 1913–14 were particularly central, and there was a resurgence of pawning during the depression of the 1930s. For example, as Webster noted in 1916,

> the recrudescence of slave dealing amongst the Mumuye ... may be attributed to the famine in 1914 which aggravated the natural tendency of these tribes to sell their children, whom they look on as their natural currency (Lovejoy and Hogendorn 1993:264).

Economic crises among the Mumuye in 1916 had forced them to pawn over 60 children through pledges by their relatives for a trifle of food or pittance of money in times when food was scarce. Child traffickers often made an initial payment of 5s. to the parents; thereafter the creditors had difficulty collecting more. In 1921, child trafficking was observed in the economically plagued Al-Kaleri district of south-west Bauchi as adoption on payment carried on between the parents and the neighbouring Fulani. Kidnapping of children with the intent to enslave or sell as slaves was also common. For example, the Mumuye not only pawned their children but also could not protect them from kidnappers (Lovejoy and Hogendorn 1993:265). It was observed that the smaller the children were the better, provided they had been weaned.

In 1924, officials of Yola in the Adamawa Province claimed that it was impossible to stamp out kidnapping of young girls and children as villages acted as child trafficking depots. During the period of economic distress, child traffickers promised to maintain the parents if they would permit them to 'adopt' and train their boys as servants and girls for 'marriage'.

In the 1930s, child stealing, slave dealing and sales of children were common phenomena. Among the Idoma of Benue, child stealing for purposes of sale to Southern Nigeria burgeoned at this time. In the Benue Province, 42 persons were convicted for trading in children and child labour. By 1934, there was extensive trafficking in children in the Nassarawa Emirate. There was equally extensive trafficking in children in Panchin Division of Plateau Province whereby parents sold their children to Fulani pastoralists and farmers.

The British considered child trafficking a gross contravention of the anti-slave trade and slavery laws. Traffickers faced sentences that ranged from two to fourteen years' imprisonment. Zang near Numan was a children trafficking centre. Through this route there was extensive child trafficking between German Cameroon and Nigeria from 1916 during the First World War. According to T.H. Haughton, in the Yola Province Annual Report, 1924,

> the past year has shown a considerable improvement in respect to slavery in the Mandated Areas, and although it cannot be denied that a relatively mild form of trafficking in children slaves still continues to exist...

The outbreak of the First World War provided profitable avenue for child traffickers, particularly in the Adamawa Province. Many of the traffickers had small girls and a few boys, kidnapped for purchase. The slave children fetched as much as £15 a head in Kano and Lokoja.

Child trafficking flourished under the British rule as food shortages and economic distress persisted. Between 1931 and 1935, sales and trafficking of children became endemic in the Mandara region of French Cameroon inhabited by the Wula ethnic group. The famine conditions, shortage of food and the general level of economic crisis resulted in the recrudescence of child trafficking. Poor parents in dire need of food supplied their children to traffickers who readily took advantage of the victims' distress. The agents were chiefly Shuwa Arabs, Kanembu and Wula who sold children to the traffickers from the Lake Chad area, Wadai, Kanem and Tibesti. The child trafficking route was from Mandara northwards through the western part of Dikwa, the north-eastern corner of Bornu Province and along the chores of Lake Chad.

The traffickers travelled by night, leaving trafficked children hidden in the bush in the daytime, thus making detection difficult. Although there were cases of children abducted by force, the majority of the trafficked children were sold by their parents for food in times of shortage. The unremitting vigilance of the Native Authorities in Borno and Dikwa, aided by close cooperation with the French authorities in Cameroon, drove the trafficking in children underground. Through the efforts of District and Village Headmen, special mounted patrols and private individuals, a total of 186 trafficking children were released while 20 traffickers were convicted.

In the Benue Province, child trafficking among the Idoma occurred in the form of child stealing. The children were sold in Western Nigeria where there was a steady demand in the cocoa plantations. During the economic depression, there was a resurgence of child stealing between the Western District of Idoma Division and Eha Amufu in the Nsukka Division of Southern Provinces. The two routes became notorious for child trafficking. Between 1931 and February 1933, after prolonged investigations and security patrols, 23 persons were convicted for child trafficking while 11 victims of trafficking were set free.

Among the Idoma, female children were regarded principally as financial assets and the 'bride prices' to be received from them on marriage constituted a source of income for the family. From 'bride price' to slave price was but a short step. Boys who had no marriageable value were sold to traffickers during the period of financial crisis. Cultural attitudes towards children and in particular girls reinforced the sale of children into slavery and children's social status made them vulnerable to trafficking. Among the Idoma, children were sold to traffickers as 'illegitimate' in the case of boys and for 'witchcraft' in the case of girls. In Igala Division of Kabba Province many children were sold as illegitimate and there was extensive trafficking in female children. In Igala Division, children without marks were sold owing to lack of money and food shortages (Abdulkadir 2004:9). Orphans became commodities for child traffickers in the 1930s.

In several instances, girls were acquired by means of purchase disguised as payment of dowry. Girl child marriage to 'stranger husbands' became a major method of child trafficking and selling children into slavery among the Idoma. In order to curtail the trend, the following marriage rules were promulgated under the Native Authority Ordinance:

(i) That it should be illegal for any parent or guardian of the Idoma tribe to give his daughter or ward in marriage to any person who is not a native of, and living in the Idoma Division, without first informing and consulting all those of his relatives whom, by native law and custom, it is his duty in such circumstances to inform and consult.

(ii) That it should in any event be illegal for any parent or guardian of the Idoma tribe to give his daughter or ward in marriage to a person who is not a native of, and living in, the Idoma Division, until she has attained the age of puberty.

In Nasarawa Division, one Habu, a notorious trafficker, was tried in 1935 for three separate charges of selling three boys with the intent that they should be treated as slaves and also on a fourth charge of buying two boys. He was sentenced to one year's imprisonment with hard labour on each of the first two charges and to five years on each of the last two; all the sentences ran concurrently. Rozoma, another notorious child trafficker, was tried and convicted of buying a young boy with the intent that he should be treated as a slave. He was sentenced to four years' imprisonment with hard labour.

In 1934, there was dramatic rise in the incidence of child trafficking in the Nassarawa Emirate. Some of the cases of child trafficking were tried in the High Court in 1935 and led to the conviction of nine persons and the release of five children from traffickers. The trafficked children were intended for sale in the cocoa farms of Southern Nigeria. Cases of child stealing and trafficking were reported to the British authorities through direct complaints by mothers of children who had been sold. Between 1930 and 1935, a total of 42 persons were convicted of the offences connected with child trafficking and 19 children were freed. Sentences ranged from two to fourteen years' imprisonment and despite the unceasing campaign by touring Administrative Officers trafficking showed no sign of decrease, probably as a result of the continuing economic difficulties experienced by the masses.

Table 4.1 Child Trafficking in the Adamawa Province, 1930–1935

Year	1930	1931	1932	1933	1934	1935
Number of cases	8	1	7	3	3	-
Persons charged	8	1	7	4	4	-
Convictions	5	-	6	4	3	-
Persons liberated as a result of convictions	4	-	-	7	6	-

Source: NAK/SNP 17/1/20216 Vol. II: Slave Traffic in Adamawa Province, Annual Report 1935.

Child trafficking endured owing to the institution of concubinage whereby non-Muslim girls were trafficked into the Emirates for this purpose since concubinage was illegal unless with slave girls. In a patriarchal society, the social construction of gender relations made girls vulnerable to trafficking for the purpose of sex slavery.

Currency scarcity in the impoverished countryside equally enabled child trafficking to flourish. In Yola, children were used as currency during the depression to obtain horses, goats, cattle and salt. There was less difficulty in child trafficking, since children were not in a position to offer resistance to enslavement or to attempt escape from captivity (Lovejoy and Hogendorn 1993:263). The strategies of child traffickers included acculturation whereby trafficked children lived with the trafficker, adopted his language, fashion and facial marks before being placed in the market for sale. The trafficked children often looked up to their traffickers, mostly Yoruba and Hausa, which made it difficult to detect their cases. In the 1930s, there was an increasing supply of child trafficking to meet the soaring market for concubines and domestic slaves largely recruited from the non-Muslim girls' population who were then kept in seclusion.

Labour constraints among Fulani nomads spurred demand for young boys who were bought to tender cattle in remote bush away from the purview of the law. Mada children in Southern Zaria on the borders of Jos were bought by Fulani pastoralists. The boys were trained to tend cattle, while the girls were often kept until they were mature enough to become concubines (Lovejoy and Hogendorn 1993:269). In 1930, in Plateau Province, children were kidnapped by unemployed young men who sold them to Fulani pastoralists and, by 1932, 92 people were convicted for trafficking in children in two districts of Plateau Province (Abdulkadir 2004:9).

Child trafficking radiated from the hills of Adamawa and the Benue Valley in four directions (Lovejoy and Hogendorn 1993:269). Trafficked children went northwards through Dikwa and Borno to the Lake Chad Basin and the Sahara Desert. Pilgrims from Northern Nigeria to Mecca often took slave children with them for sale in North Africa. This phenomenon came to the attention of the British officials as early as the 1920s (Lovejoy and Hogendorn 1993:269). The export of children to Mecca was controlled through passport policy. Impending pilgrims had to apply for passports so that their movement could be monitored. Some pilgrims often financed their journey through the sale of children of 'pagan' origin (Lovejoy and Hogendorn, 1993:275). In Yola, several men applying for passports to Mecca were denied because each of them allegedly had between four to eight trafficked children.

Many other trafficked children went southwards through River Benue. They were often trafficked by the night to the child slave market on the banks of the River Niger and sold to Nupe, Kakanda, Igala, Ebira fish and salt traders. The children were further trafficked southwards to Lokoja, Ida, Onitsha and the Niger Delta. A wealthy woman trader was noted to have purchased 200 of such trafficked children within a decade (Lovejoy and Hogendorn 1993:269). In the Igala Division, there was a boom in child trafficking partly because wealthy women who had no children of their own bought them (Abdulkadir 2004:9). In 1932, the Native Authority Police in the Idoma Division of Benue Province intercepted three truckloads of trafficked children on their way to the cocoa plantations of Western Nigeria to work as farm labourers (Abdulkadir 2004:9).

In Kano, there was a ready market for trafficked girls who were bought by rich men for the purpose of using them as concubines. They were trafficked from Adamawa by Fulani pastoralists through overland routes of Bauchi and Nafada (Lovejoy and Hogendorn, 1993:270). Traffickers used the commercial code for children by referring to them as cattle while discussing them in public. In 1933, extensive child trafficking was carried out in the Pankshin Division of Plateau Province. Children were sold by their parents to Fulani pastoralists as a result of the economic depression. Many traffickers were tried and sentenced in the Provincial Court and 15 children were released from slavery.

In the Bida Division of Niger Province, there were large-scale practices of pawnship-pledging of a third person or debtor himself/herself among the Nupe. There was a resurgence of pawning of children by parents to their debtors. By 1934, it was discovered that pawning was still prevalent in the Pategi and Lafiagi Emirates of Ilorin Province. Native Courts treated cases involving servitude as criminal cases, and instances of pawning or pledging of children were presumed to be an element of servitude since a child was not a willing pawn.

Umaisha District of the Nasarawa Emirate served as the dumping ground or depot for trafficked children to Southern Province. Children were sold at the rate of £13. Traffickers were convicted under Section 369 of the Criminal Code with sentence of two to six months' imprisonment. Notorious child traffickers in Umaisha established their trafficking depot in the town with a channel of communication in the northern bank of River Benue and the riverine districts of the Nasarawa Emirate to replace their lost markets in the Southern Province where their activities had been checked. The traffickers organized a large-scale syndicate for child trafficking and no expense was spared to obtain the goodwill of the local inhabitants. Female children between the ages of 7 and 12 were also trafficked.

In the Muri Emirate, acute food shortages and famine forced parents to negotiate their children for cash. Hausa groundnuts traders took advantage of the appalling social conditions by adding children as articles of trade (Ubah 1991:466). In most of the 1930s, famine largely arose from food shortages and insufficient income with which to buy food, which gave impetus to trafficking in children. Many poor people could not afford to buy food for their subsistence. While the poor communities sold their children to obtain food the seemingly rich procured them to reinforce their process of accumulation.

Indeed, under British rule, child trafficking occurred fundamentally in terms of structural imbalances in the access to resources among the colonized. The economic depression spurred death, diseases, starvation and massive migration. Whenever famine struck, the corollary was that people were bought and sold. In the Muslim Emirates, slave owners who ran out of money sold their slaves to generate income to maintain their household (Ubah 1991:465). Among the non-Muslims, who were largely impoverished, parents sold their children in order to save other members of the family from starvation and death (Ubah 1991:466). In 1932, starvation among the Wula hill people led to their migration to the plains in the British sphere of influence in search of food. Many sold their women and children in order to survive.

Rescued trafficked children were cared for by the Primitive Methodist Mission at Igumale and the Lucy Memorial Freed Slaves Home. Table 4.2 shows tariffs for the maintenance of such children between 1926 and 1943.

Table 4.2 Maintenance of Rescued Children, 1926–1943

Age	Rate per annum	Note
1–10	£5 each	Includes all teaching and school fees
10–13	£7	
13–16	£10	
16 and above	£13	
	II	
1–12	£6	School fees etc. To be paid extra cost 5–18 £89 plus school fees

Source: NAK/SNP 17/1/ 11834: Freed Slaves – Disposal and Subsistence of 1926–1943.

Rescued trafficked children were placed under government institutions or persons entrusted with custody. The Lucy Memorial Home was established for children who were sold by their parents or kidnappers. The home, at Wukari, was intended to liberate and train the inmates who were from different parts of Northern Nigeria. Most of these children were arrested on transit alongside their captors in the process of selling them or were arrested from those who purchased them following information given to the Native Authority Police by those who were against the use of children as slaves. Some of the lucky children got back to their parents through the help of European police while others who could not trace their ancestral homes were sent to the freed slaves' home either to engage in schooling or learning a trade to enable them earn a living.

Under the British rule, Government Freed Slaves Homes programme was short-lived. At first, a home was opened at Lokoja to take care of children rescued from traffickers, but in October 1903 it was transferred to Zungeru. In the same year another home was opened in Borno. Under the auspices of Charity of Rebecca Hussey: African Fund of Redemption of Slave Branch, schools were established for the rescued trafficked children. A sum of £270 per annum was granted as the Lagos Fund for the establishment and maintenance of schools for the liberated African children. Table 4.3 shows the expenses of the Wushishi School in the Northern Province between 1927 and 1931.

Table 4.3 Expenses at Wushishi School, 1927–1931

Name of child	Period	Number of days in the period	Maintenance grant per day	Total
Naisha	June 1927–Dec. 1931	214	3d	£213.6
Laraba	"	"	"	"
Lami	"	"	"	"
				£8.0.6

Source: NAK/SNP 17/1/10028 Vol. II: Lucy Memorial Freed Slaves Home, Wukari Proposal.

Other rescued trafficked children were placed under the custody of private individuals and families (Europeans and Africans) under the supervision of the Sudan United Mission and Lucy Memorial Freed Slaves Home. While the British government was wary of subsidizing the missionary enterprise, it was responsible for the upkeep of the children it transferred to the 'Freed Slaves' Homes for their moral and educational welfare until they reached the age of maturity. The boys went through apprenticeship schemes in printing, agriculture and government cart work while the girls were groomed for 'marriage'. Indeed, the cost of marriage of £4 paid by suitors was similar to the cost of redemption.

Child trafficking, slave dealing, kidnapping and other offences against liberty were punished under the Criminal Code, which applied throughout Nigeria and the Mandated Territory. However, child trafficking persisted arising partly from the inconsistency of the British in eradicating slavery and slave trade. Slavery in Northern Nigeria became politically expedient for the British to prevent the dislocation of the social framework and pauperization of the ruling classes, which the government aimed to preserve and strengthen.

The British Government, in a response to an enquiry from the Council of the League of Nations on the question of slavery, stated:

> In the Northern Provinces the intention and policy of the Government is not to interfere with the relation of masters and slaves (i.e., persons born in or brought into that part of Nigeria before April 1st 1901), so long as the relation is voluntarily maintained by both parties, in districts which recognise Moslem law and are under the jurisdiction of Moslem Courts.

Until the intervention of the League of Nations in the 1930s, the British were reluctant to abolish the slave trade and slavery institutions in many parts of Nigeria. According to the League of Nations Report, slavery persisted in Nigeria and indeed, in many parts of the British Africa, under the ambiguous policy of 'voluntary slavery'. The slavery abolition law was more or less ineffective in taming slavery and child trafficking. In the Southern Provinces, there were 'voluntary slaves' and the Northern Provinces, where only slaves born after 31 March 1901 were 'free'. As early as January 1902, Lord Lugard had exercised restraint in abolishing the institution of slavery. According to him, slavery should be gradually abolished in order to prevent the 'disastrous consequences' of producing

> a mass of unemployed vagrants and increase the criminal classes: in the case of women it would tend to increase prostitution: while both classes would beyond doubt bring upon themselves unforeseen misery by cancelling the obligation under which their masters lie of providing for them in sickness, or caring for their wives and children during their absence from their homes … The upper classes would be reduced to misery and starvation, and as a consequence to hostility against the Europeans who had brought this chaos about (quoted in Lovejoy and Hogendorn 1993:81–2).

The League of Nations Slavery Committee discovered that slaves born before the 31 March 1901, were expected by local custom, as administered by the Native Courts, to purchase their freedom by a system of ransom-payment of court fees. Court fees or ransom, were paid into the colonial government treasury, which meant the government derived revenue out of the slavery transactions. In Yola, in 1936, young male or female slaves, mostly trafficked children, paid £5 as ransom and court fees to secure their redemption. Slaves were mandated to pay fees that guaranteed them the right to work independent of their masters and to enable them to pay taxes and ransom for their freedom.

The British policy of non-interference equally reinforced the tax and economic base of the slave-owning ruling elites. Forced labour, otherwise known as Political Labour, was used by the local chiefs and the British in the public works and farms of the chiefs. In particular, Lord Lugard had a liberal interpretation of the Slavery Proclamation and gave concessions to slave owners. In practical terms child slaves were allowed to be sold and bought provided that the transactions were conducted within the same province (Ubah 1991:450). Child trafficking and indeed, slave trading, meant wealth to the rulers and the merchant class but the impoverished masses accepted it as a legitimate means of earning a living (Ubah 1991:452). In the Muslim Emirates of Northern Nigeria, the League of Nations discovered that the British adopted a policy of non-interference with slavery, which compromised the trafficking of young girls as concubines. The policy of non-interference was also intended to prevent economic and political instability for the British administration.

Despite the Slavery Ordinance of the League of Nations in 1936, child trafficking, particularly girls for sex-slavery or concubinage, showed no signs of diminishing. Children were exploited under the guise of adoption. In the Northern Cameroons and among the Bamileke, children were ostensibly adopted by the Emirates of Northern Nigeria and were taken away against payment of a certain amount to their families. Children were made to perform arduous tasks at a very early age. Girls and boys of 5 or 6 years carried water, wood and other children that often weighed more than themselves. Up to the late 1930s, trafficked children were still engaged in plantation agriculture owned by the aristocrats. Nevertheless, the French and the British jointly monitored the movement of traffickers along the borders through policing and patrols. Native authorities were involved in this process and many concerned individuals intercepted child traffickers and liberated the children without resort to the colonial authority.

Trafficking in the 1990s: Children in the Labour Process

In the 1990s, there was a resurgence of child trafficking in conditions of political instability under military rule and imposed neo-liberal economic reforms. These led to the greater expansion of the informal sector of the local economy and plantation agriculture, especially cocoa producing for the global economy. In both the informal sector and cocoa plantations, there was unprecedented demand for the cheap labour of children. Children were bought from their poor parents in the rural areas and in neighbouring countries while some were kidnapped or enslaved under the guise of fostering. Organized criminal networks recruited children and enslaved them with little or no remittance to the children or their parents.

In Nigeria, structural imbalances and distortions occurred in the economy in the wake of the oil boom of the 1970s. Against the background of excessive dependence on oil exports, there was a resurgence in the Nigerian economic crisis in the early 1980s owing to the devastating impact of global economic recession, collapse of crude oil prices and declining capital inflow (Obadan and Edo 2004:16). The decline of oil prices in the world market grossly affected the nation's revenue and thereby gave rise to fiscal deficits and rapid depletion of foreign exchange reserves (Obadan and Edo 2004:16). Economic crisis also manifested in galloping inflation, rising unemployment, abandoned projects, factory closures and an increasing burden of external debt. Between 1995 and 1999, the economy was characterized by sluggish growth, indicated by the GDP growth rates of 2.2 per cent in 1995; 3.4 per cent in 1996; 3.8 per cent in 1997; 2.3 per cent in 1998; and 2.8 per cent in 1999 (Obadan and Edo 2004:26–7).

The growth rate was too low for the desired improvement in living conditions of the people. Poverty remained widespread, with the incidence rising from 40$ of the population in the early 1990s to 66 per centin 1999. The sliding GDP growth rate was incapable of stemming the poverty trend. Nigeria's external reserves declined from $7.7 billion in 1997 to $7.2 billion in 1998 and $5.5 billion in 1999, tracing the sharp decline in oil. Agriculture production experienced steady growth from 3.6 per cent in 1995 to 5.5 per cent in 1998 but plummeted to 2.8 per cent in 1999.

At the end of the 1990s, Nigeria had the fifteenth lowest purchasing power in the world; per capita income was less than $1; its 10 per cent inflation rate was the 44th highest in the world; and it was the 21st highest foreign debtor. The economic crisis was characterized by weak growth, interest rate instability, diminishing capacity utilization and an unbridled rise in unsold inventory among manufacturing firms. From 60Kobo per litre in 1986 for both private and commercial vehicles the fuel price increased to N20.00 in 1999.

As the fuel price jumped and the value of the Naira collapsed, the cost of living rose and poverty spread. Governance was executed with unbridled corruption, prebendalism and predation. As the government monopoly of oil revenues shifted from a phase of control and redistribution to sheer hiding and hoarding, capital was systematically withdrawn from the economy and government officials invested abroad to finance new business enterprises or political ambition (Guyer, Denzer and Agbaje 2003:xxi). The predatory accumulation created a group of the new rich who live in 'islands' – sprawling walled fortresses, mansions and palaces with personalized social services including water, security and electricity supplies while most of the people were extremely poor and isolated. There was mass poverty and destitution.

According to Moeletsi Mbeki, head of the South African Institute of International Affairs, 'while China has lifted some 400,000 people out of poverty in the past twenty years, Nigeria has pushed 71 million people further down the poverty line'.

Nigeria is the third least developed oil exporting country, with a low human development index. The precarious economic situation forced desperate parents to send their children to work (Kar 2002:125). Parents were also seen to withdraw their children from the labour process as soon as they could afford to maintain the family or pay the children's school fees. According to Goldin, 'the higher the father's wage, the lower the probability of the child participating in the labour force, the father's unemployment sent both boys and girls into the labour force with a stronger impact on the former' (Goldin 1979:111–31).

Indeed, the supply of child labour was predicated by the living standards of a family, and children were sent to work in order to meet the subsistence needs of the family (Kar 2002:125). Poor families added children to the family labour force to generate income to meet their subsistence and school fees. Parents who were beneficiaries of the economic activities of their children had little or no impulse to discourage them from dropping out of school and entering the labour process (Isamah & Okunola 2003:64 and 71). In the 1990s, the contraction in the formal sector of the economy fuelled the dramatic expansion of the informal economy characterized by micro-enterprises, hawking and street trading. In most of urban centres in Nigeria, however, the government outlawed hawking and street trading in which police patrols and high-handedness have driven child trafficking and child labour underground. Trafficked children worked under economic spheres without labour legislation and social protection.

According to the National Human Rights Commission, Abuja, 22 million Nigerian children under the age of 15 years were part of the workforce. About 45 per cent of children hawking in Nigerian cities were products of child trafficking, especially from rural areas, poor urban neighbourhoods and neighbouring countries. The forms of recruitment used by child traffickers ranged from complete coercion through abduction and kidnapping to deception by promises of legitimate employment. In some cases children were trafficked through family networks at a time of weakening of traditional values and the unbridled quest for money.

The roll-back of the state in funding education had thrown many children out of school. By the end of the 1990s, the Federal Ministry of Education reported that 12 million Nigerian children were drop-outs. Many of them became victims of trafficking. In the early 1990s, the deepening economic crisis and widespread poverty led to a resurgence of child trafficking. Like commodities, children were bought and sold through a subterranean network of organized syndicates. Mrs Rita Akpan, the Minister of State of Women Affairs, estimated that trading in children and young women was worth N1 billion per year.

Table 4.4 gives some data for the status of primary education in Nigeria in the year 2000. Under the Basic Primary Education (BPE) scheme, states and local governments passed laws for compulsory education that were not unfortunately enforced.

Table 4.4 Primary Education in Nigeria: A Fact File, c. 2000

No. of pupils	20,900,451
No. of teachers	448,414
No. of classrooms	332,408
No. of classrooms in good condition	140,134
No. of classrooms in bad condition	192,274
Annual teachers' wage bill	N100 million

Source: *Crystal Magazine*, December 2000, p. 18.

The situation was exacerbated in the south-west where states hitherto offering free education now charged fees, which many parents, faced with diminishing purchasing power, found difficult to pay. Among females aged 15–24 who had left school 29 per cent of them dropped out because they could not pay school fees. In 1998, it was indicated that in Lagos State the annual average cost borne by families to send their children to school was N16,500 for public schools in urban centres; N9,250 for rural public schools; N43,200 for private urban schools and N28,000 for private rural schools. The number of children out of school increased: 45 per cent for females between the ages of 6 and 10 years; and 45 per cent for males of the same age. For the 10–15 year categories the figures were 35 per cent for females and 31 per cent for males.

Children were pushed out of the school into the labour process. Many parents regarded these children as income-earners and assigned them to street trading in order to fend for the family and themselves. In search of financial relief from the avalanche of economic and social distress, some parents depended on the labour of their children. Indeed, the greater majority of child hawkers, conditioned by the privation of the street, veered into crime and sex work to supplement what they made from hawking. About one per cent of GDP was spent on funding education. A large chunk of this meagre amount often went into private pockets. The assessment and collection of Education Tax was marked by massive fraud by the Federal Inland Revenue Service (FIRS), which mismanaged over N50 billion through fraudulent practices. In Kogi State, the Commissioner for Education, Chief James Akor and three other principal officers of the Ministry of Education, were indicted for embezzling N45 million out of the N136 million meant for bursary grants to students. In Kano State, the former Governor, Rabiu Musa Kwakwanso and his Commissioner for Finance, Dr Hafizu Abubakar, were indicted for misappropriating the sum of N62,689,700.00 meant for student scholarship allowances. The fraud threatened the education opportunities of Nigerian children in the state and compromised them for trafficking.

Lack of educational, vocational and economic opportunities for the youth in the rural areas made children vulnerable in the labour process, especially in the informal sector of the economy. The erosion of living standards gave impetus to many households to seek additional income by engaging in multiple modes of livelihood in the informal sector (Mustapha 1992:188). The out-of-school children were readily employed by their market women mothers as an additional workforce to generate income through hawking to supplement their sales in the competitive informal sector.

Children joined their parents in petty trading and city street hawking; participation in agricultural production, cattle grazing, marketing of fresh produce, housing construction and in the transport sector (Howard 2002:7; Araoye 2002:5). Nevertheless, some parents often withdrew their children from the labour process as soon as they could sustain the family.

Nigeria's global trafficking in children could be seen as an extension of internal trafficking, which was rife, as poor families traditionally sent boys and girls to work in wealthier homes. This often began as a form of child fostering, but sometimes it was slavery. Indeed, cultural philanthropy often ended in endemic exploitation as guardians turned the misery of the poor children to their own fortune. Hidden from the sight of the law, these children were often confined to the four walls of the home; used and denied western education, basic healthcare, adequate nutrition, leisure time and security. The children provided cheap labour and slipped into abusive conditions. They were treated like slaves and often ended up as domestic servants. The Lagos middle class has a bountiful supply of houseboys and girls brought from villages across the country by 'helpful aunts and uncles' who pocket the cash and disappear. Their parents are involved. They say to the girls, 'why don't you go with this man and work? We have no money, we have nothin to eat. You can send us money.' And so the girls go.

In 1990, Fulani pastoralists were involved in the clandestine buying of children between the ages of 7 and 11 years in Enugu (Effah 1996:14). The children were engaged in cattle rearing. Hausa traders bought children at the rates as low as N100,000 and as high as N1 million. By December 1991, the increasing menace of trafficking came to public view when 26 children of Imo State origin were deported from Libreville, Gabon. In February 1992, 250 children of Rivers State origin were deported from Gabon. In May 1995, 330 children were deported from Gabon and were kept in a camp in Calabar. The arrest of Adebisi Dan-Musa (Bisket), a seemingly notorious trafficker, for allegedly stealing 15 children for the purpose of selling them into slavery, further exposed the practice of child trafficking to the national consciousness.

Some traffickers established corporate structures for the recruitment and placement of children in the labour process. For example, Ms Sola Aderogba established Executive Maids as a child employment agency in Surulere, Lagos. According to her, children between the ages of 11 and 14 were brought to her from Akwa Ibom, Cross River, and the Republics of Benin and Cameroon. While the traffickers escaped justice, child labour was very visible in Nigerian city streets. Children worked as feet washers, househelps and hawkers as well as porters in major markets. A UNICEF survey in 1992 estimated that 54 per cent of child domestic workers were employed by civil servants and professionals while 46 per cent of employers were self-employed in urban centres. Working-class professional women constituted a major segment of users of child domestic services in urban centres.

In Kano, mainly female traffickers travelled on a weekly basis to recruit children from the area's impoverished villages. Trafficking involved female children who were engaged as domestic servants, babysitters and as hawkers of kola nuts, groundnuts and other food items. They were offered between N500 and N1,000 per month depending on their age and experience. Traffickers collected a commission of N300 to N500 per child and sometimes received gifts of foodstuffs from both parents and employers of the children. Poor parents often engaged their daughters in the labour process to supplement the family sustenance, and most importantly to save money in order to procure marriage items such as beds, utensils, wrappers and so on. Domestic work was also considered a grooming ground for the girls in terms of cooking, house tidying and trading or ultimately finding a 'rich' suitor. Some of the children absconded following exploitation by their employers and in most cases they would not return to their parents until they got married. Many of them ended up as commercial sex workers. In some states of Northern Nigeria, girls were withdrawn from schools for marriage purposes. Every year, young girls were trafficked from Ilorin to Kano to serve as domestic servants and hawkers of concoctions. Some of these girls were often further trafficked to Saudi Arabia for sex work.

In Oyo State, children trafficked from rural areas and surrounding states were put 'on hire' in Ibadan (Isamah and Okunola 2003:67). Such children were put up for recruitment by their parents or guardians, who contracted them out for wages of between N2,000 and N3,000 per year. An agreed fee was paid in advance to the parents or guardians, on the agreement that the amount would be deducted from the wages paid to the child over a period of time. In Ibadan, they were deployed to clients who used them as domestic servants or traders. Parents often put pressure on the trafficked children to remain on the job even though they were ignorant of the nature of the work children carried out or the social conditions under which they worked. In south-west Nigeria, as elsewhere in the country, child trafficking remained a highly subterranean business. In the tobacco-growing community of Elewure in Kajola Local Government of Oyo State, women and children of school age, most of them trafficked, were engaged in barns picking tobacco leaves for curing. They were offered a pittance of N100 per day for the women and less for the children, who were denied any education.

Despite the growing unemployment for highly qualified adults, there was high demand for cheap and submissive child labour in the informal sector, street hawking, hackney business (conductorship), scavenging and in cocoa plantations producing for the global market. Child scavengers, otherwise called '*kombis*', collecting scraps of iron, plastic, rubber, tin and polythene bags, earned between N3,500 and N4,000 per week. Indeed, the scavengers constituted an emerging 'special breed' of children in the labour process because of the health and social hazards they were exposed to.

In a particular case, 64 children were rescued by the police along the Onitsha–Benin expressway. The bus driver claimed he was conveying the children, who were between the ages of 5 and 16 years, from Omor village in Anambra State to spend their holidays with their parents at Ughoha town in Edo State. But the children had not a stick of luggage!

Children were being trafficked to Edo State either for forced labour or ritual purposes, as claimed by the media. In 2000, the International Labour Organization (ILO) estimated that 4,000 children were trafficked per year from Cross River State alone. Ahiazu Mbaise local government area of Imo State became one of the most notorious child trafficking and child labour zones in Nigeria. Every year children were trafficked abroad by traffickers who deceived their parents with monetary and material gifts.

About 54 per cent of those trafficked were street hawkers, while 29 per cent stayed at home and 3.5 per cent were found to be sexually abused. Many of the girls were lured into sex at a tender age, leading to an increase in the number of unwanted pregnancies and teenage mothers. Traffickers often engaged trafficked girls in illicit baby-making factories. In Enugu, Onitsha and Owerri, syndicates hoarded trafficked girls for 'mating' purposes. At Abakpa Nike, on the outskirts of Enugu, thirteen girls, mainly teenagers at different stages of pregnancy, were found by the police, quarantined in a small, dark, poorly ventilated, makeshift clinic. In 1995, police discovered the hideout of a sex syndicate called *Oju Ina* sandwiched between Oke-Arin/Idumagbo and Enu Owa in Lagos where teenage girls between the ages of 11 and 18 were camped for sex work (Effah 1996:40–1). Some of them were kidnapped or abducted and were placed under the custody of middle-aged women, who groomed them to patronize men sexually. In Kaduna, child prostitution flourished in drinking joints and dancing halls. In Kano, trafficked children aged between 8 and 10 were recruited yearly from neighbouring countries such as Niger, Mali, Senegal, Cameroon and Sierra Leone and neighbouring states like Kogi, Plateau, Katsina, Kaduna and Bauchi states in Nigeria for sex and domestic work (Muazzam 2003:43).

In a similar fashion, young children and teenagers were co-opted into street begging by old professional beggars who lured them with fabulous stories of the money-spinning advantages of street begging. The children were often subsequently recruited by robbery gangs or became victims of ritual killings and road traffic accidents. Some were used as political thugs or became 'child soldiers' in ethnic and religious conflicts. The *Almajiri* (Quranic students) were both actors and victims of the spate of ethno-religious conflicts in Northern Nigeria such as the Maitatsine religious riots in Kano; the Bulunkutu riot in Maiduguri; Yola and Gombe riots. The increase in the number of street children in Nigerian cities has worsened the crime and violence situation. According to one of the street children, '…we no dey do anything again – we dey beg and we carry load for people'. In this process, what was referred to in local parlance as 'jet age begging', using children to solicit for alms, has emerged. Such children were 'displayed' carried by women who often hired them to attract public sympathy and financial assistance. In order to prick the conscience of alms-givers, some beggars hired babies from nannies and day care centres. In Lagos, with a token of N500, some owners of day care centres 'rent out' children for at least four hours to women who disguise them as beggars in the streets. City streets have been littered with destitute and colonies of child beggars have emerged. Con-men and child traffickers have transformed street begging in Nigeria into a lucrative 'export commodity'.

Child killing and child stealing for trafficking in human parts have increased. A syndicate kidnapping children was on the prowl in Abuja suburbs at Karinwo, Gwa-Gwa satellite town and in Lagos. The 'Otokoto Seven' uprising following the ritual murder of an 11-year-old, Ikechukwu Okonkwo, a groundnut hawker in September 1996, consummated a process that had endangered Owerri for almost a decade. The rate of trafficking increased partly because of a highly organized trade in human parts business with a ready market. Traffickers often sold children to those in need of human parts for rituals. The value of a human head ranged between N3,000 and N10,000.

Across the west coast of Africa, porous borders have served as distribution points for trafficked children who were exchanged across countries in the form of imports and exports. The social dislocation of children in the West Africa sub-region through trafficking has ensured their perpetual exploitation in the labour process and perpetuated the vicious circle of the menace. Traffickers often operate with impunity and exorbitant profit at the expense of the trafficked children.

Surveys in four West African countries (Cameroun, Côte D'Ivoire, Ghana and Nigeria) revealed that of an estimated number of 284,000 engaged in cocoa farming, including the clearing of fields in cocoa farms, a total of 153,000 were involved in the application of dangerous pesticides. In Côte d'Ivoire and Nigeria, an approximate number of 2,500 working children were recruited through intermediaries for cocoa farming. The children were working in the cocoa farms and plantations under strenuous and exploitative conditions. Working conditions were worse in commercial agriculture when the children were bonded. It was not unusual to mortgage children for the debt of their parents, sometimes for life. Bonded children in the cocoa plantations were denied basic human rights and education. Cocoa production is labour-intensive and its global market of fluctuating prices led to farmers demanding the cheap labour of children. In the cocoa belt of western Nigeria, the use of migrant labour became prominent. Most of the migrant labourers were trafficked from central Nigeria to the cocoa farms by middlemen. The trend became phenomenal in the 1930s and continued into the 1990s. Child labour increased in the cocoa sector owing to the expansion in the global chocolate industry. According to Anti-Slavery International:

> The majority of cocoa farmers in West Africa are smallholders, with 22 per cent of cocoa produced on farms of less than two hectares, 65 per cent on farms of between two and ten hectares and only 12 per cent on plantations of more than ten hectares. It is difficult to be clear about labour requirements, but farms of less than two hectares will be almost entirely family run. As a result of the significant movement in the 1980s and 1990s from rural to urban areas in the region, of mainly young people, the average age of most growers is quite old. This may have led to an increasing use of paid labour on the farms and increased use of share cropping arrangements.

In Western Nigeria, labour constraints led to the continued demand for the cheap labour of young Agatu boys from Benue State of Nigeria; the Republics of Benin, Togo and Cameroon; and Burkina Faso, most of whom had no negotiating power for their income. This trend was boosted by the cocoa 'boom' of the 1990s. According to Anti-Slavery International:

> In Nigeria, exchange rate fixing complicated the effect of liberalisation in 1986, because exporting cocoa allowed the naira to be converted into a hard currency. Many companies previously uninvolved in the cocoa industry rushed to take advantage of this and it led to higher prices for farmers in the short term. In the long term, it led to problems such as defaults on forward contracts and falling quality. With foreign exchange liberalisation producer prices fell, but when access to foreign exchange was restricted once more in 1991/92 they rose again. Now that this problem has been dealt with and the system is completely liberated, farmers are receiving around 85 per cent of the FOB price.

The bulk of child labourers in the cocoa plantations of Ondo State were trafficked from Benue, Akwa-Ibom and Cross River States. In Cross River State, trafficking was often carried out during festive periods and cultural activities, especially in the months of March, April and December. In some parts of Cross River State, buses line up during these periods to convey trafficked girls and boys to Ondo State. Some of them who attended schools refused to bear their fathers' names but the traffickers' name. Twenty-four children from Ago village in Akwa-Ibom States,comprising eleven girls and thirteen boys, aged between 9 and 21 were rescued by the police from a trafficking syndicate. For each child, the trafficker was paid N3,000 as a handling charge on delivery to the cocoa plantation owners. Each child was paid N2,000 per month collected in bulk at the end of the year by the trafficker. Some traffickers do not remit the money to parents or the children. Some parents/guardians would ensure that children go to the cocoa plantations and return on a yearly basis. Trafficked girls to the cocoa plantations often served as sex slaves and many never returned. Some died in conditions of immense cruelty and their parents are told they have gone overseas.

Child labourers in cocoa plantations suffered from snake bites, pesticides and tuberculosis. Most parents remained little concerned once the traffickers unfailingly make the annual returns. Children from Cross River State were often trafficked to Cameroon, Gabon and Equatorial Guinea. Twenty children were rescued by the National Drug Law and Enforcement Agency (NDLEA) in Cross-River State. The victims, between the ages of 1 and 21 years, including six boys and fourteen girls, were rescued at Calabar-Itu Road with two men and three women traffickers. At the Ikom border, groups of children accompanied by adults often passed through to Cameroon during the farming season to work with plantation owners.

The most active trafficking route in south-eastern Nigeria is the Oron boundary (a sea route) and from private beaches in Calabar town. Usually, ships berth in the private beaches and move scores of children to Malabo in Equatorial Guinea and Gabon, where they are used as bonded labour on farm plantations. The Federal Ministry of Aviation discovered 193 unlicensed and illegal aerodromes operated by multinational oil companies. They operated uncontrolled flights that rendered Nigerian airspace porous and served as trafficking routes. In Malabo and Libreville markets, trafficked children worked as shop assistants and hawked goods rather than attend schools as traffickers had promised them. Some trafficked boys worked in agricultural plantations and the timber industry.

Children from poor families in Saki in Oyo State and Ilorin Kwara State were trafficked to Guinea, Mali and Côte d'Ivoire to work as hawkers and domestic servants. Children from Kebbi, Sokoto and Zamfara were also trafficked to Benin Republic, Togo and Mali through the Dole Kaina and Bagudo borders of Kebbi State. Children from Borno and Yobe were trafficked to Chad and Cameroon through the Baga and Doron Baga borders of Borno State, which linked with Chad, Niger and Cameroon.

In 2003, the Nigerian police estimated that between 6,000 and 15,000 children trafficked from Benin Republic were used mainly in the cocoa belt and granite quarries of Western Nigeria. The Nigerian police carried out several raids and released children working in the stone quarries and returned them to Benin Republic. Since 1991, child trafficking continued to flourish in supplying children in slave colonies at granite quarries. The slave colonies were located in Ogun, Oyo and Osun States of Nigeria. Children were trafficked to Nigeria in sacks, which were often declared as containing foodstuffs at the border.

The child slave owners had over 250 illegal routes for smuggling children into Nigeria from Benin Republic. The child slaves aged between 4 and 13 years lived and worked in appalling conditions. They were often fed once a day, lived and slept completely exposed to nature since they resided in the bush and had no shelter. The children, who earned N50 ($0.38) a week, each worked 12–16 hours, crushing enough gravel to generate N35,000 ($269). Every evening lorries delivered the gravel to construction sites in Western Nigeria. 194 of the children were liberated by the Nigerian police from the various work sites in Ogun State and deported to Benin Republic. The Nigerian Immigration Service confirmed that in March 1994, 51 prospective child slaves were liberated in Akwa Ibom State before they could be trafficked abroad. Another set of 77 children were freed between March and July; 236 others, among them 38 Beninoise and 23 Togolese, were rescued within the first two months of 1997.

Despite police surveillance and patrols, trafficking in Beninoise children continued unabated in Nigeria. One Iyabo Olasope was arrested by the police at Ojuwoye market in Mushin Lagos with twelve Sabe Beninoise children used for child labour. According to her,

> I didn't steal them neither did I kidnap any of them. They were brought to me by somebody (trafficker) to learn trade. And on each of them I paid between N500 and N600 for their services even though they're trainees. I am into direct marketing of some confectioneries, pepper, tomatoes and seasonings. And they were learning how to do this business. Beninoise children are easier to keep than Nigerian ones who are found of unruly behaviours particularly stealing.

The Sabe children were given Yoruba names by their employer and considered her as their 'biological' mother. Contrary to her claims, the stereotypes that Beninoise children are trustworthy, trafficked children particularly from neighbouring countries were often coerced into submission. Most of the trafficked children often became stranded and trapped and therefore had to rely on their traffickers and employers. A children's market or 'child labour camp' was tracked down in a five-storey building at Ojuelegba Lagos, where residents used to go and choose the children they needed for domestic work. In April 1996, this illegal market was discovered full of malnourished children, aged between 7 and 17 years old, waiting for buyers. Most of the children were employed as house-helps, shop assistants, car washers, bus conductors and scavengers collecting scraps from refuse or dump sites.

According to traffickers, girls from Benin and Togo were particularly in high demand in Lagos. More than thirty children crossed the Benin–Nigeria border every two months while twenty children were trafficked monthly through the Calabar, Sokoto and Maiduguri borders. Some aged between 8 and 15 years were bought from families for the equivalent of $30. In April 1996, a trafficker was arrested in Lagos with ten Beninoise girls aged between 10 and 12. Two suspected human traffickers were arrested by the police in Ogun State while attempting to ferry twenty-four teenagers across the border to Cotonou in Benin Republic. They included eight males and sixteen females caught in a chartered commercial bus at Owode Egbado a border town of Ogun State. The children were between the ages of 9 and 20. Traffickers were returning them to their parents at Cotonou for the Christmas break after serving as house-helps in Nigeria.

Over one million children are trafficked in several African countries annually, while traffickers generate between £100 and £150 million. Out of this number, about 60 per cent are Nigerians whose ages range between 10 and 16 years, and a majority were girls. Some of the girls were trafficked to Saudi Arabia while under the age of 18 years. The children were trafficked for the purpose of begging and sex work in Saudi Arabia. A total of 7,429 Nigerians were deported from Saudi Arabia through the Malam Aminu Kano International Airport out of which 3,032 were men, 3,823 women, 297 children and 130 destitutes. Out of the 9,952 women and 1,231 underage children deported from Saudi Arabia, the majority were from the northern states of Kano, Borno, Adamawa, Yobe, Nassarawa, Plateau, Niger, Kebbi, Kwara, Sokoto, Katsina, Gombe, Kaduna, Bauchi, Taraba and Jigawa. Three of the deported girls aged between 7 and 12 are currently under the care of the WOTCLEF coordinator, Kano State. They were deported from Saudi Arabia and could not trace their origin in Nigeria.

Again about 60 per cent of the trafficked children from Africa to Italy were Nigerians, mostly from the south-eastern states of Imo, Abia and Akwa Ibom. According to Prof. Olu Agbi, Nigerian Ambassador to Greece, most Nigerians get trapped in the intricate web of human trafficking because of their desire to seek greener pastures abroad. Every year, thousands of children are sold as slaves in Europe. Girls were sold for between Euro 70,000 to 90,000 to engage in sex work. A particular man in Akure collected as much as N400,000 to transport young boys to Turkey in order to cross the mainland Europe through Greece. But unfortunately, the young boys spent 21 days to get to Greece and most perished during the journey because they passed through landmines. Those who got to Greece engaged in hawking counterfeit compact disks (CDs). The boys had no money to reproduce the counterfeit CDs, but the Greeks and Bulgarians could do it, whereas Nigerian hawkers suffered sentences and imprisonments.

Government and NGO Intervention against Child Trafficking in Nigeria

Despite the fact that the incidence of child trafficking has been going on since the 1930s, public awareness on the issue was heightened in the 1990s with the increase in the number of deportees from Europe, Saudi Arabia and other African countries. In 1994, the late Mrs Julie Useni founded the Daughters of Abraham Foundation (DOAF) to rehabilitate trafficked girls who were engaged in sex work in Abuja. Strategic hide-outs for sex work in Abuja, which were discovered by DOAF, included Nyanya, where most sex workers lived in local hotels in search of customers; Mabushi, where they were found in crowded huts; Area I Garki, which harboured call girls who roam the streets at night, and Kado Estate, where, unlike the other three places, sex workers who dealt with foreigners and usually charged very high fees lived. During the first quarter of the DOAF campaign, over 500 sex workers were counselled at both their business places and residencies. About 150 converts were registered for rehabilitation, but only 28 of them were trained in sewing and hair dressing skills while the others ran away.

In 1996, the Women Consortium of Nigeria (WOCON) formed by Mrs Bisi Olateru-Olagbegi, assisted by the ILO's International Programme for the Elimination of Child Labour (ILO/IPEC) project, withdrew many teenagers from child labour along city streets. The Women Trafficking and Child Labour Elimination Foundation (WOTCLEF), founded by the wife of the Vice-President, Chief Mrs Amina Titi Atiku Abubakar, sponsored public enlightenment campaigns against trafficked women and children and set up a skill acquisition/education programme for the victims. WOTCLEF sponsored a soap opera on national television, *izozo*, to raise public awareness against trafficking. Under WOTCLEF's Opportunity School Project many girl children of poor background benefited from free education. Through WOTCLEF, the National Agency for the Prohibition of Trafficking in Persons (NAPTIP) was established to enforce laws against trafficking in persons, to investigate and prosecute those suspected of being engaged in trafficking including child trafficking.

The West Africa Cocoa/Commercial Agricultural Project (WACAP) is part of the ILO/IPEC project aimed at withdrawing children from cocoa farms in Nigeria. The project was supported by the Labor Department of the USA and the International Cocoa Initiative based in Geneva, Switzerland. With a budget of $600,000 from the US Department of Labor and the chocolate industry, WACAP planned to withdraw and socially protect 1,000 children; assist 150 adult members of concerned families and sensitize more than 30,000 stakeholders. The project worked in the cocoa-growing communities in which the Sustainable Tree Crop Programme operates.

In Lagos State, the government established welfare schemes for trafficked and missing children from various parts of Nigeria, and the Republics of Benin and Chad. Eighteen of the sixty-nine children whose ages were below 14 years were housed in the Lagos State Boys Remand Home, Oregun. Eighteen of them aged between 4 and 8 years were in the Lagos State Children Transit Home, Idi-Araba. Four of them within the age bracket of 9 and 16 years were in the Boys Approved School, Bierrel Street, Yaba. Four others aged below 16 years were at the Girls Approved School, Idi Araba while 25 others also below 16 years were at the Girls Remand Home, Idi Araba.

In Jigawa State, the new education law provided for the abolition of street begging and ensured compulsory child education with a budget of N1.5 billion. The law made education compulsory for the girl child and included the *Almajiri* system of education as part of the new education policy. In Abia State, the government launched the Child Advancement Programme (ASCAP), an enlightenment campaign aimed at keeping children off the streets and reducing teenage pregnancies, drug abuse and sex work. A rehabilitation and skill acquisition centre was established by the Akwa Ibom State Government for the trafficked children.

Having established that child trafficking existed in Nigeria, UNICEF in collaboration with the ILO embarked on programmes to combat child labour, trafficking and exploitation. The partnership among other things determined to improve access to basic services including health/nutrition, education and income-generating activities by at least 5 per cent in six selected cities (Lagos, Ibadan, Kaduna, Kano, Onitsha and Port Harcourt). The project aimed at improving the policy environment for Children in Need of Special Protection Measures (CNSPM) and reduce the incidence of child abuse in the selected cities. UNICEF strategies included advocacy, sensitization, capacity-building of officers and FGN/NGO partners, empowerment and service delivery; and the review of existing data on child labour in Nigeria and production of a detailed compendium (1986–1996) on child labour. Between 1997 and 1999 UNICEF Nigeria funding on these activities increased from $288,748 to $389,160.

In October 1999, the ILO began work on the International Programme for the Elimination of Child Labour (IPEC) with the support of the United States Department of Labor. The sub-regional project was entitled 'Combating Trafficking in Children for Labour Exploitation in West and Central Africa'. The project commissioned studies on child trafficking in nine African countries including Nigeria. The ILO-IPEC supported various NGOs to remove 1,000 domestic child labourers from severe exploitative situations within one year.

Conclusion

During the last seven decades, child trafficking in the labour process was marked by changes in the different economic regimes. The Great Depression, excessive taxation and forced labour impoverished many families and led to the selling of children to traffickers at a time of economic adversity. In the 1930s, many of the trafficked children became slaves on cocoa farms, cattle-rearers and concubines. Beginning from the mid-1980s and more markedly in the 1990s, the pressure of the Stuctural Adjustment Programme and globalization process weakened the Nigerian economy by increasing the number of people with low incomes, led to currency devaluation, inflation, unemployment and a general incidence of poverty. In the 1990s, the increasing economic distress arising from neo-liberal reforms gave impetus to child trafficking. Unlike the 1930s outright sale of children for food, poor parents now ensured that children participated in the informal sector of the economy by periodically remitting money for the survival of the household. The mechanism of trafficking in the 1990s differed dramatically from that in the 1930s. In the 1990s, trafficking has assumed a more global dimension with organized syndicates operating across international borders. Even though, some skirmishes of transborder child trafficking occurred in the 1930s, for example, child trafficking between Nigeria and Cameroon, and between Nigeria and North Africa, the apparatus of globalization has quickened the pace. In the 1990s, children were trafficked for the purposes of working in agricultural plantations, sex work, hawking in the informal sector, domestic work, begging, crime and ritual purposes. Trafficking has shown no sign of decrease partly because both parents and traffickers considered it as 'good' business and. indeed, as a 'poverty alleviation strategy'.

During both the 1930s and 1990s, governments imposed legislation that outlawed child trafficking rather than structurally addressing economic problems that gave rise to it. Despite patrols, anti-trafficking was rarely enforced both internally and across borders in conditions of deepening poverty. The rivalry between security officials, especially police and immigration over who has the mandate to prosecute traffickers or handle trafficking cases, has undermined efforts to curb the menace. Amid this controversy of inefficiency and corruption traffickers often escape justice. The persistent political instability, armed banditry, civil wars, cross-border smuggling and official corruption have rendered joint border patrolling in the west coast of Africa ineffective.

Trafficking in children transcended the Nigerian borders to countries within the West African region and beyond. Nigeria was a source country and served as transit and destination for other children. Nigeria was an exporter of children; it served as a depot and destination for others. In the course of the 1990s, following the Convention on the Rights of the Child (CRC) in 1989, there was a rekindled global effort and awareness to stamp out child labour and trafficking. Despite the improved policy environment outlawing child trafficking and child labour, the effort at domestication of CRC as a Child Rights Bill, and proliferation of NGOs and government programmes, child trafficking continued to assume a soaring proportion as poverty, unemployment and corruption remained unbridled. Governments still imposed bans on child labour, street begging and imposed compulsory schooling but there was a surge in child trafficking owing to economic distress in the land. The result of this trend was that of a vicious circle in which children of the poor sold their labour cheaply instead of redressing their social condition through education and highly paid work.

References

Abdulkadir, M. S., 2004, *Structuring, Struggling and Surviving Economic Depression in Northern Nigeria: The 1930s as Preview of the Present* (Professorial Inaugural Lecture), Kano: Bayero University, 31 July.

Adejumobi, S., 2004, 'Economic Globalisation, Market Reforms and Social Welfare Services in West Africa', in T. A. Aina, C. Seithy and E. Annan-Yao, eds., *Globalisation and Social Policy in Africa*, Dakar: CODESRIA.

Adepoju, A., 2002, 'Migration in West Africa', *Development* 46(3).

Araoye, M. O., 2002, *Child Labour and Sexual Exploitation in Nigeria*, Working Paper Series No. 3, Institute for the African Child, Ohio University.

Bass, L. E., 2002, *Child Labour in Sub-Saharan Africa*, London and Boulder: Lynne Rienner.

Black, M., 2002, *A Handbook on Advocacy, Child Domestic Workers: Finding a voice*, Anti-Slavery International.

Dottridge, M., 2002, 'Trafficking in Children in West and Central Africa', *Gender and Development* 10(1).

Effah, J., 1996, *Modernised Slavery: Child Trade in Nigeria*, Lagos: Constitutional Rights Project.

Goldin, C., 1979, 'Household and Market Production of Families in a Late Nineteenth Century American Town', *Explorations in Economic History* 16(2).

Guyer, J. I., Denzer, L. and Agbaje, A., 2003, 'Introduction: The Nigerian Popular Economy – Strategies Toward a Study', in J. I. Guyer, L. Denzer and A. Agbaje, eds., *Money Struggles and City Life: Devaluations in Ibadan and other Urban Centres in Southern Nigeria*, Ibadan: BookBuilders.

Howard, W. S., 2002, *Making Childhood Possible: Education and Health for Child Survival in Africa*, Working Paper Series No. 1, Institute for the African Child, Ohio University.

Human Rights Watch/Africa, 2004, *Children In Sudan: Slaves, Street Children and Child Soldiers*, New York: Human Rights Watch.

ILO-IPEC, 2001, *Combating Trafficking in Children for Labour in West and Central Africa*, Geneva: ILO.

Isamah, A. N. and Okunola, R. A., 2003, 'Family Life under Economic Adjustment: The Rise of Child Breadwinners', in J. I. Guyer, L. Denzer and A. Agbaje, eds, *Money Struggles and City Life: Devaluations in Ibadan and other Urban Centres in Southern Nigeria*, Ibadan: BookBuilders.

Kar, J., 2002, 'The Issue of Child Labour in Orissa: A Development Approach', *Indian Social Science Review* 4(1).

Kaye, M., 2002, *Forced Labour in the 21st Century*, Anti-Slavery International.

Kilbride, P., Suda, C. and Njeru, E., 2000, *Street Children in Kenya*, London: Bergin & Garvey.

Last, M., 2000, 'Children and the Experience of Violence: Contrasting Cultures of Punishment in Northern Nigeria', *Africa* 70(3).

Loconto, A., 2002, *The Trafficking of Nigerian Women into Italy*, TED Case Studies No. 656.

Lovejoy, P. E. and Hogendorn, J. S., 1993, *Slow Death For Slavery: The Course of Abolition in Northern Nigeria 1897–1936*, Cambridge: Cambridge University Press, 1993.

Muazzam, I., 2003, 'Kano: A Brief Note', in Amina Salihu, ed., *Community Empowerment Capacity Enhancement Needs Assessment: CE-CENA Initiative, A Study of Four Communities in Kano State, Northwestern Nigeria*, World Bank Institute and Centre for Democracy and Development.

Mustapha, A. R., 1992, 'Structural Adjustment and Multiple Modes of Social Livelihood in Nigeria', in P. Gibbon, Y. Bangura and A. Ofsad, eds., *Authority, Democracy and Adjustment: The Politics of Economic Reform in Africa*, Uppsala: NAI.

Obadan, M. I. and Edo, S. E., 2004, 'Overall Economic Direction, Strategy and Performance', in I. B. Bello-Imam and M. I. Obadan, eds, *Democratic Governance and Development Management in Nigeria's Fourth Republic 1999–2003*, Ibadan: Centre for Local Government and Rural Development Studies.

Olaniyi, R., 2003, 'No Way Out: The Trafficking of Women in Nigeria', *Agenda* (South Africa), No. 55.

Olateru-Olagbegi, B., 2003, 'The Current Trends in the Trafficking of Nigerian Children: Factors and Issues', Paper presented at the *Trafficking of African Children to the UK: Denouncing the 'Better Life'*, organized by Africans United Against Child Abuse, Lagos.

Osemwegie, A., 1998, *Street Children in Lagos*, Dakar: Urban Management and Poverty Alleviation.

Qvortrup, J., Bardy, M., Sgritta, G. and Winter, H., eds, 1994, *Childhood Matters: Social Theory, Practice and Politics*, Vienna: Avebury.

Reynolds, P., 1991, *Dance Civet Cat: Child Labour in the Zambezi Valley*, London: Zed Books.

Shea, P. J. and Abdulkadir, M. S., 1987, 'Economic Conditions in Igalaland in the 1930s: The archival record', Paper presented at the 32nd Congress of the Historical Society of Nigeria, University of Jos.

Ubah, C. N., 1991, 'Suppression of the Slave Trade in the Nigerian Emirates', *Journal of African History* 32.

Ubah, C. N., 1992, 'Disposal of Freed Slave Children in Northern Nigeria', *Journal of African History* 33.

UNICEF, 2002, *Child Trafficking in Nigeria: Analysis of Nigeria's Response to the Libreville Platform of Action (2000).*

US Department of Labor, 1995, *By the Sweat and Toil of Children, Vol. II: The Use of Child Labor in US Agricultural Imports and Forced and Bonded Child Labor*, A Report to the Committee on Appropriations, US Congress.

Watson, A. M. S., 2004, 'Seen but Not Heard: The Role of the Child in International Political Economy', *New Political Economy* 9(1).

White, B., 1994, 'Children, Work and "Child Labour": Changing Responses to the Employment of Children', *Development and Change* 25(4).

5

Children Exploitation in the Labour Process: Empirical Exposition from Ile-Ife, Nigeria

Dixon Olu Torimiro

Introduction

Engaging children in economic activities is a contextual issue. In a typical African setting, for instance, children are normally socialized into work. In this context, it is commonly perceived that through such a process, work culture and tradition are sustained (Odetola and Ademola 1985:57–68; Torimiro and Lawal 1998). This African context of work is being globally contested in recent times, as the children are now engaged in many questionable labour activities, perhaps, as a consequence of the poverty situation engulfing many African families (Grootaert and Patrinos 1999; Kilbride et al. 2000:60). Children are engaged in economic activities for a variety of reasons, the most important being poverty and the induced pressure upon them to escape from its trap. For instance, studies have shown that children are often prompted to work by their parents because of the poor household economic situation (Torimiro and Lawal 2001:70–4, 2002). Schooling problems may also contribute to this phenomenon, owing to the inaccessibility to schools or lack of quality education, which may spur parents to engage their children in more 'profitable' pursuits. Traditional factors such as rigid cultural and social roles in certain communities may further limit educational attainment and increase child labour (Torimiro et al. 2003:185–92).

Further, working children have become objects of extreme exploitation in terms of toiling for long hours for minimal pay. Their work conditions are especially severe, often not providing the stimulation for proper physical and mental development. Many of these children endure a life of pure deprivation. The Ghanaian experience described by Verlet (2002:78–9) led him to the critical use of the dialectics of 'good-will' and 'willingness' in describing the working conditions of the working child vis-à-vis the position of the master, which usually becomes an exploitative relationship. He noted thus:

> The master's good-will gives him the power to do what he will. His desires, his needs and moods, govern the wages, set the working hours, assign the tasks and influence the quality of the relationship. Willingness means the availability, the obedience expected of a child. Vulnerable children seeking protection and support see themselves bound over to remain meek, ever-present, ever-willing. Their labour power is malleable, flexible.

Verlet's view is germane, most expecially in any poverty-stricken environment where the owners of very limited resources are usually in control of the wills of the less privileged, not to talk of the most vulnerable, the children. It should be noted, however, that in a situation where the 'good-will' is being expressed by the child's parent(s) as the 'master', the level of vulnerability is expected to be lower and expression of the child's 'willingness' is invariably expected to be mild. However, the level of exploitative relationship and its perception in different situations are expected to vary, given the socio-cultural and economic peculiarities of different societies. For instance, children may have to be engaged in their parents' economic activities in some circumstances with little or no exploitation in order to generate money for sponsoring their education (Ajayi and Torimiro 2004). Osita (2004) also reported a common practice in Eastern Nigeria, where the male children are apprenticed to traders from an early age, in preference to going to school. According to him:

> the child usually works for a 'master', learning the details of the business over a number of years. When the young man is ready for 'freedom', the 'master' is obliged to 'settle' him by providing capital for him to set up his own business.

Globalization and Exploitation of Children in the Labour Process in Africa

For better understanding of child exploitation within the African context vis-à-vis globalization, it is imperative to take a cursory look at the extent to which the tides of globalization have contributed to the plight of the children in Africa, especially with regard to child labour. Globalization in this context is perceived as an ideological process based on the perceived persistent disparity and inequality between the North and South, which has dichotomized the state of the global economy into industrialized or agrarian, developed or developing, and rich or poor. The understanding of globalization, according to Aina (2004:3–6), is taken from a perspective that sees the world from the so-called Eurocentric or Economic North position, portraying the world from the perspectives of the dominant political and economic interest prevalent in Europe, Japan and North America. While the notion to bridge the disparity between these worlds may be applauded, the possibilities of perpetuating the Northern agenda of continual exploitation of the perceived limitations inherent in its Southern counterpart should not be undermined as 'it has provided developed countries with powerful leverage upon which to pursue their interests to the detriment of the developing world' (Agbu 2004). The gap that is expected to be bridged through its market pulls is being widened, almost on a daily basis. This situation is apparent with the consequences of the various reforms it has come to replace (Ghai 1992 Amin 1992, 1998). Aina (2004) noted that in Africa, globalisation has not only generated so much anxiety, insecurity and resistance; it has generated an almost unanimous perception of polarisation, pain and greater inequality along with a feeling of almost insurmountable threat to ordinary people's livelihoods and cultures.

One of such reforms is the Structural Adjustment Programme (SAP), which was hastily sold to many African countries. Unfortunately, several studies (Mkandawire and Olukoshi 1995; Amin 1998; Jega 2003) have not only established the failure of the reform, but also the capitalists' agenda embedded in the globalized marketing strategy. The soaring poverty level in most African countries could not be dissociated from the advent of SAP!

The major contestation is, therefore, the negative features that the 'agenda' has brought to the African continent. These include cultural breakdown, conflicts and war, greed, corruption, hunger and so on. In fact, these situations, as rightly noted by UNRISD (2003), have immensely contributed to the 'disruption of livelihood systems and institutional arrangements that, historically, have provided some degree of social protection'. This is basically a matter of lack of adequate consultation or provision for the participation of the supposed beneficiaries and stakeholders, especially the marginalized and excluded sectors such as the rural poor, peasants, poor women, children, the youth and the elderly (Aina 2004). In these situations, children are the most vulnerable. These children turn out to become objects of exploitation for different kinds of purposes, under different situations, in most parts of the African continent. The interrelationship between globalization and child exploitation is schematically represented in Fig. 5.1. By way of digressing, however, it might be suggestive to raise two fundamental questions on whether the ideology is imposed on the African nations or whether it is optional, answers to which this chapter has no mandate to provide. It might, however, become an agenda for a very serious debate.

It has severally been reported (ILO 2002; Agbu 2004) that children under different circumstances have been used as objects of trafficking, sexual violence, street begging and forced labour, to mention a few. In literature, however, many authors (e.g. Onyango and Kayango Male 1982; Ebigbo 1990:74–6; Oloko 1997:48–51; UNICEF 1997:1–15; Nkuly 2000:36–9) have further characterized the various working conditions under which child exploitative labour could be perceived, as follows: lack of freedom of movement; emphasis on the child's inferior status; overwork at tedious, exhausting jobs; emphasis on complete obedience to the employer; control of the child, managed through beatings and insults; lack of emotional warmth; expectation that the child will behave totally like an adult; expression of developmental needs by the child seen as disobedience by employers; strong belief by employers that the child's situation is good when compared to home conditions; underpayment; and an abbreviated period of childhood, with a 'push' into adulthood; full-time work at too early an age; excessive hours spent working; work that exerts undue physical, social and psychological stress; work and life on the street in bad conditions; inadequate pay; too much responsibility; work that hampers access to education; work that undermines children's dignity and self-esteem; and work that is detrimental to full social and psychological development.

Figure 5.I: Model Showing the Linkages between Globalization and African Child Vulnerability

Dark side of contestation
Insinuation of inequalities

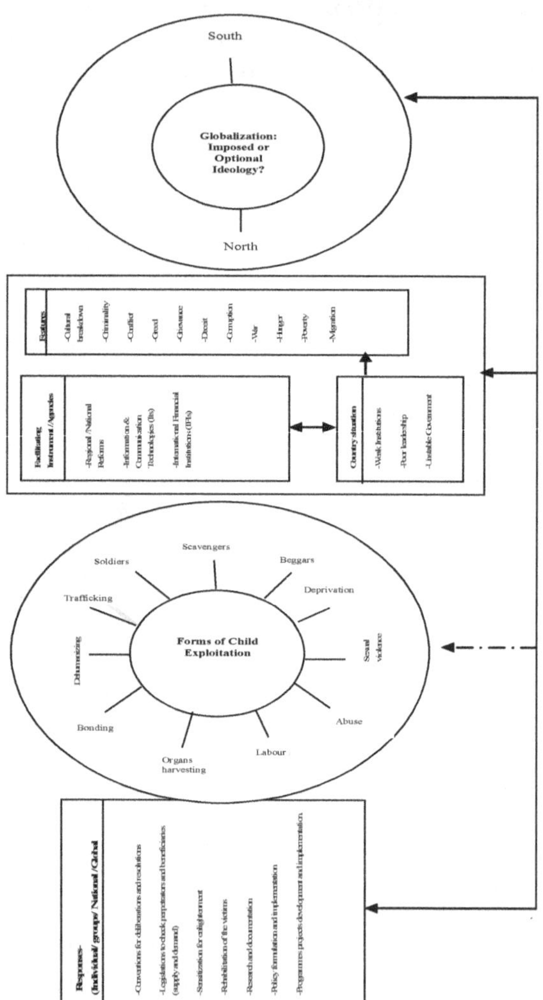

Key: Direct relationship; Inverse relationship; Indirect relationship

In recent years, child exploitation in different forms has been facilitated by globalization and modern communication and information technologies, which have made it become increasingly transnational in scope. Hence, several international events have called for immediate action to end this crime, including the Stockholm Congress against commercial sexual exploitation of children in 1996, the Amsterdam and Oslo Conferences on child labour in 1997 and the International Labour Conference Convention against the worst forms of child labour in 1998.

> The ILO Convention No. 182 defines the worst forms of child labour as slavery, debt bondage, prostitution, pornography, forced recruitment of children for use in armed conflict, use of children in drug trafficking and other illicit activities, and all other work harmful or hazardous to the health, safety or morals of girls and boys under 18 years of age (ILO 1998).

This convention has been much popularized as the major United Nations response to end the various forms of child exploitation. Other efforts from different quarters (individuals, groups, international agencies, governments and non-governmental organizations, among others) include legislation to check perpetrators and beneficiaries, sensitization for enlightenment, rehabilitation of children that have become victims, further research into the phenomenon and documentation by reports based on local and regional experiences, policy formulation and implementation to end the crime, and programmes/projects development and implementation.

Research Problem and Questions

The post-colonial era in Nigeria from the early 1960s to the mid-1970s enjoyed a rural-based economy as the major national income was basically from cash crops. This was a period when farmers took pride in marrying many wives, having many children and regarding large family size as a measure of their economic wealth, which invariably translated into high agricultural production. Their children were fully socialized into farming activities, especially in cash crop plantations. Basically, they were producing for export in consonance with the grand design of the colonial masters primarily to feed foreign industries. Though this era apparently witnessed child labour, the phenomenon was not given prominent attention at the global level, perhaps owing to the economic benefits the 'grand designers' derived therefrom. Moreover, during this period, rural people were more comfortable and could perform their basic social and economic responsibilities. However, the mid-1970s witnessed a dramatic change in the nation's economic situation, with the discovery of petroleum, mismanagement of public funds, poor leadership and weak public institutions, which significantly resulted in the abandonment of the rural sector and a decline in agricultural development. This situation made the rural areas more susceptible to the scourge of national economic recession, which culminated in high poverty levels. The situation further led to the vulnerability of children. As a way of devising coping mechanisms for survival, rural people have had to harness their children's potential by engaging them in on-farm and off-farm economic activities. Many of these children were employed in the informal urban economy or engaged as domestic servants, shopkeepers, street hawkers, building site labourers, bus conductors, industry and factory workers, to mention a few (Osemwegie 1998:52).

In recent times, there has been a dramatic increase in these activities, even in their worst forms. Also, a significant rise in child labour and child trafficking has been observed in many parts of the country. Although many invaluable efforts and interventions have been initiated through wives of political officeholders to address the issues faced by the exploited children in the various Nigerian states, however there is still the need for an empirically based expository study for proper understanding of the exploitation of children in the labour process. To be more specific, little or no research has been conducted for a proper understanding of this phenomenon in Ile-Ife in south-western Nigeria. Against this background, therefore, attempts were made to provide answers to the following research questions: What are the socio-economic conditions of these children who are engaged in economic activities? In what ways are these children engaged in labour activities that make them exploited? What are the ways of life of these children on their labour sites? What are the factors influencing their working hours and the types of work they do? How do these children perceive the jobs they are doing? And what future prospects do they perceive in what they are presently doing?

Methodology

The study was carried out in Ile-Ife, in south-western Nigeria. It lies in the tropical rain forest belt, and has an estimated population of about 282,000 people. Ile-Ife has many satellite villages that are linked by a poor road network. For the most part, the villages have poorly developed infrastructure, often without access to either electricity or pipe-borne water.

Both quantitative and qualitative data were collected. A structured interview schedule was used to elicit information from seventy (70) children (between 10 and 17 years of age), purposively interviewed on their labour sites when schools were in session. Also, on-the-spot assessment and systematic observation, where the children's daily activities were periodically observed in their labour and orderly recorded (Reynolds 1991:76), were made to generate the qualitative data. The quantitative data were analyzed using the Statistical Package for Social Science (SPSS), while the qualitative data were used to buttress the discussion. Descriptive statistics such as frequency counts, percentages, bar and pie charts were used to describe the data, while the Chi-square (X^2) and Pearson's correlation (r) were used to establish the tested hypotheses, and Contingency coefficient and Coefficient of determination were respectively used to determine the strength of associations and relationships.

Family Milieu and Socio-economic Condition of the Children Engaged in Labour

It is generally observed that many Nigerian parents in poverty have acceded to the reality of their situation by engaging their children in some economic activity in order to enable them to cope with many of their parental and household responsibilities.

For instance, in recent years, Nigeria was categorized among the eight countries in the world that are going through 'severe' poverty (where more than one-half of the population subsist on less than US$1 per day); and also among the fourteen countries that are undergoing 'severe-to-moderate' poverty (more than three-quarters of the Nigerian population has been found to be impoverished, using the US$2 a day poverty line) (ILO 2001). This condition generally has a very serious implication for household economic survival. In the context of Ile-Ife, where this study was conducted, it is interesting to note that a majority (82.86 per cent) of the children engaged in various economic activities with the consent of their parents. These children came from polygamous homes with household size of more than ten members. Their parents were mostly illiterates, engaged in various trades and informal businesses. Over 97 per cent of the children claimed they resorted to what they were doing because of the poverty situation their parents were going through and for lack of financial support to earn a living. This is in consonance with the findings of Osemweige (1998) on a study conducted on street children in Lagos.

Demographically, the children were categorized according to their gender, schooling status, age and religion in order to understand the extent to which these variables had influenced their engagement in economic activities. Male children (68.57 per cent) were found to be more engaged in the informal labour sector than their female counterparts (31.43 per cent), though most of the children (97.14 per cent) interviewed did not believe that the type of job they were doing had anything to do with their gender. About 20 per cent of the children were not enrolled in school; they were absolutely illiterates and fully engaged in various economic activities. Others had either dropped out of school at a particular level of their education or claimed to have combined their economic activities with schooling. It was, however, observed that most of the children had either abandoned their education totally or dropped out of school, because they had perpetually been at work for an average of over five years without attending school.

The age groups were categorized into two, that is, those below 15 years (45.71 per cent) and those between 15 and 17 years old (54.29 per cent). This categorization was purposefully devised (see later discussion). The two age groups are significant as they relate to the forms of work they are expected to be engaged in – these include light work, regular work, hazardous work and unconditional worst forms. In terms of religion, children (54.29 per cent) from a Muslim background were found to be more engaged in economic activities than those (45.71 per cent) of a Christian background. This further confirmed the reports of a high tendency for child labour in Islamic households compared with Christian households. In Lagos, for instance, Osemweige (1998) reported that 59.3 per cent of street children were Muslims. A total of 62.86 per cent of the children engaged in economic activities were Yoruba, born in Ile-Ife, while others (37.16 per cent) were non-Yoruba and born outside Ile-Ife. Although some of these children had their parents living in Ile-Ife, an element of trafficking was suspected, as few whose parents were living outside the study area revealed that they were brought to their labour sites by their employers. A majority (71.43 per cent) of those children who were living with their parents, though, claimed to depend on them for their livelihood, that is, they depended on their parents for their day-to-day expenses in terms of food, clothing, accommodation and other socio-economic activities. This might not be wholly correct as further enquiry revealed that most of these parents absolutely depended on the proceeds from their children's labour for their daily survival.

Some Empirical Evidence of Child Exploitation in the Labour Process

This is determined in line with the International Labour Organization's (ILO's) definition of what constitutes child labour in relation to the child's age vis-à-vis the hours spent on the labour per week and the types of labour engaged in. For the purpose of global estimates, ILO (2002) categorized the forms of work into four, under three different age groups, viz.: 5–7 years, 12–14 years and 15–17 years, in order to justify perpetration of child labour using working hours, working environment and the nature of work.

This study, however, adopted the ILO categorization with modification by categorizing the age group into less than 15 and 15–17 years for the purpose of empirical calculations. ILO described *non-hazardous work* for children as any work in non-hazardous industries/ occupations for less than 43 hours per week. Such work, if less than 14 hours per week, is tagged *light work* for the age group between 12 and 17 years. It is referred to as *regular work* for the age group 15–17 years, but considered as child labour for those less than 15 years of age. *Worst forms of child labour* are simply classified as either *hazardous work* (in specified hazardous industries/occupations plus more than 43 hours per week in other industries/ occupations) or *Unconditional worst forms* (trafficked children; children in forced and bonded labour, armed conflict, prostitution and pornography, and illicit activities). The general findings are shown in Fig. 5.2.

The study, therefore, revealed that the children were generally engaged in the worst forms of child labour of the hazardous category. About 57.14 per cent of the children usually work for less than 43 hours per week, while 42.86 per cent put more than 43 hours into their respective labour per week. The hours spent on the job vary according to the amount earned and the types of work engaged in. For those who worked for less than 7 hours per day, 14.29 per cent made a gross income of less than N150 [at a time when N140 = $US1] 28.57 per cent made between N150 and N300, and 14.29 per cent more than N300. Among those who worked for more than 7 hours per day, 25.71 per cent made a gross income of more than N300 (see Figs 5.3 and 5.4). It could be inferred from the findings that these children were working basically for their parents in order to put the household above the poverty line. As Varlet (2000) rightly put it, 'children are placed in the position of household protectors, breadwinners'.

Figure 5.2: Distribution of Children by Working Hours and Income Generated per Day

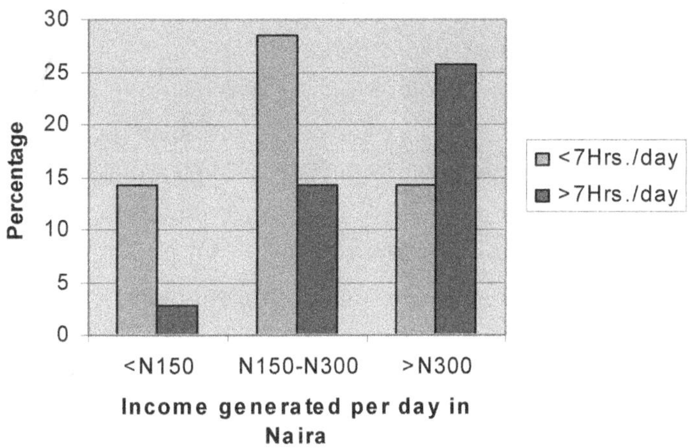

The types of work in which they were engaged included: carrying of planks in saw-mills (25.71 per cent), hawking and selling of different kinds of goods in the streets (54.29 per cent), and bus conducting in motor-garages (20.00 per cent). While 28.57 per cent of the children claimed that they did not have any problem with the jobs they were doing, these jobs were considered to be very hazardous by a majority (71.43 per cent) of the children. Hazardous work by children means any activity or occupation, which, by its nature or type has, or leads to, adverse effects on a child's safety, health (physical or mental), and moral development. Hazards could also derive from excessive workload, physical conditions of work, and/or work intensity in terms of the duration or hours of work even where the activity or occupation is known to be non-hazardous or 'safe' (ILO 2002).

Those who worked in the sawmills claimed that they occasionally sustained injuries while carrying the planks. It was, however, observed that the children might be exposed to respiratory diseases resulting from the draughts oozing from the sawdust dunghill and the dust from the milling machines, which they usually inhale while carrying the planks. Those who engaged in selling/hawking and bus conducting complained of occasional loss of money (for which their 'masters' would mercilessly beat them), failure of customers to pay, road accidents, mockery and insults from their customers, among others.

Figure 5.3: Distribution of Children by Types of Work and Income Generated per Day

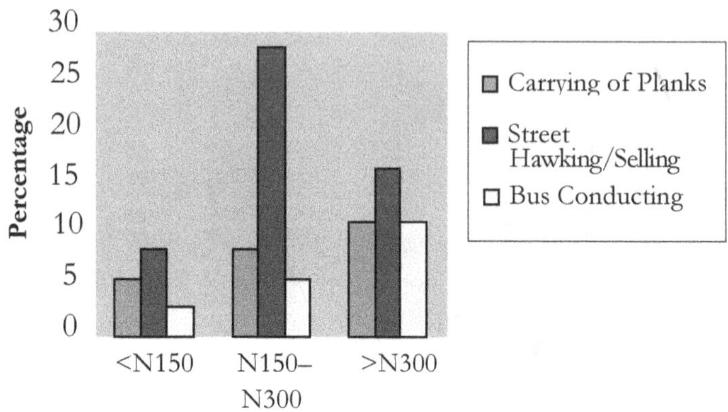

Figure 5.4: Distribution of Children by Types of Work and Hours of Work per Week

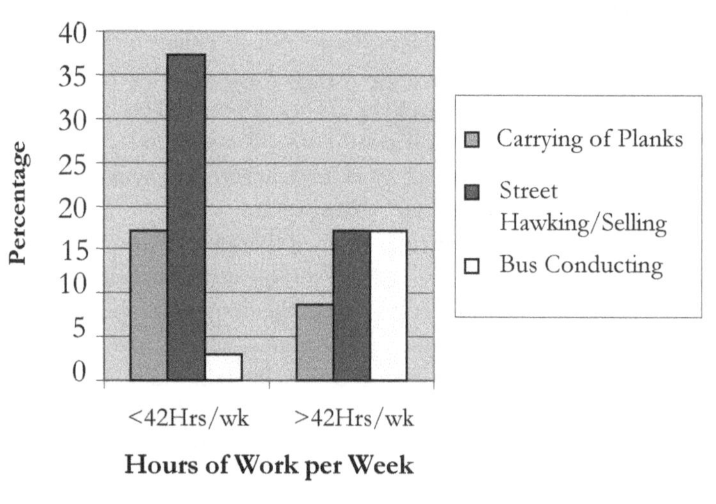

Empirically, gender, ownership of job and types of job were found to have significant association with the hours the children spent on their job per day. The two latter variables were found to exert a very strong strength of association of over 95 per cent (see Table 5.1). Also, the amount of money spent by child per day was found to significantly correlate (r = 0.34) with the hours they spent on their job per day at 0.01 level, though with a very weak strength (11.56 per cent) of relationship (see Fig. 5.5).

The child's gender is expected to be a very good factor in determining the hours he or she spends on a particular job (see Table 5.2). It was, however, observed that male children were more engaged in carrying planks at the sawmills and in bus conducting business. Culturally, some jobs have been observed to be exclusively reserved for a particular gender. For instance, tasks that are energetic are expected to be assigned to the male gender, while those that require patience and less energy exertion are ethically meant for the girls. This might be contextual, as it has to do with the prevailing culture and traditions of the studied area. However, a study conducted in Brazil found no gender differences in the number of hours worked (Araujo 1998).

Figure 5.5: Distribution of Children by the Amount Spent for Themselves per Day

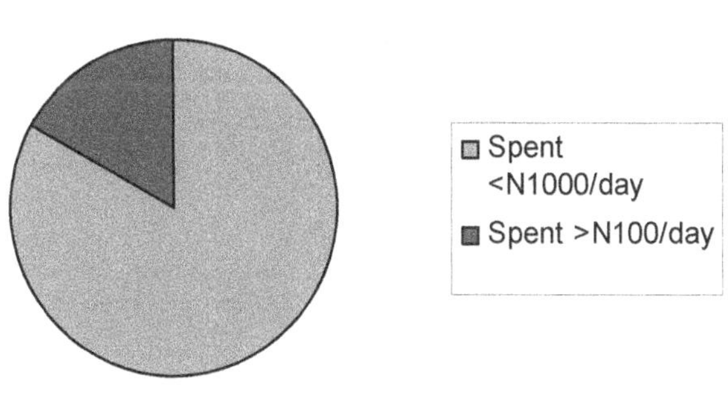

This study further revealed that most of the parents were privy to the children's engagement in labour activities and favourably supported the time they spent on the job per day. Though it was expected that many of the children (45.86 per cent, and most especially among those that were engaged in street hawking and selling) who claimed that they were working for their mothers should fare better on the job than their peers who were not working for their parents, but ironically, the contrary was observed. However, while realizing the fact that the major catalyst for the period of work by the children could not be dissociated from the amount of income they have the potential of earning, which supposedly must have been fixed by the owner of the job for each day, it could still not be discountenanced that the level of biological relationship between the job owner and the employed child would, to a large extent, influence the working hours considered for such a child per day, all things being equal. This is in line with the reasoning of Verlet (2000) when he noted that since the working children are partially responsible for household survival, their bonds with their mothers are deeper. In this circumstance, one expects the child to enjoy good welfare conditions in terms of feeding, and so on.

Table 5.1: Chi-square Analysis showing the Variables influencing the Working Hours per Day

Variables	X^2_c	X^2_t	D.F.	C
Gender	5.83*	3.84	1	0.57
Ownership of job	28.40*	25.00	15	0.96
Types of job	57.40*	54.57	39	0.99
Level of schooling	30.18	65.17	48	0.96

P values at 0.05 level of significance; C = Contingency co-efficient; * = significance
Note: X^2_c = Chi-square calculated; X^2_t = Chi-square tabulated; D.F. = Degree of freedom
Source: Calculated from the field survey, 2004.

Tables 5.1 and 5.2 further revealed that schooling is not a significant factor that could contribute to the hours a child spent on the job and the types of job he or she could do. Incidentally, many of the children, though, indicated that they were in one level of schooling or the other, but further enquiry showed that many of them had already dropped out of school. It could, however, be deduced that waning interest in school could make the children more vulnerable to long hours of labour by the employers.

Table 5.2: Chi-square Analysis showing the Variables influencing the Types of Job

Variables	X^2_c	X^2_t	D.F.	C
Gender	27.22*	27.69	13	0.96
Age	16.80	27.69	13	0.90
Level of schooling	46.14	62.43	39	0.98

P values at 0.05 level of significance; C = Contingency co-efficient; * = significance
Note: X^2_c = Chi-square calculated; X^2_t = Chi-square tabulated; D.F. = Degree of freedom
Source: Calculated from the field survey, 2004.

Some authors (Oloko 1997; ILO 2001) have equally reported that some children combine economic activities with schooling. Oloko explained that a child who does some odd jobs (which do not disturb his schooling or other aspects of his welfare) for neighbours after school to earn needed pocket money is not engaged in child labour. However, it is expected that the interest of the children will be highly sustained in their studies even if proceeds from such economic ventures are to be expended on their education.

The correlation analysis shows that age was found to be positively and significantly correlated (r = 0.24) with the amount spent by child per day at the 0.01 level. It is expected that older children should spend more than the younger children, but this study statistically showed that age as a factor has a very weak influence on the amount to be expended on the child per day, with the co-efficient of determination analysis showing that age accounted for only a 5 per cent contribution to the amount of money spent on the job per child per day. In reality however, it was observed that what was expended on a child per day was being dictated by the amount he/she made per day vis-à-vis the family budget, although these could not be statistically explained as the study did not establish any significant relationship between the amount made and the amount spent by the child per day. It was also revealed in Table 5.2 that age has no influence on the types of job the children do.

Child Culture at the Labour Sites

Child culture in this context is the way of life of the children at their labour sites. This finding was based on the systematic observation of some of the children in their various labour sites, in terms of the way they relate to their peers alongside their behaviour on the job, their break time and so on. Much of the report was based on their activities when they were in clusters.

It was generally observed that most of these children were not well fed. They often live on a very small quantity of nutritionally poor snacks (such as puff-puff, biscuits, bread, roasted yam etc.) as lunch, which they usually purchased from their co-hawkers. Many of them would not have their breakfast until about ten o'clock in the morning when they might have made appreciable sales of their goods. On the average, it was revealed that the children spent for themselves about N88 out of the income they made in a day (see Fig. 5.5). This was often spent on their breakfast and lunch, usually at the labour sites. It was also observed that some of the children, instead of spending all their money on food, secretly engaged in daily money contribution. However, how the money raised through this contribution is spent could not be ascertained.

It is also interesting to note that many of the children were very happy with what they were doing despite the high level of impoverishment apparently observed from their physical appearance. This may perhaps be related to a high level of liberty they were enjoying on the labour sites. Essentially, the street hawker or bus conductor child was observed to have derived a lot of pleasure in the company of his/her co-hawkers in the course of their daily businesses. The girls among the hawkers and the bus conductors were observed to be very lax in morals and had a high tendency to engage in early sexual activities. This was discernible from their frivolous and unethical statements and laissez-faire attitude to life.

Furthermore, it was generally observed that every job has its peak period during which the children were expected to be actively engaged for the purpose of making high income during the day. In the case of those who were hawking and selling goods, many times, during periods of very low patronage, they would be found clustering around shady places and engaged in talking with their mates. These were the places where they were usually socialized into street culture and made street friends. Many of them spent this period in relaxing, playing with their peers, feeding on snacks and quenching their thirst. In fact, this was a period when these children mostly expressed their high level of autonomy!

They often forgot that they were in employment and behaved mostly like adults. This period lasted for about three hours until later in the day when workers and students/pupils were returning from offices and schools, respectively, when patronage picked up again. When the sales are over, they would return to their recession points and take stock of their goods and account for their money before they proceeded to their employers.

For those children who were bus conductors, their peak period was usually during the early part of the day (between 7 and 11 a.m.), when they were actively engaged by their employers. Some of them were picked up from their houses by the bus drivers (their employers) while others joined their buses at an agreed location or bus stop before 7 a.m. They also had about three hours of 'recess' when the patronage would generally be low. During this period, a majority of them would join their employers to eat and thereafter spend some time in the motor parks to relax until later in the day when the business picked again. Saw-mill children workers, however, seemed to have a different way of life from those described above, because in their own case, they were treated by their 'masters' like others on apprenticeship. They were strictly under the instruction of their 'masters' and could not enjoy absolute liberty at the labour sites compared to their peers in the hawking and bus conducting businesses. In terms of morality, their situation seemed to be better off as they tended to emulate the standard demonstrated by adult site workers. They patronized the same food caterers who would come in the afternoon to supply their 'masters'. They were neater in their appearance and looked more promising, though they engaged in what was defined as a worst form of labour that is hazardous in nature.

Generally, it was revealed that the hawking/selling and bus conducting children were only unnecessarily kept on the streets or on the job for those long hours by their employers with the perception that they were always making money, whereas they oftentimes only engaged in extra-social activities that were inimical to good upbringing. Their ways of life were highly characterized by an improper way of eating and dressing, bereft of manners and full of careless talk, exhibition of immorality, delinquency and the like. This type of culture does not guarantee a proper adulthood!

Children's Perceptions about Job Preferences, Benefits Derived and Future Prospects

About 31.43 per cent of the children preferred the job they were doing to any other. Others felt that if they had the opportunity, they would prefer doing something else. Their preferences varied and included schooling (20.0 per cent) and business (11.42 per cent), while some (20 per cent) did not have anything in mind but still felt that they desired jobs that were better than what they were currently doing. However, 11.42 per cent, among those who were not hawking, considered hawking as their best option. It is generally observed that a preference for hawking over other businesses might not be unconnected to the opportunity for liberty reposed in it. It is also worthy of note that 'buying and selling' of petty goods is usually the common business for most illiterates at the study area. Apart from the fact that these children live independently on the street during working hours, it was also seen as very profitable, but condones some undesirable economic activities (such as secret financial contributions and unmonitored spending), which were there for the child to perpetuate. Among the others, 2.86 per cent preferred to be motor mechanics, soldiers or singers. On the benefits of the job, 94.29 per cent perceived the job to be their main source of income, apart from the experience and exposure they felt they were gaining. Very few (5.71 per cent) felt they were not benefiting at all from the job. Further inquiry into what they were likely to lose if they should stop doing the job revealed that many (65.71 per cent) did not believe that they had anything to lose, while 30.81 per cent counted their loss in terms of the financial benefit, which they might not be able to derive again. Few others (2.86 per cent) felt that their parents would not be able to discharge their responsibilities if they should stop.

Many (40.00 per cent) of the children perceived that the work they were doing was not good for their age, but that there was nothing they could do about it. Emotional sentiments were raised by some (8.57 per cent) of the children as a way to justify their engaging in the labour activities as a form of support for their mothers, whom they claimed they were helping. Many (65.71 per cent) of them perceived that their parents did not see anything wrong about the job, while a few (25.71 per cent) perceived that their parents did not like the job, but could not do anything. In the same vein, 65.71 per cent did not perceive that their peers or siblings could look down on them because of the job they were doing. However, about 28 per cent felt differently.

On what prospects they had regarding the job they were currently doing, a majority (57.14 per cent), interestingly, felt that there was a brighter future for them. Notable in this category were those who worked in the sawmills and many of the sellers/ hawkers. However, over 40 per cent felt that there was no future in what they were doing, mostly among the bus conductors and very few hawkers. This latter category was observed to constitute mostly those who attached prospects in life to education.

Conclusion

It is evident that many of the Nigerian children are still very much engaged in hazardous economic activities – in the category of worst forms of child labour – a situation that is not likely to stop if the current condition of extreme household poverty persists. The study reveals a high level of exploitation in the course of these children's engagement in economic activities. Most parents and even the children counted their benefits from what they were gaining from the situation without thinking about the future effects on the children. It is, however, anticipated that in the near future, these children might be trapped in a worse form of poverty than the one experienced by their parents. A majority of them may grow to be very handicapped in human capacity-building, which should have been developed through education. These children would not only constitute an unskilled generation in the future, but the country may continue to nurture the cycle and the anti-social effects would continue to manifest.

Since the poverty situation in which many of the Nigerian parents found themselves has been recognized as the major reason for engaging their children in different exploitative economic activities, it was thought that any likely solution to be proffered must be focused on poverty alleviation. In reality, a more revolutionary outcome is to plead for the genuine interest of the International Financial Institutions (IFIs) such as the World Bank and the International Monetary Fund (IMF) in reassessing their roles in connection with addressing poverty in Nigeria and in Africa. This should not be taken lightly! Moreover, continual persuasion of the parents to see the future advantages embedded in encouraging their children to go to school as against the immediate gains from child labour may contribute in no small measure to stemming the occurrence of exploitative child labour. This could be realized through public enlightenment campaigns. Locally sponsored legislation against crime could also be engendered through Local Government Councils. Law enforcement agents at the local community level need to be empowered to prosecute any perpetrator of child labour. Children found hawking, engaged in street trading or illicit activities during school hours should be sent to child welfare institutions for rehabilitation.

Acknowledgement

The author appreciates the support of CODESRIA in facilitating and funding this research through its Child and Youth Studies Institute, 2004. The assistance of M. A. Popoola (my project student) in data collection, Bayo Oloyede for painstakingly working on the model and that of Dr O. D. Kolawole (a very good colleague in my department) in editing the manuscript are also acknowledged.

References

Agbu, O., 2004a, 'The Linkages between Globalisation and Human Trafficking', Paper prepared for the Child and Youth Studies Institute on Children and the Youth in the Labour Process, CODESRIA, Dakar, 4–29 October.

Agbu, O., 2004b, 'Child Labour in Contemporary Africa: Issues and challenges', Paper prepared for the Child and Youth Studies Institute on Children and the Youth in the Labour Process, CODESRIA, Dakar, 4–29 October.

Aina, T. A., 2004, 'Introduction: How Do We Understand Globalisation and Social Policy in Africa?', in T. A. Aina, C. S. L. Chachage and E. Annan-Yao, eds, *Globalisation and Social Policy in Africa*, Dakar: CODESRIA.

Ajayi, A. O. and Torimiro, D. O., 2004, 'Perspectives on Child Abuse and Labour: Global Ethical Ideals versus African Cultural Realities', *Early Child Development and Care* 174(2).

Amin, S., 1992, 'The Empire of Chaos', *Monthly Review Press*, New York.

Amin, S., 1998, *Capitalism in the Age of Globalization*, London: Zed Books.

Araujo, C. H., 1998, *A Face Jovem da Exclusão. Perfil das Crianças e Adolescentes em Situação de Rua em Brasília*, 4 Temas, Brasília DF: CODEPLAN.

Ebigbo, P., 1990, 'The Problems of Child Abuse and Neglect in Nigeria and Strategies for Overcoming Them', in *The Nigerian Child, Now and in the Future*, Lagos: The Federal Ministry of Health and Human Services and UNICEF.

Ghai, D., 1992, *Structural Adjustment, Globalisation, Integration and Social Democracy*, Discussion Paper No. 37, United Nations Research Institute for Social Development (UNRISD), Geneva.

Grootaert, C. and Patrinos, H. A., 1999, *Policy Analysis of Child Labor: A Comparative Study*, New York: St Martin's Press.

ILO, 1998, *Trafficking in Children for Labour Exploitation in the Mekong Sub-region: A framework for action*, Discussed at sub-regional consultation, Bangkok, 22–24 July 1998, available online at: http://www.ilo.org/public/english/standards/ipec/publ.

ILO, 2001, The World of Work, *The Magazine of the ILO* 41, December.

ILO, 2002, *Every Child Counts: New Global Estimates on Child Labour*, Geneva: International Labour Office, April.

Jega, A., ed., 2003, *Identity Transformation and Identity Politics under Structural Adjustment in Nigeria*, Uppsala: Nordiska Afrikainstitutet, in collaboration with the Centre for Research and Documentation.

Kilbride, P., Suda, C. and Njeru, E., 2000, *Street Children in Kenya*, Westprint: Bergin & Garvey.

Mkandawire, T. and Olukoshi, B., eds., 1995, *Between Liberalisation and Oppression: The Politics of Structural Adjustment in Africa*, Dakar: CODESRIA.

Nkuly, J. L., 2000, Child Labour: Background paper, *African Newsletter on Occupational Health and Safety* 10(2) August.

Odetola, T. O. and Ademola, A., 1985, *Sociology: An Introductory African Text*, London: Macmillan Publishers.

Oloko, S. B. A., 1997, Child Labour, in *The Progress of Nigeria Children*, Lagos: UNICEF/FOS.

Onyango, P. and Kayango Male, D., 1982, Psychological Effects of Child Labour, in P. Onyango and D. Kayango Male, eds., *Child Labour and Health*, Journal of Eastern Africa and Development, University of Nairobi, Kenya.

Osemweige, A., 1998, *Street Children in Lagos, An Assessment Report*, Urban Management Programme, Regional Office for Africa.

Reynolds, P., 1991, *Dance Civet Cat: Child Labour in the Zambezi Valley*, London, Zed Books.

Torimiro, D. O. and Lawal, B. O., 1998, 'Rural Children's Socialization into Farming', in Y. Oruwari, ed., *Gender, Sustainable Development and Urban Poor in Nigeria: A book of readings*, Port Harcourt: Hisis Publishing.

Torimiro, D. O. and Lawal, B. O., 2001, 'Rural Children and Household Food Security Activities in Ijebu Area of Ogun State', Nigeria, *Moor Journal of Agricultural Research* 2(1).

Torimiro, D. O. and Lawal, B. O., 2002, 'Food Insecurity and Poverty Threats: Panacea for Children's Involvement in Household Food Security Activities in Lagos State of Nigeria', *Proceedings of 5th National Research Network Meeting and Conference of Children in Agriculture Programme in Nigeria*, 12–14 December, Ibadan: Nigerian Institute of Social and Economic Research (NISER) (in press).

Torimiro, D. O., Dionco-Adetayo, E. A. and Okorie, V. O., 2003, 'Children and Involvement in Animal Rearing Activities: A Traditional Occupation for Sustainability of Nomadic culture?', *Early Child Development and Care* 173(2–3): 185–92.

UNICEF, 1997, *The State of the World's Children. Focus on Child Labour*, Lagos and Oxford: Oxford University Press.

UNRISD, 2003, *Research for Social Change*, Geneva: United Nations Research Institute for Social Development (UNRISD).

Verlet, M., 2002, 'Growing Up in Ghana: Deregulation and the Employment of Children', in B. Schlemmer, ed., *The Exploited Child*, London and New York: Zed Books, in association with l'Institut de Recherche pour le Développement (IRD), Paris.

6

Internal Child Trafficking in Nigeria: Transcending Legal Borders

Oluwatoyin O. Oluwaniyi

Introduction

> 64 children in a Mercedes Benz mini bus attracted the attention of vigilant policemen on the Onitsha–Benin Expressway. When the vehicle was flagged down by the officers they became more curious at the sight of the kids on bare-feet, without travelling bags and school uniforms to suggest that they were on an excursion. The policemen from the Delta State Command, suspecting child trafficking, promptly arrested the bus driver ... he was conveying the children, who are within the ages of 5 and 16 years... (Ogefere 2004:1).

This report reveals one of the greatest challenges facing children in a globalized world. Trafficking today is a global phenomenon as children are trafficked to and from all regions of the world. About 1.2 million children are trafficked without any gender distinction for various purposes ranging from forced labour in commercial farming, petty crimes, the drug trade, prostitution, domestic service and rituals within and across borders (Ogefere 2004:1). Nigeria is not exempted as the intensity and rate of child trafficking in Nigeria today is alarming to the extent that the phenomenon has attracted global attention.

Child trafficking became glaring in Nigeria when the world media focused on the mystery surrounding the *Etireno* ship, believed to be full of children between ages 3 and 13 being trafficked to Gabon on 17 April 2001 (UNICEF 2002). Since this incident, efforts have been made by concerned bodies, including local and international non-governmental organizations (NGOs) to stem the 'slavery' of children. But while focus has been centred mostly on external trafficking of children and youths, especially girls, and how to eradicate it, internal trafficking of children from villages to cities or from one town to another has either been ignored or seen as 'normal', and hence the trend of child trafficking has tilted towards an increase in internal (intra-state or rural–urban) trafficking. In addition, traffickers have also introduced new methods of trafficking children in order to avoid the prying eyes of the police, and the traffickers will not easily or quickly give up their profitable expolitation of vulnerable children.

Though not new, the idea of placing children with other families, relations and friends is an age-long cultural phenomenon. To Akinmoyo:

> it was the norm during that period that every man and woman saw themselves as their neighbour's keeper, hence, it was a 'we' disposition to life rather than an 'I' disposition. It was normal to expect that in your absence, your neighbour will keep an eye on your possessions (Dayo 2004).

However, with pervasive economic crises coupled with the problem of debt and structural adjustment, leading to unemployment for a majority of citizens, a fall in living standards as well as increases in the costs of living, and extreme poverty of much of the populace, especially in the rural areas (Ogwumike 2001), what seemed to have been a cultural phenomenon has been exploited as a 'money-making venture whereby children are transported as commodities to be sold in the market, priced and exchanged for money like any other article in the market (Agbu 2003:2). Taking advantage of the impoverished status of rural dwellers and of the demand for cheap and malleable labour in the cities, middlemen (traffickers) in Nigeria are known to engage in internal trafficking of children from villages in Akwa-Ibom, Anambra, Abia, Cross River, Edo, Imo, Kwara, Ondo and Oyo States to the cities of Lagos, Port Harcourt, Abuja and Ibadan, to mention but a few, where most of the children are used in an exploitative manner.

In spite of the conventions and national laws guiding and protecting children from trafficking and exploitative labour as well as eradicating the use of children as slaves, such as the 1989 United Nations Convention on the Rights of the Child (UN) (UNICEF 1989), 2,000 Optional Protocol to the CRC on the Sale of Children, Child Prostitution and Child Pornography (UN)(UNICEF 2002), Convention No.182 of the International Labour Organization on the Worst Forms of Child Labour (UN)(ILO 1999; ILO-IPU 2002), 2,000 Protocol to Prevent, Suppress and Punish Trafficking in Persons, Especially Women and Children, Supplementing the UN Convention against Transnational Organized Crime known as the Palermo Protocol (ILO)(ILO 2002) and at the sub-regional level, the Libreville 2000 Common Platform for Action and A Declaration and A Plan of Action against Trafficking in Persons (2002–3)(UNICEF 2002), 2003 Anti-Trafficking law and 2003 Child Rights Act both in Nigeria, children continue to be vulnerable in the hands of traffickers and '*ogas*' (masters) either as domestics, vendors, shop-minders or prostitutes. Since the phenomenon of child trafficking is one of the most extreme forms of child labour with little attention paid to it at the policy level and in research, this study therefore intends to explore the trends of internal trafficking of children in Nigeria with emphasis on child domestics, for the following reasons. The issue of child domestics as one of the end results of internal trafficking is being ignored as unimportant when compared to the cases of prostitution, drug trading, rituals, trade in organs and street trading because child domestics are within the family household. Though they are mostly invisible, they suffer the most abuses. While they are made to work for long hours, they are poorly paid and particularly vulnerable to sexual abuse from men living within the household. And because they are hidden from public scrutiny, they are not protected by the law.

The research questions addressed in this chapter include the following: What are the dynamics surrounding the increase in internal child trafficking in Nigeria? What is the linkage between internal child trafficking and child domestic servitude? How does it take place? What are the kinds of activities engaged in by the child domestics? Who benefits more from internal trafficking and child domestic service? Is the legal framework instituted by the government adequate for alleviating this trend? If not, what are the possible interventions necessary to stem this trend?

Review of Literature on Trafficking and Children

Generally, the recognition of trafficking as a challenge to the future of children and youths is recent, yet a wealth of literature exists on the phenomenon (Effah 1996; UNICEF 1998). The extant literature on trafficking has shown that the phenomenon is not limited to Nigeria or Africa but is a common feature of poor countries such as China, Central and South America, South-East Asia, Eastern Europe and Russia where people of all ages are trafficked into a life of exploitative and forced labour such as domestic service, commercial sex, labour and the drug trade (US Department of State 2000). This phenomenon endangers the lives of children around the world.

Starting with the international legal framework, the various United Nations (UN) and International Labour Convention (ILO) documents for protecting children do not exist merely because of the children's under-age status, which has been agreed to be 0–18 years, but more importantly because of the nature of the trafficking, exploitative labour and human rights abuses these under-age people go through and the effects of child labour on the children. The 1949 Geneva Convention emphasizes that mankind owes the child the best it has to give and that the child must be protected against every form of exploitation (Langley 1994:3–7). Studies by UNICEF revealed that child work is normal and consistent with the child's evolving mental and physical capabilities but becomes exploitative when it involves beginning full-time work at an early age; working too long hours; with inadequate remuneration; excessive responsibility at too early an age; hampering of psychological and social development of the child and the inhibiting of the child's self-esteem (UNICEF/NCRIC 1986:3). Similarly, ILO sees all work as capable of depriving the child of basic education, and that results in physical injury, jeopardizing the health, safety and normal development of the child as child labour. These factors have also been recognized in the works of Black and Ennew (Black and Ennew 1993).

In addition, Article 32 of the Convention on the Rights of the Child emphasizes the right of the child to be protected from economic exploitation and from performing any work that is likely to be hazardous or to interfere with the child's education, or to be harmful to the child's health or physical, mental, spiritual, moral or social development. Articles 9, 10, 11 of same document make provisions to combat the illicit movement of the child. While the Optional Protocol to the Convention on the Rights of the Child makes it a criminal offence to sell a child for profit, the ILO asserts that child trafficking is a practice similar to slavery and forced labour, and urges all countries to prohibit and eliminate trafficking of children under 18 years of age. Child trafficking is not only similar to slavery but is slavery to all intents and purposes, taking into consideration the ways and methods by which children are deceived and transported, the bargaining and exchange of money and the eventual use to which they are put, as prostitutes, plantation workers, street vendors, in the drug trade, for ritual purposes (which involves the total elimination of the person for economic gain) and human parts trading. All these practices also existed in the past in the slave trade. And while Dottridge maintains that child trafficking is not strictly speaking slavery, as the reality of today's slavery in most parts of the world is that adults and children fleeing poverty or seeking better prospects are manipulated, deceived and bullied into working in conditions that they would not have chosen, in conclusion, he accepts that such trafficked could end up as slaves (Dottridge 2002). The Palermo Protocol provides the legal means for the prevention, suppression and punishing of traffickers.

Nigeria, in its bid to adhere to the contents of the legislation, in 2003 domesticated the UNCRC and ILO by passing into law the Child Rights Act and the Trafficking in Persons Act. While the Child Rights Act, among other things, prohibits all forms of trafficking in persons including children, Mandate XI of the Trafficking in Persons Act states that buying and selling a person for a purpose attracts on conviction imprisonment for 14 years without option of a fine, and XIII states that traffic in slaves is liable to conviction to imprisonment for life.

While the emphasis of these legal documents has been on the rights of children and their protection from trafficking and exploitative labour, the impact of these provisions on the lives of trafficked children has not been felt as the trafficking trade in children continues both within and outside the country, with the middlemen either going underground or using covert means to avoid the law enforcement agencies. What this implies is that eradicating child trafficking transcends the domestic legal framework. Some are of the opinion that the increase in this phenomenon is of global dimensions. In one of his works Agbu argues that the commercialization of humanity, including children, has emerged as a result of globalization, which has created inequalities and inequities, and consequently the migration of the poor to the rich regions of the world (Agbu 2003:1–2). To him, therefore, the result of globalization includes the loosening of barriers and political boundaries, which organized criminal gangs have capitalized on to perpetrate many heinous acts including human trafficking for the purpose of forced and child prostitution, domestic servitude, illegal and bonded labour, servile marriage, false adoption, sex tourism and entertainment, pornography, organized begging, organ harvesting and other criminal activities. This argument has also been corroborated by UNICEF UK in its report on child trafficking, though with emphasis on external trafficking. To UNICEF UK, globalization has opened borders as well as improved transportation and communication modes and, as a result, facilitated the movement of people to all parts of the world, especially to meet the demands of the labour market and commercial sex industry (UNICEF 2003:8).

Some view trafficking as originating from certain cultural practices in Africa, in which the upbringing of a child is everybody's responsibility, with children placed with other households and sometimes with wealthier relatives in the cities through direct contact with a child's parents. In return for the work performed at home, children receive education or vocational training. Many now tend to agree that this trend has changed over the years in tandem with changing global economic conditions. The neo-liberal policies of the West have led to the integration of rural subsistence economies into the wider urban metropolitan and world economy and are therefore disruptive (UNICEF 2001:206–7). The economic crises entrenched by these policies have brought about increasing unemployment, low educational levels of children, rural–urban migration, impoverishment of the masses and the break-up of extended family ties. The most affected are children who are forced to engage in hazardous activities such as child prostitution, living in the streets, drug abuse and other forms of child labour including child trafficking and becoming child domestics (Olawale 1997; Tzannatos et al. 1998:7–9). To Bass, 'children are often swept away by the economic needs of their households into different modes of child labour…' (Bass 2004:68–9). According to Human Rights Watch (2003:1), impoverishment in families has led some parents/relatives, willingly or desperately, out of deceit or the promise of a better life for them and their children, to give out their children in return for money without the knowledge of what would happen to the children. While some of these children are trafficked within the country, others are trafficked across the country's borders.

In some cases, economic factors and ignorance of risk play an important role in the trafficking of children for sexual exploitation. In this case, children are lured into Europe and the Middle East for sexual exploitation with promises of employment as shopkeepers, maids, seamstresses, nannies or hotel workers, but find themselves forced into prostitution upon arrival (UNICEF 2001). To this extent, Wennerholm argues that anti-poverty strategies or economic growth by themselves cannot eradicate the problem as long as the expanding middle-level countries such as Malaysia, Indonesia and the Philippines' financial capability and motivation for sex increases (Wennerholm 2003). Though Fitzgibbon argues that 'economic constraints may force families to give out their children for trafficking…', she does not want to totally agree that it is only the poorest families who are involved in the trade of giving out children to traffickers or middlemen for exploitative work. To her, there are other push and pull factors necessitating the trend. The push factors include exposure to the world outside the village through television or soccer clubs, and the pull factors include the demand for commercial sex exploitation, improvements in transportation and communication. Olateru-Olagbegi (2000), Social Alert and International Organisation on Migration (IOM)(2002) assert that trafficking in children results from the demand for cheap, obedient, non-unionized child manpower and malleable labour in cities and plantations, inadequate and non-existent national legislation relating to the traffic, lack of strict border policies, the burden of informal economy and corruption. However, the International Labour Organization sees the increase in the pull for trafficked children as not being based on their cheap labour; rather it is because children are easier to abuse, less assertive, less able to claim their rights, work long hours with little food and accept poor accommodation. To the ILO, therefore, it is a matter of child abuse and exploitation.

An observation from the existing literature is that the major focus has been on external trafficking of children, with few studies devoted to the internal trend. Though internal trafficking, especially in Nigeria, has received broad media coverage in the electronic and non-electronic media, and considering the number of arrests made for trafficking in children, there has been little scientific research on the matter (Oloko et al. 1992; Ebigbo 2000). Hence, this study aims to examine the trends in internal trafficking of children in Nigeria with emphasis on child domestics, as this is directly linked to the broader phenomenon of child trafficking (Human Rights Watch 2004). Such information will help in advancing knowledge in the area and enable the formulation of appropriate policy directed at solving the problem.

Conceptualizing Trafficking

Trafficking as a concept has existed as an age-old phenomenon but was generally used synonymously with trading. By the late sixteenth century, it graduated from a mere trading term to refer to the sale of illicit or contraband goods, usually, the sale of drugs and weapons across borders in order to make profit. In the nineteenth century, it became associated with illicit trade in human beings and their displacement across or within borders. However, the increase in the phenomenon in the twentieth century with the trafficking in human beings, especially children within the 8–17 age bracket, caused alarm around the world, especially in Nigeria. It became obvious that children are trafficked within and outside their countries for the commercial benefit of traffickers who sell them to end-users. The traffickers in turn use the children for domestic services, sexual gratification, agricultural work, trading and prostitution, such as the case of the '*italo*' girls scandal. 'Italo' is the local slang for Nigerian girls who do commercial sex work abroad. Since this period, various international treaties have emerged to combat the trend in trafficking, especially of children and women within and across borders, but the definition of trafficking has been burdened with different contestations. The international concern has become imperative owing to the intensity and changes in the pattern of trafficking, which makes it a criminal offence, violating the rights of the child as established in the UN Convention on the Rights of the Child.

In 1994, the United Nations General Assembly attempted a global definition for 'traffic' as:

> the illegal and underground movement of people through national and international frontiers most of them from the developing countries and from some mid-income countries whose final objective is to force women and young girls into exhausting or economic exploitation conditions to the benefit of recruiting touts, traffickers as well as other related illegal trafficking activities such as forced domestic labour, false marriage, illegal employment and false adoptions.

In the preliminary report prepared for the UN Special Rapporteur on Violence against Women:

> women trafficking means any acts that have to do with the recruitment and/or transportation of a woman or (a young girl) in or out of the national borders with a view to working or serving under violence, abuse of authority or perverting position, debt servitude, disappointment or other forms of coercion.

This definition is not complete because it evades the trafficking for boys too. The International Labour Office (ILO), viewing trafficking of children as enslavement, defines child slavery as:

> the recruitment and the legal or illegal transportation of a child – whether he agrees or not – across a border in general, but not always organized by an intermediary: parents, kinsman, teacher, procurer or local authority. At destination, the child is forced under duress or deceived into doing some works under conditions of exploitation (Muntarbhorn 1998:2–7).

In a study of child trafficking in West and Central Africa Bazzi-Veil (2000) defines trafficking as:

> a whole process and conditions whereby a child is withdrawn from parental protection and authority to be considered as market value at any moment in the process. Thus, it is made up of any act consisting of recruiting, transporting, harbouring or trading of persons involving deception, constraint or force, debt servitude or fraud resulting in a movement of a child within or outside a country.

The Palermo Protocol provides international guidance to the meaning of trafficking. Article 3(a) of the protocol sees trafficking in persons to mean:

> the recruitment, transportation, transfer, harbouring or receipt of persons, by means of the threat or use of force or other forms of coercion, of abduction, of fraud, of deception, of the abuse of power or of a position of vulnerability or the giving or receiving of payments or benefits to achieve the consent of a person having control over another person, for the purpose of exploitation.

In continuation of this definition, ILO-IPEC sees trafficking as involving the combination of movement and exploitation of a child at some stage in the process, no matter when the exploitation itself takes place. Therefore, what transforms this chain of events into trafficking is what transforms the exploitation of the child who is being trafficked, whether that exploitation occurs at the beginning or at the end of the trafficking process.

The definitions of trafficking can be simplified under the terms traffic, trafficked person and trafficker. Traffic includes any acts or attempts to committing acts involving the recruitment, transportation within or outside the borders, trade, transfer, reception or sheltering of a person, (a) involving deception, coercion (including threat or abuse of authority) or debt servitude; (b) in order to keep or detain such a person under involuntary servitude conditions (domestic, sexual), forced labour or under a situation of virtual slavery in a community that is different from the one in which such a person lives. A trafficked person is someone who is recruited, carried away, bought, sold, transferred, received or sheltered as described in the definition of Traffic, including a willing or unwilling child (defined by and in accordance with the principles of the Children's Rights Convention). A trafficker is a person who intends to commit, is an accomplice or accepts any act as described in the definition of 'traffic' (Social Alert 1998). In other words, *trafficked children are turned into commodities to be bought, sold and transported according to supply and demand.* The consequences faced by the affected children are similar to what occurred during the slave period in Africa. Such conditions include use of false promises, transport to a strange city (internal trafficking) or country (external trafficking), abduction, loss of freedom, deprivation of parental love and extreme physical abuse.

Why the Emphasis on Children

The emphasis of international concern on trafficking and actions to combat it has been placed on the thrust that children are innocent, vulnerable, malleable, dependent and lacking the type of mature, intellectual, emotional and physical capabilities present in adults and therefore should be protected from dangers or from any movement that could make the children lose such privileges or their reference point (Boyden 1996:18–22). Though historically (Aries 1965, Veerman 1992), the concept of childhood has been perceived as a recent and western invention, in the past childhood was not given any special attention or, in the words of Jenks, 'childhood did not matter at all' (Jenks 1996). Then, children of the lower classes in the West were expected to begin working at a tender age, and children who successfully survived the first dangerous years of life were quickly forced to enter the adult world and become part of it. Labour was not thought to threaten child welfare but was believed to be the most effective means of child learning and socialization, especially among the children of the poor. According to Cunningham:

> children were found to be working at the age of three or four. The birth of a child heralded the arrival of a future labourer and security for parents in later life. Children over the age of five and fourteen who were orphaned or found living in idleness or begging would be bound into agricultural service or craft (Cunningham 1991).

However, with the Reformation of the seventeenth century and the Industrial Revolution of the eighteenth and nineteenth centuries, attitudes towards children changed in the West, and mass education was gradually introduced. In order to ensure that these variables are intact, the international community developed a framework of protection for children in the form of the United Nations Conventions on the Rights of the Child as the most comprehensive instrument. According to CRC, a child is 'every human being below the age of eighteen years unless under the law applicable to the child, majority is attained earlier' (United Nations 1989).

This legal definition of a child is rejected in developing countries on the basis that it ensrines the ideas of the industrialized world and it does not reflect the true identity of the child. Sall argues that 'the material conditions necessary for the realisation of children's rights as embodied in the Convention on the Rights of the Child do not exist for many of the children born to poor parents in the developing countries' (Sall 2004:2–4). Increasing threats to survival require children to perform adult roles at tender ages in Africa, including Nigeria. At such ages, children are made to participate in productive activities rather than being protected, not as a means of contributing to their growth, but because such work is exploitative. It has been commonly argued that following the introduction of Structural Adjustment Policies, children have been taken out of the educational system and forced into adulthood at early ages through engaging in illegal activities such as prostitution, drug-hawking, street life and participation in socio-political violence in order to survive or being obliged to become breadwinners for their families. Under harsh economic conditions, the child becomes less valuable if he or she does not contribute to family labour needs. Therefore, being trafficked for an economic purpose could be an acceptable norm in such a society.

In addition, the legal definition of a child in Nigeria in particular, as generally in Africa, becomes difficult to operate given the nature of African culture, which values hard work at tender ages for growth purposes. This could be right from birth or after the performance of rituals as part of the traditional rites of passage, which is normally much less than 18 years, after which the child is perceived as an adult. As a result, using this supposed legal definition of a child in Africa is problematic for assessing who is a child, when childhood ends, whether work is regarded as exploitative for a 'child' and whether a child should be protected from exploitative work or not. Even though the Organization of African Unity, now the African Union (AU), came out with the African Charter on the Rights and Welfare of the Child in 1991, it has not been fully accepted and ratified by state parties partly becuase of the African 'concept of the child who does not have any right'. Though almost all states parties except the United States and Somalia have ratified the United Nations Convention on the Rights of the Child, child trafficking, child labour and abuse have increased on a wider scale.

In spite of the good intentions of these international legal documents in defining who a child is and how they should be treated, they have not been effective in tackling the issues of exploitation, abuse, sale of children, abduction and their use in demeaning ways. Further, in view of all the socio-economic and cultural challenges facing families, especially in Nigeria, it behoves us to know that children are the most vulnerable of all trafficked victims. At tender ages, they are taken from their family either forcibly or through deception. They are moved to faraway places where they are exposed to unfamiliar people who ruthlessly exploit their tender bodies. In the process, their survival and development are threatened, and their right to grow up within a societal or familial safety net is denied. This suggests that in addressing the issues of abuse, trafficking and exploitation in the hands of their end-users, there should be transcendence from legal framework to issues of widespread social and economic concern.

Linkage betweeen Internal Child Trafficking and Child Domestics

Internal child trafficking derives from the movement of children from their locality to another by means of threat or use of force or other forms of coercion or deception or the abuse of power or of a position of vulnerability and of giving or receiving of payments or benefits on behalf of a child for the purpose of exploitation. Children are being trafficked internally for various reasons, which include: prostitution, use as domestics or shop menders, in drug trafficking, as dancers in pubs, as bonded labour, for false adoption, in organized begging and other forms of businesses, both legal and illegal. However, the major emphasis here is internal child trafficking for the purpose of domestic servitude in urban areas. As the name implies, child domestics are children under 18 years of age who work in other people's households, doing domestic chores, taking care of children, and running errands among other tasks (UNICEF 1999:3). Internal child trafficking in Nigeria for the purpose of being commodified as domestics is not a recent development as the cultural idea of child placement with relations and richer families as part of children's developmental process led to the commodification of children's bodies in recent years. The stereotyping of some ethnic groups in Nigeria as excellent in domestic work and other forms of labour started off the commodification of such groups as the Igede in Benue State and the Yala, Okuku and Okpoma in Cross River State. However, the effects of the negative socio-economic conditions of the late 1980s not only deepened but intensified the rate and level of the phenomenon in Nigeria.

Nigeria had a total population of some 108 million in the 1980s (140 million in 2007) and a child population of nearly 55 million. It is a multi-ethnic society with diverse cultures and languages. Nonetheless, there are common features among the groups, which can be generalized, and one of these features is the age-old fostering system. Fostering was the assumption of the rights and duties of parenthood by adults who were not the child's biological parents (without the latter surrendering their rights). Fostering provided opportunities for upward social mobility for fostered children (UNICEF 2001:13). This trend continued until the early 1980s. However, this does not mean it is not still present, for, as UNICEF argues:

> to some extent, the principles of mutual solidarity still provide informal mechanisms of social security in times of adversity in a society where formal social safety nets provided by the state or employers have limited scope … the continued practice suggests a certain resilience of the values associated with the extended family (UNICEF 2001:14).

However, with the collapse of world oil market in the early 1980s, coupled with a sharp decrease in Nigeria's economic revenue, the result was an increase in internal public debt from N4.6 bn in 1979 to N22.2 bn in 1983. External debt stood at N15 bn in 1983, and with a debt of N5 bn in trade payments and the country's inability to adjust to the decline in oil earnings, the basis was set for the country's debt crisis. The state's GDP, which fell by 2 per cent in 1982, recorded a further 4.4 per cent fall in 1983 and the number of those in poverty increased from 27 per cent in 1980 to 46 per cent in 1985 (Olukoshi 1995:158, 1991:3). This situation impacted negatively on citizens as wages and salaries were not paid to workers for several months at a time. Things were worse for the peasantry. Rural unemployment increased and families could neither sustain their homes nor sponsor wards to school (Ibeanu 1993:124–53).

Efforts by the international community to alleviate this negative trend culminated in the introduction of the Structural Adjustment Programme (SAP). Its stiff conditionalities included:

- liberalization of foreign trade
- currency devaluation
- cutbacks in social expenditure such as education, health and housing
- removal of food subsidies
- tight control of money supply, and
- privatization of state-owned enterprises.

The implication of the adjustment programmes for development has been negative. Economies that were already depressed and in dire need of being boosted were simply subjected to a rigid regime of deflation that destroyed the structures of growth and exacted huge social costs that reverberated in the political arena and triggered a cycle of instability (Olukoshi 2004:23–42). Instead of alleviating the suffering of the masses, SAP further worsened it, and the negative changes were felt by both rural and urban dwellers. The consequences included:

- increase in Nigeria's debt
- stagnant economic growth
- increase in agricultural inputs and fall in prices of agricultural outputs
- unemployment of the mass of the citizenry
- impoverishment of the people, and
- lowering of health, nutritional and educational levels for tens of millions of children.

According to ITCPR (2000):

> There was no doubt that while structural adjustment had its salutary effects on economic growth, it lacked emphasis on development, which also accentuated problems of income inequality, unequal access to food, shelter, education, health and other necessities of life. It indeed aggravated the incidence of poverty among many vulnerable groups in the society.

Facing these economic crises, people both in the rural and urban centres had to explore survival strategies. As a result of the socio-economic conditions, fostering increased but, unlike in the traditional fostering method, it has been taken over by middlemen (child traffickers) who exploit the trust of parents for a profit. Once they reach the destination, children are placed with various employers who use them in all forms of service including domestic service. Though child domestic service is at the heart of child trafficking, child domestics are the most ignored, neglected and exploited group in their various engagements in homes. Therefore, there is a need for a detailed study of this phenomenon and also examine how this trend of exploitation can be reduced and in the long run eradicated.

Methodology and Limitation

The study relied on two major sources for generating data, namely, primary and secondary sources. The study explored existing literature, especially United Nations documents and reports on trafficking, reports by international and local NGOs, newspapers, media reports and journal articles. However, the literature was sparse on internal child trafficking or on child domestics specifically.

The crux of the study was the primary approach, which focused mainly on qualitative information. The location of the research study was the Ijaiye-Ogba area of Agege in Lagos State of Nigeria. This area was easily accessible to the researcher because she resides there and it was easy to make contacts and engage informants in discussion. Moreover, Lagos is one of the major destinations of trafficked children in Nigeria. Many residents in this area work either with banks, old and new generation private telecommunication companies, the federal government and state civil service. Others are in the informal sector and most of them employ child domestics. After much effort, the researcher engaged in in-depth interviews with 26 child domestics and 12 child domestics' employers through purposive and snowballing samplings Two of the child domestics were from Edo State, one from Anambra State, one from Benue State, two from Kogi, five from Oyo State, one from Ondo State, two from Ogun State and ten from Kwara State. The ratio of the child domestics shows that the phenomenon cuts across ethnic or social backgrounds, and also gender bias as two males were represented. In addition, two of the children were transported within Lagos area (though they are indigenes of Ogun and Ondo State respectively) and four of them migrated to Lagos with the assistance of employers' relations. The ages of all these children were between 10 and 17, with majority of them in the 10–12 age group.

While some of the employers were contacted directly, others were sourced through other family friends, making the snowballing method imperative. The last of this group was the traffickers of child domestics. There was access to four major groups of child traffickers. An in-depth interview was held with a trafficker in Agege. She is involved in bringing children from the eastern part of the country. Other in-depth interviews were held with three groups of child traffickers at Oyingbo, Ebute-Metta, Lagos State.

The interviews with respondents generally revolved around getting information on the:

- social backgrounds of the child domestics
- reasons for child domestics being trafficked from their environment
- modes of transportation from their environment.
- agreement between parents and the middlemen
- children's experiences as child domestics
- issues about their future
- prospects of leaving the job for the child domestics, and
- employers of child domestics managing without them.

The research study was not without its own hitches. To be sure, the fieldwork was hampered by certain limitations. The tight work schedule of employers and domestics made it cumbersome to engage them in discussions. The networks of traffickers made it difficult to interview them. Most of them denied ever being involved in the trade. Moreover, seeing a young lady researcher, they thought I was a police detective trying to spy on them. This negative perception by them hampered to a great extent the kinds of questions that could be asked. I had to devise other means such as requesting the assistance of elderly women to pretend they wanted child domestics in their homes. It was then that the research study could be carried out on the traffickers.

Recruitment of Child Domestics: The Child's Family/Middlemen/ Employer Nexus

The reality on the ground shows that internal child trafficking is rife in Nigeria, both from one state to another and from rural to urban centres of the same state. However, as this has been taken as normal, little or no serious attention had been paid to it either in the form of research, policymaking or implementation, until very recently when several NGOs began to show the world the risks children involved pass through, the abuse suffered by them at the hands of their employers and the mortgaging of the nation's children's future through the cycle of slavery in which they are engaged.

The data on the issue of trafficking children for domestic service has been classified into three types, namely: (1) process of recruitment of child domestics; (2) moving of child domestics from their homes, villages and states to cities, and the challenges involved in trafficking the children (old and new trends), and (3) the necessity of such employment and its impact on the lives of affected children, families and society as a whole. The whole process involves four major actors: the trafficker; the parents or guardians of trafficked children; the trafficked children; and the employers of trafficked children.

Process of Recruitment

Findings on the process of recruitment of child domestics have revealed that what used to be a family procedure of placing children with family members and relations for better upbringing of such children has turned out to be a purely economic transaction, for either 'push' or 'pull' factors, involving the family of the child to be recruited, the middlemen and the people who employ the trafficked children. The process of recruitment varies according to the area and conditions engendering such recruitment. However, the end result is the same.

Interestingly, the middlemen who are engaged with the task of trafficking children are also indigenes of the villages involved. The process of recruitment for trafficking can be classified into two broad groups. In the first group, some of the middlemen live in the villages and come to the cities with agricultural products such as pepper, okro, vegetables and fruits, and in the process, bring some children with them. They have friends in the cities who act as intermediaries between them and the employers of such children. This category of people forms a powerful network resembling the international traffickers (though not as sophisticated as international trafficking syndicates). The second group of traffickers comprise traffickers who are solely responsible for travelling to the rural areas, recruiting children, bringing them to the cities and placing them in households. This trend is not limited to traffickers or intermediaries in the western part of Nigeria but is common too in the eastern part. Though recruitment is seasonal, that is, traffickers only travel to the villages during festive periods such as Christmas, New Year and Easter, and the id-el Maulud, Id-el Fitri and Id-el Kabr festivals to bring children, recruitment of children from the rural areas also depends on demand in the cities, turning children into commodities that are purchased in the market when needed.

Whether as a network or sole intermediaries, the process of recruiting children for domestic work involved visiting the villages of which they are indigenes. As claimed by some intermediaries interviewed, the process of recruitment requires them to move from one household to another, identifying volunteers, who could also be a relative or friend. Some of the parents are deceived into giving out their children for placement in the cities with '*rich people*' with the promise that their children would be clothed, fed and paid for their labour services. Moreover, fon occasion, children could be encouraged by news about '*the beauty of Lagos*' and in the process unknowingly become victims. However, this is not common. Though this system still persists and thrives at a high rate – as one trafficker put it, 'man must survive in these hard times – the worsening economic conditions in Nigeria generally force some parents to put pressure on the traffickers (who are already known in the village) to take their wards with them to the city where they could earn a living, relieve the burden at home and also remit some money through it.

Another finding is that at times relations of employers assist substantially in sourcing children in rural areas, in agreement with children's parents or guardians, but without the victims' agreement, for bringing to the city in order to work as domestics. To an employer of child domestic:

> My mother brought the child along with her when she travelled to our home town in Edo State. Before then, I had one domestic servant from Benue State. She travelled for Christmas, and though she promised to come back, she did not. You see, as a banker, I faced a lot of problems when she left. I told my mother about it when she

> came around on a visit and when she travelled home, she found one for me. I think I prefer this one because she is from my place.

Transporting these children varies depending on the number of children to be trafficked and the persons involved. In most cases, children to be trafficked are gathered together at a place. They could be as few as five and more often up to 25–30 as revealed by child domestic respondents. According to a child domestic:

> Mama Seun brought us in a truck carrying agricultural products such as firewood and vegetables from my village in Kwara State. Though I did not count everybody in the truck, we were about 10–11 children inside. While some of us sat on the firewood, others sat on the floor of the truck carrying some of the vegetable on their laps. Two other women were also inside with us. I am sure that their goods were also in the truck and they were going to sell them in Lagos.

At this point, children are boarded in vehicles ranging from cars, buses and trucks depending on the number of children to be trafficked. One child domestic interviewed was transported to Lagos in a public bus from Aba and when they got to the employer's house, the trafficker claimed the transportation cost, which the employer gladly refunded. For those taken in buses and trucks, their conditions are pitiable. To a child domestic:

> We did not have any breathing space in the truck and we did not eat anything until we got to the Mama's house in Oyingbo. By the time we alighted from the truck, we were extremely tired and my legs were aching.

The children are kept either in the intermediary's or trafficker's house until employers are found for them, who either come to size up the child she wants, such as was practiced during the slave period in Africa, or the child is taken to the employer's/ customer's house by the trafficker herself.

From there, the child starts his or her work as a child domestic or in the popular parlance, '*domestic servant*', and can expect to be recycled over the years among different employers until he or she becomes a full-grown adult. Although most children are voluntarily handed over to middlemen, there have been increasing numbers of cases of children being kidnapped for trafficking. In Sokoto State, kidnapped children were sold for amounts ranging from N50,000 to N100,000 (taking N140 as equal to $1 US) to be used as labourers or for ritual purposes (Komolafe 2001:12–16). This brings to the fore questions about the reasons for trafficking of children for the purpose of domestic work in the cities, far from the families' environment, as against Article 7 of the United Nation's Convention on the Rights of the Child, which stipulates that the best place for a child is his family. This is because the best environment for meeting a child's developmental needs is the family (Apfel and Simon 1995:11). Responses from the various respondents, including the traffickers, child domestics and employers of labour, vary but they can be grouped under push and pull factors.

'Push' Factors Responsible for Trafficking in Child Domestics

'Push', as the word denotes, is the ability to use sudden or steady pressure in order to move someone or something forward and far way from oneself or to a different position. Push factors therefore means reasons or variables propelling or urging someone to move away from his or her place to another. Interviews with the respondents revealed various push factors such as poverty, peer pressure and socio-cultural practices.

Poverty

> I am 10 years old. My home town is in Ilorin. I came to Lagos with the assistance of 'Mama' after the Ileya festival to work as a child domestic. … My mother is a trader and my father is a full-time farmer. He goes to farm every Sunday evening and comes back home every Saturday evening. We are ten in the family and my parents have no money. So my mother said that I should come with Mama and other children to Lagos where I will work and have money like my senior sisters. … I knew the type of job I was coming to do because my sisters have been doing it for years.
>
> I am 12 years old from Isiala Ngwa North local government Area of Abia State. My father has 2 wives and 13 children. We are six from my mother's side and she is a full-time housewife. The children do not attend school but we follow our father to the farm every day and sell the produce of the farm. After selling the produce, the money realized is not always enough to take care of all of us. We are really very poor. Well, I don't know how they met, but when Aunty came to our house, my mother called and told me that I would be following her to Lagos where I will work and get plenty money to take away their sufferings. I'd never been to school.
>
> You need to see the conditions of living of some of these people in the rural areas. We are doing it to help them out of poverty.

The above statements by three child domestics reveal that entrenched poverty is a major push factor encouraging trafficking. The extent of the poverty shows in the fact that 69.2 per cent of the children have never been to school and their ages are between 10 and 14 years and 30.8 per cent dropped out of primary school owing to the inability to pay their school fees, or death of either parents or breadwinners of their homes. Out of frustration and the need to get out of poverty, some poor families give out their children to be trafficked for exploitative labour such as domestics with the hope that they would be fed, clothed and taken care of to achieve a better life. This hardly happens as this group of children are recycled yearly into different households and made to pass through the same exploitation until they have their own families and in some cases, their children take it up and the phenomenon becomes a vicious cycle. The frustration and desperation that lies beneath parent's willingness to give a child to traffickers are worsened by a lack of understanding of the dangers of such willingness.

Further inquiries into the lives and engagements of child domestics' parents reveal that out of the total number of child domestics interviewed, 73 per cent have both parents alive and living together, 7.7 per cent have single parents (mothers),

11.5 per cent live with their fathers and stepmothers, and 7.7 per cent do not have both parents and live with relations. The parents are engaged in different kinds of employment, with farming taking the highest proportion for their fathers and trading the highest proportion for their mothers (see Table 6.1).

Table 6.1: The Engagement of Parents

Mothers' employment	Percentage (%)	Fathers' employment	Percentage (%)
Housewives	3.8	Farmers	50.0
Farmers	27.0	Traders	11.5
Traders	34.6	Bus drivers	7.7
Load carriers	11.5	Hunters	3.8
Hair weaving	7.7	Butchers	3.8
Cloth weaving	3.8	Cleric	7.7
Food vendor	7.7	Not in any job	15.4
Plate washer	3.0		

The parents live off these trades and professions and the incomes earned are inadequate to fend for the whole family. Moreover, given the strong desire for and atachment to children; the role of women, especially in the rural areas, as child-bearers; the excessive desire of men to have a male child in a female-dominated home; and the competition that arises in polygynous homes about the number of children to bear by co-wives, the tendency to have many children within limited resources is high. Hence, parents say they have have no option but to allow their children to engage in exploitative labour as long as the returns of such labour will flow back to them. Poverty in the rural areas is just one of the results of bad governance and poor economic management in Nigeria.

The UNCTAD Report on the Less Developing Countries (LDCs), of which Nigeria is one, states that the incidence of extreme poverty has continued to increase at a fast rate and that if the trend persists, the number of people living in extreme poverty in the LDCs will increase from 334m people in 2000 to 471m in 2015 (CROP Newsletter, 2004:1). This is in line with the result of the Federal Office of Statistics that the number of people living in poverty rose from 28 per cent of the population in 1980 to 46 per cent in 1985, reduced to 43 per cent in 1992 and rose sharply to 66 per cent in 1996 (FOS 1999). As explained earlier, since the collapse of the oil boom, there has been a dramatic increase in the incidence and depth of poverty in both rural and urban areas of Nigeria. The features of poverty such as poor access to public services and infrastructure, unsanitary environment, illiteracy, ignorance, poor health, insecurity and social exclusion, and low levels of incomes have trapped the poor in a vicious cycle, affecting their coping capabilities. This trend is most rife in the rural areas where over 69 per cent of the population lives below the poverty line. This is especially so among families whose household heads are engaged in agriculture (UNICEF 2001:22–4). This does not in any way exclude the incidence of poverty in the urban centres. With the increase in migration to the cities, and a large population competing for limited resources, urban poverty rose from 3 per cent in 1980 to over 25 per cent in 1996. Two of the child domestics confirmed this negative trend as their parents live in Lagos (Ajegunle and Ikorodu), but the poor conditions of living led to a third party introducing them into the child domestics' profession.

Peer Pressure

Peer group pressure could also be identified as a factor aiding child trafficking. Some of these children bcame involved in domestic service because of pressures from friends and the middlemen who trafficked them to Lagos. To Beatrice:

> When my town girl came home, she told me a lot of good stories about Lagos, the kinds of food she ate and I could see her new clothes; and I was encouraged to join her since I had dropped out of school and there was no money at home. I joined them in the next trip.
>
> When I asked my housemaid (Adija) how she got to know Mama (middleman), she said that when Mama came to the village and met her selling wares, she called her in order to buy from her and also used the avenue to advise her to come to Lagos where she would have better money. She asked for her parents' home and in the evening, she called at the house and talked to them, and that was how she found herself in Lagos working in her house.

The conditions in the children's home made them succumb to pressure from friends and traffickers. This is to how former victims as friends have become perpetrators, though not for their own economic benefit, but they have increased the traffickers' income as well as help to reduce the poverty levels of a friend's parents/guardians.

Socio-cultural Factors

To some of the families involved in allowing their children to be trafficked to other parts of the country, especially Lagos, to live with unknown families, they see the move as part of the culture of the past, and which is still relevant today. To Adamo from Kwara State, her first time to leave her parents for Lagos was filled with fear of the unknown. She cried because she was going to be leaving the family for the very first time and her mother told her:

> Don't cry, it is part of the culture. I, your mother, also stayed with my father's family in Kaduna when I was younger and that was where I learnt this trade (selling of food items). When you live with people outside your home, it makes you strong, wise and exposed. It is just training you for your future task. Anyway, I have learnt many things, work, work and work and suffering. Though my parents are poor, I never went through this suffering at home.

This shows the persistence of the belief that either through ignorance or the economic situation the current trend of trafficking children by middlemen for profit is taken as part of the socio-cultural norm of olden days. It also brings to the fore parents' consciousness in the enslavement of their children. To this group of parents, education means nothing since they too never accessed it. The impact of this is a whole generation graduating into paupers and slaves.

These 'push' factors have contributed and continue to contribute in no small measure to endangering the lives of many Nigerian children, especially those in rural areas into a life of suffering and slavery.

'Pull' Factors

To 'pull' means to bring something along behind one while moving or to use force on (something), especially with the hands, in order to move it towards oneself or in the direction of the force. Therefore, pull factors simply mean factors necessitating the demand for child domestics. From the interviews, factors responsible for demand in trafficked children for the purpose of domestic service include: the demands of the formal and informal sectors of the economy; the burden of work at home; perceptions about children and cheap labour; and security purposes.

Demands of the Formal and Informal Sectors of the Economy

With the growth in the formal economy in cities, many governmental institutions and parastatals, private companies and corporate organizations were established to meet the needs of the state and cater for the welfare of citizens. These institutions have codes of conduct guiding those employed, and one of these codes of conduct addresses the issue of resumption to work, which is normally before 8 am and closure of work, which is normally 4 or 5 pm everyday. Some workers even work on weekends. To comply with resumption time in the office and also see to the care of the family necessitates extra hands to assist with home duties, which often include taking care of children, cooking and other household chores. Coupled with this challenge are the hitches encountered after closing of work everyday such as traffic jams, car faults and inaccessibility to transportation, so that most women get home in the evening or at night. To many of these women, getting home only to cook and see to the welfare of the home is stressful, hence, the need for a domestic help. To a female banker:

> My sister, it is not easy at all. I leave home before 6 in the morning. I live at Ogba and my office is at Lagos Island, and I have to resume by 7.30 am. With the two small kids and no other assistance, how do I cope? Don't forget that we need the money in this house to feed, clothe and do other basic things. How do I get it if I do not take my job seriously? I don't want any boss to give me query. You know that accumulation of queries is a step to being sacked, and because I don't want it, there should be somebody to assist in the home, especially to take care of the children.

To another:

> I only employ the grown-up ones between 14–20 years because of the nature of my job. I need them to assist me at home and to take care of my little children. The phenomenon cannot be eradicated because of the condition of the country.

In addition, the informal sector is not left out in the demand for child domestics. Most women, in a bid to make ends meet when faced by severe economic conditions, set up shops and other places of work where they also need the assistance of younger ones to make sales. In my interview with a young girl at Idumota, I was made to understand that a lot of girls who stay on the roadsides and call passengers to purchase goods in their shops are employed as domestics. Though some of them are particularly recruited to assist in the sales of goods, and while some of them live within Lagos and move from their own homes every morning and return in the evenings, others stay with the employers. Others are recruited not only as shop vendors at the market but to act also as domestics at employers' homes. This could also apply to other markets in Lagos State, whereby children go through double exploitation and abuse.

The Nature of Work at Home

Related to the above explanation is the nature of work at home. Most women complained about the burden of household chores being responsible for bringing about the employment of child domestics. Unlike in the olden days where siblings of couples could migrate from the village to stay with the latter, and also assist in household chores while the couples took care of their educational or vocational needs, the situation today is different. The problems now include spouse's relations monitoring a wife's activities; refusal to respect or abide by instructions from a wife; a wife's siblings being unable to cope with staying in the home; the difficulty of managing all the needs of such relations, which may include clothing, feeding, education or vocation and other needs; wives or spouses disagreeing with either of the in-laws staying in their homes; and fear by a wife or actual occurrences of spouses having intimate or sexual affairs with a wife's female siblings; all these have constrained couples from bringing relatives into their homes. Since the burden of the household chores continues to be heavy, couples have to seek alternatives, that is, employing a non-relation, most probably a very young child or a teenager, whose labour is cheap (compared to relations or adults), who can be easily abused, will abide by instructions, is less assertive, unable to claim rights, and who is not related in any way to the wives or spouses.

Most employers believe in the malleability of child domestics, even though they may not be very productive in the home. They assert that such children can be trained from tender ages to adhere to their own rules and regulations. This is in comparison to adults who are already mature and do not take to instructions easily because they are used to their old ways of doing things. Moreover, they believe that employing a child saves money. Wages paid to young children in Nigeria are currently between N2,500 and N3,500.

Security Factor

A very interesting finding from employers on why they employ children and not adults as domestics in the home is that employing children will give them a sense of security. In this argument, female adults may end up taking over their homes or snatching husbands (this phenomenon happens in some homes), which a small girl who is just growing into puberty will not be able to do. Therefore, they can go out and come back anytime of the day having the assurance that their homes are secured from '*husband-snatchers*'. To a businesswoman:

> Having a housemaid is a necessity these days, especially considering the nature of job to be done in the office and at home, but the age of the person also matters. These days, most grown-up girls are threats in our homes. They are easily lured by men with some fears instilled in them and some money. Therefore, to avoid such dangers, it is better to go for teenage children who can be overlooked by men.

Leaving homes early and returning late at night means that the bulk of the work at home is done by employed domestic servants. Such work includes taking care of the children, going to market, cooking for the whole family, general cleaning of the home and running errands, thereby usurping the roles of the wives. These blurred distinctions about the role of wives and domestic servants have sometimes included taking over of the former's sexual role in the home. This problem has not only led to insecurity in most homes, it has also brought about cases of separation and divorce among couples.

Complementary Needs

From the above, trafficking of children for domestic work is a complementary phenomenon. While the children or parents of trafficked children and traffickers need the employers of these trafficked children for economic benefits and as part of survival strategies, the employers need the children for labour benefits. It becomes a symbiotic relationship. Can we then begin to see this phenomenon simply as a form of child abuse or as a trend that might continue as long as there is monetary exchange, especially so in the face of lingering increase in economic hardship in Nigeria with consequences for the already rural poor? No less than 92.6 per cent of the employees believed that domestics are a necessity and cannot be eradicated because the household chores must be done and the economic situation in the country has not improved. In addition, it is a way of supplementing family incomes for traffickers and parents of trafficked children. Though all the child domestics interviewed agreed that they are paid, the money is paid to the 'Mama' who brought them, and the exact amount paid by their employers is hidden from them. However, of all the child domestics interviewed, only two of them were being sponsored by their employers to access education, both at the secondary level. To those employers, they believe that since the children refused to leave like others, and have shown their intention to stay, they decided to assist their parents by sponsoring their education.

When the child domestics were asked whether they would prefer to leave domestic service work and live with their parents, most of their responses were negative. Here are some of their answers:

- I want to learn fashion designing as my senior sister who just got married. If I stop this job, I will not have money to learn fashion designing (Basirat, 10 years old).

- I agreed to do this job because of the situation on the ground. If I stop this job, it will affect my family but my God is a miraculous God, He will surely assist us (Dorcas F., 16 years old)
- My madam is very wicked but if I leave this job, what will happen to my parents? It is because they are very poor that they told me to come to Lagos (Beatrice, 12 years old).
- If I go home now, it is to go and suffer because the money from farm proceeds is not always enough to take care of all of us (Charles, 13 years old).
- I will like to stay in Lagos, work for some time and open my own supermarket like my boss (Aminat, 12 years old).
- I enjoy my stay with Mummy Seun because if I go back to my parents' place, I will not see this kind of enjoyment like the food, television, the house is very beautiful and the clothes too (Fausat, 10 years old).
- If I had not stayed with Mummy Ola, I wouldn't have had the opportunity to go to secondary school (Shade, 17 years, staying with her employee for four years now).

These responses do not show that they all enjoy the kinds of services they render. Some of the the children said, 'I do all the cleaning in the home'; 'I sell kerosene, wash plates and do general cleaning'; 'I do normal job generally and then we go to the market where she is selling'; 'though you will eat, she will curse you and send the remaining of the curses to your parents'; 'I do all the household chores including backing and feeding the baby and also being sent on errands'; 'I don't sleep until late in the night and have to wake up early the next day'. Apart from all these comments, they also suffer other effects to the extent that when a girl was asked about her experiences, she kept quiet for some time and just burst into tears. Some could not say anything because of the presence of the inhabitants. These assertions reflect that the symbiotic relationship is more beneficial to one party (employers) than the other, especially considering the meagre amounts the children were paid monthly, which have to be shared between the traffickers and parents of trafficked children.

Placement or fostering of children in the traditional set-up resulted in the exploitation of most of the children who were turned into slaves in the homes of and for foster parents and their children either from the start or over time. Therefore, it could only be imagined the extent of exploitation of children who are formally trafficked for labour services. Some of the children trafficked for domestic purposes end up being sexually abused, among other forms of exploitation they pass through. They suffer physical injuries resulting from beating; work for long hours; suffer social trauma resulting from exclusion, starvation, lack of access to education and vocational training, and unequal treatment; and suffer psychological trauma resulting from not being a family member. There has been the wide-held notion that trafficking has thrived so far because it is less risky. But this is a wrong perception given the dangers children face. Apart from road mishaps that could occur, the way children are packed in the buses or trucks impacts negatively on their health, and the way and rate they are moved around different households can only create mental instability.

State Interventions and Policy Implications

Child trafficking for any purpose is defined and condemned in the United Nations Children's Rights Convention and other documents relating to the protection of the child from trafficking, hazardous and exploitative labour. As at today, Nigeria is a signatory to the 1989 United Nations Convention on the Rights of the Child, 1999 (No. 182) ILO Convention, and 2000 Optional Protocol to the United Nations Convention on the Rights of the Child respectively. Articles 11, 12, 32, 34 and 35 of the UN CRC, among others, state clearly the right to protection of the child from exploitation, abuse and trafficking. The Child Labour Convention (No. 182) regards selling and trafficking of children as 'the worst forms of child labour', and its accompanying Recommendation (No. 190) provides additional and powerful weapons for the elimination of all forms of child slavery (Haspel and Jankanis, 2000:3–7). Moreover, the Optional Protocol regards trafficking of children for whatever purpose as being one of the worst forms of child exploitation. ILO recommendations constitute hazardous labour under the Worst Forms of Child Labour Convention includes work that 'exposes children to physical, psychological or sexual abuse' or involves 'particularly difficult conditions such as work for long hours or during the night or work where the child is unreasonably confined to the premises of the employer'. Under these criteria, most child domestic work would constitute hazardous labour.

In a bid to incorporate the international legislations into the national law, the federal government under President Olusegun Obasanjo established the Office of the Special Assistant to the President on Human Trafficking and Child Labour in 2001. The Office was charged with:

- co-ordinating all the activities of Human Trafficking and Child Labour in the country and making direct input to government in form of policy formulation;
- advising the President on issues relating to human trafficking and child labour;
- initiating and developing programmes of action, which could help alleviate the problem;
- co-ordinating and collaborating with all governmental and non-governmental organizations involved directly or indirectly with human trafficking and child labour;
- gathering relevant data and information on issues relating to human trafficking and child labour;
- influencing governmental policies, which could serve as a means of eliminating and reducing the scourge of human trafficking and child labour;
- working with international organizations with specific interests in the subject area (Akinmoyo 2004).

In order to make these responsibilities more effective, the law created the National Agency for the Prohibition of Traffic in Persons (NAPTIP). This was established as a means of enforcing the Trafficking in Persons (Prohibition) Law Enforcement and Administrative Act 2003. The agency has responsibility for investigating and prosecuting offenders, counseling and rehabilitating trafficked children and public sensitization.1 The responsibility of NAPTIP is to arrest, prosecute and sentence to '*life imprisonment*' anybody caught trafficking children and women. NAPTIP gives Nigeria leverage over other West African neighbours as being the first country in the region to establish an anti-trafficking agency and enact anti-trafficking laws. To further entrench the United Nation's CRC in national legislation, the Child Rights Act was instituted in 2003, made possible by the efforts of various NGOs, prominent among them being the Women Trafficking and Child Labour Eradication Foundation (WOTCLEF), founded by Titi Abubakar, wife of the current Vice-President of Nigeria, as well as international organizations such as UNICEF.

Evidence has shown that enforcement agencies have been effective in arresting some of the culprits. Apart from daily reports in the newspapers, television and radio, my observation of the traffickers during the interviews revealed that either most of them were aware of these laws or some of them had been caught, therefore putting others on the defensive. This was noticed in the first interview with the first set of traffickers, where they gathered as foodsellers who were not willing to reveal their identity as traffickers of children for domestic service. Though they are known for bringing children from the villages, especially from Oyo and Kwara States, they all denied ever knowing anything about domestics and were directed to see somebody else, who happened to be their chairperson or head of the network. Immediately when some questions were put to her, she reacted by saying:

> I don't understand what you are saying. I don't know anything about child domestic business. I have never been involved in bringing any child. It is only when they bring them from the villages that we dispatch them to those who need them… what is the big deal about child domestics? I was also a child domestic when I was young. It does not kill but makes somebody wise. But as I said, I don't know anything about how they get to Lagos. You can only ask me questions about what I sell….

However, despite the legal guarantees as provided for by the national and international communities, and the punitive measures laid down by national legislation, the traffic is still going on as the demand for domestics intensifies and as economic conditions worsen in the country. This is a serious violation of the basic rights of children such as the right to freedom of opinion, the right of not being forced to do any work likely to harm one's physical and mental health, the right to keep contact with one's parents, the right of not being separated from one's parents unwillingly, the right to education, the right to freedom and safety and the right to free movement.

Challenges to Policy Implementation

Effective implementation of this legislation has been hindered by certain factors, among them the increasing numbers of arrests of culprits forcing traffickers to design new ways of transportation to avoid the attention of law enforcement agencies. For the groups of traffickers, including the woman from the East, they confirmed that owing to the pressures from law enforcement agents, they have created new ways of operation or trafficking. Some of the new trends include: conveying children in goods-carrying trucks and buses, therefore giving the impression that they are travelling to sell goods; not conveying them in full view as before; as the woman from the East said, she travels to bring children in accordance with an order (either boy or girl or one or two children) made by customers (the employer of the children), and she does not take more than three at a time, in order to convince enforcement agents that they are her own children. Two conclusions can be made from these new trends of transporting trafficked children since the inception of the anti-trafficking laws. First, traffickers make considerable profits from this transaction; hence it becomes difficult for them to stop it. Second, the number of children trafficked every day shows that there is a high level of demand for domestics in the cities, especially Lagos, therefore creating a boom business for traffickers or middlemen.

In addition, it is a known fact that most of the decision-makers and enforcers of the law have child domestics in their own homes. For these groups of people, it will be rather difficult to prosecute traffickers because the law can be bent to suit their own intent and purpose. In research study carried out by one NGO, it was gathered that most of the law-makers and enforcers in Nigeria were not aware of any law known as the Child Rights Act.

Systemic corruption is also on the increase at the level of trafficking. Instead of criminalizing traffickers and prosecuting them, law enforcement agencies release them on bail and they continue to perpetuate the crime. Since the coming into force of the Child Rights Act, which makes the sentence for those involved in the selling or abduction of children 25 years and the Trafficking Act, which puts the sentence as life imprisonment, at the time of writing, of the number of people that have been arrested, none has been prosecuted or found guilty in a court of law.

A major obstacle to the success of policies is the lack of public awareness, especially of trafficked children and the parents of the dangers of trafficking, and the inability to report traffickers and abuse in the hands of employers to the law enforcement agencies. This has made it possible for this type of child abuse to continue.

Another obstacle to policy implementation is that much of the emphasis by the state and NGOs has been on issues of external trafficking or trafficking across Nigerian borders. Even when there are reports on internal trafficking, attention is removed from child domestics because of their invisibility. In other words, in spite of the laws and documents on anti-trafficking and forms of child labour, there are no specific laws protecting child domestics in Nigeria.

All these factors have undermined the efforts of the government and the international, national and local NGOs.

Conclusion

From the foregoing, it will be realized that internal trafficking has many faces, one of which is the issue of child domestics. This dimension is important because internal trafficking of children for domestic service appears benign when compared to other cases such as trafficking for the purpose of prostitution, street trading, labouring on farms, rituals and trade in human parts; yet it is the most exploitative and harmful form of child trafficking. The traffickers or intermediaries who indulge in moving children are not the only culprits here, for parents of trafficked children and the people who employ them, including the lawmakers and law enforcement officials in Nigeria, are also guilty. While the needs of the cities are high, including economic needs, therefore necessitating the high demand for child domestics, the current and lingering economic crisis in the country, which feeds into inacessibity to education, poor infrastructure, impoverished subsistence living, the high incidence of illiteracy and recrudescence of bad old practices such as placing children into unknown families has increased the rate of the phenomenon. This shows that tackling the problem is not a one-way process but entails concerted efforts by the state and non-state actors at intervention on both demand and supply sides.

In terms of suggestions, efforts that should be made by the state, and non-state actors include:

- First and foremost, the most crucial effort, which will also aim at the root cause of the phenomenon, is alleviating or in the long run removing poverty mostly at the rural level. Nigeria is not devoid of poverty-alleviation programmes. The earliest poverty alleviation programmes started 1972 withYakubu Gowon's National Accelerated Food Production Programme and the Nigerian Agricultural and Cooperative Bank, entirely devoted to funding agriculture, especially in the rural areas. This was followed in 1976 with Gen. Olusegun Obasanjo's 'Operation Feed The Nation'; in 1979, by Shehu Shagari's Green Revolution; in 1983, by Gen. Muhammadu Buhari's 'Go Back to Land Programme'. Ibrahim Babangida's era saw the establishment of the Directorate of Food, Roads and Rural Infrastructure (DFRRI), establishment of the Peoples Bank of Nigeria, community banks, National Directorate of Employment (NDE), Better Life for Rural Women Programme; then in 1983, it was the turn of the Maryam Abacha's 'Family Support Programme' and 'Family Economic and Advancement Programme' among others. In recent times, under the Peoples Democratic Party-led government, it is now the Poverty Alleviation Programme (PAP) encapsulated under the National Economic and Empowerment Strategy (NEEDS) of 2004 and the State Economic and Empowerment Strategy (SEEDS). Suffice it to say that though all these interventions were well -ntentioned, their execution left much to be desired. The increasing poverty rate in the country is evidence of the failure of most of these programmes.

  Therefore, any programme aimed at alleviating and eradicating poverty must not only target the basic needs of the rural areas, because poverty in Nigeria is largely a rural phenomenon, but there should be total commitment from every actor to ensure that it is successful. This holistic approach should include creating employment for all unemployed graduates or school leavers; providing a welfare package for the old and vulnerable, including children and women; diverting much of the emphasis of national budgets from defence to other forms of human security; and provision of basic social amenities such as water, health facilities, shelter and electricity supply to reduce rural–urban drift. Moreover, since the poverty ratio in the urban areas is competing with that in the rural areas as seen from the discussions and the placing of children from the urban centres into other households owing to poverty and also encouraging traffickers from thriving by trafficking children, efforts should be directed at embarking on similar projects for urban dwellers.

- Second, the government should resuscitate programmes such as the Better Life for Rural People and the establishment of community banks. The Better Life for Rural People should actually target the rural poor and involve introduction to and training on best practices such as the use of modern agricultural techniques, and modern resources to enhance productive capacity. The community banks should also be established to give out soft loans to rural people to embark on projects on their professions. This project should have a human face, and there should be total political will on the part of succeessive governments to make it work. There should be a monitoring agency to oversee the kinds of projects the loans are used for and to administer the progress of such projects to deter people from using the loans for wrong reasons such as marrying more wives or organizing parties. The end result will be increase of rural incomes.
- Third, education should be made compulsory and free from primary to secondary levels. This will avert the claim by parents that poverty hinders children from attending school. The 'free' part of the package includes non-payment of school fees till the end of secondary education and provision of materials such as books and desks at little or no cost at all. At this point, it will also be important to say that employment opportunities should be provided for secondary school leavers and university graduates, thereby creating alternatives to child domestic labour.
- Fourth, there should be concrete sensitization of rural dwellers and advocacy at the community level to show the dangers inherent in the cultural practice of placing children with wealthier families for the purpose of fostering and their rights in case of malpractice. This is because access to the law by rural dwellers is problematic. This programme should transcend broadcasts on the television and radio but should include house-to-house education and dramas at the community levels on the dangers associated with child trafficking and domestic service, and other purposes of child trafficking such as ritual purposes. The sensitization programme should be done in villagers' languages in order to put across the message and the themes should totally capture the essence of the programme. In addition, the programme should also educate on the need to embark on family planning, that is, the need to have children that can be adequately taken care of by rural families.
- Fifth, it was realized from the interviews with employers that it will rather be a difficult task eradicating child domestics because of the demands of urban living. The government should provide codes of conduct that will guide and protect children with monitoring welfare agencies. The codes of conduct

should emphasize the age at which a child can be employed for domestic purposes, the conditions under which the child should work, including the compulsory education, health and social needs of the child, payment of parents directly rather than via intermediaries, and constant checking by welfare officers on the well-being of such domestics. Every domestic employed should be registered with the proper state agency. It will be important to say here that corruption at the level of welfare officers makes it necessary to put in place legal sanctions against malfeasance on their part.

- Sixth, welfare packages should be given in all organizations to women, especially, mothers, to create opportunities for them to have enough time to take care of the home front and especially their children. Without this measure, trafficking of children for the purpose of domestic work will increase at a more unacceptable rate, and the efforts of the government and non-governmental organizations will be futile.

The study shows that the legal framework has not been effective in stemming the nature and rate of trafficking in Nigeria. This, however, does not mean that it should be thrown out, for the fact remains that it forms the first step in protecting victims as well as prosecuting culprits. Therefore, efforts should be focused on ensuring strict adherence to these laws and regulations. To make the legal framework a success, corruption, which has eaten deep into the fabric of the Nigerian system and has become an institution on its own, should be strongly tackled.

Legally, there is confusion in the legal framework on internal and external trafficking as much of the concentration is on external trafficking. Therefore, internal trafficking should be given special focus and attention should be paid to trafficking for the purpose of domestic service with the aim to punishing traffickers and employees for the exploitation and abuse of these children. Moreover, trials of culprits should be expedited and culprits should be punished accordingly.

The basis for the combating of internal child trafficking lies within the structural and precipating factors that bring about trafficking for domestic purposes. The fact that children pass through danger right from their states of origin to the destination sites should spur state and non-state actors to ensuring that all the processes of trafficking are checked before Nigeria becomes a '*slave trade*' country.

References

Agbu, O., 2003, '*Corruption and Human Trafficking: The Nigerian Case*', *West Africa Review*, Vol. 4, No.1.

Akinmoyo, D. E., 2004, *Keynote Speech*, 3rd Annual AFRUCA Conference in London, UK.

Albert, I. O., 1997, 'Youth, Street Culture and Violence in Kano', *Nigeria, Proceedings, Youth, Street Cultures and Urban Violence in Africa*, Ibadan: IFRA/African Book Builders, 1997.

Apfel, R. J. and Simon, B., 1995, 'On Psychosocial Interventions for Children: Some Minders and Reminders', *UNICEF Review*.

Aries, P., 1965, *Centuries of Childhood: A Social History of Family Life*, New York: Vintage Books.

Bass, L. E., 2004, *Child Labour in Sub-Saharan Africa*, Boulder: Lynne Reinner.

Black, M. and Ennew. J., eds., 1993, *Street and Working Children*, Summary Report of Innocenti Global Seminar, 15-25 February, Florence: UNICEF International Child Development Centre.

Boyden, J., 1996, '*Social and Cultural Meanings of Childhood*', *Development*, No. 1.

CROP Newsletter, 2004, Vol.11, No. 3, September.

Cunningham, H., 1991, *The Children of the Poor*, Oxford: Blackwell.

Dottridge, M., 2002, 'Trafficking in Children in West and Central Africa', *Gender and Development*, Vol. 10, No. 1.

Ebigbo, P. O., 2000, *Child Trafficking in Nigeria: The State of the Art*, Abidjan: Study for IPEC/ILO.

Effah, J., 1996, *Modernized Slavery: Child Trade in Nigeria*, Lagos: Constitutional Rights Project.

Federal Office of Statistics, 1999, *Poverty Profile for Nigeria*, 1980-1996, Lagos: Federal Office of Statistics.

Haspel, N. and Jankanis, M., eds., 2000, *Action Against Child Labour*, Geneva: ILO.

Human Rights Watch, 2004, 'Child Domestics: The Most Invisible Workers', June 10.

ILO, 2002, *ILO Convention 182 Concerning the Prohibition and Immediate Action for the Elimination of the Worst Forms of labour*, ILO Eighty-Seventh Session, Geneva: International, Labour Office, 17 June, 1999.

ILO, 2002, *Unbearable to Human Heart: Child Trafficking and Action to Eliminate it*, Geneva: ILO.

ILO-IPU, 2002, *Eliminating The Worst Forms of Child Labour: A Practical Guide to ILO Convention No. 182*, Geneva: ILO.

International Labour Organisation, 2002, *Every Child Counts: New Global Estimates on Child Labour*, Geneva: IPEC, April.

IOM, 2002, 'New Global Figures on the Global Scale of Trafficking', *Trafficking in Migrants Quarterly Bulletin*, No. 23, April.

ITCPR, 2000, *Nigeria: Poverty Reduction Plan*, Background Paper for the Consultative Group on Nigeria, Prepared for the Consultative Group on Nigeria, Prepared by the Inter-Ministerial Technical Committee on Poverty Reduction for the Federal Ministry of Finance, Abuja, October.

Jenks, C., 1996, *Childhood*, London: Routledge.

Komolafe, F., 2001, 'Child Labour Loses Over 4,000 Kids in One Year', *Sunday Magazine*, 15 July.

Laetita, B-V., 2000, *Sub-regional Study on Child Trafficking for Economic Exploitation in West and Central Africa*, Executive Summary.

Langley, P., 1994, *Indicators of the Role and Conditions of Children in the Development Processes in Africa: A Critical Comment*, Paris: UNESCO.

Muntarbhorn, V., 1998, *Trafficking in Children for Labour Exploitation in Mekong Sub-region*, Geneva: ILO.

Ogefere, S., 2004, « Police Rescue 64 Children from Suspected Traffickers », *The Guardian*, 6 August.

Ogwumike, F., 2001, 'An Appraisal of Poverty Reduction Strategies in Nigeria', *CBN Economic and Financial Review*, Vol. 39, No. 4.

Okechukwu, I., 1993, 'Deteriorating Conditions of Nigerian Peasantry', Okwudiba Nnoli, ed., *Dead-End to Nigerian Development. An Investigation on the Social, Economics and Political Crisis in Nigeria*, Dakar: CODESRIA.

Oloko, S. B. A., 1992, *Situational Analysis of Children in Difficult Circumstances (CEDC* Report for UNICEF in collaboration with J. Shindi, A. Olowu, R. A. Mohammed, B. Arikpo and O. Shoyombo.

Olukoshi, A., ed., 1991, *Crisis and Adjustment in the Nigerian Economy*, Lagos: JAD Publishers.

Olukoshi, A., 1995, 'The Politics of Structural Adjustment in Nigeria', Thandika Mkandawire and Adebayo Olukoshi, eds., *Between Liberalisation and Oppression: The Politics of Structural Adjustment in Africa*, Dakar: CODESRIA.

Olukoshi, A., 2004, 'Globalisation, Equity and Development: Some Reflections on the African Experience', *Ibadan Journal of the Social Sciences*, Vol 2, No 1 September.

Sall, E., 2004, 'Childhood Paradigms Against the Backdrop of Poverty Situations in Developing Countries (Africa)', Paper Presented at the *Workshop on Children and Youth in the Labour Process,* held at CODESRIA, Senegal from October 3-29.

Social Alert, 1998, 'SOS Trafficking on the Tracks of Stolen Childhood: A Comparative Analysis of Child Trafficking in the World', *Research on Economic, Social, and Cultural Rights*, No. 2, December.

Tzannatos, Z. and Fallon, P., 1998, *Child Labour: Issues and Directions for the World Bank*, Washington DC: Social Protection, Human Development Network.

UNICEF/NCRIC, 1986, *Child Protection in Nigeria: Summary of Research Findings on Protection and Violation of Children's Rights*, Lagos: UNICEF.

UNICEF, 1989, *United Nations Convention on the Rights of the Child*, New York: UNICEF.

UNICEF, 1998, *The State of the World's Children 1997: Focus on Child Labour*, New York: Oxford University Press.

UNICEF, 1999, *Child Domestic Work*, New York: UNICEF Child Development Centre.

UNICEF, 2001, *Children's and Women's Rights in Nigeria: A Wake-Up Call*, Abuja: UNICEF.

UNICEF, 2002, *A World Fit for Children*, New York: UNICEF.

UNICEF, 2002, *Child Trafficking in West Africa: Policy Responses*, Florence: UNICEF Innocenti Research Centre.

UNICEF, 2003, *End Child Exploitation: Stop the Traffic*, London: UNICEF.

U. S. Department of State, 2000, *Victims of Trafficking and Violence Protection Act 2000.*

United Nations, 1989, *United Nations Conventions on the Rights of the Child*, New York UNICEF.

Veerman, P. E., 1992, *The Rights of the Child and the Changing Image of Childhood*, Dodrecht: Martnus Nijhoff.

Wennerholm, J. C., 2003, 'Crossing Borders and Building Bridges: The Baltic Region Networking Project', *Gender and Development*, Vol. 10, No. 1.

7

Le phénomène *Vidomègon* : une autre forme de trafic d'enfants dans les villes de Cotonou

A. Ludovic Couao-Zotti

Résumé

La question du trafic et de l'asservissement des enfants n'est pas nouvelle dans le contexte socioéconomique béninois. Mais elle est devenue préoccupante au cours de ces deux dernières décennies, parce que les enfants sont utilisés à des fins lucratives. L'étude, au-delà de la simple description du phénomène, vise à en approfondir la compréhension et élargir le champ d'investigation. Elle est également la contribution à une meilleure connaissance de la pratique du *Vidomègon* (Enfant placé chez quelqu'un) dans ses pires formes. C'est pourquoi l'analyse et l'interprétation des informations recueillies ont pris en compte les enfants victimes et les personnes qui sont identifiées comme les exploiteuses. Dans une telle logique, il a été remarqué que le phénomène apparaît aujourd'hui comme une réponse des familles aux situations de précarité fluctuante. Par ailleurs, le phénomène revêt plusieurs formes au regard de la situation de précarité des familles où les enfants sont potentiellement des enfants à risque destinés à l'exploitation. Leur jeune âge attire, à cause de la main-d'œuvre bon marché qu'ils représentent et de leur extrême malléabilité.

La Convention des Droits de l'enfant, pourtant ratifiée par le Bénin, ne semble pas être appliquée dans toute son ampleur. La non-application correcte, ajoutée au déchirement de la famille et la pauvreté grandissante constituent des facteurs de mise en esclavage des enfants.

En tenant compte des résultats auxquels est parvenue la présente étude, on s'interroge de plus en plus sur les possibilités des pouvoirs au niveau central et local à faire face, de manière efficace à la lutte contre toutes les formes de violences et d'abus faits à l'encontre de l'enfant. Il est vrai qu'en prenant à cœur la problématique du phénomène *Vidomègon,* le Gouvernement de la République du Bénin a mis en place des programmes et structures de lutte contre le trafic des enfants, dans le cadre de la coopération bilatérale et multilatérale. Dans le domaine de la prévention, des programmes d'IEC sont initiés. Le côté répressif de l'action des pouvoirs publiques a permis, avec les campagnes de sensibilisation, à faire reculer le phénomène, dans sa dimension transfrontalière, mais sur le plan interne, le fait de s'être un peu trop focalisé sur l'extérieur, n'a pas permis de mesurer à sa juste valeur, le malheureux sort que vivent des milliers d'enfants à l'intérieur des quatre murs des maisons : « *Silence, ici on exploite et on maltraite* ».

Introduction : la problématique du *Vidomègon*

La problématique du *Vidomègon* ou « placement » des enfants, est un phénomène séculaire et est donc une tradition dans la culture africaine et plus précisément au Bénin. Le terme de placement, dans son acceptation commune, constitue un acte autorisant le déplacement d'un enfant dans une famille autre que celle de nature biologique.

En effet, confier son enfant ou le placer dans une famille d'accueil revêtait, il y a encore quelques décennies, un sens et une marque de confiance réciproque entre deux familles et communautés. L'enfant y était accueilli comme faisant partie intégrante de sa nouvelle « famille » De ce point de vue, il bénéficiait de tous les soins, participait pleinement à la vie familiale comme tous les autres enfants, sans distinction, et s'y intégrait aux plans sociocuturel et économique.

Mais à partir des années 80, l'actualité nationale a été, de plus en plus marquée par plusieurs cas de maltraitance, de meurtre, d'abus sexuel d'enfants, en somme, de violences de tout genre envers les enfants. Il s'est révélé, selon les données empiriques et les observations, que la plupart de ces enfants violentés, sont ceux placés auprès de personnes autres que leurs parents biologiques. Ce sont des enfants qui présentent toutes les caractéristiques de personnes marginalisées, dont les conditions d'existence sont des plus précaires.

Au cours de ces quinze dernières années, la question est devenue si préoccupante que les pouvoirs publics et les organisations de la société civile (Organisations non gouvernementales, Associations, Clubs de réflexion…) ont décrit la situation comme un phénomène, d'où le vocable phénomène *Vidomègon* (dans une langue locale du sud du Bénin « Enfant placé chez quelqu'un ». Plusieurs ONG s'investissent dans la prise en charge des enfants en situation difficile, et il est apparu que celles-ci récupèrent de plus en plus d'enfants victimes de maltraitance et mauvais traitements. De plus, on remarque un accroissement du nombre d'enfants de la rue dans les grandes agglomérations des villes comme Cotonou, Porto-Novo et Parakou et leurs arrière-pays.

Malgré les mesures de sensibilisation et de répression prises et les moyens matériels et humains mis en œuvre pour éradiquer le mal, il existe encore des poches de résistance aussi bien en zones urbaines que rurales. Il a même été constaté que le phénomène est alimenté et entretenu par un véritable réseau national et international de trafiquants et de placement d'enfants, qui tirent des profits financiers de cette activité.

Au regard de ce qui précède, s'est posée la question ci-après : En quoi le phénomène *Vidomègon* constitue une autre forme de trafic d'enfants dans la ville de Cotonou ?

La réponse à cette question a permis de mieux cerner le phénomène du trafic des enfants et du *Vidomègon*, dans toutes ses dimensions et, partant, d'en dresser le profil caractéristique, ce qui a conduit à élaborer des approches de solutions en vue d'atténuer à défaut de l'éradiquer, cette nouvelle forme d'esclavagisme des temps modernes.

Le cadre de l'étude

Le thème relatif à l'étude sur le phénomène *Vidomègon* : une autre forme de trafic d'enfants dans la ville de Cotonou a suscité un intérêt particulier, du fait du débat qu'il suscite actuellement, de l'ampleur qu'il a pris depuis environ deux décennies et de ce qu'il est beaucoup plus perceptible dans le Département du Littoral, à Cotonou, Commune et ville du Bénin où les activités économiques sont les plus intenses. Dans cette logique, il est plus facile de récolter suffisamment des données susceptibles de répondre adéquatement à la question de l'étude.

La population de la présente étude a été constituée sur la base d'un échantillon de 250 sujets, âgés de 7 à 16 ans, rencontrés à leurs lieux de travail, dans les marchés et dans la rue. Quelques-uns ont été interrogés près de leurs domiciles. Ils sont au total 200 filles et 50 garçons. Leur répartition s'est établie, selon les catégories d'âges ci-après :

- 7 à 9 ans : 103 dont 78 filles et 25 garçons ;
- 10 à 13 ans : 130 dont 110 et 20 garçons ;
- 14 à 16 ans : 17 dont 12 filles et 05 garçons.

Le choix porté sur ces différentes tranches d'âge est parti du constat général que la plupart des enfants n'ont pas de précision exacte sur leur âge. Pour être plus proche de la détermination des âges, il a fallu opérer des catégorisations en fonction de la taille, des traits du visage, de la logique et de la maturation du raisonnement.

Par ailleurs, on s'est intéressé à certains adultes (50), parmi lesquels sont représentés des tuteurs et tutrices des enfants interrogés, parce que ceux-ci ont indiqué leurs domiciles. Cet intérêt s'est manifesté afin d'avoir l'avis de ces personnages plus ou moins acteurs du phénomène. Ceci devrait aider à l'analyse et l'interprétation des informations recueillies auprès d'eux. On a également cherché à savoir s'il existe un lien de cause à effet entre le statut économique des parents et la situation de placement de leurs enfants. L'entretien a été consacré à des enfants qui présentent des indices de pauvreté, à partir de l'habillement et du faciès.

Au cours de l'étude, il a été expliqué aux enfants qu'ils devront répondre le plus sincèrement possible aux questions portant, entre autres, sur la façon dont ils se sont retrouvés à Cotonou et pour quels motifs, sur les types de relations et les liens de parenté ou entre eux et leurs tuteurs/tutrices d'une part, et la nature des activités menées, d'autre part. Les enfants ont été également priés de donner leurs impressions et perceptions sur la situation qu'ils vivent en ce moment-ci. Les déclarations et les témoignages des uns et des autres ont permis de collecter des données nécessaires à une analyse approfondie du phénomène.

Les difficultés rencontrées

Certains tuteurs et tutrices d'enfants (45) ont été questionnés sur la perception qu'ils ont du *Vidomègon.* Ils devront également se prononcer par rapport aux relations interpersonnelles et au traitement qui est fait à ces enfants. La collecte des informations qualitatives a été particulièrement difficile à cause de la réticence des adultes à répondre aux questions. Il fallait souvent changer d'interlocuteurs, par souci d'avoir des informations exhaustives. Pour celles qui ont répondu avec plus ou moins d'enthousiasme, le développement de leurs arguments a mis en évidence un malaise sur la problématique du *Vidomègon.*

Par ailleurs, tous les enfants rencontrés n'ont pas voulu se prêter aux questions des enquêteurs. Plusieurs parmi ceux âgés de 8 à 10 ans se sont sentis mal à l'aise au cours de la conversation et au bout de trois minutes, ils se sont enfermés dans un mutisme injustifié, répondant simplement par « oui » ou « non », puis l'instant d'après, s'en sont allés sans se signaler. Ceci n'a pas permis d'obtenir la totalité des informations désirées. Même certains parmi les plus âgés sont demeurés craintifs et anxieux au cours de l'entretien. Ainsi, 2/5 des entretiens se sont révélés incomplets et il a fallu, à chaque fois, pour maintenir l'échantillon de base, rechercher et observer d'autres enfants.

Pour les enfants qui ont été repérés dans des ateliers de coiffure, de mécanique et de vulcanisation, il fallait être extrêmement prudent, pour ne pas attirer l'attention de leurs patrons ou traiter de voleur, car le risque était grand d'être brûlé vif, sans pouvoir se défendre, si quelqu'un criait « au voleur ». Le pied de grue au coin des ruelles a été parfois long (en moyenne 2 heures pour rencontrer un enfant).

Les résultats de l'étude

Le milieu de provenance des enfants

Au Bénin, le trafic des enfants est un phénomène relativement nouveau et est surtout né du développement du secteur tertiaire. Force est de constater que ce trafic se fait à partir de trois critères principaux : l'âge, la situation familiale et le sexe de l'enfant. L'étude a fait ressortir que, généralement, les enfants dont l'âge varie de 7 à 9 ans et de 10 à 13 ans sont les plus nombreux à subir le sort de *Vidomègon*, parce qu'ils représentent, pour l'ensemble de la population enquêtée, plus de 93 pour cent. De manière plus spécifique, les enfants de 9, 10 et 11 ans sont au total 130, soit 52 pour cent de l'effectif.

Une étude de l'ONG Anti-slavery, en collaboration avec Solidarité d'Afrique et du Monde (ESAM), réalisée en 1998, a conclu et mis en exergue, à partir des différentes arrestations opérées, que les intermédiaires ou les trafiquants recruteurs des enfants constituent de faux dossiers de voyage, pour les enfants, avec des fausses pièces d'état civil. Il s'agit là du trafic pour l'extérieur.

Mais sur le plan intérieur, la situation est plus dramatique car, le phénomène est beaucoup plus caché et moins visible. En focalisant l'attention sur l'extérieur, on a tendance à oublier que le destin de milliers d'enfants se joue, pourtant, dans les contrées et surtout dans les villes, où les enfants constituent une main d'œuvre docile, moins exigeante que l'adulte, en matière de rémunération, mais surtout manipulables à volonté. Ils sont recherchés parce qu'ils sont économiquement et financièrement rentables pour ceux qui les emploient. C'est ce que la présente étude a fait ressortir en déterminant la proportion des enfants entre 9 et 11 ans, qui représente un peu plus de la moitié de ceux qui sont pris en compte dans le travail.

En tenant compte des conclusions de la Conférence nationale organisée au Bénin en 1997 sur le trafic des enfants, deux réunions sous-régionales ont eu lieu à Cotonou (1998) et Libreville (2000) à l'instigation du Bénin. On a estimé que près de 250 000 enfants (dont 72 pour cent de filles) ne vivent pas avec leurs parents biologiques et n'étaient pas scolarisées.

La présente étude a confirmé ce constat datant de près d'une dizaine d'années. Sur les 250 sujets interrogés, 23 filles contre 14 garçons vivent avec un membre de la famille élargie (tante, oncle, grand'mère). En fait, 213 enfants vivent au domicile des personnes qui n'ont aucun lien de parenté avec la famille des enfants, ce qui signifie qu'ils ont été simplement placés à des fins économiques. Dans ces conditions, ils sont susceptibles d'être exploités dans diverses activités, soit comme apprentis, soit comme employés de maison, revendeurs, etc. et c'est d'ailleurs le cas chez ces enfants.

Il convient de faire remarquer que l'étude a révélé que 82 pour cent de ces enfants, sont issus de familles paysannes et ouvrières vivant des situations de précarité. Plus de 11 pour cent des sujets ont des parents qui sont sans profession actuellement, bien que ces derniers aient, auparavant, exercé des métiers comme la vannerie, la soudure artisanale et la blanchisserie, pour ne citer que les plus importants. Le développement de nouveaux types d'activités a rendu certains métiers moins rentables du point de vue financier, ce qui a conduit à leur abandon pur et simple. Par ailleurs, 7 pour cent de ces enfants ont déclaré que leurs parents, le père en particulier, a un emploi saisonnier mais instable : démarcheur en immobilier, garde-vélo, conducteur de taxi-moto...Quant aux informations relatives à leurs mères, les enfants, dans la plupart des cas, ont souligné que celles-ci sont des femmes au foyer, avec généralement pour activité, le petit commerce. Ce type d'activité, comme on peut le constater, n'assure que très partiellement la subsistance familiale. Pour celles qui ont une qualification, ce sont des puéricultrices, couturières, tresseuses de cheveux sans outils de travail et sans occupation réelle et qui se convertissent de temps en temps à des travaux aussi variés que diversifiés (balayeuses de rue, domestiques, lessiveuses, etc.).

Dans cette logique, il est utile de rappeler ici, la perception des travaux du Sommet mondial sur le développement social tenu en mars 1995 à Copenhague, qui ont établi les diverses formes de la pauvreté. Le caractère multidimensionnel de la pauvreté s'appuie sur deux types d'études ayant permis d'établir le profil de la pauvreté au Bénin :

- les Enquêtes légères auprès de Ménages (ELAM), qui ont étudié le phénomène de pauvreté dans les milieux urbains ; et

- les Études sur les Conditions de Vie des Ménages en milieu rural (ECVR) qui ont, quant à elles, appréhendé la pauvreté en milieu rural.

La pauvreté monétaire analysée selon les indicateurs habituels d'incidence (P0), de profondeur (P1) et de sévérité (P2) a été évaluée en référence à des seuils annuels de pauvreté qui s'établissent respectivement à 74 886 F CFA par tête en 2002 et à 82 224 F CFA en 2006.

Les résultats des enquêtes ont montré que la pauvreté au Bénin varie considérablement selon les zones de résidence, l'incidence étant de 27 pour cent en moyenne en milieu urbain contre 40,6 pour cent en zone rurale. L'incidence de pauvreté, de manière générale, se serait accrue par rapport à 2002, passant de 28,5 pour cent à 36,8 pour cent. De même, la profondeur de la pauvreté (P1) se serait accrue sensiblement au cours de la période, passant de 11 pour cent en 2002 à près de 14 pour cent en 2006 avec un écart plus marqué en milieu rural, dans un environnement où le taux moyen de croissance économique est de 3,5 pour cent sur la période 2004-2006.

Avec un taux annuel moyen d'accroissement de la population évalué à 3,2 pour cent au cours de la décennie passée, les performances de l'économie doivent être consolidées, car il a été établi que pour réduire significativement et durablement la pauvreté, une croissance réelle d'au moins 7 pour cent équitablement et judicieusement répartie est nécessaire. Or, actuellement, on est encore loin du compte. Lorsqu'on considère, par ailleurs, la pauvreté d'existence à travers un indice composite de niveau de vie, on note sur la base des données du Recensement Général de la Population et de l'Habitat (RGPH3) que le phénomène a touché près de 43 pour cent de la population en 2002 dont 3 fois plus d'individus en milieu rural qu'en milieu urbain (59,1 pour cent contre 17,7 pour cent). À partir de ces données, il est établi un lien entre la pauvreté, la vulnérabilité et le travail (trafic) des enfants.

Selon les déclarations des enfants enquêtés, 40 pour cent se trouvent en 2e ou 3e position dans la fratrie. Il faut souligner que ces enfants sont issus de familles polygames, pour la plupart et ont vécu, jusqu'à leur départ de la maison familiale, avec, en moyenne, 4 à 5 frères et sœurs. Des études (RGPH3) ont montré en 2002 que la pauvreté des ménages augmentait proportionnellement à leur taille. Les ménages de plus de 6 personnes affichaient des incidences de pauvreté deux fois plus élevées que ceux de moins de 3 personnes aussi bien en milieu rural qu'en milieu urbain.

En 2006, cette relation entre le niveau de vie et la taille du ménage se confirme tant du point de vue de la pauvreté monétaire que de la pauvreté non monétaire. Ce rapport est passé de 2 en 2002 à 3 pour la pauvreté monétaire. Les conséquences qui découlent de cette situation obligent à l'exode, particulièrement vers Cotonou, la ville la plus développée économiquement au Bénin. Mais, même à Cotonou, les poches de pauvreté se sont élargies, ce qui conduit certains ménages à rechercher des *Vidomègon* pour les aider à mener, parallèlement à leurs métiers, d'autres types d'activités, génératrices de revenus supplémentaires pour le ménage.

Les régions de provenance des enfants interrogés sont généralement considérées comme pauvres du point de vue des infrastructures socioéconomiques. Certains enfants (13 pour cent) proviennent des régions comme Zè et So-Ava dans le Département de l'Atlantique, d'autres, les plus nombreux (53 pour cent) sont arrivés des arrières pays des villes de Bohicon et d'Abomey dans le Département du Zou. Par ailleurs, 23 pour cent sont issus des villes de Comè et Lokossa, dans le Mono. Enfin, 11 pour cent viennent de la région du Département des Collines et du Borgou.

Il ressort de ces chiffres que les enfants sont arrivés de cinq Départements sur douze et que deux Départements sur cinq, qui totalisent à eux seuls 76 pour cent des enfants, viennent en tête des pourvoyeurs de *Vidomègon*. Ces données mettent en exergue la forte corrélation entre le faible niveau d'accès de la région aux services sociaux de base et aux infrastructures pouvant développer des activités génératrices de revenus, la capacité des parents à subvenir aux besoins fondamentaux de leurs progénitures et le placement de ces dernières en ville.

La réduction des opportunités d'emploi dans ces zones et l'insuffisance des infrastructures économiques ont fortement concouru à l'appauvrissement des familles. Ceci est illustratif, de manière assez claire, des conditions difficiles d'existence des populations dans ces Départements. L'analyse a permis de conclure que l'un des facteurs déclencheurs du phénomène *Vidomègon*, est la dégradation des conditions de vie et d'existence.

En effet, selon les données présentées dans le Document de Stratégie de Réduction de la Pauvreté au Bénin (2003-2005), et le Document de Stratégie de Croissance pour la Réduction de la Pauvreté (SCRP) 2007-2009, dans les deux régions pourvoyeuses du plus grand nombre d'enfants placés, l'appareil de production, s'il existe, est rigide et cette rigidité se caractérise, en particulier dans le secteur des services, par l'informel, la faiblesse du micro- financement et l'obsolescence des outils, des infrastructures et des méthodes de production.

Selon les mêmes sources, la mise en œuvre de différentes politiques et mesures économiques ces dix dernières années n'a pas suffi à réduire la pauvreté, particulièrement en milieu rural. Cette situation pourrait s'expliquer par l'inefficacité des mesures de redistribution des maigres revenus tirés de la légère croissance économique au milieu des années 1990, les difficultés du monde rural à obtenir une rémunération optimale de sa production alors que d'autres acteurs du système de production et de commercialisation dans les grandes villes captaient des marges de profits.

Les résultats de l'étude font apparaître également, que 9 pour cent des filles âgées de 14 à 16 ans, ont, avec l'accord de leurs parents et de leur propre volonté, suivi certaines personnes chercheuses de *Vidomègon* de passage au village, pour aller travailler comme domestiques, vendeuses ou ouvrières dans des gargotes, à Cotonou. Les motifs de leur départ, c'était gagner de l'argent. Elles se retrouvent aujourd'hui, malgré elles, dans une situation de grande difficulté, chez des femmes qui, pour les maintenir dans leurs conditions de dépendance, usent de menaces de toutes sortes et n'hésitent pas, dans certains cas, à user du châtiment corporel. Malheureusement, ces filles n'ont manifesté, à aucun moment, le désir de retourner au village auprès de leurs parents par peur de retomber dans une précarité plus sévère.

Par ailleurs, parmi les enfants enquêtés, on a pu déceler 30 filles et 8 garçons orphelins de père et de mère ou de l'un des deux parents, dans la tranche d'âge entre 8 et 11 ans. Dans ces cas, le fait de confier les enfants, à une famille pouvant leur assurer un meilleur avenir, s'est avéré, dans maints cas, pour le parent vivant, une porte de sortie de la misère. Dans le cas des enfants demi-orphelins, 66 pour cent sont confiés à des parents proches et 34 pour cent à des inconnus et donc placés. Quant aux orphelins à part entière, ce sont les oncles et tantes qui les ont pris en charge dans une proportion de 80 pour cent.

L'analyse du niveau de vulnérabilité de ces enfants a montré que ceux-ci sont nombreux à vivre dans des conditions socio-économiques défavorables, si l'on tient compte des disparités importantes entre zones urbaine et rurale et entre couches sociales. Cette situation de pauvreté et de faible accès aux services sociaux de base, constitue un terrain favorable pour l'exploitation des enfants.

Les témoignages des enfants âgés de 10 à 13 ans font état de ce qu'ils ont été déplacés sans leur consentement parce que les parents en ont décidé ainsi. Il convient de remarquer que, dans la plupart des familles l'autorité parentale et celle des adultes est partout présente et dans une certaine mesure, très pesante dans la vie des enfants. Une autorité envahissante qui met l'enfant dans des situations de dépendance. Les décisions sont prises sans que les enfants aient à donner leur avis et toute résistance à des décisions parentales, en l'occurrence du père de famille, est considérée comme un manquement grave. C'est d'ailleurs pour cette raison qu'à la question posée aux enfants : « Est-ce qu'on vous a demandé votre avis avant de vous emmener à Cotonou ? » La réponse a été « non » pour 70 pour cent des enfants. Pour les 30 pour cent restants, ils soutiennent que leur avis, bien qu'ayant été demandé, n'a pas eu de poids devant les arguments développés par les parents pour les envoyer à Cotonou. Devant la décision de certains parents, de faire transférer leurs enfants vers les centres urbains, ces derniers ont un sentiment d'impuissance, car ils se sont retrouvés dans un contexte de rapport de force continuel, favorable aux parents.

En outre, et paradoxalement, 80 pour cent des enfants n'ont manifesté aucun grief contre leurs parents. Au contraire, 69 pour cent âgés de 7 à 10 ans ont estimé que c'est pour leur propre bonheur qu'ils sont arrivés à Cotonou, parce que cela soulagerait les parents et leur procurerait un revenu mensuel. Apparemment, ces enfants se satisfont du bien-être qu'ils peuvent procurer aux parents indépendamment de ce qu'ils vivent chez leurs nouveaux « maîtres » Par contre, 80 pour cent de ceux entre 13 et 16 ans ont beaucoup insisté sur la satisfaction personnelle qu'ils peuvent tirer d'un travail quelconque : satisfaction matérielle d'une part, satisfaction psychologique d'autre part.

En outre, en focalisant l'attention sur la façon dont les enfants sont déplacés et ensuite placés dans des familles, l'étude a voulu s'appuyer sur l'hypothèse selon laquelle, il existe des réseaux organisés de trafic d'enfants à l'intérieur du pays, relayés par leurs complices à l'extérieur.

L'analyse des informations recueillies auprès des enfants a permis de confirmer cette hypothèse. En effet, la plupart des enfants (61 pour cent) ont soutenu, au cours des discussions, qu'ils ont été transportés à Cotonou par des personnes inconnues, avec le consentement de leurs parents, principalement celui du père. Dès qu'ils sont arrivés à destination, ils ont été accueillis, nuitamment, par des femmes à des endroits précis, puis conduits vers des domiciles. Par ailleurs, d'autres enfants (29 pour cent) ont déclaré avoir été transféré à Cotonou par des proches de leurs parents (oncle, tante, cousins, amis, etc.) qui ont souhaité les prendre en charge pour leur éducation et leur assurer le bien-être matériel et psychologique nécessaire à leur développement. 75 pour cent des enfants ont affirmé, qu'ils voyageraient bientôt dans un autre pays pour y rester quelques mois et revenir. Cette affirmation met en lumière le fait que les enfants passent une période transitoire chez certains tuteurs et tutrices avant de prendre une autre direction, pour une autre destination, certainement pour aller travailler dans des champs de café et de cacao, en Côte d'Ivoire, servir dans des maquis ou dans des maisons au Gabon, en tant que domestiques et dans des carrières de concassage de pierres au Nigeria, etc.

En leur posant la question de savoir s'il leur est arrivé d'avoir en idée de s'enfuir du domicile, 25 pour cent ont déclaré avoir déjà fugué, au moins une fois, mais ont été rattrapés et corrigés, c'est-à-dire battus, ce qui les en a dissuadé, du moins pour le moment. Par ailleurs, 42 pour cent ont envie de quitter leurs tuteurs/tutrices, mais sont dans l'attente de trouver l'occasion propice. Les 33 pour cent restants ont du mal à se déterminer par peur de représailles. Entrent dans cette catégorie, les enfants âgés entre 7 et 12 ans. Les garçons sont plus fugueurs et représentent un taux plus élevé (16 pour cent) que les filles (9 pour cent) Pour les plus âgés (de 13 à 16 ans), ils ont été très discrets par rapport à cette question, ne voulant même pas y répondre.

Les conditions de vie et de travail à destination

Au cours de l'étude, il a été identifié plusieurs types de ce placement dont les principaux sont : le placement-vente à travers lequel est placé dans une famille sous contrat moyennant une somme de 15 000 à 20 000 F CFA ; le placement semi-rémunéré qui est une forme de contrat temporaire tacite ; et le placement simple en échange d'une prise en charge de l'enfant.

De ces trois types de placements, l'étude a révélé que le premier cas concerne 62 pour cent des enfants, tandis que dans le second, on en retrouve 12 pour cent. Quant au dernier, 25 pour cent des enfants en sont victimes. Ces chiffres sont illustratifs du « marchandisage » et de la « chosification » de l'enfant. Dans de telles situations, les risques de l'exploitation des enfants sont élevés.

L'étude a, par ailleurs, recensé une gamme variée d'activités qui se mènent généralement dans nos villes et même au sein des familles. Ce sont des travaux domestiques, le commerce, des travaux dans des ateliers d'artisans (maçonnerie, mécanique, coiffure, soudure, confection de tenues).

L'enquête n'ayant pas pris en compte tous les types d'activités existantes, celles recensés sont directement liées aux enfants interrogés. C'est pour cette raison qu'ont été définis quelques types d'activités que sont : les activités domestiques, le petit commerce, la mécanique, la maçonnerie, la confection de vêtements et vulcanisation.

Il faut souligner que la participation des enfants à l'activité économique n'est pas toujours considérée comme une mauvaise chose en soi par leurs tuteurs et tutrices. Certains ont soutenu qu'elle est même bénéfique. En vertu de la Convention 138 de l'Organisation internationale du Travail (OIT), le travail, qui ne nuit pas aux études, est autorisé à partir de l'âge de 12 ans. Malheureusement, force est de constater que les enfants (120, soit 48 pour cent) entrant dans le cadre de la présente étude, travaillent dans des conditions qui enfreignent les normes de l'OIT : d'abord, plusieurs sont âgés de moins de 12 ans, ensuite certains ne fréquentent plus l'école et d'autres ont du abandonner les classes du fait de la situation de précarité de leurs familles. 47 pour cent, dont la majorité représentée par des filles, ont déjà mis pied à l'école avant d'abandonner, faute de moyens pour le financement des études.

L'enquête a révélé aussi que le niveau, le plus élevé de scolarité atteint par ces enfants est la classe de CE1, alors que le plus bas niveau est le CI. Dès lors, la durée moyenne de survie de ces enfants dans le système scolaire n'excède pas trois ans. Retirés pour l'une ou l'autre raison liée directement à la pauvreté, ces enfants sont prédisposés au travail et à l'exploitation à des fins commerciales et économiques. Un point sur lequel tout le monde semble s'accorder est qu'il existe généralement un lien élevé entre le fait qu'un enfant ne fréquente pas l'école et son placement (en ville). On soutient généralement que c'est parce qu'un enfant n'est pas scolarisé qu'il est placé, mais on peut également dire que c'est le fait d'être placé qu'il n'a pu aller à l'école. Bien souvent, il semble que les enfants travaillent parce qu'ils ne vont pas à l'école. Celle-ci coûte bien trop cher pour les familles démunies. Les droits d'inscription, les frais de transport, l'achat des livres, du matériel scolaire et de l'uniforme pour un seul enfant, représentent parfois l'équivalent d'une année de revenu alors qu'une famille peut avoir au moins 3 ou 4 enfants. De toutes les façons, de tels enfants sont considérés comme des enfants, courant un risque très élevé de devenir *Vidomègon*.

Selon le représentant de l'UNICEF au Bénin interrogé par Radio France international le 11 juin 2007, le Bénin serait non seulement un pays où la pratique du travail des enfants placés est très présente, mais aussi il constitue un pays de transit ou d'accueil des enfants venant des pays frontaliers.

On a distingué, au cours de l'étude, une première catégorie de 59 enfants âgés entre 7 et 11 ans, travaillant à la fois comme domestiques et revendeuses d'une part, comme domestiques et apprentis d'autre part. La seconde catégorie concerne 34 enfants âgés de 12 à 16 ans, cumulant également plusieurs activités. Mais le point commun des activités effectuées par ces deux catégories d'enfants est avant tout, l'activité domestique, c'est-à-dire le ménage : lessive, vaisselle, le nettoyage de la maison, la garde d'enfants, etc.

Il a été constaté que la majorité des domestiques sont des filles (93 pour cent) alors que les garçons sont impliqués à 7 pour cent dans ces mêmes travaux. La comparaison entre ces deux chiffres est illustrative de la différence de traitement des genres en matière de division du travail. En réalité, les garçons, même s'ils sont conviés à des tâches domestiques, le sont de toutes les manières moins que les filles. Le nombre de garçons allant vendre au marché ou dans la rue est faible. Ainsi, sur cinq enfants vendeurs on a dénombré seulement 1 garçon pour 4 filles.

Par contre, les garçons qui vivent avec leurs tutrices, et plus particulièrement avec leurs tuteurs artisans, y sont en même temps apprentis, bien qu'exécutant des activités domestiques.

Parmi les 50 garçons recensés au cours de l'étude, 14 sont apprentis mécaniciens, 8 apprentis maçons, 8 apprentis vulcanisateurs, 12 apprentis tailleurs. Leurs âges varient de 8 à 14 ans. Ceux âgés de 7 ans sont au nombre de 8 et revendent des objets divers pour le compte de leurs tutrices en même temps qu'ils exécutent des travaux domestiques. Parmi les enfants de 16 ans, il n'y a aucun garçon.

Il faut souligner que, contrairement aux filles *Vidomègon*, les garçons passent beaucoup plus de temps à l'atelier qu'à la maison. Il a été constaté d'ailleurs que deux apprentis sur quatre, dorment à leurs lieux de travail, parfois avec le tuteur, mais souvent seul, afin de prévenir tout vol par infraction, du matériel de travail. En réalité, ils jouent le rôle de gardiens, dans des quartiers malfamés, exposés de ce fait aux pires dangers de la nuit.

L'étude, en mettant en exergue le statut des *Vidomègon*, a fait ressortir le fait que plus de 95 pour cent vivent au domicile de leurs tuteurs et tutrices, sans que ceux-ci soient forcément des proches de leurs parents biologiques. 75 pour cent des filles sont avec des personnes sans lien avec la famille alors qu'ils sont 35 pour cent de garçons dans la même situation. D'un autre côté, on a dénombré 30 filles et 8 garçons orphelins de l'un ou des deux parents. Un enfant orphelin, vivant dans des conditions de précarité, est caractérisé par sa vulnérabilité, parce que plus désavantagé par rapport aux autres enfants dont les deux parents sont vivants et c'est d'ailleurs pour cette raison qu'on les retrouve parmi les sujets *Vidomègon* interrogés.

D'après les données recueillies, de tous les enfants interviewés, ceux âgés entre 9 et 16 ans, sont économiquement les plus actifs, parce que vivant avec des tuteurs et/ou tutrices exerçant, entre autres, des activités commerciales. Les filles se livrent, dans leur majorité, à des activités telles que la vente des produits vivriers saisonniers, des produits manufacturés, de la glace, etc. On les retrouve également dans des ateliers de couture et coiffure et dans des gargotes comme serveuses, lorsque la tutrice est la tenancière de l'atelier. On en a dénombré 64 entre10 et 16 ans.

Il est vrai que personne ne sait précisément combien ils sont, ces enfants exploités à Cotonou, car les statistiques sont difficiles à établir. En effet, le désir a été grand de connaître le nombre exact des filles et garçons entrant dans l'échantillon de notre recherche, et qui travaillent à plein temps ou à temps partiel, pour aider leurs parents et tuteurs dans les tâches ménagères ou autres. Les visites à domicile ont donc permis rencontrer des parents, des tuteurs et d'autres personnes afin de se faire une idée exacte de la situation réelle de vie des enfants placés auprès de ces familles.

Partout où l'étude a été menée, les adultes interrogés ont montré et soutenu la nécessité pour les enfants d'aider leurs parents et les personnes adultes dans les petits travaux à la maison ou hors de la maison parce que les enfants, eux-mêmes, en tirent le plus souvent un sentiment de fierté. Cela constitue une forme de formation. L'une des tutrices interrogées à déclaré ceci : « Le *Vidomègon* est une nécessité pour nous, fonctionnaires et commerçantes, parce qu'ils doivent garder la maison, exécuter de petites tâches et aller chercher nos enfants à l'école. Dans certains cas, ils doivent nous aider à vendre et à surveiller les marchandises quand nous devons nous absenter. » Comme on le voit, cette déclaration est chargée de sens. En effet, il ne fait l'ombre d'aucun doute que le *Vidomègon* est un enfant à tout faire et qui ploie sous la multitude des responsabilités qui lui sont confiées malgré son jeune âge.

Les hommes interviewés, quant à eux, n'ont pas voulu trop en parler. Il s'est avéré que le sujet est sensible au regard du sentiment d'inconfort qu'il déclenche chez les adultes interrogés. Toutefois, il a été constaté, dans les déclarations faites par les enfants, celles faites par leurs tutrices et celles venant de personnes tierces, des contradictions assez expressives. En effet, la description de diverses situations met en exergue les conditions de pénibilité des travaux exécutés par les enfants. Ils sont réduits à la servitude parce qu'obligés de consacrer toutes leurs journées à des tâches qui sont susceptibles de nuire à leur santé. Plusieurs enfants (235) ont décrit leurs journées de travail qui durent en moyenne 14 à 16 heures. La plupart sont réveillés dès 6 heures du matin pour aller se coucher autour de 22 heures le soir sans toutefois avoir le droit de faire la sieste dans l'après-midi.

Selon ces mêmes enfants, les conditions de travail sont très difficiles, surtout à cause de leur durée. La lessive, par exemple leur prend entre 6 et 10 heures par semaine. En présentant aux enfants une liste de travaux qu'ils exécutent ou sont supposés exercer, ils devaient choisir dans un ordre décroissant des plus répugnants et éprouvants pour eux aux plus supportables. Pour les filles, quel que soit l'âge, vient en tête, la lessive (46 pour cent), suivie du commerce ambulant (23 pour cent) et la préparation du repas (11 pour cent) En ce qui concerne les garçons, les travaux les plus détestés sont le commerce ambulant (67 pour cent), la lessive (30 pour cent), le travail à l'atelier (15 pour cent).

Comme on peut le constater, la tendance générale est que les trois premiers travaux que les filles n'aiment pas exécuter se retrouvent également en partie chez les garçons, car tous considèrent ces travaux comme des corvées. Malgré la dureté des travaux exercés, les enfants n'en tirent apparemment aucun bénéfice. Au contraire, les tuteurs et surtout les tutrices manifestent très souvent leur insatisfaction par rapport à eux, les taxant de tous les maux.

En cherchant à approfondir les questions relatives à leur rémunération financière par rapport à la main-d'œuvre qu'ils représentent, on a été surpris de constater, selon les déclarations de certaines tutrices (30 pour cent), qu'une partie de l'argent est envoyée aux parents et que le reste est gardé pour la confection des habits et l'achat des chaussures pour les fêtes. En fait, puisque qu'en parlant ici du travail des enfants, on fait allusion à ceux qui opèrent dans le secteur informel, il est difficile de quantifier la valeur réelle du travail fourni par ces enfants. Mais une chose est claire, ils sont exploités parce qu'ils travaillent nuit et jour afin de gagner de l'argent pour les adultes et nourrir, dans une certaine mesure, leurs familles restées au village.

Tout se passe comme si les droits de ces enfants sont relégués au second plan. C'est un phénomène à la mode dans nos grandes villes, de voir dans une famille sur 150, une fille ou un garçon (rarement) servir de bonne à tout faire. Tout le monde a tendance à condamner le phénomène, à faire des marches et à le dénoncer, mais dans les arrière-cours, il y a des choses reprochables qui sont faites aux enfants.

En somme, nombreux sont ces enfants font de la vente ambulante pour le compte de leur famille d'accueil et ne sont pas rémunérés pour ce qu'ils font. De ce point de vue, ils sont astreints au travail sous forme de pratiques serviles que l'environnement social ne veut pas condamner

Le climat relationnel au sein de la nouvelle « famille »

En se basant sur la définition que les Nations Unies donnent de la violence en tant que *recours intentionnel à la force physique ou au pouvoir, réel ou induit, lorsque celui-ci provoque ou risque de provoquer des blessures physiques ou psychologiques, la mort, un retard dans le développement ou des privations*, les résultats de l'enquête menée révèlent une prévalence de la violence au sein du cercle familial et plus particulièrement à l'encontre des enfants *Vidomègon.*

En effet, il est admis par l'étude que la vulnérabilité de l'enfant *Vidomègon* est exacerbée par des facteurs comme son déplacement, son placement, la pauvreté, et l'isolement social. Notons que la plupart de ces enfants viennent de groupes qui sont marginalisés dans notre société, notamment les enfants vivant dans la pauvreté. Cette violence constitue une violation des droits de l'enfant et revêt de nombreuses formes. Certaines bénéficient d'une importante couverture médiatique. D'autres sont plus insidieuses et moins reconnaissables. Malheureusement, elles se produisent dans des lieux où les enfants devraient être protégés.

Les dernières dispositions législatives en droit de la famille consacrent l'enfant comme sujet de droit qu'il faut absolument protéger. La jurisprudence reconnaît l'application directe de la Convention internationale des droits de l'Enfant. *Pourtant, les scènes de violence auxquelles sont témoins les enfants et dont ils sont l'objet constituent des brèches dans la protection de l'enfant.* Le traitement fait aux enfants *Vidomègon* n'échappe pas à cette logique qui est connu de tous. D'ailleurs, à l'occasion de la journée de l'Enfant africain qui a lieu en juin 2007, l'UNICEF a mis l'accent sur la traite des enfants afin de maintenir la dynamique dans la lutte contre la violence à l'égard des enfants qui se développe de plus en plus sur le continent.

En demandant aux adultes en charge de *Vidomègon* de déterminer les types de punitions qu'ils infligent, suite aux manquements, la liste est longue mais seulement trois des plus importantes sont mises en exergue. Il s'agit du châtiment corporel (coups, gifles) des punitions verbales (insultes, cris, menaces, critiques) et des privations (argent de poche, nourriture, sortie). Les raisons avancées pour infliger des punitions aux enfants sont variées : vol, mensonge, retard dans l'exécution des activités à eux confiées, impolitesse, etc. En somme, ils seraient punis pour mauvais comportements et mauvaise conduite. Même si la plupart des adultes interrogés soutiennent que les coups et gifles interviennent très rarement, néanmoins 80 pour cent des enfants ont estimé en être victimes puisqu'ils sont battus, en moyenne, une fois par semaine et 100 pour cent sont insultés et humiliés à une fréquence élevée (4 ou 6 fois/jour), devant d'autres personnes.

Il a été même remarqué sur certaines parties du corps (bras et torse) d'une trentaine d'enfants, des traces cicatrisées de coups ayant certainement occasionné des blessures. « Il n'y a pas d'objet qui ne serve à me frapper, pourvu qu'il soit à portée de la main », déclare un garçon de 10 ans. « Avant hier, poursuit-il, mon patron m'a donné deux gifles parce que je ne suis pas vite revenu d'où il m'a envoyé. Et pourtant j'y suis allé à pied ». Cette situation, qui est particulière à cet enfant, est malheureusement le quotidien des milliers d'enfants à Cotonou. Visiblement, ils sont maltraités et plusieurs relatent avec amertume et ressentiment les différents sévices dont ils sont l'objet. Nombreux sont, parmi eux, qui nourrissent l'espoir de quitter cette situation, mais se trouvent dans l'impuissance de retourner chez leurs parents, surtout lorsqu'ils ne savent pas par où y aller, avec quels moyens et pour quelles perspectives. Une quinzaine d'enfants ont raconté comment ils ont pu tromper la vigilance de leurs tuteurs et tutrices pour s'enfuir de la maison. Pendant deux ou trois jours, ils ont séjourné dans la rue, dormant là où le sommeil les a pris et quémandant argent et nourritures à quelques adultes, avant d'être rattrapés par leurs tuteurs et reconduits à la maison.

Les enfants ont par ailleurs souligné que leurs tutrices ne leur accorde jamais confiance et les traitent de menteurs ou menteuses, chaque fois qu'il leur est permis de se défendre des accusations. Les propos de 3 tuteurs et 17 tutrices ont confirmé ce climat de suspicion entre les enfants et eux. Ainsi, lorsqu'on leur a demandé de donner leurs impressions sur leurs « enfants », ils ne tarissent pas de qualificatifs les plus négatifs mais finissent par reconnaître, de manière assez subtile, leur utilité dans la maison. En les accusant de tous ces maux, ils voulaient prédisposer les enquêteurs à cautionner les mauvais traitements infligés à ces enfants.

À la question « Qui sont les personnes qui vous frappent ou vous insultent ? », les enfants ont déterminé avec précision certains membres de la famille. Les adultes (tuteurs et tutrices) viennent en tête avec 68 pour cent, suivis de leurs enfants (23 pour cent), qui sont, le plus souvent plus âgés qu'eux. Viennent ensuite les parents des tuteurs tutrices 9 pour cent (tantes, mères, cousines, neveux et nièces) séjournant ou ayant séjourné quelques jours ou semaines dans la maison. Il est utile d'insister ici sur le fait que le Vidomègon est vulnérable, à tout point de vue du fait de son statut et de ses caractéristiques socioéconomiques. Certains parmi eux ont même soutenu que même les plus petits qu'eux dans la famille, leur portent des coups sans qu'ils ne puissent les leur rendre, par peur de représailles des adultes.

À l'autorité répressive des adultes, s'ajoutent donc les caprices des autres enfants à leur égard, toutes choses dont les effets négatifs varient d'un enfant à l'autre. On a donc remarqué chez certains enfants, une attitude négative et hostile, l'angoisse permanente, de l'apathie, de l'indifférence. Chez d'autres, on remarque de l'aigreur et une tension intérieure, perceptible dans la voix et le regard. Des enfants qui, en général, sont toujours sur la défensive dès qu'on les aborde pour parler. Certains foyers sont pour ces enfants, de véritables camps « de concentration » où règne la terreuret où la moindre erreur de comportement, le plus léger manquement se paie très cher.

Il est vrai, comme l'ont souligné certains parents, que l'enfant a certes des devoirs, mais il a aussi des droits. On doit se rendre à l'évidence que, dans la plupart des familles béninoises, si ce ne sont pas toutes, on frappe de temps en temps les enfants et personne ne crie au scandale. Ainsi, dans le cas de la présente étude, l'une des questions à se poser n'est pas tant de savoir s'il faut frapper l'enfant *Vidomègon* ou non, mais surtout d'avoir le sens de la mesure. C'est pourquoi, nous faisons la distinction entre ce qu'il est permis d'appeler punition à des fins éducatives et maltraitance.

Ici, plus qu'ailleurs, les enfants ci-dessus décrits, se trouvent moins dans la situation de la punition à caractère éducatif que dans celle de la maltraitance et l'on sait l'extrême influence qu'elle exerce sur la formation de la personnalité. On se rappelle d'ailleurs, dans son article 19, la Convention internationale des Droits de l'Enfant (CIDE) adoptée par l'Assemblée générale des Nations Unies le 20 novembre 1989, qui a défini la maltraitance comme une forme de violence physique ou psychologique que pourrait subir un enfant.

Les actions entreprises par les pouvoirs publiques

Sur le plan économique

En partant du fait que les facteurs déterminants du trafic d'enfants et de leur mise au travail forcé sont liés à la paupérisation des populations rurales, principalement, au chômage endémique qui en explique également l'extension et au recours à une main-d'œuvre domestique bon marché et docile, le gouvernement du Bénin a mis en œuvre un ensemble de mesures tendant à faire profiter, à la plus grande partie possible de la population, surtout des zones rurales.

Le potentiel de croissance de l'économie béninoise est dépendant de l'agriculture, parce que le secteur rural 70 pour cent de la population active et contribue pour environ 36 pour cent à la structure du PIB, procure environ 88 pour cent des recettes d'exportation du pays et participe à hauteur de 15 pour cent aux recettes de l'État. L'agriculture joue ainsi un rôle essentiel dans le processus de développement économique et social. Malgré ces performances, il y a un paradoxe criard, car il a été constaté que la pauvreté est plus forte en milieu rural qu'en milieu urbain. Sur les dix dernières années, elle a régressé en zone urbaine alors même qu'elle s'est aggravée dans le monde rural.

Les plus récentes mesures prises par le Gouvernement sont celles contenues dans le Document de Stratégies de Réduction de la Pauvreté (2003-2005). En effet, la stratégie gouvernementale visait, entre autres, l'amélioration du revenu du monde paysan à travers la promotion de sa participation à la production rurale. Pour soutenir cette stratégie, une série de projets et de programmes a été initiée et figure dans le Cadre de Dépense à Moyen Terme (CDMT). Par ailleurs, la Déclaration de

Politique de Développement rural (DPDR) et son Plan stratégique opérationnel sont disponibles et constituent le document sectoriel de base portant la stratégie de développement du monde rural que le Gouvernement est a mis en place.

Pour atteindre ses objectifs de développement du secteur agricole, des actions ont été développées à travers différents projets et sous programmes contenus dans le CDMT. Il s'agit :

- de l'appui à l'amélioration de la productivité agricole ;
- des infrastructures rurales ;
- de la gestion durable des ressources naturelles ;
- de l'appui au développement des marchés agricoles ;
- de l'administration et la gestion des services.

Étant donné que le développement du secteur agricole va de pair avec l'épineuse question foncière, le Gouvernement a mis en place avec l'appui de la Banque Mondiale, un Projet de Gestion des Forêts et Territoires riverains (PGFTR) afin de contribuer à la gestion durable et rationnelle des ressources naturelles renouvelables du pays en tant que Programme d'appui à la Direction des Forêts et des Ressources naturelles (DFRN).

Sur le plan éducatif

L'examen des statistiques scolaires de ces dix dernières années a révélé que, bien qu'il existe des améliorations sensibles en matière d'accès à l'éducation, des disparités subsistent entre les zones urbaines et rurales d'une manière générale. Ceci prive une grande partie des enfants béninois d'aller à l'école et de s'y maintenir, sur une longue durée.

En effet, l'accès à l'enseignement primaire est plus ou moins universel en zone urbaine, alors que dans les zones rurales, le taux d'accès est de l'ordre de 86 pour cent pour les garçons et seulement de 64 pour cent pour les filles, encore que, d'une zone rurale à l'autre, on enregistre de grandes inégalités d'accès des filles à l'éducation. Par ailleurs, 39 pour cent des garçons ruraux et 14 pour cent des filles rurales terminent le cours primaire. Comme on peut le constater, des efforts restent à faire dans la perspective de la scolarisation universelle au primaire et de l'accès équitable entre filles et garçons. Et pour être logique avec les ambitions de développement, la politique éducative mise en application, vise entre autres, l'égalité des chances pour tous les enfants en âge scolaire. Ainsi, il a été procédé à la poursuite de la subvention de la gratuité de l'inscription dans les écoles primaires publiques, à la promotion de la scolarisation des filles et l'appui aux communautés pour l'inscription et le maintien des élèves à l'école, spécialement les filles.

L'analphabétisme étant une cause profonde de pauvreté, le Bénin vient de se doter d'une Politique nationale d'Alphabétisation et d'Éducation des Adultes (PNAEA). Cette politique a servi de cadre de référence à l'élaboration et à la mise en œuvre de divers programmes éducatifs répondant aux besoins, préoccupations et aspirations des acteurs et des bénéficiaires. D'un autre côté, le programme *Appui au développement communautaire* a permis de modifier progressivement les comportements des populations de plus de 60 villages en faveur du respect des droits de l'enfant grâce à l'alphabétisation et la formation de 3 200 personnes en matière de planification locale et à l'appui à l'installation d'unités génératrices de revenus au bénéfice des enfants.

En agissant de la sorte, le Gouvernement a pour ambition d'éradiquer l'analphabétisme au Bénin. Le Document de Stratégies de Réduction de la Pauvreté (2003-2005) a révélé que la réduction du taux d'analphabétisme est passée de 68 pour cent en 2001 à moins de 60 pour cent en 2005 et passera, si cette tendance est maintenue, à 50 pour cent à l'horizon 2010, au sein de la population de la tranche d'âge de 15 à 49 ans. Ces progrès, malgré leurs faiblesses, ont favorisé l'émergence d'un environnement de plus en plus lettré et réduit le taux d'analphabétisme des femmes et des jeunes filles de 79,65 pour cent en 2001 à 60 pour cent en 2005.

Les actions réalisées durant les trois (3) années (2003-2005) ont contribué à maintenir un nombre important d'enfants dans le système éducatif, évitant, par la même occasion, qu'ils soient l'objet de trafic interne ou externe.

Sur le plan juridique

Au niveau du trafic, du travail et de la maltraitance de l'enfant, il semble que les réponses juridiques sont, à certains égards, insuffisantes. Dans la mesure où le Bénin ne dispose pas d'un arsenal juridique en la matière, il est difficile de contrecarrer efficacement les trafiquants, mais le gouvernement déploie des efforts pour se conformer aux normes, en matière de lutte contre le trafic des enfants.

Le Gouvernement a retenu pour la période 2007-2009 de « garantir à l'enfant et à l'adolescent le respect de leurs droits et l'accès équitable aux services sociaux essentiels » à travers :

- la protection de l'enfance et de l'adolescence contre les maltraitances et la traite des enfants ;
- la promotion de l'accès des enfants filles et garçons aux services sociaux essentiels ;
- l'amélioration de l'état alimentaire et nutritionnel des enfants ;
- le renforcement des capacités des structures oeuvrant au profit des enfants ; et
- la réinsertion familiale et sociale des orphelins et enfants vulnérables

Il a été initié, à cet effet, un projet de Protection, qui a permis une plus grande sensibilisation sur les problèmes liés au trafic des enfants. Ce projet a suscité une plus grande implication des communautés à la lutte contre le trafic en appuyant la création de 500 comités locaux de lutte dans les zones dites à risque. Une loi interdisant le trafic des enfants a été déjà votée par l'Assemblée nationale en janvier 2006, dont la promulgation pourra renforcer les capacités nationales. Mais, au même moment, en attendant la promulgation de cette loi, d'anciennes lois ont été utilisées pour juger, au cours de l'année 2005, 83 affaires liées au trafic d'enfants, dont 20 ont abouti à des peines d'emprisonnement allant de trois à douze mois. Afin d'apporter une assistance aux enfants victimes de trafic, le Ministère de la famille est en coopération avec des organisations internationales, des ONG et un réseau de 1 141 comités locaux de lutte contre le trafic des enfants, disséminés à travers le Bénin.

Depuis 2003, l'Unicef, en partenariat avec l'État béninois, a mis en place un comité mixte chargé de superviser l'élaboration d'un Code de l'Enfant afin de garantir une meilleure protection juridique à l'enfant. En effet, l'institution appuie le gouvernement du Bénin dans les six villes les plus touchées par le phénomène : il s'agit de mettre en œuvre des activités de prévention et de prise en charge des apprentis. Cette action s'articule autour de plusieurs axes : la sensibilisation, des cours d'éducation non formelle, la réinsertion scolaire des enfants de moins de 14 ans, des séances d'écoute et de conseil. Ces actions sont renforcées aujourd'hui à travers des partenariats d'ONG béninoises).

Le Bénin, se trouvant dans un environnement sous-régional marqué par la criminalité transfrontalière, a signé, en 2005, un accord bilatéral avec plusieurs pays de l'Afrique de l'Ouest, pour une collaboration dans la lutte contre le trafic des enfants.

Mesures à prendre pour l'avenir

Des mesures s'imposent à plusieurs niveaux :

- le renforcement de la surveillance des zones dites à risques afin d'assurer une approche intégrée des problèmes liés au trafic, aux familles des enfants, à la santé, à l'éducation et à la réhabilitation des enfants ;
- la mise en œuvre d'une véritable politique de développement rural, induisant une amélioration sensible des conditions de vie et d'existence ;
- le renforcement des activités économiques par l'octroi de crédit aux parents ce qui leur permettrait d'être nantis financièrement pour maintenir les enfants sur place ;
- une plus grande responsabilisation des autorités locales concernant le contrôle et l'éradication du trafic d'enfant ;
- la mise en place de Comités villageois permanents de sensibilisation des familles ;
- le développement de nouvelles stratégies de prévention et de lutte contre le phénomène, parce que celles qui existent ont montré leurs limites ;
- la promulgation de la loi sur l'interdiction du trafic des enfants ;
- une meilleure concertation entre l'État, les ONG et les associations afin de diffuser l'information ;
- le renforcement de la législation et des dispositions légales permettant de punir les trafiquants ;
- l'éducation du public pour la mise en application des Conventions relatives aux droits de l'enfant ;
- la coopération internationale entre la police, la douane et les ambassades pour un meilleur contrôle de la sortie des enfants ;
- la mise en place d'un système continu de recueil d'information sur le trafic interne des enfants (recensement des enfants par tranche d'âge) afin de constituer

une banque de données et d'élaborer un programme de prévention ou la création de registres de trafic et de violence envers les enfants ;

- le dépôt de lois rendant le signalement de maltraitance et de trafic obligatoire ;
- l'élargissement du *Code de criminalité* et de la *Loi sur la preuve au Bénin en la matière.* Ces infractions comprennent : la violence physique criminelle envers un enfant, la négligence criminelle envers un enfant, la violence psychologique criminelle envers un enfant, l'homicide d'un enfant, et le manquement à signaler des crimes soupçonnés envers les enfants ;
- l'assurance que le *Code de criminalité* comporte des dispositions de condamnation pour une meilleure protection des enfants ;
- l'amélioration de l'expérience des enfants témoins et la facilitation de leur témoignage dans les procédures criminelles ;
- le prolongement des délais pour le dépôt de plaintes dans les cas de violence envers les enfants ;
- l'information des enfants de leurs droits, et leur apprentissage de la façon d'identifier la maltraitance, demander de l'aide, et éviter une nouvelle victimisation ;
- l'accroissement de la connaissance de la violence et du trafic des enfants et son incidence au cours de différentes périodes de la vie ;
- l'amélioration de l'échange de renseignements entre les organismes gouvernementaux et les ONG ;
- l'accroissement de l'efficacité des réactions et interventions au niveau local et national ;
- l'amélioration du soutien et des services aux enfants.

Conclusion

Ce travail ne prétend pas être exhaustif mais il s'est assigné comme but d'attirer l'attention sur les problèmes relatifs à la traite des enfants, dans toutes ses dimensions. L'étude a pu mettre en exergue certains aspects du phénomène, difficiles à appréhender et auxquels des solutions idoines devront être trouvées.

Il a été constaté que les droits de l'enfant béninois sont, dans une large mesure, bafoués, consciemment ou non, par des personnes qui ont, eux-aussi, été enfants, avant de devenir adultes, d'une part, et qui sont supposés connaître la loi en la matière. Au moment où il est clamé haut le rejet de l'asservissement de l'enfant, des milliers de ménages continuent impunément, dans nos villes, de vivre en marge des lois de la cité, en posant, chaque fois que l'occasion leur est permise, des actes délictueux, nuisant gravement au développement intégral de l'enfant.

Eu égard à l'étendue du trafic et de la mise en esclavage des enfants, au Bénin, ainsi qu'à la complexité et à l'énorme incidence de la question, une prévention, une identification et une réaction efficaces est une tâche énorme mais essentielle. La résolution d'une pareille problématique exige l'engagement et la coopération continus au niveau central, intermédiaire et local, de praticiens et de décideurs à l'échelle nationale.

Références

Adihou, A. F., 2000, « Rapport sur le trafic des enfants entre le Bénin et le Gabon », *Anti-Slavery* : Avril

Adepoju, A., 1999, *La famille africaine (Politiques démographiques et développement)*, Paris: Karthala.

Almeida-Topor, H. d', 2003, *L'Afrique au 20e siècle*, Paris: Armand Colin.

Almeida-Topor, H. d', 2002, *Rapport sur le Développement en Afrique (Développement rural et réduction de la pauvreté)*, Paris: Economica.

Baldry, A. C. and Farrington, D. P., 2000, « Bullies and Delinquents : Personal Characteristics and Parental Styles », *Journal of Community & Applied Social Psychology*, 10(1): 17-31.

Bénin, Ministère de l'Enseignement primaire et secondaire (MEPS) et Ministère du Plan, 2006, *Plan décennal 2006-2015.*

Bénin, Ministère de l'Enseignement primaire et secondaire (MEPS) et Ministère du Plan, 2006, Plan d'Action national pour l'Éducation pour Tous (PAN/EPT), in *Plan décennal 2006-2015.*

Bénin, Ministère du Plan, 2005, *Lettre de Politique éducative le 23 février.*

Bénin, Ministère du Plan, 1996, *Déclaration de Politique de Population (DEPOLIPO) révisée en 2006.*

Bénin, Ministère du Plan, 2006, *Stratégie de Croissance pour la Réduction de la Pauvreté (SCRP) sur la période 2007-2009.*

Beziat M., 1999, Secrétaire général du CCEM, Mission d'enquête au Bénin du 9 septembre au 5 octobre.

Bocquier, P. et Traoré, S., 2000, *Urbanisation et dynamique migratoire en Afrique de l'Ouest (La croissance urbaine en panne)*, Paris: l'Harmattan.

Committee on the Rights of the Child, 2006, *General Comment No. 8. The Right of the Child to Protection from Corporal Punishment and Other Cruel or Degrading Forms of Punishment (articles 19, 28(2) and 37, inter alia).*

Cousinet, R., 1952, *La Formation de l'éducateur*, Paris: PUF.

Deuxième rapport périodique du Bénin sur la mise en œuvre de la Convention relative aux droits de l'enfant (1998-2002)

Destremau, B. et Lautier, B., 2002, « Femme en domesticité », *Revue Tiers Monde*, 170, avril-juin.

Dunne, M. and Leach, F., 2004, 'Institutional Sexism : Context and Texts in Botswana and Ghana'. Paper presented at the 7th Oxford International Conference on Educational Development, 9–11 September 2003, Oxford.

EMIDA, 2000, *enquête sur les violences éducatives faites aux enfants dans les familles et à l'école primaire au Cameroun*, Yaoundé: EMIDA/UNICEF.

Gayet, D., 1995, *Modèles éducatifs et relations pédagogiques*, Paris: A. Colin.

Gloton, R., 1974, *L'Autorité à la dérive*, Paris: Casterman.

Herrera, R., 2006, « Objectifs du millénaire pour le développement : lutte contre la pauvreté ou guerre contre les pauvres ? », *Alternatives Sud*, vol. 13, n°. 1, pp. 185-199, janvier.

Houssaye, J., 1996, *Autorité et éducation. Entre savoir et socialisation, le sens de l'éducation*, Paris: ESF.

INSAE Bénin, 2002, *Troisième Recensement Général de la Population et de l'Habitation (RGPH3).*

International Labour Office, 2002, *Every Child Counts – New Global Estimates on Child Labour, International Programme on the Elimination of Child Labour (IPEC) – Statistical Information and Monitoring Programme on Child Labour (SIMPOC),* Avril, Genève: International Labour Office.

International Labour Office, 2006, *The End of Child Labour : Within Reach*, Geneva: International Labour Office.

James, M., 1994, *Domestic Violence as a Form of Child Abuse : Identification and Prevention, Issues in Child Abuse Prevention*, National Child Protection Clearinghouse, Melbourne, Australia.

Krug, E. G. et al., ed., 2002, *Rapport mondial sur la violence et la santé*, Genève: OMS.

Krug, E. G. et al., ed., 2002, *World Report on Violence and Health*. Geneva: World Health Organization.

Lobrot, M., 1971, « Des mots, des mots… Comment ? Pourquoi ? », *L'École des Parents*, 7, pp. 42-46.

Monestier, M., 1998, *Les Enfants esclaves*, Paris: Le Cherche Midi.

Nieuwenhuys, O., 1996, 'The Paradox of Child Labor and Anthropology', *Annual Review of Anthropology* , Vol. 25: 237-251.

Nieuwenhuys, O., 2001, 'Who Profits from Child Labor ?' (Children Labor and Reproduction), Amsterdam : University of Amsterdam.

OIT, 1999, « Convention n° 182 sur les pires formes de travail », *Bulletin Officiel du Travail, de l'Emploi et de la Formation professionnelle No 2001/22 du 05/12/ 2001, Journal officiel du 18/ 11/ 2001.*

ONU, 2000, Sommet du Millénaire de septembre.

ONU, 1989, Convention on the Rights of the Child (Adopted by the General Assembly of the United Nations on 20 November.

OSD (Orientations Stratégiques de Développement) du Bénin, 2006-2011, Cotonou, République du Bénin.

Osofsky, J. D., 1999, « The Impact of Violence on Children », *The Future of Children-Domestic Violence and Children*, Vol. 9, no. 3, Louisiana State University.

Pilon, M., 1997, Ménages et familles en Afrique (Approches des dynamiques contemporaines) Séminaire CDEP-ENSEA-INS-ORSTOM-URD, Centre for Afrikastudier, Paris: CDEP, Vol. 15.

PNUD, M. S., 2006, Stratégies pour l'atteinte des OMD, août.

Rapport national du Bénin sur le Suivi du Sommet mondial pour les enfants (Cotonou, décembre 2000), Cotonou, République du Bénin.

Richter, L., 2004, *The Importance of Caregiver-Child Interactions for the Survival and Healthy Development of Young Children,* Genève: Organisation Mondiale de la Santé.

Stratégie de Croissance pour la Réduction de la Pauvreté (SCRP) sur la période 2007-2009, Cotonou, République du Bénin.

UNFPA, 2000, *État des populations dans le monde*, New York: UNFPA.

UNICEF, 2004, *Analyse régionale sur l'exploitation sexuelle en Afrique de l'Ouest et du Centre : évolution de la situation, progrès accomplis et obstacles à surmonter depuis le Congrès de Yokohama en 2001*. UNICEF, West and Central Africa Regional Office.

UNICEF, 2005, *Memories of Childhood Violence*, Eastern and Southern Africa, Regional Office.

UNICEF, 2006, *Derrière les portes closes (L'impact de la violence domestique sur les enfants). Traduction du rapport rédigé conjointement par The Body Shop International, l'UNICEF et le Secrétaire Général des Nations Unies.*

UNICEF, 2006, « Rapport annuel de l'Observatoire des droits de l'enfant de la région océan indien », *La violence contre les enfants dans la région de l'océan indien. Mauritius,* New York: UNICEF.

UNICEF, 2007, *The State of the World's Children 2007*, New York: UNICEF.

Vision de l'enfant au 21e siècle, Rapport de la réunion régionale de novembre 1999 à Abidjan, Abidjan, Côte d'Ivoire.

Weber, S., 1976, *Modèles dominants et aspirations à l'éducation. Un exemple au Brésil,* Paris: CNRS.

WHO, 2002, *Preventing Child Maltreatment : A Guide to Taking Action and Generating Evidence,* Geneva: WHO.

Youssef, R. M. et al., 1998, 'Children Experiencing Violence (ii) : Prevalence and Determinants of Corporal Punishment in Schools', in *Child Abuse & Neglect,* 22: 975–985.

8

Problématique du travail des enfants et stratégies de survie au Congo Brazzaville

Etanislas Ngodi

Le Congo Brazzaville connaît actuellement une situation fortement marquée par les effets des crises socio-économiques et des mutations culturelles d'une part, et d'autre part, par les conséquences des conflits armés de ces dernières années. Cette dynamique interne a entraîné le développement du secteur informel en milieu jeune. Le travail des enfants qui s'inscrit dans ce contexte semble lié aux stratégies de survie et d'accumulation. L'ampleur du phénomène demeure difficile à évaluer, compte tenu de l'absence des travaux en sciences sociales sur la complexité du phénomène des enfants et surtout des données statistiques. D'où l'intérêt de cette contribution qui se propose d'examiner la place du travail des enfants dans les dynamiques économiques et sociales au Congo, en relation avec la pauvreté et les stratégies de survie des enfants.

Au regard de l'émergence d'un système de débrouillardise, un questionnement apparaît nécessaire pour comprendre les dynamiques et les perspectives historiques sur le rôle des enfants dans le processus du travail. Trois questions peuvent constituer l'ossature de ce travail : Pourquoi le travail des enfants au Congo Brazzaville ? Quelles sont les activités qui concourent aux stratégies de survie des enfants ? Quel est le rôle de l'État et la place des législations face à ce fléau social ?

Ambiguïté et contexte du travail des enfants au Congo Brazzaville

Défis d'une approche méthodologique

Le problème du travail des enfants au Congo Brazzaville montre la nécessité de disposer des statistiques plus précises et détaillées. Or, à notre parfaite connaissance, les sources disponibles ne sont généralement pas adaptées pour mieux saisir l'ampleur du phénomène. Il y a quelques années, le Bureau International du Travail (BIT) avait publié le chiffre de 250 millions d'enfants au travail dans le monde. Ce chiffre a été repris dans nombreuses publications et par diverses organisations pour stigmatiser le phénomène. Ces données ont montré la nécessité de disposer de statistiques actualisées pour les différents pays.

Au Congo, l'analyse du marché du travail se heurte à la faiblesse de l'information statistique disponible. Les sources statistiques classiques (recensements, enquêtes) ne sont généralement pas adaptés pour saisir le travail des enfants. L'analyse s'observe à trois niveaux.

- En premier lieu, l'information relative au travail des enfants est fragmentaire. Les investigations réalisées par des services statistiques (CNSEE, ONEMO) sont fort peu nombreuses et ne permettent surtout pas de mieux explorer le phénomène. Les recensements et enquêtes auprès des ménages ne tiennent pas souvent compte de la contribution des enfants. Cela s'explique par plusieurs raisons : tout d'abord l'enfant est défini comme une personne de moins de 18 ans conformément à la Convention des Nations Unies relative aux droits de l'enfant (1989) et à la Convention 182 du BIT sur les pires formes de travail de l'enfant (1999). En conséquence, le travail des enfants est souvent minoré. Ensuite, les questions sur l'activité telles que définies dans les questionnaires des recensements ne s'adressent souvent qu'aux personnes au-dessus d'un certain âge. Ce qui complexifie d'ailleurs le phénomène. Enfin, l'attention accordée souvent aux enfants de la rue comme groupe cible engagé dans le marché du travail.
- En second lieu, les insuffisances conceptuelles contribuent à renforcer la faiblesse quantitative de l'information statistique relative au travail des enfants. La définition de l'enfant tient compte des dispositions législatives, fixant l'âge de 18 ans. Quant au travail, il découle qu'il s'agit des activités économiques au sens de la comptabilité nationale, c'est-à-dire que le travail couvre toutes les activités destinées à une production qui sera soit commercialisée, soit auto-consommée. D'après l'UNICEF, une distinction devrait être établie entre le travail acceptable et le travail intolérable qui participe à l'exploitation sociale de l'enfant. En effet, le travail acceptable procure à l'enfant assurance et fierté, assure sa formation même si par ailleurs il ne préserve pas « sa scolarité, son repos et son loisir ». Le travail intolérable par contre considéré comme les pires formes de travail des enfants entrave le développement physique et mental de l'enfant.
- En troisième lieu, la précarité des informations est accentuée par l'incertitude méthodologique des études disponibles. D'une part, la représentativité des échantillons n'est pas toujours assurée et d'autre part, l'exploitation des données demeure parfois très partielle, faute de méthodologies.

Aujourd'hui, l'insuffisance des données chiffrées ne permet pas d'avancer des chiffres sur le nombre d'enfants impliqués dans le marché du travail au Congo Brazzaville. L'absence des enquêtes nationales n'offre donc pas la possibilité de quantifier et/ou mesurer l'importance du travail des enfants, sa distribution géographique et les tendances de son développement dans le pays. Dans les quelques rapports disponibles, on note deux approches. D'un côté, l'approche protectionniste défendue par les organisations du système des nations unies (UNICEF, Banque Mondiale, FNUAP) qui abordent le travail des enfants sous l'angle de l'exploitation et de la victimisation et de l'autre l'approche socio-économique qui sous-tend le travail des enfants dans le cadre surtout des stratégies de la socialisation. On présente très souvent les enfants comme des couches marginalisées et exclues des processus économiques et qui cherchent des moyens d'assurer leur subsistance et atténuer les conditions d'extrême pauvreté. Ce qui fait intervenir la notion de stratégies de survie, appréhendée comme une nouvelle méthodologie de recherche qui permet de rendre compte et interpréter les activités des enfants.

L'ambiguïté du phénomène du travail des enfants nécessite une approche interdisciplinaire. La multiplication des activités, la mobilité des enfants et les difficultés liées aux définitions des concepts sont autant de problèmes d'ordre méthodologique.

Spécificités nationales et travail des enfants

Le travail des enfants au Congo Brazzaville trouve sa place dans un contexte de crise généralisée. La compréhension des dynamiques de ce fléau social nécessite la mise en perspective de la situation socio-économique et politique des années 1980 et 1990. Il convient de ce fait de distinguer le cadre macro-économique du Congo, la crise socio-culturelle et les crises politiques successives.

Contexte socio-économique

Le travail des enfants au Congo constitue la conjoncture de plusieurs éléments déterminants. le phénomène peut être appréhendé à travers multiples facettes. En effet, le contexte macro-économique issu des programmes d'ajustement structurel des années 1980, les rigidités structurelles et l'absence relative des politiques de l'emploi ont contribué à exacerber les déséquilibres sur le marché du travail. Ce contexte caractérisé surtout par la récession économique, les migrations des ruraux vers les centres urbains et l'inadaptation du système éducatif ont aggravé la crise. La réorientation de la politique économique a eu des répercussions sensibles sur l'emploi. D'une part, les licenciements liés à la restructuration du secteur para-public favorisent le chômage et d'autre part, des mesures de limitation des recrutements à la fonction publique aggravent le désœuvrement des couches sociales.

Le contexte macro-économique de l'économie a exercé de puissants effets sur le marché du travail. Il a contribué à réduire les revenus de plusieurs groupes vulnérables. Le ralentissement du processus économique explique la mise en œuvre au cours des années 1980 des programmes d'ajustement structurels avec l'appui du FMI et de la Banque mondiale. Ces programmes remettent en cause l'intervention de l'État dans le domaine économique et social, par le biais d'une régulation conjoncturelle et d'une normalisation structurelle. Ce rééquilibrage macro-économique a affecté tout le secteur public. Les différentes reformes macro-économiques mises en œuvre sous forme de programmes d'ajustement structurel ont en effet imposé des restrictions budgétaires drastiques à l'État, obligé de se désengager des charges sociales. La crise de ces programmes s'est traduite par des déséquilibres budgétaires, l'aggravation de la dette, le désengagement de l'État, le développement du secteur informel. Il s'ensuit la suppression des emplois, l'arrêt des recrutements dans la fonction publique, les licenciements. Ce qui va sans doute avoir des incidences dans la gestion des familles. À cet égard, la rue apparaît comme un espace de bien-être, de développement de sociabilité, d'apprentissage et de travail pour les acteurs sociaux, dont les enfants.

Dès lors, les modèles de vie deviennent de plus en plus dépravés, créant du coup des conditions qui rendent difficile l'expression des groupes sociaux. La précarité socio-économique, la dégradation des conditions scolaire, le manque d'insertion sociale, la dépravation des mœurs et des valeurs morales, l'alcoolisme et le tabagisme sont autant de manifestations de cette crise multisectorielle. Le chômage et la généralisation de la crise entraînent des comportements anormaux dans la société congolaise : placement des enfants, exploitation du travail des enfants, prostitution, etc.

Les rapports sont de plus en plus mercantilisés du fait de la promotion des valeurs inadaptées à l'idéal humain. Cette dégradation des valeurs morales de référence s'empire avec les conflits armés. Les différentes crises politiques en effet ont accentué la détérioration du contexte macro-économique, la destruction du tissu social et les principales unités de production. C'est ce contexte ambigu qui permet d'envisager la problématique du travail des enfants au Congo Brazzaville. Les enfants évoquent dans le marché du travail, le moyen de faire face aux conditions de vie difficiles, à la misère des parents, au manque de soutien et à la survie. L'économie des moyens consiste à travailler pour le bien être de tous. Le processus du travail des enfants intervient dans les relations de survie, de sociabilité et de reproduction sociale.

Déliquescence de l'État

Dans le contexte du cheminement du développement du Congo et de l'évolution récente de l'environnement macro-économique, l'appréciation du marché du travail en liaison avec la pauvreté revêt une importance particulière. En effet, la précarité de la situation économique et sociale a entraîné la déconfiture de l'État au Congo. Le ralentissement de la transition économique, aggravé par la faiblesse administrative et institutionnelle à gérer la crise a eu des répercussions énormes dans la vulnérabilité des enfants : pauvreté des parents, manque de soutien, émigration et/ou chômage.

La force la plus puissante qui a poussé les enfants à un travail dangereux et débilitant sera donc l'exploitation de la pauvreté. Pour une famille pauvre, la petite contribution du revenu d'un enfant ou l'aide qu'il apporte à la maison et qui permet à ses parents d'occuper un emploi peut faire toute la différence entre la faim et la satisfaction des besoins élémentaires. Les parents des enfants qui travaillent sont souvent sans emploi ou sous-employés, et ils recherchent désespérément un travail qui leur procure des revenus sûrs. Alors, pourquoi est-ce à leurs enfants qu'on offre un emploi ? Parce qu'on peut payer les enfants moins cher ; parce qu'ils sont plus dociles, plus malléables (on peut en général leur demander tout ce qu'on veut ; ils remettent rarement en question l'autorité) ; parce qu'ils risquent moins de s'organiser contre l'oppression et ne répondent pas aux coups. (UNICEF 1997).

La vulnérabilité des enfants permet de voir la dimension symbolique et instrumentale des pratiques de survie des enfants pour s'accommoder de la culture de débrouillardise. Le travail permet le développement du processus de sociabilité, d'apprentissage, de socialisation et d'affiliations diverses. L'influence des variables socio-économique des ménages semble nécessaire. Le taux de pauvreté très élevé dans les ménages entraîne le processus d'instabilité familiale. Il s'ensuit des divorces, le manque de ressources, l'encouragement des enfants à intégrer le processus du travail et les dislocations multiples. L'incapacité des ménages à satisfaire leurs besoins essentiels met à profit la main d'œuvre infantile. La déstructuration familiale a une grande influence sur le travail des enfants. Dans les conditions de précarité économique, il est clair que le travail précoce devient un impératif qui s'impose. Le manque de soutien justifie l'implication des enfants dans le processus du travail.

Plusieurs recherches à travers le monde ont débouché sur la conclusion selon laquelle, la pauvreté est la cause principale du travail des enfants et des jeunes. (Bernard Schlemmer 1996). La pauvreté est généralement avancée pour légitimer le travail des enfants. En effet, dans la plupart des pays en développement, l'incidence des crises économiques a eu pour conséquence le développement du secteur informel et le recrutement de la main-d'œuvre infantile. Dans le cas du Congo, du fait de la pauvreté, de nombreux parents n'hésitent pas à abandonner leurs enfants ou de les inciter dans le processus du travail. La socialisation de l'enfant par le travail fait de la pauvreté une véritable monnaie d'échange de la misère des parents. Ce qui induit une demande importante d'enfants dans la perspective de satisfaire les besoins élémentaires de la famille.

Le désengagement de l'État du secteur socio-économique va entraîner l'accentuation des déséquilibres sur le marché du travail, inhérents à la déstabilisation de l'économie, l'expansion de l'emploi dans le secteur informel. Dans ce contexte, l'existence du phénomène du travail des enfants peut être imputable à la déscolarisation et non scolarisation des enfants. La baisse du taux de scolarisation au cycle primaire ces dernières années passant de 98,6 pour cent en 1987 à 79 pour cent en 1998 démontre la situation de récession économique généralisée. Les couches défavorisées deviennent les candidats potentiels et effectifs du travail précoce. La déscolarisation et la non scolarisation trouvent leurs origines aux récents développements de la crise socio-économique des années 1980 qui a plongé le Congo dans le marasme économique, les ruptures salariales, les réformes structurelles austères et aux conflits socio-politiques depuis 1993.

La perception de l'école par les groupes sociaux n'est pas toujours positive. La décision d'envoyer un enfant à l'école n'est pas seulement une question de dépenses, mais aussi une question de coût indirect substantiel en termes de travail. L'accès à l'école et l'obtention d'un diplôme ne garantissent pas de trouver un emploi au Congo. C'est pour ces raisons que certains parents ne perçoivent pas la nécessité de continuer à envoyer leurs enfants à l'école, mais préfèrent les orienter vers l'apprentissage d'un métier (menuiserie, maçonnerie, artisanat, commerce, etc.) au détriment de la scolarisation.

Les conflits armés

Depuis 1990, on assiste à plusieurs bouleversements et recompositions internes au Congo Brazzaville. Les avatars du système des partis uniques, l'endettement progressif, le bidouillage politique, la dénaturation des pouvoirs, la prédation et la criminalisation de l'économie du fait des programmes d'ajustement structurels et de la corruption, les conflits armés ont participé à la faillite de l'État congolais. La violence est apparue comme un mode de production, de redistribution du pouvoir, un moyen de sécurisation économique, un circuit d'ascension politique et de recomposition des élites. Ce qui va sans doute contribuer à fonder une rupture sociale dans le champ politique, l'échec de la socialisation, la perte des valeurs, les inégalités du développement et la marginalisation des couches sociales. La dynamique de la gestion harmonieuse et intégratrice des contradictions politiques conduit à la mise en place des stratégies de reclassement, de revalorisation et d'intégration dans le système global de survie des groupes sociaux. La croissance de la pauvreté, l'aggravation des déficits budgétaires, la progression rapide du chômage, la réduction des dépenses sociales viennent s'ajouter à la désalarisation et la mort de l'État providence.

La crise de l'État sous ses différents aspects amène dans les rues des cohortes de désœuvrés, accélérant de ce fait le phénomène du travail des enfants. Les conflits armés ont donc accéléré le phénomène du travail des enfants.

Activités et conditions de travail des enfants au Congo Brazzaville

Le travail des enfants au Congo Brazzaville a atteint ces dernières années des proportions inquiétantes suite à la démission de l'État et à l'ampleur du désastre économique. Ceci est d'autant plus vrai que les activités enfants liées à la survie se développent de manière dangereuse et incontrôlée dans les différents centres urbains congolais. Les marginalisés ne savent plus à quel saint se vouer pour survivre. D'où la restauration de l'appareil étatique est un impératif qui s'impose.

Problèmes de classification des activités

La classification des activités des enfants dans les centres urbains congolais paraît complexe. Dans l'accroissement des activités informelles à Brazzaville, les enfants jouent un rôle moteur. On ne peut compter la quantité inquiétante d'enfants qui travaillent dans la rue et pratiquent ce qu'il convient d'appeler les petits métiers du secteur informel. Les enfants et les jeunes y trouvent dans le secteur informel un moyen de survie et de repositionnement. Ce secteur joue un rôle d'adoption et d'accueil des migrants et des marginalisés des centres urbains.

Les enfants travailleurs sont constitués par des garçons et filles. Mais la proportion la plus importante est celle des garçons (70 pour cent). La plupart des enfants travaillent, d'une manière ou d'une autre. Le type de travail qu'ils effectuent varie selon les sociétés et les époques. Le travail peut être une partie essentielle de l'éducation d'un enfant et un moyen de transmission d'un précieux savoir-faire parental. Dans certains pays, les enfants aident souvent à l'atelier ou dans un petit commerce, acquérant ainsi avec le temps les compétences d'un professionnel. Ailleurs, des adolescents travaillent quelques heures par semaine pour se faire de l'argent de poche. De l'avis du Fonds des Nations unies pour l'enfance, ce genre de travail est bénéfique, renforçant ou favorisant le développement physique, mental, spirituel, moral ou social de l'enfant sans compromettre sa scolarité, ses loisirs et son repos.

C'est une autre réalité que désigne l'expression « travail des enfants ». On parle de ces enfants qui travaillent de longues heures pour des salaires de misère, souvent dans des conditions dangereuses pour la santé. Ce type de travail « est manifestement destructeur ou synonyme d'exploitation ». Car l'exploitation des enfants comme prostitués n'est pas acceptable en quelque circonstance que ce soit. La même chose est vraie du « travail des enfants en servitude », expression employée largement pour désigner la mise en esclavage de fait des enfants pour rembourser les dettes contractées par leurs parents ou leurs grands-parents. Et également des industries connues pour les graves risques qu'elles présentent pour la santé et la sécurité. On ne saurait tolérer que des enfants, quels qu'ils soient, puissent être employés à ces travaux dangereux (UNICEF 1997).

La plupart des enfants qui travaillent sont des domestiques, qu'on a qualifiés d'enfants « les plus oubliés du monde ». Le travail de maison n'est pas forcément dangereux, mais il l'est souvent. Les enfants placés en servitude domestique sont souvent mal payés, si tant est qu'ils le soient. Leurs conditions de travail dépendent entièrement des caprices de leur maître. Les petits domestiques sont privés d'affection, d'école, de jeu et d'activités sociales. Qui plus est, ils sont exposés à la violence physique et aux agressions sexuelles. Une autre forme est l'exploitation sexuelle des enfants à des fins commerciales. On estime que, chaque année dans le monde, au moins un million de jeunes filles tombent par naïveté dans les griffes de proxénètes. Les garçons aussi sont souvent exploités. Par les dommages physiques et affectifs qu'elle inflige – sans parler de l'infection par le VIH –, cette exploitation est l'une des formes de travail des enfants les plus dangereuses (Unicef 2002, 2003).

Un fort pourcentage d'enfants exercent divers métiers qui sont la vente, la mécanique, la soudure, la restauration. Certains sont à des tâches que l'on jugerait trop dangereuses pour des adultes. Beaucoup souffrent de tuberculose, de bronchite ou d'asthme. Des milliers d'autres enfants ont fait de la rue leur lieu de travail. Ils exercent des petits commerces comme activités productrices. De nombreux enfants travaillent dans les marchés, dépôts, terminus de bus. Le petit commerce fixe ou ambulant vient largement en tête, ils sont des milliers à proposer des sachets d'eau et divers produits dans les lieux publics. Environ 52 petits métiers ont été identifiés : Petit commerce (vente à la sauvette des petits articles, de l'eau ; vente dans les kiosques et placards) ; Prestations de service (chargement de bus ; portage des colis et bagages ; lavage des voitures ; démarcheurs ; vidangeurs des latrines ; domestiques ; prostitution ; serveurs dans les bars et restaurants) ; Artisanat (cordonniers ambulants ; cireurs des chaussures ; souffleurs dans les ateliers de fabriques de marmites, de bijouterie, de tôlerie ; apprentis dans les ateliers de menuiserie/maçonnerie, de mécanique, d'électricité, de plomberie, de vulcanisation, de sculpture, de vannerie ou de poterie) ou les loisirs (animateurs des radio-matanga ; danseurs, chanteurs ; disco joker).

Les enfants sont souvent amenés à mettre en œuvre la stratégie consistant à mener plusieurs activités à la fois. Ils sont tantôt cireurs, porteurs, vendeurs, serveurs, mendiants, tantôt shayeurs (commerçants ambulants), fouilleurs de poubelles, ramasseurs d'ordures, laveurs ou gardiens de voiture ou tout simplement domestique ou apprentis. Dans le processus du travail des enfants, le secteur informel intervient comme stratégie de lutte contre la pauvreté, phénomène crucial qui menace la stabilité du pays et surtout son développement durable.

Situation de construction sociale

Le travail des enfants constitue une nouvelle approche dans les sciences sociales, permettant de rendre compte des processus de positionnement social, d'appropriation fictive et de production des biens de services à l'œuvre. L'état de vulnérabilité de pauvreté et d'exclusion des enfants sensés développer des stratégies de survie, incite à y réfléchir. La précarité des conditions de travail des enfants s'explique par l'absence de consensus sur le volume du travail, l'inadaptation des contrats, l'âge minimum d'admissibilité au travail et les types d'activités appropriées.

Certains enfants travaillent plus de 12 heures par jour, alors que la durée journalière de travail est de 8 heures pour les adultes. Les filles font beaucoup plus de l'aide familiale extérieure (commerce) et elles ne perçoivent qu'un repas en compensation. Ces enfants subissent des conditions d'exploitation extrême et ne bénéficient d'aucun encadrement, d'aucune aide psychologique ou matériel et pire encore d'aucune protection sociale.

Le rôle des enfants dans les transformations sociales et le développement économique est parfois interprété dans le sens de victimisation de l'enfant. C'est dans ce cadre qu'il convient de parler de « l'exploitation » en adoptant une vision marxiste qui renvoie à la confiscation d'un surtravail. Les activités que les enfants entreprennent qu'elles soient légales ou marginales, répondent à la culture de rue. La rue constitue dans le processus du travail des enfants, l'espace ou s'opérationnalise et se développe de nombreux problèmes vécus (maladie, violence, prostitution, décrochage scolaire.). Elle est aussi un espace de travail, de vie, de bien-être et de développement (sociabilité, apprentissage, socialisation et affiliation diverses).

Le travail expose les enfants à divers dangers tant pour la santé et le développement psychique. On note la consommation abusive de drogues et de stupéfiants, l'exposition des enfants à divers produits toxiques, la contravention de la loi et les conditions pénibles du travail. Les enfants ne cotisent à aucun fonds de retraite et n'appartiennent à aucun syndicat. Les congés sont inconnus, ils sont mal payés, la sécurité sociale hors de propos, etc.

La conséquence du phénomène du travail des enfants est que des dizaines de millions d'enfants sont exposés à de grands dangers. Ces dangers peuvent venir de la nature du travail ou des conditions dans lesquelles il est accompli. Les accidents du travail sont plus graves chez les enfants et les adolescents que chez les adultes. Tout d'abord parce que l'anatomie d'un enfant diffère de celle d'un adulte ; son bassin et sa colonne vertébrale peuvent facilement se déformer s'il porte du lourd. Ensuite parce qu'un enfant est plus vulnérable qu'un adulte aux radiations et aux substances chimiques toxiques. Les risques de maladies professionnelles, les troubles de croissance peuvent altérer les capacités physiques et mentales de l'enfant durant toute sa vie active. En effet, les maladies contractées par les enfants dans le cadre du travail sont nombreuses : paludisme, céphalées, maux de tête, crise de nerf, fièvre, diarrhées ou dysenterie, carie dentaire, gale, plaie, teigne, maux de côtes, rhume, toux, épilepsie, hémorroïde, vertiges, varicelle, hernie, angine, courbatures, oreillons, fièvre jaune, colopathie, appendicite, anémie, etc. De plus, les enfants ne sont pas physiquement aptes à supporter de longues heures d'un travail épuisant et monotone qui est très souvent leur lot. Enfin, la plupart des enfants n'ont pas conscience du danger et ne savent pas grand-chose des précautions à respecter.

La jeune fille, dans le processus du travail est exposée et s'expose. Dans le domaine musical, par exemple, la jeune fille est exposée sur la scène musicale comme une marchandise, dressant la victime sur le chemin de la prostitution avec le risque évident de la contamination et la propagation du VIH/SIDA.

Dans la domesticité, il s'établit très souvent un type de relation d'exploitation masquée par un paternalisme mal défini. La fille ainsi engagée n'a pas de tâche précise à accomplir, répond à la demande comme tout enfant le ferait dans sa famille et même au-delà et fait face aux mille et un besoins de son employeur : ménage, gardiennage, courses au marché, etc. Il y a une sorte de domestication des rapports de travail avec toutes les conséquences y afférentes. Il ressort que la jeune fille est oppressée par une double exploitation : au niveau de ses employeurs (travail sous-rémunéré, mal défini, non respect des heures de travail légales, manque d'un contrat de travail établi en bonne et due forme sous prétexte de sa minorité, maltraitance, simulacre d'adoption, etc.), et au niveau de ses parents (usurpation quelquefois du droit de jouir de son salaire). La domesticité est aussi un facteur favorisant les abus sexuels de toute sorte.

Cette situation précaire dans laquelle travaillent les enfants pose le problème de protection des enfants et de respect des chartes et conventions ratifiées au niveau national et international par le Congo Brazzaville.

Les effets de l'exploitation sur le développement psychologique, affectif et intellectuel des victimes sont graves eux aussi. Les enfants sont privés d'affection. Coups, insultes, privations punitives de nourriture et agressions sexuelles sont très fréquents. Ainsi la plupart des enfants qui travaillent sont condamnés à connaître toute leur vie pauvreté, malheur, maladie, analphabétisme et échec social.

En outre lorsqu'un enfant donne sa confiance, il la donne entièrement, sans réserve. Si donc cette confiance est trahie, les répercussions sur le jeune esprit sans défiance sont terribles. Des personnes et des lieux autrefois synonymes de sécurité ou de soutien sont devenus sources de danger et de crainte. Le monde de l'enfant est de moins en moins prévisible et maîtrisable (Kelly 1997).

Conséquence de ces actes horribles, dont beaucoup se commettent pendant des années, certains enfants grandissent avec des difficultés relationnelles et psychiques qu'ils gardent à l'âge adulte. Si l'enfant reste tant meurtri une fois sa confiance trahie, c'est parce qu'on a profité de lui pour la raison qu'il est un enfant. Cependant, beaucoup d'enfants agressés sexuellement n'en parlent jamais, réaction que les pervers escomptent bien. Ces dernières années, de plus en plus de cas de maltraitance d'enfants sont signalés partout dans le monde, de sorte qu'aujourd'hui l'accumulation est telle qu'on ne peut pas nier ou ignorer les faits. Dans ce contexte vouloir éradiquer le phénomène de l'exploitation des enfants, c'est s'attaquer à un géant.

Stratégies de survie ou de débrouille des enfants

Niveaux de survie et zones d'action

On entend par stratégie de survie, toute activité, qui vise à renforcer le pouvoir d'achat et à lutter contre la misère. Cette dernière est un des principaux facteurs de désintégration des familles. Ces stratégies sont un palliatif à un ordre socio-économique défaillant. Toutes les activités liées à la débrouille font partie de ces nouveaux canaux de repositionnement et de survie. La notion de stratégies de survie s'applique à des populations très défavorisées. Elle intervient comme réponse à la compréhension et à l'interprétation des conditions d'existence des couches marginales ou exclues des progrès économiques.

C'est dans ce cadre de manque que le travail apparaît comme mode de recomposition des équilibres sociaux. Dans cette trajectoire, les enfants qui se lancent dans le processus du travail cherchent des moyens d'assurer leur subsistance ou d'atténuer leur condition de vie. (Schoemaker 1987). Les stratégies économiques consistent à maximiser le nombre de personnes qui participent aux activités rentables de l'unité domestique. Elles dépendent des facteurs démographiques, aussi bien de tout un ensemble de mouvements sociaux qui interagissent entre eux, impliquant d'autres dimensions et indicateurs sociologiques. Misère et survie apparaissent comme un couple difficile à départager dans les villes congolaises. Il découle de cette adresse que la jeunesse est, de plein pied dans les activités de survie à cause du contexte social dans lequel elle évolue. Les différentes stratégies servent dans le réaménagement des fonctions à l'intérieur des communautés (Duque et Pastrana 1973:177).

Pour faire face à la crise généralisée, il se dessine des espaces de repositionnement qui permettent aux exclus sociaux de survivre. La participation économique de chaque membre de l'unité familiale semble nécessaire. La socialisation par le travail dénote une certaine vision des choses. Le travail des enfants apparaît donc comme un signe de responsabilité, de discipline et d'honnêteté de la part de l'enfant. La survie des enfants par l'exercice des métiers précaires apparaît sans conteste dans les villes congolaises. En proie au dénuement profond, les enfants dont l'âge oscille entre 7 et 18 ans se trouvent être condamnés à pratiquer les petits métiers susmentionnés qui, sans doute, ne procure pas grand-chose à sa victime si ce n'est l'apaisement journalier de la famine. La maturité sociale des enfants qui ne dépend pas nécessairement de l'âge est la condition sine qua non de leur insertion sociale.

D'après les enfants enquêtés à Brazzaville, ils se considèrent matures et socialement disposés à participer aux activités économiques qui leur permettent de survivre. La manière la plus commune pour gagner de l'argent est mendier, vendre, porter, voler, nettoyer, laver ou ramasser. Pour de nombreuses filles, se prostituer ou servir sont des verbes courants. Et pourtant, ces enfants appartiennent à la tranche d'âge de 8 à 17 ans. Les enfants travailleurs sont très actifs dans l'économie informelle. Leurs activités échappent au paiement des impôts (TVA, revenus, etc.), des charges sociales, ou au respect des législations. Ils sont parfois dans les activités mafieuses mettant en place des réseaux mafieux dans le cadre de la criminalisation même de l'État telles la contrebande, la contrefaçon, la corruption ou le recel de biens volés, le trafic de drogue, la prostitution, etc. L'émergence de cette nouvelle forme de capitalisme tend à prendre en ligne de compte les aspirations de toute une population paupérisée.

Les jeunes filles sont de plus en plus nombreuses dans le marché du travail. Certaines sont utilisées dans l'économie domestique des foyers et ménages. L'assistance ménagère s'est progressivement estompée pour devenir une opportunité économique ouverte à cette catégorie sociale. D'autres sont danseuses dans les orchestres, petites bonnes, vendeuses ou encore comme petites « londoniennes » dans la prostitution, la production pornographique et autres abus sexuels.

Opportunités et contributions économiques

Au Congo Brazzaville, face à la déconfiture et à la désertion des pouvoirs publics, le secteur informel a pris une importance considérable dans les milieux économiques. Les différentes activités de ce secteur jouent un rôle dynamique dans l'économie du fait de leur caractère rentable, productif et créatif. La contribution du secteur informel au PIB de l'économie non observée du pays est de 40 pour cent environ. La survie des populations entières en découle.

Même si aujourd'hui de nombreuses campagnes médiatiques sont menées dans le sens de la protection des enfants ou de la lutte contre l'exploitation des enfants dans le processus du travail, la problématique du travail des enfants dans les villes congolaises reste d'actualité. Elle suscite un intérêt croissant à cause des enjeux économiques et sociaux qui entourent la dynamique du travail. Les enfants dans de nombreuses familles pauvres sont considérés comme des travailleurs actifs, porteurs de stratégies de survie d'insertion et de changement. Dans la plupart du temps, les revenus obtenus par les enfants sont journaliers ou mensuels. Les revenus journaliers peuvent varier entre 500 et 10 000 F CFA selon les activités, les lieux ou points de stationnement et les périodes. Pour les enfants travaillant sous la direction des patrons, les revenus mensuels sont très loin du SMIG officiel (50 000 F CFA). Les enfants gagnent entre 5 000 et 15 000 F CFA. Pour les petites bonnes le revenu varie en fonction du volume horaire. Les salaires attribués sont de l'ordre de 7 000 à 25 000 F CFA. L'argent payé à la jeune fille n'est toujours pas considéré comme un véritable « salaire », mais plutôt comme une gratification, une récompense pour l'encourager dans ses efforts. Les « tuteurs » estiment qu'ils doivent trouver leur propre gratification aux efforts qu'ils consentent pour guider et protéger, former et contrôler la jeune fille sous leur autorité. Dès lors, les parents sont reconnaissants envers ceux qui d'une part les soulagent de leurs responsabilités et d'autre part leur permettent d'avoir de quoi se nourrir, résolvant de ce fait le problème de la socialisation de leur fille.

Les revenus du travail des enfants sont utilisés pour la survie. Les enfants ont tendance à assouvir les besoins élémentaires et des instincts de débrouillardise. Ce qui constitue parfois de supports pour de nombreuses familles. L'épargne vise à réaliser des projets pour l'amélioration des conditions de vie ; l'assistance aux parents ; l'achat des fournitures scolaires. Cette micro-économie se manifeste par la multiplication des fonctions productrices et renforce le rôle de l'enfant dans la reproduction sociale. Les bénéfices moyens réalisés mensuellement par plusieurs acteurs de l'informel confirment que ceux-ci vivent de leurs revenus. Ces revenus quoi que insuffisants sont utilisés pour la survie. Le niveau de profit et la valeur de ce travail demeurent précieux dans le contexte de précarité économique.

La revalorisation des stratégies de survie constitue aujourd'hui une nouvelle approche permettant de rendre compte des processus de positionnement social, de production et d'appropriation fictive des populations marginalisées. Ces stratégies dans le cas du Congo Brazzaville reflètent les imprécisions, les tensions dynamiques et les contradictions des processus d'intégration sociale des enfants dans une société qui connaît des mutations importantes. Au bout de compte, la participation des enfants dans la gestion familiale fait du travail un moyen de développer des sociabilités et des réseaux de survie des acteurs sociaux. Les différentes stratégies de survie développées influent sur les statuts et rôles attribués aux enfants dans la société congolaise.

Rôle et place de l'État et des législations au Congo Brazzaville

Le travail des enfants est un nouveau fléau social qui mérite d'être analysé par la communauté des chercheurs africains en Sciences sociales. Les stratégies de survie des enfants travailleurs s'inscrivent dans une vision diachronique et synchronique. Des solutions irréfléchies et non structurelles axées unilatéralement sur l'abolition immédiate du travail des enfants existent.

Conventions relatives au travail des enfants

Évolution historique des textes relatifs aux droits de l'enfant

Dans plusieurs sociétés, l'enfant a une place importante dans la famille, et pas seulement l'avenir de l'enfant, son futur établissement, mais sa présence et son existence nue. (Donzelot 1977:15). Dès lors, la protection de l'enfant apparaît nécessaire. Il apparaît clairement que vouloir le meilleur pour l'enfant, c'est aussi chercher à éradiquer le pire. Il a besoin d'être protégé et soigné pour éviter que le monde puisse le détruire. Mais ce monde aussi a besoin d'une protection qui l'empêche d'être dévasté et détruit par la vague de nouveaux venus qui déferle sur lui à chaque nouvelle génération (Arent 1972:239-240).

Il est de plus en plus reconnu aujourd'hui que la grande nouveauté du XXe siècle est l'apparition des droits de l'enfant. En Occident, le droit à la protection concerne la création des tribunaux pour enfant (1912), la suppression de l'incarcération (1935), la création du juge des enfants (1945) et la protection judiciaire (1958). Ces droits avaient fait l'objet d'une Déclaration des droits de l'enfant, par l'ONU en 1959.

La Convention internationale sur les droits de l'enfant adoptée en 1989 a été saluée par une surenchère emphatique dans les discours politiques de tout bord : il faut tout faire pour l'enfance. Cette Convention, tout en réaffirmant le droit à une protection, ajoute le droit aux libertés d'opinion, d'expression, de pensée, de conscience, de religion, d'association. Ce qui s'inscrit comme une pression sociale face à l'utilisation de l'enfant comme moyen de compréhension narcissique. Au terme d'une lecture attentive des 54 articles de la Convention, il convient de noter que tous les articles se valent et sont importants. Dans le domaine qui nous concerne, notamment le travail des enfants, la Convention mentionne la protection de l'enfant contre l'exploitation économique (Art.32) et sexuelle (Art.34), vente, trafic et enlèvement des enfants (Art.35). L'article 32 insiste sur la nécessité de protéger l'enfant contre les travaux forcés, dangereux et à hauts risque (industries, mines, etc.).

Au regard de cette Déclaration, de nombreux textes, influencés par le BIT et l'OMC ont été ratifiés. Les protocoles additionnels ont concerné la Résolution portant sur l'élimination des pires formes du travail des enfants de 1996, la Déclaration des principes fondamentaux du droit au travail de 1998 et à la Convention 182 en 1999.

Dilemmes développementaux et intervention des conventions internationales

Les différentes conventions internationales, notamment la Convention sur les droits de l'enfant et la Convention 182 mettent un accent particulier sur l'éradication des pires formes d'exploitation de l'enfant dans le processus du travail. Ce qui n'est d'ailleurs pas synonyme de mettre fin au travail des enfants. Il convient dans certaines conditions d'évaluer les coûts économiques de l'implication des enfants dans le marché du travail.

La Convention 182 stipule l'interdiction de recrutement d'un enfant de moins de 18 ans (Art.2), les pratiques de nouvelles formes d'esclavage comme le trafic des enfants, les recrutements forcés dans les conflits armés, la pornographie et la prostitution (Art.3). Nombreux sont les pays qui ratifient les conventions sans pouvoir les appliquer. On peut dès lors se demander quelles sont les obligations et motivations de ces textes internationaux sur la résolution des fléaux comme le travail des enfants. Le problème de base demeure sans doute l'occidentalisation des textes qui ne tiennent pas toujours compte des réalités sociales, culturelles, économiques ou politiques des pays africains.

L'influence des experts de l'OIT, des partenaires au développement et des bailleurs de fonds internationaux font faire certaines choses aux États africains. Aujourd'hui, les obstacles à l'applicabilité des Conventions internationales constituent des dilemmes dans le milieu des académiciens en Sciences sociales. La standardisation des normes internationales, la revalorisation des procédures de ratification des textes et la socialisation des enfants doivent constituer des éléments d'une nouvelle problématique. Si les lois internationales sont manipulées par les grandes puissances, il en est de même pour les protocoles additionnels et législations nationales qui remettent en cause le rôle des États. L'implication des ONG et des Institutions comme l'UNICEF dans la vulgarisation des idéaux visant la protection des enfants est d'un grand intérêt.

Législations nationales et politiques mises en œuvre

Il est encourageant de savoir que le travail des enfants est maintenant reconnu comme un problème mondial. Des initiatives telles que le congrès de Stockholm sur l'exploitation sexuelle des enfants à des fins commerciales, où 130 pays étaient représentés, ont contribué à attirer l'attention sur ce fléau. Par ailleurs, des pays légifèrent à présent contre le tourisme sexuel et la pornographie infantile. Certains même fichent les pédophiles connus et restreignent leurs possibilités de contacts avec des enfants. Il y a ceux aussi qui s'efforcent d'améliorer la vie des enfants en élaborant une législation de protection de l'enfance. Ceux enfin – pays ou personnes – qui boycottent les produits fabriqués par des enfants. On ne peut évidemment que saluer de tels efforts pour faire disparaître l'exploitation des enfants, mais il faut être réaliste et reconnaître que le phénomène est enraciné profondément dans la société humaine. Il serait naïf de penser qu'une solution aussi simple que l'élaboration de nouvelles lois offrira une protection totale aux enfants. Alors qu'on a déjà voté bien des lois, le problème perdure. Le fait qu'il faille protéger par un impressionnant arsenal législatif le droit naturel à avoir une enfance est en soi une mise en accusation des adultes crapuleux du monde.

Les lois ne protègent pas les enfants de façon absolue. Il suffit pour s'en convaincre de regarder les résultats de la formidable législation qu'est, par exemple, la Convention des droits de l'enfant, dont beaucoup d'États sont signataires. Or, on sait avec certitude que bon nombre de ces États, écrasés sous des contraintes économiques, ne font pas assez pour enrayer l'exploitation de leurs jeunes citoyens. La maltraitance des enfants demeure un problème international majeur.

Au Congo Brazzaville, les textes régissant le travail des enfants ne relèvent pas du hasard. Ils sont le résultat des Conventions et Chartes internationales. Les principales règles de loi sur l'âge minimum d'admissibilité au travail, le salaire, la durée du travail et le congé ne sont inscrites nulle part et font l'objet de polémique.

Étant donné que les enfants ont des aspirations professionnelles, ils sont donc disposés à apprendre un métier. Le système éducatif devrait tenir compte de leurs aspirations en diversifiant les possibilités éducatives par l'apprentissage des métiers adaptés aux besoins pratiques des enfants. Il convient aussi que la famille et l'État puissent orienter les enfants en tenant compte de leur prédisposition naturelle. Il convient de développer des programmes qui aboutissent non peut-être à éradiquer le travail des enfants, mais l'exploitation des enfants.

La question de l'enfance au Congo préoccupe aussi bien les pouvoirs publics que les associations et organisations non gouvernementales qui mettent en œuvre plusieurs stratégies. Au niveau gouvernemental, deux structures s'occupent de l'enfance en difficulté. Ce sont : l'Administration pénitentiaire et la Direction générale des Affaires sociales.

L'Administration pénitentiaire, relève du Ministère de la Justice (Direction de la Protection de l'Enfance et Direction de l'Éducation surveillée) et a pour mission d'assurer l'instruction des jeunes délinquants, la réinsertion sociale, la protection et l'assistance éducative des délinquants mineurs ou en danger moral. De nombreux enfants qui échappent à tout contrôle parental ou familial et social, intègrent difficilement ces structures. Ce qui développe les activités multiples des enfants dans les villes congolaises.

La Direction générale des Affaires sociales, placée sous la tutelle du Ministère de la Santé, de la Solidarité et de l'Action humanitaire se préoccupe aussi de la question de l'enfance difficile. Mais elle est actuellement marquée par des difficultés liées au manque de moyens financiers et de ressources humaines qualifiées. En somme, au niveau gouvernemental, le problème du travail des enfants reste entier. Les initiatives communautaires sont développées par des ONG et associations locales avec l'appui des bailleurs de fonds extérieurs et des institutions internationales. Elles comprennent principalement l'éducation des enfants. Dans les foyers, les stratégies consistent à l'assistance des enfants (alimentaire, soins médicaux, etc.), avec pour finalité leur réinsertion familiale, scolaire et professionnelle (placement en apprentissage chez les artisans).

L'encadrement et le soutien psychoaffectif sont ponctuels dans certains foyers (Père David, Don Bosco, la Maison de l'espoir, AMURT, le Centre Père Jarot, le Centre d'accueil Ndouenga, etc.). Ces structures accueillent, hébergent et assistent très souvent enfants orphelins, abandonnés ou en détresse. Ce qui ne règle pas le problème de survie des enfants qui vivent avec ou sans parents. La plupart de ces structures sont confrontées aux nombreux problèmes qui limitent leurs interventions : faiblesse et insuffisance des ressources financières et matérielles ; faible participation, insuffisance quantitative et qualitative des spécialistes ; extrême mobilité des enfants ; manque de coordination et de politiques conséquentes en matière du travail des enfants, etc.

La politique actuelle n'encourage pas les maisons ou les institutions d'accueil. Il existe un certain nombre de structures publiques et privées (Médecins d'Afrique) qui interviennent en matière d'aide auprès des orphelins et des enfants vulnérables. Quelques difficultés d'intervention ont été identifiées parmi lesquelles :

- le manque de moyens financiers et matériels qui entrave le développement de leurs actions ;
- le manque du professionnalisme et de formation du personnel, en particulier dans le domaine des compétences sociales et éducatives. Les intervenants auprès des enfants sont peu qualifiés, « formés » sur le tas. La plupart sont des bénévoles tout juste indemnisés pour leur transport, ce qui ne permet aux structures de capitaliser de l'expertise ;
- un travail de réseau peu développé, qui ne permet pas de miser sur la complémentarité et le renforcement mutuel et d'obtenir des économies d'échelle ;
- les conséquences matérielles et psychologiques de la guerre (dégâts matériels désorganisation des dispositifs de soutien, disparition totale des initiatives qui fonctionnaient avant la guerre).

Les approches de solution sur le travail des enfants doivent intégrer une vision systémique, pour obtenir une synergie des efforts dans l'orientation et l'encadrement des enfants. Ces approches impliquent toutes les institutions sociales : la famille, l'école, l'État, églises et autres organisations communautaires. Pour y parvenir il faut des stratégies d'intervention visant à promouvoir un développement humain durable dans lequel ressort de façon explicite la volonté d'assurer et de garantir les droits fondamentaux des enfants. La résorption du phénomène complexe du travail des enfants suppose que des spécialistes de l'enfance soient mobilisés pour questionner ces enfants-travailleurs et pour les orienter plus efficacement qu'ils ne le sont aujourd'hui. Nous pensons qu'il est difficile d'éradiquer le travail de l'enfant, mais ce qui convient de faire, c'est d'assainir les conditions de travail, de faire converger la nécessité de travailler, l'éthique professionnelle et le cadre éthique adéquat. Cette réglementation devrait fixer un certain nombre de principes : l'âge minimal, les conditions de travail, les salaires, etc.

Les stratégies à mettre en œuvre pour lutter contre l'exploitation des enfants dans le processus du travail doivent consister à :

- ouvrir l'accès aux opportunités d'emplois à tous en multipliant les investissements intérieurs capables de créer des effets d'entraînement ;
- assurer l'applicabilité des traités internationaux ratifiés, à l'instar de la Convention des Nations Unies du 20 novembre 1989 sur les Droits de l'Enfant et la Charte Africaine de 1990 relative au Droit et au Bien-Être de l'Enfant ;
- identifier les secteurs dans lesquels œuvrent le plus souvent les enfants, ce qui est difficilement évaluables aujourd'hui ; valoriser certaines activités actuellement exercées par les enfants en développant leur esprit d'entreprise ;
- promouvoir l'éducation à la vie familiale à l'école, dans les familles, dans les églises, dans les quartiers au moyen des campagnes d'Information-Éducation-Communication afin de sensibiliser les parents actuels et potentiels sur les responsabilités parentales vis-à-vis des enfants. Ce qui contribuera ainsi à diffuser la Convention relative aux Droits de l'Enfant ;
- mettre en place un système d'orientation scolaire tenant compte des aspirations et prédispositions personnelles des enfants. À côté de l'école actuelle qui

n'offre pas d'autres perspectives pour l'enfant qui ne s'y adapte pas, l'école des métiers par l'approche atelier d'apprentissage pourrait bien associer le besoin d'alphabétisation aux possibilités de réalisation sociale de l'enfant. Une revalorisation de l'école professionnelle est indispensable.

Conclusion

La problématique du travail des enfants au Congo Brazzaville doit être traitée à travers un processus pragmatique. La responsabilisation des États africains demeure au cœur de toutes les stratégies. Les organismes au développement et partenaires bilatéraux doivent soutenir les forces locales qui œuvrent à l'amélioration du bien-être des enfants. Le travail des enfants est une question complexe imbriquée dans la culture et l'économie d'une société. Le rôle de l'enfant dans la production sociale et la reproduction dans le cadre des relations de socialité et de survie ne doit pas être remis en jeu.

Références

Association Panafricaine Thomas Sankara (2000), *Réinsertion sociale des enfants de la rue à Brazzaville,* Brazzavill: UNESCO Congo.

Agnellis, S., 1986, *Les enfants de la rueel'autre visage de la ville*, Paris: Berger- Levraut.

Arent, H., 1972, *La crise de la culture*, Paris: Gallimard.

Banque Mondiale Congo, 2004, *Rapport d'enquête sur les orphelins de Moungali,* Brazzaville: BM.

Bonnet, M., 1999, *Le travail des enfants. Terrain de lutte*, Lausanne 20, Cahiers Libres.

Bonnet, M., 1992, « Le travail des enfants en Afrique », *Revue Internationale du Travail*, vol.732, 1993, n°3, BIT.

Bureau International du Travail, 1998, *Éradiquer les pires formes de travail des enfants. Guide pour la mise en œuvre de la convention n°182 de l'OIT.*

Celerier, I., 2002, « Comment protéger les futurs orphelins », *Bulletin Transcriptase Sud* n°106, p. 49.

Congo Brazzaville, 2000, *Rapport national sur le suivi du sommet mondial pour les enfants*, Décembre, Brazzaville.

Danzelot, J., 1977, *La police des familles*, Paris: Minuit.

Douma, J. B. et al, 2001, Les causes de mortalité des moins de 15 ans dans une ville africaine, cas de Pointe-Noire.

Hunter, S., 1990, 'Orphans as a Window on the AIDS epidemic in Sub-Sahara Africa : Initial Results and Implication of Study in Uganda', *SOC.SCI.MED*, 31, pp 681-690

Hunter, S. and Williamson, J., 2000, *Children on the Brink,* Executive Summary, USAID, pp. 1-10.

Kabwebwe, A., 1997, *Enquête méthodologiques et statistiques sur le travail des enfants,* Genève: BIT.

Kelly, C., 1998, *Child Abuse & Neglect,* UNICEF.

Laberge, D., 2000, *L'errance urbaine,* Montréal: Multi monde.

Lucchini, R., 1996, *Sociologie de survie*, Paris: PUF.

Makave, V., Ani, C. and Grantham-McGregor, 2002, 'Psychological Well-being of Orphans in Dar El Salaam', *Acta paediatr*, 346, pp. 1907-1910.

Massamba, H., 2002, Le travail des enfants en milieu urbain au Congo, Groupe de Recherche en Politique sociale (Grepolis). Brazzaville.

Manier, B., 1999, *Le travail des enfants dans le monde*, Paris: La Découverte.

Mendelievich., E., 1980, *Le travail des enfants*, BIT

Michel., G., 1998, « Enfants de, à, dans la rue », in *Langage et culture des enfants de la rue*, Paris: Karthala.

Mboussou, F., 2003, Situation des orphelins du VIH/Sida à Brazzaville in transcriptase n°111 Octobre.

Médecins d'Afrique (2004), Prise en charge des orphelins enfants vulnérables. Brazzaville.

Mukoyogo, C. M., Williamson, G., 1992, *Orphelins du SIDA : une perspective communautaire en Tanzanie, Londres*, Dar es Salam: Actionaid, AMREF, World in Need (Collection Stratégies pour l'Espoir n° 5), pp. 9-13. OMS, 2001, *Situation sanitaire au Congo*. Washington.

Palloni, A. and Julée, Y., 1992, 'Some Aspects of the Social Context of HIV and its Effects on Women, Children and Families', *Population Bulletin of United Nations*, 33, pp. 64 – 87.

PNUD, 2002, Analyse de la situation des femmes et des enfants du Congo de 1970 à 2000, Brazzaville.

Tessier, S., 1998, *À la recherche des enfants des rues*, Paris: Karthala.

Toto, J. P., 1999, « Déterminants économiques et socioculturels des enfants de la rue en Afrique : des développements méthodologiques récents » in, *La Population africaine au 21e siècle*, Troisième conférence africaine de la population, Durban/Afrique du Sud, 6-10 Décembre, vol. 3, pp. 355-364.

Toto, J. P., 1994, *Les enfants et les jeunes de la rue à Brazzaville*, Dakar: UEPA.

UNICEF, 1997, La situation des enfants dans le monde. New York.

UNICEF, 2000, Enquête sur les enfants qui vivent et travaillent dans la rue à Brazzaville.

UNICEF-Congo, 2001, Prise en charge des orphelins du SIDA à Brazzaville.

UNICEF-Congo, 2002, Analyse de la situation des enfants et femmes du Congo.

UNICEF, 1992, Analyse de la situation des enfants et des femmes au Congo, Brazzaville.

9

Étude sur le travail des enfants dans l'agriculture : Région de Meknès-Tafilalet, Maroc

Hassan Khalouki

L'enfant est placé à la croisée des chemins, il vit sous l'influence de la famille, du milieu géographique et socio-culturel dont il est issu ; la religion, l'histoire lui tracent les normes et le système de valeurs à suivre, l'enseignement qu'il reçoit, les médias auxquels il a accès, lui ouvrent de nouveaux horizons.

L'ensemble contribue à la formation de sa personnalité et à son insertion dans le circuit de production. Seulement les recherches et les travaux qui ont analysé tout ce processus se sont souvent limités à l'enfant en général sans distinction de sexes, la distinction des secteurs et des branches est souvent ignorée en faveur d'une perception urbaine et industrielle.

Le travail des enfants

Le travail des enfants constitue un phénomène largement répandu dans le monde, particulièrement dans les pays en développement. On estime que 250 millions d'enfants de 5 à 14 ans travaillent aujourd'hui dans le monde, souvent dans des conditions qui entravent gravement leur développement physique, émotionnel et spirituel. Un consensus s'établit progressivement au sein des gouvernements et de la société civile qui estiment que des efforts doivent être immédiatement déployés pour protéger tous les enfants contre les travaux qui nuisent à leur santé en adoptant des mesures préventives et en les soustrayant à des situations dangereuses.

Actuellement, il existe trois accords internationaux importants, qui sont complémentaires et fournissent un cadre aux politiques et aux progrès visant à lier éducation et abolition du travail des enfants, à savoir :

- la Convention relative aux droits de l'enfant (1989) ;
- la Convention 138 et la recommandation 146 (1973) de l'OIT sur l'âge minimum d'admission à l'emploi ;
- la Déclaration mondiale sur l'éducation pour tous (1990).

Au Maroc, le travail des enfants bien qu'il soit un phénomène très ancien et largement observé, reste très peu caractérisé et encore mal connu. Selon les dernières estimations de la direction de la statistique (Ministère du plan et de la prévision économique), sur 9,8 millions d'enfants, il y aurait environ 642 000 considérés comme actifs, soit 6,5 pour cent. Parmi ces enfants travailleurs, 82 pour cent se trouveraient en milieu rural (prés de 523 000 enfants).

Ces chiffres placent le Maroc parmi les pays les moins touchés par ce phénomène dans les pays en développement, particulièrement en Afrique où les taux d'enfants actifs dépassent 40 pour cent de la population d'enfants de moins de 14 ans. Toutefois, les estimations officielles sont à prendre avec beaucoup de précaution du fait qu'il s'agit d'un phénomène qui n'est pas toujours aisément déclaré et sa détection par des enquêtes de portée nationale est parfois très difficile.

Travail des enfants dans l'agriculture

Le travail des enfants dans l'agriculture est souvent invisible, parce qu'ils aident leurs parents dans leurs taches ou dans d'autres formes d'organisation du travail. Parce que ce travail n'est pas reconnu et qu'il n'émarge pas facilement aux statistiques, il passe largement inaperçu, ce qui crée un cycle de pauvreté et hypothèque l'avenir des enfants, puisque leur accès aux études et à la formation est fortement réduit.

Selon l'Organisation internationale du travail (OIT), l'agriculture fait partie des trois secteurs les plus dangereux pour les travailleurs (après les mines et la construction). La moitié de tous les décès liés au travail, relève du secteur agricole. Malheureusement, des enfants figurent parmi ces décès.

De par le monde, la plupart des enfants qui travaillent se trouvent dans les champs et dans les pêcheries, non dans des usines. Ce constat fondamental sur le travail des enfants est souvent ignoré en faveur d'une perception urbaine et industrielle de ce qu'est réellement le travail des enfants. Cette négligence du travail des enfants en milieu agricole, combinée à la perception largement répandue que les enfants qui travaillent dans les fermes sont moins à risque qu'en milieu urbain, continue de prévaloir aujourd'hui. Cette attitude culturelle véhicule une perception erronée du travail des enfants et fait en sorte que les lois qui devraient protéger les enfants ne s'appliquent pas dans la plupart des milieux agricoles où ils travaillent.

Cette négligence du travail des enfants en milieu rural s'explique par au moins cinq facteurs :

- ceux qui étudient les problèmes du travail des enfants et élaborent des programmes pour le combattre sont habituellement basés dans les villes et sont davantage susceptibles de concentrer leurs efforts sur les problèmes du milieu urbain, comme les enfants de la rue, qui sont visibles et à la portée de main ;
- les régions rurales sont souvent éloignées, au double plan géographique et culturel, ce qui empêche les chercheurs et les concepteurs de programmes, basés en ville, d'y passer de longues périodes ;

- le coût de la recherche sur le travail des enfants en milieu rural est relativement élevé du fait du temps et des exigences quantitatives et qualitatives en moyens humains qu'elle nécessite :
- dans plusieurs pays, les gouvernements mettent d'abord l'accent sur la situation urbaine, ce qui reflète souvent une négligence volontaire de la part des groupes d'intérêt ;
- plusieurs décideurs nationaux et internationaux supposent que le travail des enfants dans un environnement rural « idyllique » ne peut être néfaste pour les enfants, de fait, cette forme de « solidarité familiale » est perçue comme entièrement bénéfique.

En agriculture, la culture constitue un facteur extrêmement important dans la négligence de longue date du travail des enfants en milieu rural. La situation du travail des enfants dans le milieu rural reste très méconnue à travers le monde. Les données provenant de pays qui disposent de statistiques relativement fiables sur le travail ou d'études spécifiques sur le travail des enfants indiquent dans l'ensemble un pourcentage beaucoup plus élevé d'enfants travaillant en milieu rural qu'en milieu urbain, commençant à travailler plus jeunes (à 5, 6 ou 7 ans) et pouvant travailler un nombre de jours et d'heures plus élevé. Les fillettes sont particulièrement susceptibles de commencer à travailler plus jeunes et à se voir refuser l'accès à l'école.

Un rapport publié récemment par le BIT affirme que prés du tiers de la main d'œuvre agricole dans certains pays en développement est formée d'enfants. Ce n'est que récemment que des études spécifiques du BIT ont permis de prendre la mesure de la contribution du travail des enfants à la production d'aliment et de produits agricoles par pays.

Voici quelques cas d'études (Bangladesh, Brésil, Kenya, Malawi, Égypte) :

- *Bangladesh* : 82 pour cent des 6,1 millions d'enfants économiquement actifs, travaillent dans l'agriculture ;
- *Brésil* : 3 millions d'enfants travaillent dans les plantations de sisal, de thé, de canne à sucre et de tabac ;
- *Kenya* : les enfants forment le quart de la main-d'œuvre agricole ;
- *Malawi* : la majorité des enfants habitant dans les plantations de tabac y travaillent (78 pour cent des enfants ayant entre 10 et 14 ans et 55 pour cent des enfants de 7 à 9 ans) ;
- *Égypte*: plus d'un million d'enfants ayant entre 7 et 12 ans sont engagés chaque année dans la lutte contre les infestations de vers dans les feuilles de coton.
- *Maroc* : le monde rural abrite la plus grande densité des enfants qui travaillent pour le compte de leur propre famille ou pour de petites entreprises ou exploitations agricoles. Le travail au sein de l'enceinte familiale peut aller de la simple aide dans le ménage jusqu'au travail dans le champ dans des conditions physiques déplorables, en passant par l'approvisionnement en eau potable ou en combustibles (petites filles), la bergerie (petits garçons) et l'entretien et l'alimentation des animaux.

Le travail pour le compte de tiers prend des formes variées et dénote le plus souvent des conditions difficiles voire même dangereuses pour le développement normal des enfants. Ces travaux répondent à des objectifs à la fois économiques (réduction des charges de main d'œuvre de l'exploitation familiale, participation à la trésorerie de la famille,..), sociaux (participation dans le soutien de la cohésion de famille,..) et culturels (valeur du travail, valeur de l'argent, normes et schéma culturels admis,…).

Dans tous les cas, le travail des enfants est à la fois une cause et une conséquence du sous-développement local marqué par l'ampleur de la pauvreté, l'absence d'infrastructures de base et la marginalisation des ressources humaines particulièrement dans le milieu rural. Il empêche les enfants de fréquenter l'école et d'améliorer leur situation durablement.

Les conditions dans lesquelles beaucoup d'enfants travaillent en milieu rural sont méconnues au Maroc. Beaucoup de questionnements doivent être compris et élucidés afin d'asseoir une stratégie cohérente et efficace d'intervention en faveurs de ces enfants, notamment :

- Quels travaux agricoles sont exécutés par les enfants et dans quelles conditions ?
- Quelles sont les situations réelles de leur environnement quotidien ?
- Quels sont les impacts du travail des enfants en agriculture ?
- Quels sont les mécanismes qui régissent ce phénomène ?
- Quels mécanismes régissent la relation école-travail ?

Méthodologie

Il s'agit d'une méthode de recherche permettant de comprendre une réalité ou une situation sociale spécifique dans un contexte socioculturel particulier. Elle utilise plusieurs stratégies de collecte de données et d'informations quantitatives et qualitatives. Elle consiste en une recherche sur les populations à travers des entretiens avec de petits groupes d'individus et l'observation.

Objectifs de l'étude

Les objectifs assignés à l'étude découlent de la problématique posée plus haut et se présentent comme suit :

- la caractérisation des situations de travail des enfants dans l'agriculture (TEA) ;
- l'estimation de l'impact du travail des enfants dans la zone d'étude ;
- l'identification et la description des conditions réelles du TEA dans la zone étudiée ;
- l'étude des interactions agissant sur la relation école-travail et la compréhension des forces, pressions et comportements agissant vers l'une ou l'autre direction ;
- la détermination des bases pour l'instruction de programmes d'intervention visant à améliorer la situation des enfants travaillant en agriculture ou, le cas échéant, à abolir les formes dangereuses de travail.

Impératifs d'une recherche sur le travail des enfants

- très peu ou pas d'informations disponibles sur le travail des enfants dans les structures administratives des pays ;
- manque d'informations fiables sur les dynamiques sociale, économique et culturelle qui régissent la relation enfant-travail-école ;
- nécessité d'évaluer les risques physique et psychologique auxquels beaucoup d'enfants sont exposés, afin de pouvoir formuler des projets et des programmes d'actions.

Nécessité de limiter les aspects de la recherche

Du fait de l'incapacité à étudier l'ensemble du travail de l'enfant dans un laps de temps réduit, il est impératif de concentrer l'étude sur des aspects bien délimités. À titre d'exemple :

- les types de travaux effectués par les enfants et impacts du travail des enfants ;
- identification et description des conditions de travail des enfants ;
- dynamique de la relation entre l'école et le travail : attitude des parents et des enfants ;
- évaluation de l'étendu des situations dangereuses, nocives et particulières vis à vis de la santé physique et psychologique des enfants ;
- bases adéquates pour l'instruction de programmes d'intervention et de projets.

Zone de l'étude

L'étude concerne une région qui présente la caractéristique de la diversité de l'environnement physique et humain. Elle comprend des zones distinctes ; la plaine et oasis, le piémont des montagnes et la montagne.

La majorité de la population de la région est localisée dans le milieu rural et la proportion des enfants ayant moins de 15 ans représente 35 pour cent de la population de la région. L'agriculture constitue l'activité économique principale en milieu rural et renferme plus de 82 pour cent de la population active de la région. Le taux d'analphabétisme atteint 84 pour cent en milieu rural et 38 pour cent en milieu urbain, ce taux atteint 90 pour cent chez les femmes.

La région bénéficie de plusieurs programmes de développement relatifs à l'équipement en infrastructures de base dans le milieu rural ainsi que des projets de lutte contre la pauvreté avec le concours de plusieurs organismes nationaux et internationaux.

Le choix de la région répond à l'énorme déficit en matière d'information sur le travail des enfants en milieu rural et notamment dans l'agriculture, principale activité économique de la région.

Sources d'informations

La méthodologie adoptée se base sur les éléments et sources d'information suivants

- la documentation de l'UNICEF et du BIT relative aux recherches sur le travail des enfants ;

- les aspects méthodologiques développés par les consultants dans le domaine de recherche sur le travail des enfants ;
- les expériences capitalisées dans le domaine de la recherche sociale et de développement ;
- la connaissance du domaine agricole et de la région de l'étude ;
- discutions et entretiens avec les personnes et les organisations reconnues ;
- observations ; information visuelle, conversations (enfants, parents, employeurs, enseignants).

Les enfants sont l'élément central de la recherche. Ils constituent des pourvoyeurs individuels de données et sont la source d'information la plus importante. Ils peuvent contribuer au processus de collecte d'information à travers la participation dans les discutions de groupes (informateurs clés).

Les enfants travailleurs peuvent intervenir de façon limitée dans les phases ultérieures du processus (comparaison des résultats, opinions sur les programmes à mettre en place…).

Analyse des Résultats de l'étude

Importance du travail des enfants en l'agriculture dans la région.

Le travail des enfants en agriculture est une réalité, il est banal et généralement toléré par pratiquement toutes les composantes de la société.

À travers les différents groupes de discussions menés auprès des parents, instituteurs et enfants, il se dégage que le travail de l'enfant est un phénomène social courant qui touche l'ensemble des ménages et toutes les zones étudiées.

Les statistiques recueillies à travers les enquêtes montrent que ce phénomène touche à peu prés la moitié des enfants âgés de 7 à 15 ans, avec des degrés différents selon la région, le niveau de vie et les conditions socio-économiques de l'enfant et de sa famille.

Tableau 1 : Importance du travail des enfants en agriculture par zone

Région	Nombre de ménages	Nombred'enfants	ETA	%
Montagne	36	85	45	53%
Piémont	96	224	119	53%
Plaine	80	158	76	48%
Total	212	467	240	51%

Il ressort du tableau ci-dessus que le travail des enfants en agriculture est légèrement plus élevé en zones de montagne et de piémont avec 53 pour cent. La zone de plaine, offrant une infrastructure de base et socio-économique relativement plus importante, reste moins touchée par ce phénomène.

Néanmoins, il a été constaté que les enfants de la montagne et du piémont partent en plaine pour chercher du travail rémunéré dans les fermes modernes irriguées.

Causes du travail des enfants en agriculture

Conditions de développement humain

♦ La pauvreté

Comme partout dans le monde, la pauvreté est la première cause de travail des enfants en agriculture. La plupart des parents interviewés ont déclaré être incapables à subvenir aux besoins essentiels (terre agricole ne dépassant guère 2ha par ménage, surtout en zone de montagne et de piémont), et d'autre part, le revenu du ménage a significativement chuté suite à plusieurs années de sécheresse et la réduction des opportunités d'emploi.

Le travail des enfants constitue une manière à la fois de :

- réduire les charges de l'exploitation agricole familiale à travers l'apport de force de travail non rémunéré (main d'œuvre familiale) ;
- échapper aux frais de scolarisation des enfants qui ne vont plus à l'école ;
- contribuer financièrement aux dépenses des ménages, à travers la rémunération du travail des enfants chez les tiers.

La survie des ménages est très liée à l'apport de revenus extérieurs d'un ou de plusieurs membre de la famille (généralement fils et filles) qui travaillent en ville ou à l'étranger.

♦ Analphabétisme et ignorance des parents

L'analphabétisme des parents est généralisé et leur niveau de conscience quant aux impacts du travail des enfants est très faible.

Les populations paysannes vivent en marge de la société. À titre d'exemple, 10 à 20 pour cent des ménages n'ont pas d'état civil et 10 à 15 pour cent n'ont pas d'acte de mariage.

La non-scolarisation des enfants est due aux effets directs conjugués de la pauvreté, l'analphabétisme et l'ignorance des parents. Les enfants non scolarisés ayant tout leur temps libre sont très vite attirés par le travail agricole dans l'exploitation familiale ou pour les tiers.

♦ Conditions familiales

Les conditions familiales constituent un facteur déterminant quant au travail de l'enfant et surtout le « timing » et la précocité de ce travail.

Il est généralement constaté que le garçon aîné n'est pas scolarisé à cause de son implication avec son père dans les travaux agricoles et l'aide de la famille, surtout si le patrimoine agricole du ménage est important. De même, la fille aînée est généralement engagée dans les travaux de ménage ainsi que dans les travaux liés à l'élevage.

La mort ou l'absence du père condamne le garçon aîné à prendre la responsabilité de chef de famille à un stade très précoce (dès l'age de 12 ans) et implique directement la rupture de sa scolarisation s'il est scolarisé. Les enfants orphelins sont généralement privés de scolarisation à un stade très précoce et se trouvent obligés de travailler pour assurer leurs besoins quotidiens et ceux de leurs familles.

♦ Coutumes

Le travail des enfants trouve aussi son explication au niveau de la valeur social du travail dans les coutumes de la région. Le travail a une valeur sacrée et le soutien de la famille confère à l'enfant une valeur sociale au rang des adultes. L'auto-prise en charge et l'indépendance financière est une valeur très prisée par les enfants à un âge très jeune.

En définitif, le stade « enfance » de l'enfant n'existe pratiquement pas dans le vécu des populations rurales pauvres. D'autres valeurs viennent justifier le travail de l'enfant comme une adaptation à un environnement précaire sans merci où il n'y a place ni au divertissement ni à l'épanouissement.

Faiblesse des infrastructures

♦ Infrastructures de base

Le niveau d'équipement en infrastructures de base dans les zones visitées est très faible. Il est comparable à la situation générale des zones rurales les plus marginalisées.

• Accès à l'eau potable

Le taux d'accès à l'eau potable (adduction d'eau potable par branchement individuel ou existence d'une borne fontaine) dans les douars visités ne dépasse pas 46 pour cent en moyenne. Il est de 55 pour cent en plaine et de 42 pour cent en montagne. Le reste de la population est approvisionnée en eau à partir de puits privés non contrôlés (29 pour cent), de sources (20 pour cent), ou encore à partir des eaux des oueds et des seguias (10 pour cent).

• Électrification

Sur 43 douars enquêtés, seulement 12 sont électrifiés, soit 28 pour cent. Le taux d'électrification des douars est plus élevé dans la région du piémont avec 43 pour cent et atteint 19 pour cent dans la plaine. En terme de ménage, le taux de raccordement est de 15 pour cent dans l'ensemble, avec un faible niveau enregistré dans la plaine de 19 pour cent. Il en résulte que les conditions de vie dans les douars visités sont très défavorables.

• Réseau routier et désenclavement

La région est très enclavée. Le réseau routier est très peu développé et la plupart des douars visités sont difficilement accessibles. Le degré d'enclavement s'accentue en allant de la plaine vers la montagne.

♦ Infrastructures socio-économiques

Les infrastructures socioéconomiques sont très peu développées dans les douars visités reflétant la situation générale dans la zone d'étude. A ce propos, on note particulièrement :

- l'éloignement des collèges : aucun douar n'est doté d'un collège et le collège le plus près se situe à plusieurs dizaines de kilomètres, ce qui explique le taux très élevé (plus de 95 pour cent) de rupture de scolarisation des enfants ayant terminé les études primaires ;
- l'inadaptation du système scolaire : beaucoup d'enfants et de parents critiquent le système scolaire adopté qui ne répond point aux besoins spécifiques des enfants du milieu rural. Ce système est lourd, inefficace et inadapté aux conditions de vie des enfants ruraux ;

- l'absence de la formation professionnelle : il y a un besoin important de formation professionnelle pratique et rapide pour la qualification d'une main d'œuvre analphabète et très peu professionnelle ;
- l'éloignement et le sous-équipement des centres de Santé : dans la plupart des douars, l'accès à un centre de santé prend des heures puisque la distance à parcourir est supérieure à 10 km et atteint parfois plus de 50 km. En plus, les centres de santé existant ne peuvent pas assurer à la population rurale le service sanitaire demandé du fait du sous-équipement de ces centres qui manquent de personnel et de matériel, indispensables à un service sanitaire de base adéquat ;
- inexistence d'infrastructures et d'activités de promotion de la jeunesse ; A l'exception de quelques terrains de football caillouteux et très dangereux quant à la pratique d'un sport quelconque, il n'y a aucune infrastructure de jeunesse et sport. La jeunesse rurale est laissée pour compte. La notion de « l'enfance » est même oubliée ;
- la quasi-absence d'activité économique extra-agricole : l'activité agricole reste la principale source de revenu et d'emploi dans les douars visités, à l'instar de l'ensemble de la zone d'étude. La précarité du secteur agricole face à l'aléa climatique (sécheresse et autres catastrophes climatiques) et le caractère très traditionnel des systèmes de production agricole pratiqués font que les revenus des ménages sont médiocres, voire nuls, et les moyens de survie viennent souvent de transfert d'argent des membres de la famille travaillant dans d'autres secteurs en ville ou à l'étranger.

♦ Développement communautaire

Dans la quasi-totalité des douars visités, il existe une association ou une ONG. La majorité d'entre elles s'occupent de la gestion du réseau d'eau potable où elles sont créées dans le cadre de projet de développement (programme rural). Les autres organisations n'ont ni moyens de travail ni programmes d'actions. Leur capacité de développement institutionnel est très faible ne permettant pas de générer des cycles de développement local.

Ces organisations qui disposent de ressources humaines et de volontaires soucieux du développement de leurs localités, nécessitent un encadrement et des moyens de travail pour participer activement à l'amélioration de leur cadre de vie. Elles constituent la voie obligée pour une sensibilisation à l'éradication du travail des enfants, particulièrement en agriculture.

Caractérisation du travail des enfants en agriculture

Catégories des travaux effectués par les enfants

Le travail des enfants en agriculture se caractérise par la présence de 3 grandes catégories de travail, selon le type de rémunération pratiqué :

♦ Travail familial non rémunéré (TFNR)

Il s'agit du travail des enfants dans leurs exploitations agricoles familiales. C'est un cas quasi-généralisé puisque les enfants contribuent de façon plus ou moins importante dans les travaux agricoles et dans les tâches de l'élevage pratiquées sur le patrimoine foncier familial. C'est un travail qui peut être permanent pour enfants non scolarisés et pour les opérations à caractère continu et permanent dans le temps, comme le gardiennage et les divers travaux agricoles. Il peut être occasionnel pour les enfants scolarisés qui apportent leur aide au cours des périodes de vacances et dans les situations d'activités de pointe comme la période de labour ou encore les périodes de récolte des produits agricoles.

Il y a lieu de noter ici l'importance des travaux effectués par les filles qui contribuent à la fois aux travaux agricoles ainsi qu'aux travaux ménagers. Le secteur de l'élevage est très présent dans cette catégorie de travail, particulièrement l'élevage extensif.

♦ Travail familial rémunéré (TFR)

Ce type de travail est de faible importance et absent dans la zone montagneuse pauvre. Il est pratiqué plutôt dans les exploitations agricoles relativement plus « viables » situées en zone de plaine.

Le travail familial rémunéré concerne surtout les travaux liés à une recette financière immédiate pour l'exploitation agricole familiale comme le commerce de légumes ou la récolte de produits agricoles et leur vente à proximité de l'exploitation agricole (olives) ou encore le transport des denrées.

♦ Travail pour tiers rémunéré (TTR) (permanent et occasionnel)

Le travail des enfants chez autrui constitue un véritable emploi soumis aux conditions d'offre et de demande de la force de travail ouvrière en agriculture. Il se concentre dans les zones à haut potentiel agricole (ici la zone de plaine et les périmètres irrigués) et dans les périodes de besoin intense en main d'œuvre. Les employeurs les plus importants sont les fermes et les grandes exploitations agricoles. Ce type de travail qui n'inclue pas les enfants scolarisés, concerne aussi bien les garçons que les filles. La distinction entre les deux sexes est perceptible dans les conditions de rémunération.

Classification du travail des enfants en agriculture.

Le recensement de l'ensemble des travaux observés ou identifiés permet de faire la classification suivante :

♦ Travail familial non rémunéré (TFNR)

Fille

- Gardiennage de troupeau-zones proches ;
- Coupe et transport de fourrages ;
- Alimentation des animaux ;
- Entretien des bergeries et d'étables ;
- Petit élevage.

Garçon

- Gardiennage de troupeau-zones éloignées ;
- Travaux agricoles et labour ;
- Semis, épandage d'engrais, traitements agrochimiques.

Fille et garçon

- Irrigation ;
- Récolte d'olives, amendes, prunes et noix, raisins et autres...

♦ Travail familial rémunéré (TFR)

Garçon

- Commerce de fruits et légumes ;
- Plantation, entretien et récolte de légumes.

Fille et garçon

- Récolte d'olives.

♦ Travail pour tiers rémunéré (TTR) (permanent et occasionnel)

Garçon

- Gardiennage de troupeau – zones éloignées ;
- Travaux agricoles et labour ;
- Semis, épandage d'engrais, traitements chimiques ;
- Transport de produits agricoles.

Fille et garçon

- Récolte d'olives et d'agrumes ;
- Plantation et récolte de pommes de terre ;
- Semis et récolte de pois ;
- Plantation et coupe de menthe.

Il se dégage de l'analyse des différents travaux, que les filles sont plus concernées par le travail permanent et non rémunéré et que les garçons sont plutôt concernés par les travaux rémunérés et faisant appel à l'utilisation de machines et engins agricoles ainsi que des produits chimiques et pesticides.

Conditions de travail des enfants

Durée de travail

La durée de travail des enfants varie en fonction du type de travail, de la saison et de la scolarisation de ceux-ci. Elle diffère également selon qu'il s'agit d'une fille ou d'un garçon.

Pour les enfants non scolarisés, il s'agit souvent de travail permanent et à caractère continu bien que les travaux effectués changent d'une saison à l'autre. Pour ces enfants, la durée de travail dépasse 8 heures par jour et peut atteindre jusqu'à 12 heures par jour (voir encadré ci-dessous).

Durée de travail permanent des enfants non scolarisés :
*Gardiennage-élevage : 8 à 12h/jour ; *Maraîchage : 8 à 10 h/jour ; *Travaux agricoles : 12 h/jour.

Le gardiennage de troupeau dans des zones lointaines est le travail qui peut débuter à l'aube et se terminer au coucher du soleil, chaque jour. De ce fait, la durée maximale de travail est atteinte pendant la saison estivale où la durée du jour atteint jusqu'à 14 heures.

Les autres travaux au niveau des champs, ont plus ou moins un caractère saisonnier et sont discontinus dans le temps. La période de labour constitue la première saison de pointe avec des durées de travail atteignant jusqu'à 12 heures par jour. Cette opération se fait parfois dans des conditions très particulières (premières pluies, conditions d'accès à la parcelle, disponibilité de la semence et des engrais ...) limitant le temps qui lui est imparti, ce qui oblige l'agriculteur à la réaliser coûte que coûte, dans un délai bien réduit.

Les travaux des enfants dans les grandes exploitations agricoles concernant surtout la conduite des cultures maraîchères (légumes) depuis le semis ou la plantation jusqu'à la récolte. De telles opérations nécessitent beaucoup de main d'œuvre recrutée quotidiennement ou hebdomadairement dans les places d'offre de force de travail (Moakaf). La durée de travail dépend de plusieurs facteurs dont le nombre d'ouvriers travaillant dans la parcelle, le délai de livraison de la production, la saison, la volonté de l'employeur et le salaire journalier. Elle varie de 8 à 12 heures par jour.

Pour les enfants scolarisés, les travaux effectués sont semi-permanents ou occasionnels et se concentrent dans les jours fériés et les vacances. Les enfants effectuent divers travaux agricoles, la récolte de fruits et légumes, le gardiennage et la conduite de l'élevage. Les horaires de travail sont similaires au travail permanent pour les non scolarisés.

Au cours de l'année scolaire, le travail des enfants porte le plus souvent sur une demi-journée ou sur deux périodes : le matin avant d'aller à l'école (6 heures à 8 heures) et l'après-midi (16 heures à 18 heures).

Dans tous les cas, le travail des enfants scolarisés est, au minimum, de 4 heures par jour et, au maximum de 8 heures par jour (voir encadré ci-dessous). Les horaires du travail sont organisés en dehors de la classe.

Durée de travail des enfants scolarisés : Travail semi-permanent :

---

* Gardiennage et élevage : 4 à 6 h/jour ;
* Travaux divers : 4 à 8 h/jour.Travail occasionnel :
* divers travaux agricoles ;
* Vacances (été) et jours fériés ;
* horaires hors classe.

Concernant la différence entre fille et garçon, il y a lieu de signaler que généralement, la fille travaille plus que le garçon dans la mesure où elle s'occupe de façon permanente de tous les travaux à l'intérieur de la maison (travaux d'élevage et travaux ménagers). La durée totale de travail de la fille est majorée d'au moins 2 heures par jour de travaux supplémentaires de ménage, d'entretien des locaux d'élevage, d'alimentation des animaux, ...

Age de mise au travail des enfants

Les enfants commencent à travailler à un âge très précoce. Les garçons sont mis au travail vers l'âge de 9 ans tandis que les filles sont exploitées dès l'âge de 5 ou 6 ans.

Les filles sont mises au travail à un âge plus précoce
Fille : 5-9 ans Garçon : 9-12 ans

Les parents, particulièrement le père, sont les personnes décisives quant à la mise au travail de leurs enfants. Les travaux effectués en jeune âge se rapportent au gardiennage en zone proche de la maison et à l'entretien des locaux de l'élevage.

Environnement de travail

Les enfants travaillent dès leur jeune âge dans des conditions qui peuvent être qualifiées parfois de très dangereuses vis à vis de leur sécurité et de leur développement physique et psychologique. L'environnement de travail des enfants en agriculture est marqué par les caractéristiques suivantes :

- isolement et éloignement du Douar : le gardiennage du troupeau en montagne, forêts et parcours amène l'enfant berger à parcourir de longues distances pour parvenir aux lieux de pâturage. L'enfant berger est souvent seul dans la nature, très éloigné de son douar et sans moyens de protection contre toute agression humaine ou animale ;
- dans tous les travaux agricoles, il n'y a pas de respect des règles de sécurité au travail : les enfants travailleurs sont habillés n'importe comment. Il ne porte pas d'habillement protecteur et parfois ils ont les pieds nus et s'exposent à plusieurs risques physiques. Leur travail les amène à manipuler du matériel agricole et des produits dangereux sans aucune initiation, ni protection. Les outils utilisés sont souvent inappropriés provoquant des déformations corporelles irréversibles. Il n'y a pas de moyens de premiers secours et en cas d'accidents, les enfants ont recours à certains moyens traditionnels après plusieurs heures de souffrance ;
- le travail des enfants dans les champs les expose aux coups de soleil et aux intempéries. Ils passent de longues heures à l'extérieur sans abri ni protection ;
- le travail des enfants dans les étables et les écuries les amène à côtoyer pendant longtemps des animaux d'élevage dans des conditions d'hygiène très rudimentaires.

Conditions de rémunération

La rémunération financière des enfants travaillant en agriculture concerne le travail rémunéré chez les tiers (TTR) et dans une moindre mesure le travail familial rémunéré (TFR).

Dans ce qui suit nous allons considérer uniquement la rémunération du travail des enfants chez les tiers, en l'occurrence les fermes et les grandes exploitations agricoles.

Tableau 2 : Rémunération du travail des enfants en agriculture

Travail	Garçon	Fille
Gardiennage	30 à 35 DH/j	-
Maraîchage	30 à 35 DH/j	20 à 30 DH/J
Récolte d'olives/agrumes	20 à 30 DH/j	15 à 20 DH/J
Récolte de raisins	35 DH/j	20 à 25 DH/j
Irrigation	15 DH/j	-
Travaux agricoles-labour	35 à 40 DH/j	-
Transport (blé)	100 DH/semaine	-

Il ressort de ce tableau que :

- d'une façon générale, la rémunération du travail des enfants représente 60 à 75 pour cent de la rémunération habituelle des adultes (40 à 50 DH) ;
- la rémunération est faite sur la base d'un salaire journalier, mais elle est perceptible souvent en fin de semaine ;
- pour la plupart des travaux agricoles (à l'exception du gardiennage), la rémunération porte uniquement sur les journées effectivement travaillées. Aucun jour férié n'est payé et les congés ne sont pas pris en compte ;
- les travaux les plus rémunérés correspondent à des journées entières de tâches dures et pénibles (labour, travaux agricoles d'entretien) ;
- les filles ne sont pas concernées par l'ensemble des travaux agricoles. Elles travaillent en tant qu'ouvrières agricoles dans les fermes et grandes exploitations, particulièrement dans les opérations de récolte et d'entretien des cultures maraîchères. Leur rémunération est généralement inférieure à celle des garçons de 5 à 10 DH/jour.

Valorisation financière du travail des enfants par les parents employeurs

Dans le cas du travail non rémunéré des enfants dans leur propre exploitation familiale, il a été jugé utile de donner une valeur financière estimative du travail des enfants. Pour ce faire, il a été demandé aux parents employeurs de valoriser le travail de leurs enfants en répondant à la question : combien vous faut-il d'argent par mois pour que votre enfant ne travaille pas ? Ou encore, si votre enfant ne travaille pas, combien vous faut-il d'argent par mois pour embaucher de la main d'œuvre salariale ?

Il s'est avéré alors que le travail de l'enfant dans l'exploitation familiale est survalorisé par les parents qui estiment sa valeur entre 1 000 et 1 500 DH/mois pour le garçon et entre 300 et 600 DH/mois pour la fille.

Le calcul estimatif de la valeur de la force de travail d'un enfant (fille ou garçon) de 12 ans travaillant 200 jours par an correspondrait à 500 DH/mois en moyenne. Cette valeur correspond aux frais de la main d'œuvre salariale que le chef d'exploitation doit engager pour compenser le travail de son enfant.

La contribution des enfants travailleurs par ménage varie de 300 à 2 000dh/ mois, selon le nombre d'enfants qui sont mis au travail.

Le temps libre des enfants travaillant en agriculture (ETA)

Lors des interviews avec les ETA, il a été procédé à la définition du calendrier journalier qui est répartie entre le temps imparti à l'école (y compris les déplacements pour se rendre à l'école), le travail, le ménage et le temps libre, les résultats sont consignés dans le tableau ci-après.

Tableau 3 : temps libre des ETA

% temps libre	0%	10%	20%	30% et plus
Filles	41%	34%	13%	3%
Garçons	16%	26%	30%	29%
Total	26%	29%	23%	19%

Il ressort que le temps libre de l'ETA est très réduit et ne répond aucunement aux normes de divertissement des enfants en jeune âge. 26 pour cent des ETA n'ont pas de temps libre, soit 41 pour cent des filles est 16 pour cent des garçons. Seuls 19 pour cent des ETA ont un temps libre dépassant 30 pour cent (ou 3 à 4 heures par jour), soit 29 pour cent des garçons et seulement 3 pour cent des filles. Il en résulte que les filles travaillent plus que les garçons et que leur temps libre est très faible.

Le peu de temps libre dont disposent les ETA est toutefois dissipé dans la rue dans des conditions ne permettant aucun divertissement physique ou moral à l'enfant. L'absence de toutes infrastructures de jeunesse et de sport conjuguée à l'ignorance et à la négligence (involontaire) des parents font que les enfants sont laissés à leur sort sans aucun encadrement éducatif ou pédagogique.

Risques et situations dangereuses

Les conditions dangereuses dans lesquelles les enfants travaillent les exposent à plusieurs risques et accidents dangereux. Les situations les plus fréquentes qui ont été identifiées sont :

Accidents

- morsure de serpents : plusieurs cas de décès ont été enregistrés parmi les enfants bergers et au cours du travail au champ. La non disposition des moyens de secours et l'éloignement des centres de santé qui d'ailleurs ne sont pas équipés seraient à l'origine de l'incapacité à secourir les enfants mordus ;
- accidents de véhicule sur la route ou de tracteurs et machines agricoles : les ETA sont amenés à se déplacer sur de langues distances pour se rendre au lieu de travail. Ces déplacements peuvent être mortels lors de la traversée d'une route. Aussi les enfants bergers en s'occupant plus du rassemblement du troupeau s'exposent dans plusieurs situations à des accidents mortels. Plusieurs cas d'accidents d'engins agricoles ont été également signalés ;
- coupure et blessure au contact de machinerie : Certaines manipulations, hasardeuses et sans initiation, de machines agricoles peuvent entraîner des accidents graves comme les coupures enregistrées lors de manipulation de motopompe d'irrigation ;

- chutes de falaises et tombées d'arbres : Il arrive que des enfants bergers soient entraînés dans des chutes de falaises de pentes accentuées, ce qui provoque des blessures et des cassures. Lors de la récolte d'olives ou de noyer par exemple, plusieurs cas de tombées d'arbres à hauteur élevée ont été enregistrés. Les traitements des cassures se font le plus souvent par des moyens traditionnels.

Santé-Maladie

L'environnement de travail des ETA est propice au développement de certaines maladies et déséquilibres sanitaires. Les principaux risques identifiés à ce niveau concernent :

- les mauvaises conditions d'hygiènes (étables, bergerie, irrigation, labour,...)

Autres risques et situations dangereuses

D'autres risques graves sont également identifiés à travers les discussions menées avec les enfants et les instituteurs. Ils concernent :

- le viol de filles et de garçons en situation d'isolement et sans défense ;
- le vol et l'agression d'enfants ;
- la peur et les troubles psychologiques liés à l'isolement prolongé et à la solitude.

Perception du travail des enfants en agriculture

De façon générale, le travail des enfants en agriculture passe inaperçu aux yeux de la société rurale. C'est un phénomène normal, habituel et ordinaire. Le travail des enfants en agriculture n'inquiète personne et l'on peut dire qu'il y a une indifférence sociale face au travail des enfants.

Les discussions menées avec les différentes catégories sociales peuvent être considérées comme une première sensibilisation à une situation perçue jusque là comme normale. Les questions posées ont été une occasion aux enfants, aux parents et aux instituteurs de réfléchir, pour la première fois pour certains, au phénomène du travail des enfants. Cette réflexion aura sans doute des répercussions sur la manière de voir et de percevoir les ETA.

L'attitude des personnes interviewées sur la question a été donc spontanée et sincère.

Perception des enfants

La majorité des enfants justifie leur travail par la nécessité d'aider leur famille soit en apportant de l'argent ou en travaillant auprès de sa famille. Le caractère sacré du travail et la possibilité d'avoir de l'expérience dans la vie sont aussi des justificatifs avancés. Cependant, la majorité d'entre eux trouve les travaux agricoles pénibles à très pénibles et aspire à apprendre un autre métier moins pénible et plus rémunérateur.

Perception des parents

Une grande partie des parents interviewés se déclarent contre le travail des enfants, mais affichent leur incapacité à changer la situation puisqu'ils sont dans le besoin immédiat et impératif de l'aide de leurs enfants. Il rapporte que malgré tout, les jeunes ne veulent plus travailler en agriculture et qu'ils les encouragent à travailler dans d'autres secteurs, notamment en ville.

Perception des instituteurs

Tous les instituteurs ne sont pas contre le travail des enfants, et ce malgré l'impact de ce phénomène sur la scolarisation des enfants. Certains d'entre eux sont même pour le travail des enfants qui aident leurs parents.

Relation travail-école

Pour les enfants qui travaillent en agriculture, trois situations se présentent :

- l'ETA va à l'école en parallèle avec son travail ;
- l'ETA a rompu sa scolarisation après avoir été à l'école pour quelques années ;
- l'ETA n'a jamais été à l'école.

La répartition des différentes situations est donnée dans le tableau suivant :

Région	Enfants en classe	Enfants en rupture de scolarité	Enfants non scolarisés
Montagne	18%	47%	34%
Piémont	38%	37%	25%
Plaine	56%	45%	21%
Total	33%	42%	25%

Il en ressort que :

- un tiers des enfants travaillant en agriculture sont encore en classe. Ce taux diminue en allant de la plaine (56 pour cent) vers la montagne (18 pour cent) ;
- le quart des ETA n'ont jamais été scolarisés et sont par conséquent analphabètes. Cette fraction atteint 34 pour cent en zone de montagne ;
- une grande partie des ETA ont quitté l'école, soit 42 pour cent. Ce taux est important dans toutes les régions et concerne plus de filles que de garçons ;
- la rupture de la scolarisation concerne aussi bien la fin de l'enseignement fondamental (garçons et filles) que les premières années d'E.F (plus de filles). La rupture de la scolarisation est une conséquence directe de plusieurs facteurs combinés dont la mise au travail de l'enfant, les conditions de vie de celui-ci marquées par la pauvreté, l'ignorance et la négligence ainsi que l'inadaptabilité et l'inefficacité du système scolaire (voir encadré ci après).

Cause de la non-scolarisation des ETA
Non scolarisation : - Pauvreté, - Analphabétisme et ignorance des parents, - Besoins de main d'œuvre familiale (fils aîné, importance du travail), - Besoin de filles pour travaux ménagers, - Coutumes (filles), - Eloignement de l'école.
Rupture : - Pauvreté, - Besoins de main d'œuvre familiale (Mort ou absence du père), - Inexistence de collège proche, - Inadaptation du système d'enseignement avec les besoins des parents, - Mauvaise image de marque de certains instituteurs ou d'école. - Echec scolaire ou insuffisance de communication enfant-instituteurs.

Impact du travail des enfants sur leur scolarisation

L'analyse de l'impact du travail des enfants sur leur scolarisation met en évidence deux types de processus selon qu'il s'agit d'une fille ou d'un garçon.

Pour la fille

Les conditions de travail sont très défavorables et contraignantes. La fille est sollicitée à la fois pour les travaux agricoles, souvent l'élevage, et pour les travaux ménagers qui incluent aussi la corvée de l'approvisionnement en eau et l'apport du bois. Les forces physiques et intellectuelles de la fille sont épuisées en dehors de l'école, ce qui affaiblit sa capacité à suivre les cours et à assurer sa présence en classe. Il en résulte un échec scolaire.

De plus, le manque de moyens, qui est incompatible avec l'échec de la fille, conjugué avec la culture coutumière des parents qui préfèrent garder leur fille à la maison au lieu de la laisser traîner dans les champs militent pour que, finalement, la fille rompe sa scolarisation à un stade plus précoce.

Pour le garçon

Pour le garçon, d'autres valeurs entrent en jeu. Bien que la scolarisation du garçon ne pose pas de problèmes coutumiers, sa rupture de scolarisation peut être induite par différentes raisons dont les plus importantes concernent :

- l'insertion précoce dans le monde de travail ;
- la valeur sacrée du travail (aide de la famille, auto-prise en charge…) ;
- le gain d'argent : orientation vers les valeurs matérielles et perception d'une certaine inutilité de l'école surtout qu'elle produit des chômeurs ;
- du fait de ces raisons, le garçon commence à afficher son désintérêt vis-à-vis de l'école et ne s'investit plus dans les études, ce qui se solde par l'absentéisme et l'échec scolaire.

L'inexistence de collège proche constitue également un autre facteur très important de déscolarisation des enfants qui ont fait des efforts pour surmonter les contraintes précitées et sont parvenus à terminer les études fondamentales.

D'autres facteurs familiaux peuvent être déterminants dans la déscolarisation ou la non-scolarisation du garçon :

- le garçon aîné n'est pratiquement jamais scolarisé puisqu'il constitue une main d'œuvre familiale potentielle et une aide précieuse du père ;
- la mort ou l'absence du père ou d'une autre personne clé de la famille entraîne souvent la déscolarisation d'un ou de plusieurs enfants de la même famille, soit parce que la famille s'appauvrit ou parce qu'il y a un besoin pressant de main d'œuvre familiale.

Perspectives d'avenir

À travers les éléments de discussions développés plus haut, il ressort que le phénomène du travail des enfants en agriculture est une contrainte qui vient s'ajouter aux autres conditions de vie défavorables dans lesquelles des milliers d'enfants vivent une souffrance journalière chronique et aiguë.

L'enfance en tant que phase de développement physique, psychologique et culturel est pratiquement absente dans le vécu des jeunes populations rurales. Les enfants sont responsabilisés et chargés de fardeaux lourds dès leur jeune âge sans qu'ils puissent avoir l'occasion de saisir et de comprendre leur situation.

L'environnement de développement des enfants en milieu rural produit une spirale de pauvreté qui enchaîne les générations actuelles et futures. L'ignorance et la pauvreté produit des enfants analphabètes, ignorants et incapables de sortir de la spirale de la pauvreté puisqu'ils ne sont ni préparés au changement, ni outillés de savoir et savoir faire indispensables à toute tentative de changement.

Pour ces enfants, le présent est très mal vécu et l'avenir leur fait peur. Le seul espoir de ces jeunes est de partir ailleurs, loin d'un environnement rural hostile sans moyens de vie, sans protection et sans avenir, loin de ce secteur de l'agriculture dont le travail est très pénible et ne payant pas, et loin aussi de cette marginalisation largement vécue par les jeunes ruraux.

Ces enfants en souffrance sont la problématique du développement humain de demain que le pays devra résoudre. En l'absence de toute mesure d'intervention et de changement favorable de situation de ces jeunes, on doit s'attendre à certaines conséquences irréversibles telles que l'augmentation de la pauvreté, de l'exode rural, de l'immigration clandestine, du taux de criminalité et autres déséquilibres sociaux dont la correction nécessite beaucoup de moyens et de temps.

Il est donc impératif de placer l'enfance rurale au centre de préoccupation des Pouvoirs Publics et des organisations de développement local. Une telle perspective permettra de s'inscrire dans une logique de développement durable basée avant tout sur les hommes et les femmes de demain.

Il est nécessaire d'instaurer un système d'intervention contre le phénomène de travail des enfants en agriculture à travers la synergie de l'ensemble des parties prenantes.

Les axes d'interventions de cette approche qui implique l'ensemble des partenaires de développement local sont les suivants :

L'État

Les principales interventions devant être prises par l'État s'articulent autour des axes suivants :

- la lutte contre la pauvreté et l'ignorance en milieu rural à travers des programmes de développement local ciblés et orientés vers les populations les plus démunies ;
- la mise en place des infrastructures de base socio-économiques ainsi que les infrastructures communautaires de protection de l'enfance et de développement de la jeunesse et des sports ;
- la promotion de la famille rurale à travers des programmes de sensibilisation et d'orientation en matière d'éducation et de planification familiale ;
- l'instauration d'un Programme national d'éradication des travaux permanents des enfants et d'aide aux enfants travaillant à mi-temps en agriculture ;
- l'élargissement de la protection légale des enfants par la mise en place de lois interdisant la mise au travail des enfants en agriculture avant l'âge de 15 ans et la veille à l'application de la loi sur la protection de l'enfant.

L'école, le Ministère de l'Éducation nationale et les organismes de formation professionnelle

L'école et le Ministère de l'Éducation ainsi que les organismes de formation professionnelles peuvent jouer un rôle important dans l'amélioration de la situation de milliers d'enfants ruraux, et ce, à travers :

- la sensibilisation et l'alphabétisation des enfants et parents ;
- l'adaptation des programmes scolaires (contenus, durée, moyens de communication, …) aux réalités locales et aux besoins spécifiques de chaque zone ;
- la construction de collèges, de centres de formation professionnelle à la proximité des populations rurales.

Les ONG (Associations de développement) et les Communes rurales

L'intervention des ONG et des CR peut être organisée autour des axes suivants :

- la sensibilisation des parents aux programmes d'alphabétisation ;
- la mise en œuvre de projet de développement en faveur des adultes et lutte contre la pauvreté ;
- l'encadrement des enfants en situation difficile ;
- la formation professionnelle.

Les Employeurs (Grandes fermes privées et publiques)

Les fermes et les grandes exploitations devront jouer leur rôle de fermes patriotes respectant les droits fondamentaux des enfants, et ce en assurant :

- l'établissement de code de conduite strict dans la manière de recrutement des ouvriers ;
- l'application de la loi relative au travail des personnes mineures et des chartes de protection de l'enfant ;

- l'allégement des conditions des enfants contraints à travailler à travers des programmes intégrés de travail-formation-encadrement.

Conclusions

Sur le plan méthodologique

La méthodologie adoptée pour la réalisation de ce travail est une méthode très intéressante pour caractériser des phénomènes sociaux dans le monde rural. Le coût ainsi que le temps nécessaires compensent à notre avis largement le « manque » de précision dans les chiffres et les résultats quantitatifs. L'étude est cependant limitée par :

- l'étalement des travaux agricoles sur toute l'année : il a été montré plus haut qu'il y a généralement 3 périodes de pointes, la période de préparation des terres en automne, la période d'entretien des cultures en fin hiver-début printemps et la période de récolte de la plupart des cultures annuelles en été ;
- l'inaccessibilité temporaire à certaines zones : l'enclavement de la zone d'étude rend l'accès aux douars très difficile particulièrement quand les conditions climatiques sont défavorables ;
- l'incompréhension des populations des activités de recherche, car dans un milieu analphabète, il faut beaucoup plus de temps pour acquérir la confiance des personnes interviewées.

Sur le plan des résultats

Le travail des enfants en agriculture est quasi généralisé à travers toute la zone de l'étude et concerne un enfant sur deux. Ce phénomène est ordinaire aux yeux des composantes sociales à tel point qu'il passe inaperçu. On note par ailleurs le manque d'information et d'études se rapportant aussi bien au niveau régional (où il n'y pas d'information sur le travail des enfants) qu'au niveau national (où le travail des enfants en agriculture n'est pas étudié).

Ce phénomène grave est le résultat cumulé de :

- la faiblesse des Indicateurs de Développement Humains de la région ;
- la défaillance du système éducatif ;
- du manque de sensibilisation quant aux impacts et conséquences à court, moyen et long terme.

Plusieurs travaux sont exécutés par les enfants dans des conditions déplorables comportant des risques substantiels sur le développement physique et moral des enfants. La majeur partie des ETA sont employés comme main d'œuvre familiale au sein de l'exploitation agricole de leurs parents ou proche-parents et ne perçoivent aucune rémunération contre le travail qu'ils effectuent de façon permanente ou occasionnelle.

Les filles sont mises au travail à un âge plus jeune (5 ou 6 ans) et sont doublement exploitées dans les travaux ménagers. Le nombre d'heures de travail des filles dépassent souvent 10 heures par jour (contre 7 à 8 heures pur les garçons) et la rémunération de leur travail chez les tiers représente généralement ¾ de la rémunération des garçons.

Les travaux les plus dangereux identifiés sont :

- le métier de berger dans les régions montagneuses et forestières de la région ;
- le travail intensif dans les grandes fermes de la plaine ;
- l'enfant chef précoce de famille pour cause de décès ou d'immigration du père.

Les perspectives d'avenir de ces enfants s'annoncent très difficiles. Le phénomène de travail des enfants produit des adultes désorientés n'ayant pas vécu d'enfance, analphabètes et pauvres. Leur avenir est incertain et affichent une attitude négative face à leur vie.

L'atténuation des conséquences graves qui pourraient en découler passe par une lutte durable et structurée contre le travail des enfants et l'amélioration des conditions de vie des populations rurales. Ces objectifs nécessitent le concours des efforts de l'ensemble des parties concernées, à savoir l'État, les collectivités locales, les ONG, les employeurs et la population.

Recommandations

Au niveau de l'intervention, il est recommandé de :

- promouvoir des actions de développement local (scolarisation, santé, amélioration des revenus, micro finance, ...) ;
- intégrer la composante « enfant » et la lutte contre le travail des enfants dans les différents programmes à travers des actions spécifiques de sensibilisation et de lutte contre le travail des enfants ;
- mener une campagne de sensibilisation et de mobilisation sociale des populations contre le travail des enfants en agriculture à travers le réseau des ONG locales ;
- initier et développer, en collaboration avec les partenaires publics et privés concernés, une stratégie nationale de lutte contre le travail des enfants en agriculture ; en l'occurrence les travaux les plus dangereux, les métiers de berger permanent et de chef de famille précoce et dans les entreprises et grandes fermes intensives en tant que « ouvriers (es) agricoles ».

Références

Antoine, P. et Diouf, P. D., 1988, « Urbanisation, scolarisation et mortalité des enfants », *Annales de l'IFORD*, vol. 12.

Almeida-Topor, Hélène d', 1992, *Les jeunes en Afrique : évolution et rôle,* Paris: L'Harmattan.

Bequele, A. and Boyaden, J., 1988, *Combating Child Labour*, Geneva: ILO.

Bonnet, M., 1993, « Le travail des enfants en Afrique », *Revue Internationale de Travail* n° 3.

Bop, C., 1990, « Les laissés pour compte », *Vie et Santé*, Avr.

Desai, S. de, 1992, 'Children at Risk: The Role of Family Structure in Latin America and West Africa', *Population and Development Review*, vol 18.

Grant, J, P., 1990, *La situation des enfants dans le monde*, N Y: UNICEF.

Jully, R., 1989, « L'enfant et l'ajustement structurel à visage humain » *Environnement Africain,* vol. VII.

Koudou, K. R., 1990, Pratiques éducatives et développement moral : ... Thèse d'État, Toulouse.

Koton, D., 1987, « Identification des problèmes socio-économiques des mères et enfants au Kivu », Cahiers du CERPRU.

Lauras-Locoh, T., 1990, « Évolution de la famille et transition démographique en Afrique », *RISS*, n° 126, Nov.

Locoh, T., 1995, *Familles africaines ; population et qualité de vie,* Paris: CEPED.

Mansaray, A., 1991, « Les marginalisés de l'éducation ; quels groupes et pourquoi ? », *UNESCO-Afrique*, mars.

Ngakoutou, T., 1991, « La jeunesse Africaine face aux changements socio-économiques et culturels », *UNESCO-Afrique*, mars.

OCDE, 1983, *Les études et le travail vus par les jeunes,* Paris: OCDE.

OCDE, 1986, *L'enseignement au féminin ; études internationales sur la façon dont filles et garçons sont élevés et instruits,* Paris: OCDE.

Sahoo, U. Ch., 1990, 'Child Labour and Legislation', *Economic and Political Weekly*, vol. 25, n°46.

UN, 1990, *Droits de l'enfant*, NY: NU.

10

Problématique de la prostitution infanto-juvénile à Kinshasa : cas des *Tshel*

José Mvuezolo Bazonzi

La prostitution est une réalité mondiale : elle existe aujourd'hui dans toutes les sociétés, bien que le débat autour de ce sujet embarrasse plus d'une société et semble être un tabou dans certains milieux africains. D'ailleurs, les écrits sur le sujet, surtout s'agissant de la prostitution infanto-juvénile, sont rares, et la recherche demeure peu aisée et tout à fait délicate.

À travers le monde, ce phénomène est souvent lié au tourisme, au trafic des drogues, à la pauvreté et aux stigmates des conflits armés. Et les régions du monde les plus touchées restent sans conteste l'Amérique latine, l'Asie du Sud-Est et l'Afrique subsaharienne.

Au cours de la décennie écoulée, il a été observé à Kinshasa, capitale de la République Démocratique du Congo (RDC), l'intensification d'un phénomène encore très peu répandu sur le continent africain, celui de la prostitution des jeunes enfants, dont l'âge varie entre 10 et 16 ans. La plupart de ces enfants ont déserté l'école et le toit familial, et se livrent au « travail du sexe » qui semble rémunérateur. L'ampleur du phénomène nous a inspiré la présente recherche.

En effet, la République Démocratique du Congo traverse depuis bientôt quatre décennies, une crise multiforme qui semble se pérenniser et qui apparemment n'a pas encore dit son dernier mot. Car, depuis les années 70, ce pays est passé par plusieurs tribulations, en l'occurrence la zaïrianisation (1973),[1] les effets drastiques des programmes d'ajustement structurel communs aux pays du Sud (1980 -), les pillages de triste mémoire dans la capitale (1990 et 1992), et les guerres meurtrières à travers le pays (de 1996 à 1997 et de 1998 à 2003), sans oublier l'insuffisance chronique d'une bonne gouvernance qu'accable la rémanence des effets pervers des mouvements de rébellion spontanés, opérant à l'est du pays, principalement dans la région du Nord Kivu. Cet état de choses a eu pour conséquences notamment le déplacement interne des populations fuyant les affrontements armés (ce qui a produit les « déplacés de guerre internes »), l'éclatement de la cellule familiale, la désorganisation du système de production et l'effondrement de l'économie nationale.

Jusqu'en l'an 2000, l'économie congolaise était caractérisée par l'hyper-inflation, la dépréciation constante de la monnaie nationale, le Franc Congolais, la baisse des activités de production et la dégradation des infrastructures socio-économiques. Cette crise fulminante a ainsi renvoyé près de 80 pour cent de la population active au chômage et a de surcroît porté un coup fatal à la jeunesse qui désormais perd tout espoir d'embauche et ne sait plus où donner de la tête pour obtenir un emploi rémunérateur.

Face à cette crise multiforme, la population congolaise en général et kinoise en particulier, s'est trouvée désemparée et a développé des réflexes de survie en créant des petits « boulots » informels. Mais ces derniers ne sont pas souvent très rentables et ne permettent pas aux individus d'assurer la satisfaction complète de leurs besoins ainsi que ceux de leurs familles, loin s'en faut. Ainsi, il est fréquent qu'au sein d'une même famille, homme, femme et enfants se mettent à « travailler » en vue de subvenir aux besoins vitaux communs. Dans ce piège de la pauvreté, les jeunes enfants sont sacrifiés à l'autel de la débrouillardise.

C'est dans ce contexte à la fois pénible et macabre que plusieurs enfants et jeunes Kinois vont se trouver obligés de travailler en lieu et place de fréquenter l'école. Et, à défaut du « travail formel » qui n'est pas si disponible sur le marché kinois, les jeunes filles vont s'adonner à qui mieux mieux au « travail informel » du sexe, faisant fi des retombées liées à ce genre d'activité. À Kinshasa, le terme *tshel*[2] désigne ces enfants et jeunes prostitués qui, à corps défendant, consentent des rapports sexuels à tout venant contre de l'argent.

Nous considérons comme « travail informel », toute activité économique échappant au cadre institutionnel et réglementaire, et dans le cas d'espèce, toute prestation de service sexuel en échange d'une rétribution pécuniaire préalablement négociée et s'opérant en marge de toute réglementation. Le caractère « informel » de ce type de prostitution est renforcé par le fait que c'est une activité non enregistrée et non contrôlée par les services publics ; en outre, elle est non conforme et même contraire à la loi, en dépit du fait qu'elle s'exerce au vu et au su de tous, et en ce qu'elle utilise une catégorie de personnel « inapproprié ».

Plusieurs types d'approches apparemment et partiellement complémentaires, débattent aujourd'hui des causes de la prostitution. Pour certains, la prostitution, considérée comme étant « le plus vieux métier du monde », serait un phénomène naturel et donc prisé par les hommes dont l'instinct sexuel serait plus fort. D'autres approches attribuent la prostitution à la société bourgeoise qui aurait légitimé l'inégalité entre les sexes et l'hégémonie masculine (Maurer 1992:25-26). D'après ces modèles d'explication moralisants, seuls les hommes malades fréquenteraient les prostituées. Or il n'en est rien, car il n'en est pas toujours ainsi dans la société. Ainsi, il s'avère nécessaire d'explorer d'autres modèles d'explication.

L'approche selon laquelle la prostitution fonctionnerait d'après les lois de l'offre et de la demande dans une société en proie au consumérisme peut être évoquée, sans pour autant que cela implique pour nous un jugement de valeur ou une quelconque adhésion à cette approche, qui du reste, n'est pas exclusive ou l'unique plausible. Toutefois, dans un contexte de libéralisation et de globalisation, les individus, victimes des images de désir véhiculées par la mondialisation, sont très influencés par le consumérisme (Nyamnjoh 2004:1). Dans un tel environnement, tout se vend, tout s'achète ; ainsi en est-il de la force de travail physique ou intellectuel, des idées, et bien sûr le sexe n'échappe point à cette règle. Dans ce type de marché, et selon que la société est phallocratique, les hommes constituent la demande, et les femmes l'offre. Toutefois, la question ne semble pas aussi simple que cela, car plusieurs facteurs – comme nous le verrons par la suite – sont enchevêtrés dans les arcanes de ce phénomène.

C'est ainsi que, dans une ville comme Kinshasa, où vivent près de huit millions d'habitants, et où se côtoient la misère, le chômage et le sous-emploi pour la majorité de la population avec l'insolente aisance matérielle d'une minorité d'individus nantis, la prostitution infanto-juvénile devient un phénomène à la limite du fléau. En effet, beaucoup d'enfants et de jeunes, dont les familles ont été disloquées à cause du chômage chronique des parents, du phénomène de « désalarisation »,[3] et de fréquents conflits armés qui ont perduré à travers presque tout le pays et provoqué des « déplacés internes », se sont retrouvés à Kinshasa, sans ressources ni espoir.

Par ailleurs, la mauvaise gouvernance et la dégradation généralisée des conditions de vie en RDC, semblent favoriser le travail informel des enfants, notamment dans la prostitution, qui est du reste une « activité économique » échappant aux normes et réglementations, dans un environnement miné par d'interminables conflits violents. Ainsi, dans un tel environnement, la prostitution infanto-juvénile tend à s'amplifier en milieu urbain, creuset du désoeuvrement de la jeunesse. Elle semble aussi s'aggraver par la persistance du phénomène de l'éclatement de la cellule familiale et la déperdition scolaire chronique.

La prostitution infanto-juvénile

La prostitution : un fait social ancien, récurrent et récursif

La prostitution est un phénomène de société touchant autant les hommes que les femmes, et aussi bien les adultes que les jeunes. Elle n'est pas un fait social nouveau en soi. Elle a existé depuis l'aube de l'histoire dans la plupart des sociétés humaines. C'est d'ailleurs à ce titre qu'elle est parfois considérée comme le plus vieux métier du monde. Dans la Bible par exemple, plusieurs écrits attestent l'existence des prostituées.[4]

Qu'est-ce que la prostitution ? La plupart des êtres humains sensés savent ce que c'est. J. G. Mancini, dans une excellente étude sur la prostitution et le proxénétisme, en a donné une excellente définition que nous nous permettons de rappeler ici :

> La prostitution est le fait, pour une femme de pratiquer, contre rétribution, librement et sans contrainte, alors qu'elle ne dispose d'aucun autre moyen d'existence, des relations sexuelles habituelles, constantes et répétées, avec tout venant et à la première réquisition, sans choisir, ni refuser son partenaire, son objet essentiel étant le gain et non le plaisir (Mancini 1965).

Il est intéressant de souligner que les réalités sociales sont si complexes et si évolutives qu'aujourd'hui les individus des deux sexes se « prostituent », prostituer signifiant dégrader, avilir quelque chose par un usage autre que celui auquel il est normalement destiné.

Toutefois, dans le cadre de cette étude, la définition de Mancini nous est d'une grande utilité, étant donné que dans la société congolaise actuelle, la prostitution masculine n'est pas encore développée. C'est pourquoi, empruntant le prisme de l'analyse micro-économique classique, nous observons dans le cas d'espèce que l'offre est constituée presque exclusivement par les jeunes filles, alors que la demande est étendue à presque toute la gent masculine, dès l'âge pubertaire. Loin de nous donc toute idée de discrimination sexuelle ou tout penchant sexiste discriminatoire.

Par ailleurs, bien que la prostitution puisse être considérée comme un travail à part entière, il n'en est pas moins vrai que sous sa « variante » infanto-juvénile, elle représente bien un épiphénomène au sein de la société africaine actuelle, loin s'en faut. Le travail ennoblit l'homme : il est sans conteste l'un des facteurs majeurs en faveur de l'intégration sociale de l'individu, mais lorsqu'il est exercé par certaines catégories d'individus et surtout lorsque certaines conditions ne sont pas réunies, il peut effectivement devenir très problématique et susciter tout de même un ensemble de questions.

Il en est ainsi du « travail » effectué par les jeunes enfants qui se lancent dans la prostitution pour survivre en milieu urbain. C'est donc un problème délicat, comme l'affirme Mamane Boukari (1997:2) dans un rapport sur le travail des enfants :

> Problème sérieux, le travail des enfants l'est dans tous les pays tant au Nord qu'au Sud, si l'on en juge par les formes abominables d'exploitation des enfants, qui y ont recours : prostitution, pornographie, travail dangereux, adoption, travail dans des conditions qui n'ont rien à envier à l'esclavage.

À Kinshasa, le terme prostitution est exprimé, dans la langue locale par le terme générique *kindumba*.[5] En revanche, les personnes qui s'adonnent à la prostitution, c'est-à-dire les prostituées, sont désignées par plusieurs vocables : *ndumba, bula, mungando, londonienne, etc.* Si le terme *ndumba* est un terme générique pour désigner une prostituée, par contre, *mungando* désigne plutôt une prostituée adulte professionnelle, et *londonienne*, une jeune prostituée. Mais il importe de souligner que le terme « *tshel* » est un nouveau vocable pour identifier un autre type de professionnels du sexe que sont les enfants et les jeunes de 10 à 25 ans, bien que celles-ci n'acceptent pas d'être appelées par ce vocable qu'elles jugent péjoratif. Ainsi, il arrive que la prostitution soit pratiquée par des enfants, et en particulier par des jeunes filles de moins de 18 ans.

Depuis les temps immémoriaux, la pratique de la prostitution sacrée a existé dans plusieurs civilisations. Quelques exemples peuvent être tirées de l'histoire de l'humanité. Dans l'Égypte antique, le dieu Amon autorisait les prêtres d'avoir des rapports sexuels avec les plus belles filles. Cette pratique a continué d'exister dans les civilisations grecque, romaine et ptolémaïque (Maurer 1992:28).

Actuellement encore, des traditions existent et se perpétuent dans de nombreux pays notamment en Inde (dans sa partie australe), où les enfants sont conduits à la prostitution par une pratique religieuse appelée le *Devadasi* ; une pratique semblable existe également au Népal (Maurer 1992:28).

En outre, la prostitution enfantine touche sévèrement plusieurs pays du Sud-Est asiatique, comme le Cambodge, la Thaïlande, la Malaisie, les Philippines, etc. Ces pays sont en fait la cible des touristes sexuels en provenance du Nord, à la recherche d'aventures et de fantasmes divers. Toutefois, ce phénomène n'est pas « stéréotypique » des pays asiatiques, loin s'en faut. En Amérique, des pays comme le Brésil, sont aussi bien touchés par ce fléau. Dans ce pays, en effet, aucune loi n'interdit la prostitution, bien qu'il soit défendu de l'encourager, et il y existe environ 9 millions de prostituées dont plus de 2 millions sont des enfants et des adolescents (Maurer 1992:27, 29).

Et depuis plus d'une décennie, l'Afrique contemporaine ne paraît pas être épargnée par ce type de prostitution. Dans plusieurs villes africaines en effet, à cause notamment de la situation économique particulièrement précaire et de l'exode rural prononcé, la prostitution des jeunes est devenue une réalité sociale banale. À Kinshasa par exemple, les enfants de la rue constituent l'un des réservoirs qui fournissent les prostituées infanto-juvéniles, sans oublier les filles désoeuvrées et déscolarisées des quartiers pauvres qui sont une sorte de poche noire qui alimente l'offre sur le marché kinois du sexe.

Esquisse du marché du sexe à Kinshasa

Selon l'entendement commun, le marché d'un bien quelconque est le lieu de rencontre entre la volonté des consommateurs exprimée par leur demande et les désirs des producteurs (entrepreneurs) exprimés par leur offre. Ainsi, comme tout marché, celui du sexe à Kinshasa fonctionne selon la loi de l'offre et de la demande.

En principe si le demandeur (consommateur) et l'offreur (entrepreneur, c'est-à-dire l'agent économique qui offre le bien ou le service sur le marché) sont rationnels, ils doivent constamment répondre à une préoccupation centrale, celle de satisfaire leurs aspirations primaires. Pour le premier, il s'agit d'acquérir sur le marché une combinaison de biens (dans le cas d'espèce, boisson alcoolisée ou non, tabac, « sexe » ou service sexuel, plantes ou extraits de plantes aphrodisiaques ou supposées l'être, etc.) qui lui procure une satisfaction maximale, tandis que pour le second, il s'agit d'obtenir le « volume » de production (nombre de passes ou séances) qui lui donne un profit maximum.

C'est donc dans cette logique qu'il faut comprendre et interpréter le caractère mercantiliste et souvent rude des négociations auxquelles se livrent la prostituée et son « client », la première n'offrant ses services sexuels au deuxième que contre paiement préalable desdits services. Paulette Songué (1986:12), qui a eu le mérite d'étudier la prostitution au Cameroun, le dit avec des mots crus :

> Au niveau le plus bas de la prostitution, cet engagement est clair, et les clauses sont établies verbalement dès le premier contact, avec le tarif et les modalités de la « passe ». (…) Ce contact revêt un caractère commercial, avec comme priorité leprofit.

Le marché kinois du sexe est aussi caractérisé par une concurrence féroce, concurrence à laquelle se livrent les offreurs, à différents endroits ou points d'activité. Et si l'on considère la qualité et les quantités de services vendus sur ce marché ainsi que les prix pratiqués, tout laisserait à croire qu'il s'agit bien d'un marché idéal, un marché à concurrence pure et parfaite. Car les éléments caractéristiques de ce type de marché semblent être réunis, à savoir l'atomicité de l'offre et de la demande, l'homogénéité du produit, la transparence du marché, la mobilité parfaite des offreurs et des demandeurs, c'est-à-dire la liberté d'entrée et de sortie, et l'impersonnalité des relations dans le marché.

Mais en réalité, il n'en est rien : les conditions de la concurrence parfaite ou du marché idéal ne sont pas faciles à réunir, ainsi qu'il en est de tout type de marché en économie réelle (emploi, monnaie, etc.). C'est ainsi que certaines prostituées, surtout de la catégorie *haut de gamme*, agissent comme des producteurs en situation monopolistique : elles fixent souvent, en échange de leurs services, des prix prohibitifs, des prix « à prendre ou à laisser ». Toutefois, comme la concurrence parfaite est une utopie, ainsi le monopole pur est inexistant. En effet, pendant que certaines prostituées *haut de gamme* se pavanent sur le Boulevard du 30 Juin (la principale artère de la ville), dans les boîtes de nuit select et les grands hôtels de luxe, d'autres professionnelles, *moyen* et *bas de gamme* négocient leurs services à des prix plus ou moins « raisonnables », des prix « populaires » sur la Place de la Victoire à Matonge, à Yolo, à Bandalungua ou ailleurs.[6] Avant d'aborder l'offre dans ce marché, examinons premièrement la demande.

La demande

L'objectif de toute activité économique se trouve dans la satisfaction des besoins, laquelle requiert la disponibilité des biens. Du point de vue économique, le besoin exprime tout ce que l'on désire. Et l'aptitude qu'a un bien de satisfaire un besoin désigne son utilité. C'est ainsi qu'il est communément admis que les besoins constituent le moteur central du mécanisme économique. Un bien, c'est-à-dire une chose susceptible de satisfaire directement ou indirectement un besoin ou un désir humain, peut être matériel ou immatériel. Un service constitue un bien immatériel ; c'est le cas des actes posés par certains professionnels dans le cadre de leur métier, tels que les médecins, les avocats, les coiffeurs, les mécaniciens, les transporteurs, et bien sûr les prostituées.

Par ailleurs, les besoins de l'être humain sont illimités, satiables et substituables. C'est pourquoi, pour prétendre à plus de satisfaction, le consommateur peut être obligé d'utiliser une certaine quantité d'un bien ou une combinaison de biens. Et, à la limite de son revenu (contrainte budgétaire), le consommateur rationnel désireux d'obtenir le maximum de satisfaction doit maximiser sa fonction d'utilité.

La demande (ou la consommation) d'un bien peut être affectée par la modification du revenu (du consommateur), du prix de ce bien (ou service) ou du prix des autres biens. Dans la demande prostitutionnelle, à côté du service de la prostituée, il y a des biens tels que le tabac, l'alcool et les plantes aphrodisiaques qui sont prisés. Cette demande est d'autant plus importante que de nombreuses cultures africaines postulent que le besoin des rapports sexuels chez l'homme n'est pas maîtrisable. D'où le mari peut, si le besoin se fait sentir, avoir des relations sexuelles avec d'autres partenaires, surtout moins âgées, étant donné que la rumeur qui veut qu'agir ainsi procure de la puissance et même de la chance, court encore les rues.

> [En effet,] les sociétés africaines ont connu de multiples formes d'inégalités sociales entre les sexes. Les femmes sont soumises aux hommes de multiples manières et ce, tout au long de leur existence. [...] La persistance de ces contradictions a augmenté une crise de personnalité et d'identité de la femme, les réflexes édictés par ce statut « d'être inférieur, de ce fait incapable et constamment à la barre » ont fini par éclipser ceux afférents à son noble rôle dans la société. Ce statut social inférieur de la femme influe sur l'acte sexuel qui est [encore] perçu [de nos jours] comme devant satisfaire principalement les besoins de l'homme (Musuamba 2001:7-8).

Par ailleurs, la trilogie sexe, drogue et finance est une donne importante quant à l'évaluation de la demande prostitutionnelle. Les individus se comportent en petit ou grand consommateur, en partie en fonction de leur revenu et de leur inclination psycho-émotionnelle. À cela s'ajoute le fait que la plupart des acteurs de cette demande sont également influencés par certains facteurs culturels, notamment la recherche inconditionnelle du plaisir (hédonisme) et le libéralisme croissant des mœurs, consécutif à un pseudodynamisme culturel. En effet, dans un monde globalisé qui devient un « village planétaire », l'image du Nord, fortement médiatisée, est perçue au Sud comme un « must » : c'est un appât culturel incontournable et irrésistible, influencé par l'omniprésent consumérisme dont parle Nyamnjoh (2004:1).

In loco, ces acteurs sont aussi exposés aux multiples sollicitations des *Tshel* qui, par leur accoutrement provoquant et choquant, et surtout par leur « professionnalisme », induisent la genèse des stimuli sexuels : on parle de « bip ».[7]

Il faut enfin avouer que les besoins exprimés dans le cadre de cette demande sont plus ou moins complexes, en ce sens qu'ils englobent aussi bien des besoins physiologiques et semi-vitaux que des besoins psychologiques voire culturels. Ainsi, ces acteurs se recrutent le plus souvent dans le rang des célibataires endurcis, des veufs, des divorcés, des jeunes pubères, des mariés et des touristes à la quête de l'aventure sexuelle et du fantasme érotique extraconjugal. Somme toute, auprès de qui s'adresse cette abondante demande ?

L'offre

Comme la demande, l'offre suppose une relation entre la quantité offerte d'un bien ou d'un service, sans en oublier la qualité, et son prix. Dans ce marché, les principaux acteurs de l'offre sont d'une part, les prostituées elles-mêmes et d'autre part, les proxénètes (entremetteuses principalement) qui agissent souvent comme intermédiaires incontournables. Parfois, la culture inculque et prédispose la femme africaine à adopter un comportement qui favorise le phénomène de semi-prostitution :

> Dans de nombreux pays africains, les femmes survivent économiquement grâce à la prostitution ou autres activités sexuelles. Et sans être considérées et sans [même] se considérer elles-mêmes comme des prostituées, de nombreuses femmes ont des relations sexuelles avec un homme en échange d'un soutien financier ou matériel (Musuamba 2001:13).

Il est vrai que beaucoup de femmes recourent à la prostitution comme mode de survie. Cependant, certaines trouvent en cette activité une source transitoire de revenu, en présence ou à l'absence d'un travail rémunéré. Ce phénomène de semi-prostitution, qui touche par ailleurs moult étudiantes et fonctionnaires, n'est pas à extrapoler au niveau de toute la gent féminine. Ce serait faire fausse route au risque de s'y méprendre, tant il est si vrai que la dynamique sociale dans la société africaine autorise plusieurs créneaux de solidarité en faveur de la femme. Avec ou sans emploi, la femme trouve toujours quelqu'un qui lui vient en aide, et pas nécessairement en échanges de services sexuels, mais surtout et souvent par sollicitude masculine, l'image de la mère génératrice aidant, laquelle image est fort incrustée dans le psychisme masculin.

Par ailleurs, [si] « le corps féminin est apparu longtemps comme une source de débauche, de dépravation – donc de désordre social » (Lewin 2002:13), il n'est pas cependant moins vrai que ce corps n'a jamais cessé d'intriguer et il continuera d'intriguer les hommes, tant il est vrai que le corps féminin est à la fois le creuset de la beauté, de la sexualité et de la maternité. En effet, c'est le lieu par excellence de l'expression de tous les fantasmes masculins.

À Kinshasa, les enfants de la rue, les filles mères, les filles désoeuvrées et déscolarisées, les filles et femmes déplacées de guerre, et bien d'autres constituent des proies faciles et une offre bon marché, eu égard aux différents prix pratiqués par les unes et les autres ainsi que leur activisme sur le marché du sexe. Cependant, cet « activisme » n'est pas exempt de problèmes et lourd de conséquences. Parmi lesquelles, nous épinglons le risque encouru par rapport aux infections sexuellement transmissibles (IST) et le VIH/SIDA, étant donné que ce risque est souvent perçu comme la fille aînée de l'incidence de cette pandémie sur le métier du sexe.

Pauvreté et VIH/SIDA : véritables défis pour la RDC

La crise généralisée survenue après les deux pillages (1991 et 1993) a engendré une kyrielle de chômeurs dans le pays. En effet, on estimait en 1995 que 5 pour cent seulement de la population active de Kinshasa avait un emploi stable et « rémunérateur » dans le secteur formel.

> Une manifestation majeure de la crise (…) est le processus de « désalarisation » massive de l'activité économique, lié à la suppression d'emplois du fait de la fermeture d'entreprises (…), et en particulier dans le secteur public, à la valeur dérisoire de rémunérations qui, en outre, ne sont plus assurées qu'irrégulièrement (De Villers 2002:12).

À cela sont venues se greffer les affres de la guerre (1996, 1998 -) et sa cohorte de conséquences dramatiques : déplacés de guerre, personnes victimes des violences sexuelles, infection à VIH/SIDA, etc., le tout faisant le lit du dénuement et de la pauvreté totale de la population.

Le phénomène de la pauvreté en RDC

La pauvreté est la fille aînée du sous-développement. C'est ainsi que la lutte contre la pauvreté est apparue, au cours de cette décennie, comme étant le cheval de bataille tant pour les institutions de Bretton Woods que pour les pays concernés.

La RDC est confrontée à de graves problèmes de développement. En effet, malgré ses ressources naturelles abondantes et diversifiées – et qui ne sont du reste que des potentialités –, la majorité de sa population croupit dans une misère indescriptible, comme le témoignent la plupart des indicateurs du développement humain tels que l'alphabétisation, la nutrition, la santé ou l'espérance de vie. Et le tableau demeurera sombre tant que des efforts musclés ne seront pas conjugués pour enrayer la pandémie du VIH/SIDA aggravée par la guerre et mettre définitivement un terme à la guerre et aux différents conflits armés, notamment dans la partie orientale du pays. Aujourd'hui, en outre, la lutte contre la pauvreté constitue un défi majeur pour la RDC.

Dans ce pays, la pauvreté est un phénomène de masse ; elle est non seulement répandue parmi la population, mais elle est aussi visible auprès de l'élite technocratique ; elle est profonde et grave car elle touche aussi bien le monde rural que les cités urbaines. Son ampleur est donnée par la proportion des personnes qui vivent en dessous du seuil de pauvreté unique, soit 1 dollar par personne par jour. Actuellement, on estime que 80 pour cent de cette population vit en dessous de ce seuil. Et cette situation n'est pas sans conséquence manifeste sur le vécu quotidien de la population congolaise dont les plus jeunes membres développent, bon gré mal gré, une dynamique migratoire axée vers le nord et ayant pour destination de prédilection l'espace Schengen.

Déjà en 1999, Mbaya et Streiffeler décrivaient les effets de la crise économique qui s'est amplifiée par la suite, en des termes des plus explicites.

> La crise économique a engendré des comportements particuliers chez les jeunes congolaises aussi bien dans les centres urbains qu'en milieu rural. Dans les centres urbains, si les garçons peuvent se passer du savon, de la crème et d'autres besoins de toilette élémentaires, il n'en est pas le cas pour les jeunes filles. Les jeunes filles des ménages vivant en deçà du minimum vital vont au gré du vent en mettant leur corps en jeu pour avoir de quoi manger, s'habiller décemment, payer les frais scolaires, se faire soigner dans un hôpital, assister financièrement et matériellement les parents et les autres membres de famille (Mbaya et Streiffeler 1999:86).

Sida, pauvreté et croissance économique

En RDC, comme dans la plupart des pays africains touchés par ce fléau, l'épidémie de VIH/SIDA a fait augmenter la pauvreté et la mortalité des adultes et des enfants. Ce qui ne manque pas d'annihiler tous les efforts entrepris quant à la croissance économique, à la réduction de la pauvreté ainsi qu'à la formation du capital humain (Banque Africaine de Développement 2002:132).

Il faut également signaler l'impact négatif que jouent les conflits armés et les guerres civiles en Afrique, sur les performances économiques. La RDC est l'un des pays africains, à l'instar du Soudan, de la Somalie, de la Sierra Léone, du Burundi, etc., qui sont plongés dans la guerre depuis bientôt une décennie. Ces conflits armés ont produit une multitude des blessés et des morts, et de nombreux réfugiés et « déplacés de guerre » (espèce de réfugiés « internes »), privés de leur espace de vie et de leurs moyens de subsistance. Ces différents conflits constituent donc un obstacle majeur au développement des régions concernées. Ils sont aussi synonymes de désinvestissement, non production, chômage, pauvreté, déperdition scolaire, famine, dérive politique en régime « autocratique », insécurité de toute sorte, violation massive des droits humains, etc.

Au demeurant, ce problème risque de s'aggraver si rien n'est entrepris pour le résoudre. En effet, la persistance de la guerre et de l'instabilité politique dans la région des Grands Lacs par exemple, [pour revenir au cas du Congo], a des effets [néfastes], immédiats et indirects, sur l'économie des ménages et des pays en conflits ([au] niveau macroéconomique), ainsi que sur la santé des populations, par le biais de la propagation des IST et du VIH/Sida, à cause de la vulnérabilité économique [de ces dernières] et du recours à la prostitution comme moyen de survie dans les zones urbaines (Banque Africaine de Développement 2002:133).

En outre, ce phénomène contribue à accroître la pression sur les infrastructures sociales et physiques déjà insuffisantes des villes d'accueil vers lesquelles affluent les personnes fuyant les zones où sévissent les conflits armés. Et de ce groupe, les personnes âgées, les femmes et les enfants constituent les individus les plus fragiles et les plus exposés à toute sorte d'abus, d'exploitation et de violence.

La propagation du VIH/SIDA repose avant tout sur le comportement intime de l'être humain. Ainsi, dans une société où la majorité de la population est jeune et où ces jeunes sont sexuellement très actifs, la probabilité d'infection aux IST et au Sida est relativement forte. La lecture des taux de prévalence du VIH chez les jeunes de trois pays de la région des Grands Lacs où sévissent les violences sexuelles post conflit armé est plus qu'éloquente : [8]

En 1999, le taux de prévalence du VIH chez les jeunes de 15 à 24 ans était de :
4,31 – 5,84% (filles) contre 1,66 – 3,32% (garçons) pour la RDC ;
9,04 – 12,23% (filles) contre 3,48 – 6,96% (garçons) pour le Rwanda ;
9,86 – 13,34% (filles) contre 3,80 – 7,59% (garçons) pour le Burundi.

Dans la région des Grands Lacs où perdurent des conflits armés, les militaires ont souvent des relations sexuelles avec la population civile, soit par commerce normal, soit, et le plus souvent, par viol qui est devenu une véritable arme de guerre. Si l'on considère le nombre considérable des déplacés de guerre présents à Kinshasa, on peut alors réaliser la vulnérabilité de sa population face au Sida, et particulièrement la catégorie des professionnelles du sexe appelée *Tshel.* Or :

> Le VIH/SIDA peut intervenir tout au long de la vie. [Et] même s'il affecte aussi bien les hommes que les femmes, celles-ci sont plus vulnérables à cause de facteurs biologiques et épidémiologiques, de la violence sexuelle, d'un statut socio-économique peu élevé et de l'absence de pouvoir de négociation avec les partenaires masculins. En Afrique subsaharienne, 55 pour cent des 28,1 millions d'adultes infectés par le VIH sont des femmes ; chez les jeunes, le nombre de femmes infectées est *quatre* fois plus élevé que celui des hommes (ONUSIDA/OMS 2002).

En outre, bien que le taux de prévalence du SIDA en RDC soit relativement faible par rapport à ses voisins de l'Afrique australe et de l'est, le poids démographique de sa population en majorité jeune reste un sujet d'inquiétude :

> Selon les estimations, le taux de prévalence national du VIH/SIDA est de 4,2 pour cent. Ce chiffre est certes inférieur à celui rencontré dans bon nombre de pays d'Afrique de l'Est et australe mais environ un million d'enfants congolais ont perdu leurs parents en raison de l'épidémie (Human Rights Watch, 2006:4).

Le métier de *Tshel*

La législation congolaise en matière de travail interdit d'embaucher les individus âgés de moins de 18 ans, la capacité de contracter étant tout de même fixée à 16 ans. En outre, la prostitution des mineurs est interdite.[9] Elle constitue une infraction punissable d'après les prescrits du Code Pénal Congolais. En dépit de ce dispositif juridique, le métier de *Tshel* existe et se pratique allègrement. La dynamique sociale aidant, ce nouveau « métier » tend à s'imposer comme créneau de survie par prédilection pour les jeunes générations des milieux urbains.

Être Tshel à Kinshasa

De prime abord, nous voudrions signaler que ce n'est pas un métier à proprement parler ; mais il tend à le devenir par la force des choses à cause notamment de la forte précarité socio-économique en milieu urbain, et par le fait que ces enfants et jeunes, « artisans » engagés dans ce métier, en font effectivement une profession, fût-elle transitoire, et en tirent leurs moyens de subsistance, bien qu'elles ne s'en vantent point publiquement. Au premier contact, les *Tshel* se présentent comme des agents de négoce.

En quoi consiste ce métier ?

Ce métier consiste à aborder les passants au carrefour des grandes agglomérations, au niveau des marchés, de grandes places publiques, aux abords des hôtels et bistrots, autour des bars populaires appelés *ngandas*, au niveau des cimetières désaffectés, au niveau de certaines rues non suffisamment éclairées mais bordées d'arbres, à la croisée des chemins, etc., en les incitant à avoir des rapports sexuels avec soi, et ce, moyennant paiement préalable d'une modique somme d'argent. Ceci est bien sûr du racolage, comme toute prostituée professionnelle sait en user. En revanche, les *Tshel*, pour exercer leur métier, usent d'un racolage subtil et raffiné, on dirait des virtuoses patentés dans leur art. Pour ce faire, ces jeunes utilisent plusieurs astuces allant de la saine flagornerie au doux harcèlement, en passant par la supplication angélique. Dans ce métier, tout est négociable et le client n'est pas roi.

D'où proviennent ces jeunes ?

Leur positionnement stratégique au cœur de la ville, notamment à Matonge, et sur le boulevard du 30 juin en plein centre ville, les fait remarquer des paisibles citoyens chaque soir et surtout les week-ends. La plupart d'entre elles proviennent des quartiers pauvres et périphériques de la ville. Elles semblent être le symbole du niveau de désagrégation culturelle, morale et familiale de la société. Le surplus d'énergie que regorgent les jeunes – véritable potentiel créatif – ne semble pas être canalisé pour être transmuté en force réellement constructive pour le renouvellement et la revivification de la société. Si les jeunes filles semblent avoir un faible pour le métier du sexe et sont effectivement enclines à la prostitution, les jeunes garçons en revanche basculent souvent dans la violence sans coup férir.

Dans sa problématique des enfants en situation difficile, Fabrizio Terenzio (1995:22-23) note que :

> La jeunesse africaine récemment urbanisée, a connu en l'espace d'une génération, deux événements d'une portée considérable : la place prépondérante qu'elle a pris dans la société qui rajeunit de jour en jour [...], et la perte de sa fonction sociale, fort bien définie dans la société traditionnelle et qui n'a pas de statut dans la société moderne [...]. C'est donc à une jeunesse marginalisée par la ville mais majoritaire que nous avons à faire. Elle recèle en son sein une considérable énergie pour construire ou détruire la société. Les enfants et les jeunes qui actuellement recherchent leur survie dans les rues des grandes villes, illustrent la réaction créative de la population, mais constituent également le symptôme annonciateur d'une poussée de l'injustice, de la misère, et de ses effets, parmi lesquels : l'irruption de la violence urbaine.

Et parlant des enfants et des jeunes dans les villes, évoluant dans la rue, il pense que « le phénomène de rupture familiale est au centre de beaucoup de leurs histoires personnelles » (Terenzio 1995:27). C'est ainsi que beaucoup de ces filles entretiennent des rapports solidaires et chaleureux avec leurs « collègues ». Il suffit de les observer dans leur milieu de « travail » pour s'en rendre compte : elles se comportent en véritables « consœurs » lorsqu'elles se rencontrent dans la rue, à la manière des journalistes, et comme des vraies professionnelles, arborant cigarette à la bouche et démarche altière. Ce qui rend parfois leur racolage caractéristique et perceptible.

De temps en temps, certaines d'entre elles s'organisent en bande, et au regard de la loi, elles ne semblent pas être celles qui font des infractions. Au contraire, des policiers procèdent quelquefois à des guets-apens et à des extorsions de leurs clients, et ce, souvent avec leur propre complicité. Et cela ne semble émouvoir personne dans la société, en dépit du dévoilement de certains épisodes malheureux que subissent quelques victimes. En revanche, certaines personnes, soucieuses d'assouvir leurs fantasmes érotiques presque dans une barbarie tropicale, et comme pour satisfaire leur curiosité sexuelle, bravent le risque et encouragent ce genre de transaction.

Ces jeunes sont-elles indépendantes ?

Après une minutieuse observation dans leur milieu de travail, nous avons noté que la plupart des *Tshel* exercent leur métier en tant qu'indépendantes. Toutefois, une petite frange d'entre elles dépend d'une « matrone », chez qui elles versent une certaine somme d'argent au pro rata des opérations. Le montant rétrocédé varierait entre 10 et 20 pour cent des recettes totales. Ces chiffres semblent indiquer que le proxénétisme n'a pas encore atteint des proportions inquiétantes dans la ville de Kinshasa.

Profil des Tshel

Avant de dresser le profil des *Tshel*, voyons d'abord qui sont-elles, que signifie ce terme et quelle symbolique se cache derrière ce vocable.

Le terme Tshel

Aussi invraisemblable que cela puisse paraître, l'origine de ce terme ne semble pas être connue de façon précise. Toutefois, l'enquête menée auprès des jeunes Kinois a révélé qu'il s'agit d'un terme d'origine argotique lingala, utilisé par ces derniers, pour désigner les toutes jeunes prostituées. Selon eux, ce terme comporte les significations suivantes : petite fille prostituée, jeune et belle nocturne (12 à 18 ans), jeune professionnelle du sexe, fille libre, etc., et ne concerne pas les prostituées professionnelles adultes appelées *mingando*. De plus, ce terme, qui semble chargé d'une émotion négative signifierait également « petite pute à tout faire », et nierait toute la dignité liée à leur travail. En fait de dignité, y en a-t-il dans ce métier ? Et en réalité, ces filles n'aiment pas qu'on les appelle *Tshel*,[10] même si vraisemblablement, elles se pavanent dans les rues et qu'elles s'affichent comme étant des vraies prostituées. Elles aiment plutôt être appelées « *chouchou* », « *chérie* », « *mama moke* » (petite maman), « *tantine* », « *petite* », « *sœur* » ou « *petite sœur* », etc.

Le profil proprement dit

L'observation des *Tshel* dans leur milieu de production nous a permis de percevoir qu'elles sont très jeunes, certaines affichant une mine fort angélique. La *Tshel* est un individu dont le profil joue contre toute tentative de stéréotypage. Tantôt, elle est d'un niveau d'instruction modeste, tantôt, elle a un *background* scolaire suffisant. Et certaines sont très douées en langues : ainsi, la *polyglottie* n'est pas une vertu rare chez les *Tshel haut de gamme* (de catégorie supérieure) et expérimentées – celles qui ont du métier et qui ont usé leurs fesses sur le banc de l'école – bien qu'elles aient un faible pour le lingala, la langue parlée à Kinshasa. En fait, c'est le propre du commun des Kinois de « mépriser » les langues « étrangères ».

Par ailleurs, plusieurs entretiens approfondis et répétés avec ces jeunes ont révélé qu'elles sont plus ou moins instruites, bien qu'une bonne partie d'entre elles aient à peine terminé leur cycle primaire. Ce phénomène touchant également une minorité d'intellectuelles, il n'est pas rare en effet de rencontrer une jeune ayant terminé son cycle d'études jusqu'au diplôme d'État et arborant ainsi un joli petit cursus pré-universitaire.[11] Par contre, plusieurs d'entre elles ont reconnu n'avoir pas été si loin ou du tout sur le banc de l'école mais elles ont reconnu posséder une ancienneté de plus de six années. Ce qui laisse présager que l'âge probable de leur « enrôlement » sur le trottoir se situerait invraisemblablement vers les 11 ou 12 ans, parfois même un peu en deçà.

En ce qui concerne le statut matrimonial de leurs parents, retenons que plusieurs d'entre elles sont issues des ménages polygamiques, des parents séparés ou divorcés ou tout simplement des parents reconvertis à une nouvelle religiosité et remariés. Et donc plusieurs se sont retrouvées toutes seules, abandonnées à leur propre sort, et sommées de se débrouiller pour survivre. Comment s'y prennent-elles pour survivre ? Arrivent-elles à gagner un revenu suffisant leur permettant de faire face à leurs besoins fondamentaux ? Voilà autant de questions qui intriguent le premier venu dans ce labyrinthe d'adeptes de Vénus.

Le revenu généré

Il est vrai que ces questions nous ont également personnellement préoccupé au fur et à mesure que nous effectuons cette recherche. Chaque jour qui passait nous faisait découvrir une réalité et un monde différent de celui d'où nous venions. Il nous semblait chaque jour partir vers une autre planète, une planète à la fois insolite et familière, car ses habitants étaient à la fois semblables et différents à ceux que je laissais dans ma planète de départ…

Comme dans tout métier, toute prestation procure un revenu. Dans le cas sous examen, le niveau du revenu est fonction de la qualité des services rendus, de l'assiduité au travail, de la force physique et psychologique, du temps et de la saison, de la fidélité et de l'abondance de la clientèle, de la fidélisation des clients et de la capacité de négociation. En effet, le service a un coût, et le coût varie d'un individu à l'autre, selon le standing du client, le jour, l'heure, l'endroit, ou l'habileté de négociation avec le client, etc. Nous parlons d'habileté et non de capacité, car dans ce « métier », le premier contact est capital, et la négociation de la rémunération du service est une grande bataille pour la professionnelle.

Nous avons tenté d'évaluer le revenu mensuel généré par ce métier par la plus basse catégorie, en tenant compte de certains facteurs et aléas de ce métier. Ainsi, lorsque l'on prend en compte les différents types de services offerts par les *Tshel* (massage, passe, nuitée) et les différents « tarifs » y correspondants, on peut effectivement évaluer leur revenu moyen. Toutefois, étant donné que le niveau de production est fort variable, nous avons intégré dans le calcul du revenu virtuel, un *facteur correctif f* en fonction de 26 jours ouvrables par mois, 20 jours par mois de pleine activité possible, 2 à 3 clients par jour, et 4 nuitées correspondant aux 4 week-ends du mois.[12]

Étant donné le registre fort variable des prix pratiqués sur ce marché, une passe peut se négocier entre 1 et 7 US $, tandis que la nuitée entre 5 et 30 US $. Selon le modèle de calcul utilisé, le revenu individuel peut donc aller de 20 à 180 US $, tandis que le revenu mensuel virtuel (modèle théorique) pourrait osciller entre 50 et 460 US $. Autant ces chiffres peuvent « émerveiller » le lecteur, autant ils peuvent le révolter. Car en effet, la réalité est toute autre. La dureté de ce métier ne se raconte pas, elle doit se vivre pour être mieux saisie. Pourtant, il ne nous a pas semblé intéressant de procéder à des récits biographiques de telle ou telle *Tshel*, pas plus pour les dévaluer que pour louer leur mérite ou la réussite de l'une ou l'autre. Car, comme Paulette Songué (1986:6) avec les prostituées de Yaoundé, nous sommes d'avis que :

> Les récits autobiographiques auraient plutôt pour résultat d'appeler le lecteur à l'apitoiement sur leur condition, ou alors de grossir ou surévaluer les mérites de la prostitution, là où la prostituée a « réussi ».

D'ailleurs, la plupart du temps, il est nécessaire voire indispensable pour les *Tshel*, de combiner d'autres petites activités afin de nouer les deux bouts du mois, surtout après une période non productive (maladie, malaises divers). En outre, quelques individus ont affirmé avoir d'autres sources de revenu, afin de subvenir aux innombrables besoins qu'exigent leur métier (habits, produits de maquillage, etc.). Il s'agit notamment du petit commerce (épices, produits cosmétiques, pains, etc.), de la tresse des cheveux, … Certaines sont temporairement occupées comme danseuse dans une petite formation musicale du quartier, ou comme comédienne dans une petite troupe de théâtre populaire en gestation,… D'autres encore ont carrément avoué s'adonner au vol, surtout en compagnie des clients riches. A ce propos, les touristes en font souvent les frais. Et au Congo, les éléments militaires de la MONUC en ont souvent été victimes, surtout au début de leur mission à Kinshasa, car ils tombaient de temps en temps dans leur traquenard.

Corrélation entre niveau d'instruction et revenu

Nous nous sommes également intéressé à la question de savoir s'il existe une corrélation entre le niveau d'instruction des *Tshel* et leur revenu, ou en d'autres termes si leur niveau d'instruction influence leur revenu. Une première évaluation préliminaire, fondée sur les données disponibles tirées de notre enquête, semble effectivement montrer l'évidence d'une corrélation linéaire entre le niveau d'instruction des *Tshel* et leur revenu.[13] Mais ce revenu n'est pas exempt de coûts. Quelle est la nature de ces coûts ?

Coûts liés au métier

L'exercice de tout métier ou de toute activité économique suppose l'existence des coûts. La plupart des individus ont reconnu le caractère informel de leur métier et ne disposaient donc d'aucun document administratif, ni de fiche de contrôle médical, bien qu'ils aient affirmé suivre un traitement médical en cas de maladie. Toutefois, les principaux coûts pour ce métier concernent le logement, l'habillement, les soins médicaux, les produits de toilette et de beauté les produits de coquetterie, la nourriture, le transport, les appels téléphoniques et l'aide à la famille, et parfois les frais scolaires pour les membres de famille (jeunes frères et jeunes sœurs).

Par ailleurs, ils ont reconnu faire face à certains autres coûts fortuits, notamment des amendes transactionnelles versées auprès des agents de police de manière parfois inopportune, ou alors des extorsions voisines des rackets, orchestrées par des hommes en uniforme ou non, armés et non identifiés. Certaines professionnelles sont également tenues de verser des petites sommes d'argent, des pourboires ou des commissions à d'éventuelles entremetteuses ou matrones, voire à des entremetteurs (là où ces personnages existent).

Facteurs déterminants et statut sérologique

La plupart des personnes interrogées estiment que ce sont des raisons économiques (pauvreté) qui les ont poussées dans la prostitution malgré leur jeune âge. D'autres motivations ont été évoquées, notamment le plaisir sexuel (car il y en a qui adorent vraiment le sexe et des nymphomanes pourrait-on dire), et l'obligation ou la contrainte, dans une moindre mesure. En revanche, une bonne partie d'individus ont affirmé exercer le métier du sexe pour les raisons suivantes : déception dans le mariage (précoce), négligence des parents, vengeance vis-à-vis de la société. Il faut souligner que la promiscuité qu'on trouve dans certains quartiers populaires favorise la sexualité et le mariage précoces de beaucoup de jeunes. Ceci est déterminant pour leur avenir sexuel.

À la question « Connaissez-vous votre statut sérologique (VIH/SIDA) ? », plusieurs sujets ont déclaré connaître leur statut sérologique qu'ils ont supposé être négatif ; plusieurs autres ont avoué être ignorants sur ce sujet, et ce, pour les raisons ci-après : « j'ai peur ou j'aurai des soucis si je connais mon statut », « je suis bien portante et je n'ai pas besoin d'être informée sur mon statut », « je n'ai pas d'information sur ça et ça ne m'intéresse pas », ou « je risque de mourir si je sais ».

Usage du préservatif et tenue de travail

La plupart des personnes interrogées ont affirmé qu'elles faisaient un usage systématique du préservatif lors de rapports sexuels, et plusieurs nous ont déclaré : « je n'ai pas le sida, car j'exige toujours la capote ». Cependant, lors des entretiens répétés que nous avions eu avec ces jeunes personnes, certaines d'entre elles ont reconnu qu'elles pouvaient être tentées par l'aventure des rapports non protégés, lorsqu'elles se trouvaient en face d'une forte somme d'argent. Ce comportement irrationnel a surtout été observé lorsqu'il s'agissait des partenaires venus de loin (expatriés, compatriotes venant de loin, touristes divers, etc.) et manipulant des devises.

Ainsi que l'exigent certains métiers, les *Tshel* ont aussi un accoutrement tout à fait particulier à leur métier. On n'irait pas jusqu'à dire qu'elles ont un uniforme, mais bien un « quelque chose » de commun qui ressemble à cela, un accoutrement singulier. Il s'agit la plupart du temps des habits moulants, des tenues provocantes (« sexy »), des vêtements attirants et favorables au racolage gestuel : mini-jupe *kibenda,*[14] mini-blouson transparent, pantalon jeans taille basse, blouse à dos nu, pantalon serré, blouson *body*, etc. Mbaya et Streiffeler (1999:88) les ont décrites en ces termes :

> Elles s'habillent drôlement et portent le plus souvent des mini-jupes ayant une fente (« *mundelo* »)[15] qui laisse voir tout le dessous par devant ou par derrière : question d'exciter l'instinct sexuel des passants pour en décrocher un et obtenir de lui de l'argent après l'acte sexuel.

Difficultés du métier et desiderata des Tshel

L'exercice de tout métier comporte des difficultés, celui des *Tshel* ne fait pas exception hélas. Les principales difficultés de ce métier ont pour noms : intégration dans la « bande » c'est-à-dire le groupe, sévisses corporels, escroquerie, attaques par des bandits, agression par des « *shégués* » (enfants de la rue), insolvabilité de certains clients familiers dont les militaires, les policiers et les aînés timbrés du quartier (les « *bayayas* »), tracasseries policières, risée des voisins, fuite du client, rabattement inconsidéré de prix, infections sexuellement transmissibles ou non, stature physique et exigences de certains clients, menaces de la matrone en cas de chute prononcée des recettes (pour celles qui en ont), baisse du tarif à cause de la conjoncture ou de la crise économique généralisée, clients douteux et insolvables, risques divers.

Un extrait d'un récent rapport réalisé par Human Rights Watch sur les enfants de la rue en RDC est plus qu'explicite :

> Une fonctionnaire (...) a indiqué qu'en dehors des civils, les soldats et les policiers étaient aussi responsables d'abus sexuels sur les filles de la rue. Dans le cadre de son travail, elle a découvert qu'au moment de leurs méfaits, les auteurs utilisaient rarement, voire jamais, de préservatifs, faisant ainsi courir le risque aux filles de contracter des maladies sexuellement transmissibles, notamment le VIH/SIDA. A ses yeux, les violences sexuelles à l'égard des filles compliquent davantage encore leur réhabilitation et rend d'autant plus difficile une réinsertion réussie au sein de leur famille, en particulier lorsque les filles ont des enfants nés d'un viol. Les victimes de viol peuvent être âgées d'à peine huit ans (Human Rights Watch 2006:22).

Somme toute, ces braves filles ont reconnu que leur métier était difficile : pour cela, une action des pouvoirs publics constituerait un salut pour elles. Quant à leur avenir, plusieurs ont émis le vœu de devenir femme d'affaires, ou de se marier carrément (« devenir un jour une épouse avec un mari et des enfants »), malgré tout. Également, elles aimeraient bien bénéficier de la compréhension de la communauté, et surtout obtenir l'aide et le soutien de l'État. Comment dès lors réaliser ce rêve ?

Connaître les *Tshel* : constat et caractérisation

Loin de nous l'idée de condamner les acteurs impliqués dans la prostitution infanto-juvénile, ou porter un jugement de valeur sur cette réalité sociale ; en revanche nous voulons, au terme de cette étude préliminaire sur ces jeunes professionnelles du sexe appelées « *Tshel* », établir un constat qui permet leur caractérisation. Ce constat pourrait servir de terreau à toute recherche ultérieure sur le terrain kinois ou d'ailleurs, et permettre une meilleure posture de recherche comparative concernant le même objet sur d'autres terrains.

À l'observation, les *Tshel* se présentent comme des jeunes filles âgées de moins de 18 ans. En réalité, la plupart des filles que l'on trouve sur le trottoir sont âgées de moins de 14 ans. Or à cet âge, l'individu n'est ni suffisamment développé physiquement et psychologiquement ni assez autonome et robuste pour exercer un métier aussi éprouvant.

Elles se recrutent parmi les couches pauvres de la société, plusieurs ayant déserté l'école et le toit familial dès la prime enfance ; elles vivent soit en bande, à leur propre compte, dans un logis appelé « maquis », soit encore en famille.

Poussées par l'instinct de survie, la précarité de la situation socio-économique du pays et la misère, elles se jettent dans la rue, leur unique espace d'épanouissement et espoir de survie. Si certaines ont encore leurs parents vivants (qui d'ailleurs sont soit chômeurs soit sous-payés, et largement irresponsables), d'autres sont orphelines et donc seules. Cette survie basée sur le métier du sexe les expose constamment à des agressions de tout genre. Par exemple, leur vulnérabilité face au Sida semble établie. En effet, « tentées » par certains clients véreux, beaucoup de *Tshel* concèdent des rapports sexuels non protégés. De plus, elles ne sont pas exemptes des sévisses corporels et mauvais traitements physiques de la part des « mauvais clients » qui ne sont rien d'autres que les éléments de la police et de l'armée.

N'étant pas encore des femmes mûres, elles sont pour la plupart des enfants et des jeunes en pleine croissance. La naïveté de leur âge les expose souvent à des embûches et dangers divers parfois innommables. Et dans les conditions actuelles du pays, le rêve de « femme d'affaires » ou de « femme épouse et mère » qu'elles semblent chérir n'est qu'une chimère.

Certes, cette activité leur procure tout de même quelque revenu. Mais ce revenu est faible, et parfois insuffisant pour satisfaire les besoins fondamentaux. Pour améliorer leur revenu, elles sont presque obligées de développer d'autres atouts et aptitudes susceptibles d'attirer et d'augmenter leur clientèle, ou alors elles s'adonnent à d'autres activités secondaires ou tertiaires tel le larcin auprès des clients, afin « d'arrondir » leurs fins du mois.[16]

Le revenu qu'elles tirent de leur « job » est modeste : il est à peine au-dessus du seuil de pauvreté. Tout ce qui est gagné est directement consommé sans épargne aucune. Dès lors, aucune amélioration sensible de leurs conditions de vie n'est possible, à moyen terme. Et en l'absence de toute qualification professionnelle, leur insertion sociale future pose problème.

À la lumière de ce constat, l'on réalise que l'avenir des milliers de jeunes qui, à travers la ville de Kinshasa s'adonnent à ce « métier de *Tshel*, est plus qu'hypothéqué. Dans ces conditions, comment ces jeunes peuvent-elles sortir de la trappe de la pauvreté ?

Notes

1. La « zaïrianisation » c'est la nationalisation des entreprises et autres sociétés industrielles intervenue en 1973 en RDC, alors appelée « Zaïre ». Elle fut suivie par la radicalisation. Voir aussi: Pourtier 1991:30.
2. Le terme *Tshel* désigne une jeune prostituée âgée de 10 à 25 ans. Cf. infra.
3. Impaiement (absence de salaire) dans la fonction publique et donc perte du pouvoir d'achat. Voir aussi G. De Villers 2002:12.

4. Voir La Bible dans Jérémie 3:1-5 (allégorie), Proverbe 6:24-28, 7:6-18, Siracide 9:6, Luc 7:36-50, etc.
5. En *lingala*, la langue parlée à Kinshasa, tout comme en *kikongo* d'ailleurs (langue parlée à l'ouest de la RDC), « kindumba » signifie prostitution, « ndumba », « bula » et « mungando » (« mingando » au pluriel) désignent les prostituées ou femmes libres en général.
6. La plupart des quartiers de la ville sont touchés par ce phénomène. Les *Tshel* sont ainsi catégorisées : *haut, moyen et bas de gamme*, selon leur standing de vie. On les appelle aussi, contre leur gré, *fioti-fioti* (tout petit).
7. Par analogie, le « bip » des jeunes prostituées est comparé au « bip » des appareils cellulaires utilisés pour appeler ou faire signe à un correspondant. Et ces bips peuvent être le fait de laisser entrevoir l'intérieur des cuisses en position assise, le nombril, les seins, etc.
8. Cf ONUSIDA 2000:125.
9. La Loi n° 015/2002 du 16 octobre 2002 portant *Code du Travail* est clair en son article 3 qui stipule que : « Toutes les pires formes de travail des enfants sont abolies. L'expression « les pires formes de travail des enfants » comprend notamment : (…) b) l'utilisation, le recrutement ou l'offre d'un enfant à des fins de prostitution, de production de matériels pornographiques ou des danses obscènes ; (…) d) les travaux qui, par leur nature ou les conditions dans lesquelles ils s'exercent, sont susceptibles de nuire à la santé, à la sécurité, à la dignité ou à la moralité de l'enfant ».
10. Pour certains, le terme *tshel* serait dérivé du mot anglais shell ; ainsi il signifierait personne qui s'occupe de l'« échange de l'argent contre le sexe ». Pour d'autres, ce terme serait dérivé des expressions lingala « tshela nga », « ko tsha » qui signifient respectivement « fais pour moi », « faire ».
11. Dans le système éducatif congolais (RDC), le Diplôme d'État est l'équivalent du « Baccalauréat » français.
12. Calcul du facteur correctif (f) dans l'évaluation du revenu. Pour calculer le revenu mensuel moyen virtuel, il faut tenir compte de 26 jours ouvrables (31 jours du mois diminué des jours de l'indisponibilité menstruelle), 20 jours de pleine activité possible selon le niveau de la demande évalué forfaitairement à 2 ou 3 clients par jour, et de 4 nuitées de pleine production qui correspondent aux 4 week-ends du mois. Mathématiquement, on a: (1) (13x2) + (13x3) / 2 = 32,5 ; (2) 32,5 / 2 = 1,625 ; (3) (4x0, 25)=1 ; (4) (1,625+1)= 2,625. Le facteur du revenu mensuel moyen virtuel (f) est donc égal à 2,625.
13. Pour ce faire, il nous a semblé bon de recourir à la théorie de la corrélation. Ainsi, nous basant sur les données de l'enquête, et après quelques calculs statistiques, nous avons obtenu les coefficients de corrélation (r = 0,77) et de signification (R = 0,593). L'outil statistique montre qu'il existe bien une corrélation entre les deux variables. Les deux variables sont le niveau d'instruction (x) et le revenu (y). L'on peut dès lors estimer la droite de régression Y = a+bx qui est égal à Y = 3,01+15,94 x. Ainsi, pour chaque niveau d'instruction, on peut estimer la variable dépendante Y. Toutefois, une enquête à plus grande échelle serait la mieux indiquée pour valider ces résultats préliminaires fondés sur un échantillon modeste.
14. « *Kibenda* » signifie ce qui tire. La mini-jupe qualifiée de kibenda est celle qui fait découvrir les cuisses en position assise.
15. « *Mundelo* » est la fente intentionnellement longue, qui est placée sur la jupe, favorable au racolage gestuel.

16. Il existe une forte corrélation entre le niveau d'instruction et le revenu gagné (r = 0,77). Cependant le coefficient de signification est peu élevé (R = 0,593). Cela signifie sans doute que le niveau d'instruction n'est pas l'unique variable qui expliquerait la hauteur du revenu. En effet, certains atouts et aptitudes propres à un métier s'acquièrent sur le « terrain ». Et dans le monde de la vente des services, plusieurs facteurs sont indispensables à la conquête d'un marché : il s'agit notamment de l'habileté à négocier, la coquetterie, la santé et la robustesse physique, etc.

Références

Arnvig, E., 1993, « Prostitution enfantine au Cambodge : l'ONU a-t-elle détourné le regard ? », *Tribune internationale des droits de l'enfant*, Genève, 10 (3):4.

Banque Africaine de Développement, 2002, *Rapport sur le développement en Afrique. Développement rural et réduction de la pauvreté en Afrique*, Paris: Economica.

Bazonzi, J. M., Makaya, V. M. et Kinuani, L. M., 2004, *Analyse socio-économique du secteur informel en RDC : cas des cireurs des chaussures dans la ville de Kinshasa,* Kinshasa: Facultés Catholiques de Kinshasa, document ronéoté.

Biaya, T. K., 2000, *Les jeunes, la violence et la rue à Kinshasa. Entendre, comprendre, décrire*, Séries Nouvelles Pistes, Dakar: CODESRIA.

Boukari, M., 1997, « Note introductive », *Emploi, Travail et Droit de l'Enfant,* Dossier documentaire, ENDA T.M., Dakar: ENDA, p. 2.

David, P., 1994, « Casques bleus de l'ONU et prostitution enfantine : après le Cambodge au tour du Mozambique », *Tribune internationale des droits de l'enfant.*11 (1): 16-18.

De Villers, G., 2002, in De Villers G. et al. (dir.), *Manières de vivre. Économie de la « débrouille » dans les villes du Congo/Zaïre*, Cahiers Africains, n° 49-50, série 2001, Paris: L'Harmattan.

Human Rights Watch, 2006, *Quel avenir ? Les enfants de la rue en République démocratique du Congo*, Volume 18, No. 2(A).

http://www.afrik.com/dossier 201.html.28décembre2004.

http://www.unicef.fr/index.cfm?id=oi_pre_unicef_2951.28décembre2004.

Journal Officiel de la RDC, 2002, *Loi n° 015/2002 portant Code du Travail,* Kinshasa, 43e année, Numéro Spécial, Cabinet du Président de la République.

Kpatindé, F., 2004, « Scandale à la Monuc », *Jeune Afrique /L'Intelligent*, n°2264, p.74-75.

Lecaillon, J. et Pondavon, C., 1998, *Analyse micro-économique. Cours et exercices corrigés*, Paris: Cujas.

Lewin, R., 2002, « Avant-propos. On revient de loin », in Coenen, M.-T., (dir.), *Corps de femme : sexualité et contrôle social*, Bruxelles: De Boeck Université.

LIZADEEL, 2003, *Situation des droits de l'enfant en RDC*, revue trimestrielle, n° 03, Kinshasa: LIZADEEL.

Lukusa, G. M., 1999, *Congo/Zaïre. La faillite d'un pays. Déséquilibre macro-économique et ajustements (1988-1999)*, Cahiers Africains, n° 37-38, Paris: L'Harmattan.

Mansini, J. G., 1965, *Prostitution et proxénétisme*, Paris: PUF.

Maurer, M., 1992, *Tourisme, prostitution, sida,* Paris: L'Harmattan.

Mbaya, M. et Streiffeler, F., 1999, *Secteur informel au Congo-Kinshasa. Stratégies pour un développement endogène*, Kinshasa: Éditions Universitaires Africaines.

Musuamba, M.-L. N., 2001, *Genre et VIH : « être femme à l'heure du Sida en Afrique »*, Kinshasa: Saint Paul.

Ngambu, F. N., 1996, *Manuel de sociologie et d'anthropologie*, Kinshasa, Presses Universitaires Kongo, Collection Manuels Universitaires, n° 001.

Nyamnjoh, F. B., 2004, *Fishing in Troubled Waters: Disquettes and Thiofs in Dakar*, Dakar: CODESRIA, p. 1-2.

OMS, 2005, *Santé de la femme : stratégie de la Région africaine*, Bureau Régional de l'Afrique, Brazzaville, 2005, p. 3.

ONUSIDA, 2000, *Rapport sur l'épidémie de VIH/SIDA*, Genève, p. 125.

ONUSIDA/OMS, 2002, *Rapport sur l'épidémie mondiale de VIH/SIDA*, Genève, 2002.

ONUSIDA/OMS, 2004, *Fiches épidémiologiques sur le VIH/SIDAet les maladies sexuellement transmissibles* : *République démocratique du Congo*, p.2.

Pourtier, R., 1991, « L'inéluctable défi des transports » in *Politique Africaine. Zaïre : un pays à reconstruire*, Paris, Karthala, n°41, p. 30.

Quivy, R. et Van Campenhoudt, L., 1995, *Manuel de recherche en sciences sociales*, 2e éd., Paris: Dunod.

Reynolds, P., 1991, *Dance civet cat. Child Labour in the Zambezi Valley*, London: Zed Books.

Songué, ÉP., 1986, *Prostitution en Afrique : l'exemple de Yaoundé*, Paris: L'Harmattan.

Terenzio, F., 1995, « Problématique des enfants en situation difficile », ENDA, *Enfants en recherche et en action : une alternative africaine d'animation urbaine.* Séries Etudes et Recherches, n°181-182-183, Dakar: Enda-Editions, pp.22-31.

Werner, J.-F., 1993, *Marges, sexe et drogues à Dakar : ethnographie urbaine*, Paris: Karthala.

11

Enfants et jeunes dans le métier de la danse au sein des groupes musicaux modernes à Kinshasa

Léon Tsambu Bulu

Introduction

Le travail des enfants, économique ou contraint, reste une question sociale et politique à cause des préjudices qu'il fait subir « à leur développement mental, physique et émotionnel » (http://www.droitsenfant.com/), mais aussi à l'avenir même d'une nation. Cette étude effectue une plongée dans le monde du showbiz congolais (RDC) afin de comprendre et expliquer une forme particulière du travail des enfants et des jeunes au sein des groupes musicaux modernes à Kinshasa, où ils sont engagés comme danseurs au point d'être devenus, surtout les filles, les acteurs les plus attendus des spectateurs des prestations vivantes et le point de mire des consommateurs des vidéoclips, frisant ainsi une sorte de voyeurisme.

Autant la question musicale congolo-kinoise dans son ensemble souffre d'ostracisme heuristique, autant les réflexions thématiques et critiques sur le travail juvénile dans le secteur de la musique populaire urbaine n'ont jusqu'à ce jour bénéficié d'un intérêt majeur. Car l'on a souvent tendance à n'insérer le travail de cette catégorie sociale que dans le registre de la domesticité, de la prostitution choisie ou forcée, des micro-métiers de la rue, dans l'agriculture, l'artisanat et l'industrie, l'armée comme cela se décline dans les études et statistiques du BIT et de l'Unicef. Lorsque De Boeck traite de la question de l'enfance kinoise, c'est en termes d'une catégorie sociale d'oisifs (mais vivant parfois de petits métiers, de prostitution ou de larcins), de flâneurs diurnes et nocturnes appelés « shege », et particulièrement ceux « stigmatisés comme sorciers » (*ntshor*) – jetant ainsi le pont entre le jour et la nuit, le visible et l'invisible, l'exotérique et l'occulte –, victimes d'une exclusion sociale maternée par le nouvel imaginaire hyperreligieux des églises néopentecôtistes qui, à la fois et paradoxalement, produisent une rhétorique de diabolisation de la figure du sorcier tout en offrant à ce dernier un cadre de « rédemption ». En plus, il fait allusion à une sous-catégorie d'entre elles, les *fioti-fioti* ou *kamoke*[1] ou encore les *nyonyo*,[2] devenues célèbres par leurs prouesses professionnelles dans la danse (De Boeck 2004). Il faut cependant noter que toutes les *Fioti-fioti*, *Nyonyo* ou petites filles danseuses ne se recrutent pas dans la rue.

Wrzesinska qui pose de façon globale la problématique de l'enfance et de la jeunesse en Afrique, et particulièrement en RDC, passe en revue différentes stratégies de résorption du fléau, notamment la resocialisation (réinsertion ou placement en famille) des enfants de la rue et constate que pour les adolescents et jeunes adultes, la vie professionnelle ne leur est pas favorable à cause de la récession économique qui a entraîné aussi celle de l'emploi (Tshikala 2002:60). D'où, à mon avis, cette dynamique vers les professions libérales comme la danse et la musique qui ne réclameraient à la base que le talent naturel et le capital physique du corps. À son tour, Nicole Manimba (2000), citée par Inswan Sabakar (2004), s'interroge sur les déterminations psychologiques et sociologiques de l'engouement des filles vers la profession de la danse au sein des groupes musicaux à Kinshasa, et ce au détriment de l'école. La récession de l'emploi, la crise salariale, l'hyperprogrammation musicale télévisée (en situation de pluralisme médiatique) militent pour ce choix. Dans ce même ordre d'idées, Isabelle Kapinga (2002), au bout d'une enquête menée auprès de 50 filles danseuses prestant au sein des groupes musicaux de la capitale congolaise, confronte les variables d'âge, de scolarité, de revenu professionnel de la danseuse et de sa famille pour aboutir à une détermination du métier par la précarité sociale individuelle (intellectuelle) et collective (structurelle) avant de s'appesantir sur les conséquences sociales inhérentes à l'exercice de cette activité. Cependant, sa conclusion lui paraît contradictoire car, constate-t-elle, malgré le faible revenu salarial, la danseuse arbore des toilettes luxueuses ou coquettes, évocatrices d'une prostitution camouflée. Madibwila Itumba (2003), dont l'étude dégage des accointances avec celle de Isabelle Kapinga, n'a pas manqué de mettre en exergue la corrélation entre pratique féminine de la danse, consommation de la drogue, abus sexuels au sein du groupe musical et prostitution en dehors du groupe.

Il relève de toutes ces études que dans le contexte de leur travail, en l'occurrence au sein des groupes musicaux, les jeunes travailleurs sont en quête d'émancipation économique et sociale. Ce que cette réflexion tente de revisiter. Cependant, hormis Madibwila qui l'a à peine effleurée, aucune étude précitée n'aborde la question de gestion et de rapport de force au sein des groupes musicaux qui devrait expliquer d'autres formes d'exploitation des travailleurs(euses) de la danse. Car l'image qu'offre en l'occurrence la femme dans la profession musicale est maquillée de suspicions : qu'elle mène une carrière de chanteuse, de musicienne ou de danseuse, en solo ou en groupe, qu'importe son âge et son talent, elle est inféodée à l'imperium phallocratique pour se maintenir ou émerger (Tsambu Bulu 2001). En considérant l'espace musical populaire en général et celui de la danse en particulier comme un champ (Bourdieu), tout effort d'intelligibilité de la question sous étude va consister à considérer l'économie du travail des enfants et jeunes danseurs au sein des groupes musicaux à Kinshasa comme ne participant pas uniquement de l'ordre de la quête du profit matériel et financier (économisme), mais aussi, sinon en priorité ou en synergie avec l'ordre de la quête du profit symbolique qu'offre le métier : la célébrité, le prestige, les rêves et plaisirs de voyage pour l'Occident et l'expression d'une passion.

Cette étude se focalise sur le métier de danseuse tout en faisant un clin d'œil à l'enfance masculine à travers un cas insolite, celui d'un enfant de 7 ans devenu star par la danse, afin de montrer l'autre visage du métier. Pour ce faire, quelles sont les déterminations sociologiques et psychologiques à la base du choix du métier de la danse au sein des groupes musicaux modernes kinois ? Comment se définit l'influence des médias dans le choix et l'exercice de ce métier ? À quelles formes d'exploitation sont soumis(es) les travailleurs(euses) de la danse au regard des rapports de force et des agents en présence ? Quels sont les conséquences et risques auxquels s'exposent-ils ? Voilà autant de questions auxquelles tentera de répondre cette étude qui ne manque pas d'évaluer, à l'aune des normes internationales et nationales, la situation d'un travail qui continue à se masquer derrière des apparences ludiques. Ont tour à tour la parole à travers des entretiens semi-directifs : un maître chorégraphe, un agent de casting (recrutement) des danseuses, deux parents ou tuteurs, quatre danseuses et un danseur répartis dans les catégories sociales d'enfants et de jeunes selon le critère d'âge[3] de l'ONU. Après avoir situé dans le contexte historique congolais la profession de la danse, intervient l'exposition de 5 cas empiriques des jeunes travailleurs, lesquels cas sont soumis ensuite à la raison sociologique pour comprendre et expliquer les mécanismes sociaux du métier. Une conclusion boucle cette étude qui capitalise les résultats d'études antérieures et n'affiche aucune prétention d'avoir épuisé la problématique du travail des enfants dans le monde musical et de la danse.

La pratique professionnelle de la danse dans la conscience historique de la scène kinoise

La pratique musicale africaine se définit par essence comme une osmose entre le jeu instrumental et le chant qui se dilue dans la danse, en communion avec le public. Musique et danse ne s'excluent pas au point que le chanteur assure à la fois le statut de danseur qui pourrait en même temps s'appliquer à l'instrumentiste et au public. Cette logique s'est transposée dans la musique moderne, à la seule différence, et non la moindre, qu'il s'est creusé un hiatus entre l'artiste ou l'exécutant, placé sur une scène surélevée, et le public, en contrebas, d'où il lui voue une admiration dévote, réduit au rôle passif de consommateur d'une performance préfabriquée. C'est pour lutter contre cette passivité du public que les arts du spectacle comme la musique, recourent aux techniques d'excitation sensorielle du public consommateur afin de plaire à son goût.

Dans les années 1940, à l'aube de la musique populaire urbaine congolaise, des chanteurs comme Antoine Wendo, Baudouin Mavula, Henri Bowane, Léon Bukasa… ont évolué comme des bardes, des individualistes, avant de s'agréger dans des groupes qui de ce fait constituaient des cadres de prédilection pour le spectacle dont la danse demeure le servomoteur. L'arrivée de la femme sur la scène musicale urbaine au Congo passe par le rôle vocal. Dans un champ artistique d'essence phallocratique, Lucie Eyenga, Martha Badibala, Tekele Monkango, Marcelle Ebibi (Camerounaise), Marie Kitoto… se sont illustrées dans les années 1950 par la profession de la voix plutôt que par la danse. Elles évoluaient, séparément ou en fusion avec leurs pairs masculins, dans les maisons de disque de l'époque : Ngoma, Opika, CEFA, Loningisa, Esengo. La tradition va se poursuivre après l'indépendance. Ainsi va-t-elle se révéler en 1963, au sein d'OK Jazz, la chanteuse Henriette Borauzima (Stewart, 2000:117-118). Elle va se retrouver plus tard (1966) aux côtés de Tabu Ley Rochereau qui, pour des besoins de marketing, la surnomma « Miss Bora » (Stewart 2000:127). Mais bien avant Henriette Bora, Photas Myosotis évolua aux côtés de Tabu Ley au sein du groupe African Fiesta.

Il a fallu attendre l'année 1970, lors du passage de Rochereau à l'Olympia pour que la femme, d'abord employée comme chanteuse, occupe le devant de la scène dans le nouveau rôle spécifique de danseuse dans lequel elle sera sociologiquement minorisée. À la tête de cette révolution dictée par les enjeux du showbiz se trouve Rochereau : *he had (…) opened the door for women to play more substantive roles in the bands*,[4] note Gary Stewart qui fait encore remarquer que Rochereau voulait ainsi délivrer la scène musicale de l'emprise phallocratique (Stewart 2000:188).

Sur les traces de Tabu Ley Rochereau et de ses *Rocherettes*, la chanteuse Abeti Masikini, dite la Tigresse, n'hésita pas à incorporer des danseuses au sein de son groupe Les Redoutables. C'est avec un spectacle chorégraphié par les *Tigresses* que la madone fit à son tour un triomphe dans le music-hall parisien de Bruno Coquatrix. Franco à son tour s'entoura des *Francorettes* alors que le Trio Madjesi inventa ses *Madjesiennes*. L'existence des groupes essentiellement féminins comme TAZ Bolingo en 1986 n'escamotait pas la nouvelle tradition. Le génie créateur de Tabu Ley, inspiré par Claude François et ses *Claudettes*, fit donc école au point que, malgré une entrée en veilleuse de la pratique, il est de mode, à partir de Koffi Olomide et ses *Koffiettes* dans les années 1990, que tous les groupes musicaux kinois se relookent en se dotant d'une section chorégraphique composée des danseuses et rarement des danseurs. C'est alors que face aux *Koffiettes* de Koffi, aux filles d'Empire Bakuba et aux *Zaïkorettes* du groupe Zaïko Langa-Langa, de loin plus âgées et à peine sorties de l'adolescence pour quelques-unes, Papa Wemba innove avec les *Fioti-fioti* en 1996. Elles ont quatorze ans au moins et seize-dix-sept ans au plus. L'idée de Papa Wemba à son tour va faire école sur la scène congolo-kinoise. La scission du groupe Wenge Musica BCBG TT 4x4 en 1997, qui alors ne bénéficiait que des services chorégraphiques d'une seule fille jusqu'à sa mort, met en place deux nouveaux groupes concurrents ayant chacun son armée de danseuses « fioti-fioti » qui finissent par se faire une notoriété nationale et extra-africaine que seule les *Koffiettes* détenaient. À noter par ailleurs que, féminisé à 90 pour cent et éphémère, le métier paraît moins alléchant aux hommes qu'aux filles dont on rechercherait le sex-appeal à l'image des chanteuses comme Tshala Muana et Mbilia Bel qui traînent un passé des danseuses. Les exigences du showbiz tournées vers l'exploitation psychologique du corps de la femme pour des besoins de marketing et d'audience, le progrès technologique dont est tributaire la technique du vidéoclip imposent à la musique congolaise, de nature festive, de nouveaux enjeux sur la scène physique (salle de spectacle) et/ou virtuel (vidéo, clip). C'est ainsi qu'il faudra noter que jusqu'à ce jour, tous les groupes anciens ou nouveaux, par effet de mode et pour besoin de marketing, s'emploient à utiliser des enfants, adolescentes ou jeunes sur scène et dans les vidéoclips.

Jeunes professionnels de la danse et du spectacle dans les groupes musicaux : exposition des cas

Sous cette section de notre étude se déclinent six cas d'enfants et jeunes répartis selon le sexe autour de deux cas masculins et de quatre cas féminins. Selon l'âge nous avons deux cas d'enfants (moins de 18 ans) et quatre cas de jeunes (au moins 18 ans). Cette conception sémantique trouve sa justification dans les textes institutionnels internationaux tels ceux de l'Unicef alors que certains auteurs partent des critères anthropologiques culturels (F. de Boeck 2004) pour définir si pas l'enfance, du moins la jeunesse. Mais il faudra reconnaître que tous ceux qui se retrouvent dans la fourchette de la jeunesse ont débuté leur métier encore enfants et que cette étude, suivant les exigences méthodologiques, revisite le trajet historique de chaque sujet enquêté. De ce fait, notre étude prend plus en charge la situation sociale de ces danseurs plus en tant qu'enfants que jeunes, car même jeunes, ils ne sont qu'au début de cette étape.

Cas Béni Lomboto

Debout sur ses sept ans (2004), Lomboto, qui vit en famille monoparentale, combine scolarité et danse dans un groupe musical. Il est considéré comme une source d'espoir pour sa mère qui, dès qu'elle a aperçu les talents de son fils à 5 ans, était prête à l'introduire dans le métier. Petite star du showbiz devenue aujourd'hui l'objet des convoitises des grandes stars kinoises, sa mère, qui utilise parfois le « nous » pour exprimer l'opinion commune avec le père de l'enfant, déclare que Lomboto n'est pas à vendre malgré la précarité de sa vie. Voici mes entretiens séparés avec la mère et l'enfant :

Récit de la mère (Bijou Lomboto)

> Béni Lomboto a débuté la danse de scène et sa scolarité l'année dernière (2003). Dans son ancienne école, il était à la base du chahut et de la distraction de ses camarades de classe à cause de son vedettariat ; mais parfois c'est la maîtresse elle-même qui à la fin de la classe lui demandait de danser. D'où la décision de l'inscrire dans une autre école où on devait le prendre pour un enfant normal comme ses camarades. À chaque récréation le directeur d'école le place dans son bureau. Ses résultats du premier trimestre font état d'une bonne performance (84 pour cent). Déjà à 5 ans, Lomboto faisait ses premiers pas dans la danse à partir de la maison, devant l'écran de télévision, puis dans la rue. Nous étions alors près à aller proposer ses services à Werrason sur la musique de qui il dansait.

La vie de scène de Lomboto commence par ses fréquentations et ses prouesses à l'entrée du bar où le groupe de Félix Wazekwa tient ses séances de répétition. Lomboto a été finalement « engagé » dans le groupe. La télévision bien sûr l'a influencé par le fait qu'il voyait sur le petit écran les danses qu'il imitait. J'ai conféré avec Wazekwa au point de conclure que Lomboto va combiner la danse avec l'école plutôt que d'étouffer son talent. Et Wazekwa soutient et la carrière et l'école de l'enfant. À l'initiative de l'employeur, il était prévu la signature d'un contrat de travail de manière à fixer le salaire de l'enfant… mais sa matérialisation avec l'administration de l'orchestre n'a pas encore eu lieu.

Bien sûr que l'enfant s'est tapé de la popularité au point que quand tu sors avec lui, d'autres enfants parfois vous suivent. À la station de bus, une voiture finit par s'arrêter pour vous embarquer. Il arrive aussi que des visiteurs nous surprennent à la maison, adultes ou enfants. Au début de son vedettariat il subissait certaines agressions de la part d'autres enfants dans le sens de lui ravir de l'argent chaque fois qu'on l'envoyait à la boutique du coin.

Aujourd'hui quand il a une production scénique, je l'accompagne. Pour une production nocturne, il passe toute sa journée au siège du groupe, il s'endort jusqu'à 22-23 heures pour aller, dans la même voiture que le président, au concert qui se termine au petit matin. Il rentre le lendemain au siège pour dormir avant que j'aille le récupérer les après-midi. Il nous raconte des histoires autour des habits, des jouets ou de l'argent reçus. Il me ramène tout l'argent qu'il gagne. À la maison quand ses images passent à la télé, nous les regardons tous et lui-même s'en ravit.

Le métier de Lomboto ne m'aurait apporté qu'un capital social. J'ai été reçue en audience par des ministres et par le Gouverneur de la Ville grâce à Lomboto. Je n'insiste pas sur l'argent parce que l'enfant lui-même ne pense pas à l'argent au point que quand nous l'avons mis à l'épreuve, dans le sens de lui proposer d'aller évoluer dans le groupe de Werrason, sous prétexte de gagner mieux, il refusa d'un trait. Parce que ce qui compte encore pour lui c'est l'art plutôt que l'argent. Que Wazekwa propose de l'amener vivre en Europe, comme tu le dis, serait une bonne chose. Je dois pourtant regretter la convoitise des leaders des autres groupes musicaux, en l'occurrence celui qui nous a proposé un montant de 2 500 $ et des téléphones cellulaires pour lui « vendre » Lomboto. Mais non, Lomboto n'est pas à vendre, ni de jour ni de nuit, en dépit de ma vie misérable. Il faudra que nous évitions l'erreur de décider à la place et contre la volonté d'un enfant si capricieux. Car s'il refuse de travailler dans tel groupe nous aurions à payer les pots cassés comme déjà chez Wazekwa, il y a des jours où il observe une grève de travail.

Dans l'éventualité d'une somme d'argent importante payée en guise de salaire par son patron, je me proposerais d'aider avec ça les frères, les grands-parents, les petits frères, la famille de Lomboto ainsi que la personne qui a prophétisé sur son avenir.

Récit de Béni Lomboto

Hein! je me prends pour une star, de la manière dont je danse. Dans la rue je me considère comme tout enfant. Je joue. Mais je suis l'objet de curiosité de la part d'autres enfants, comme à l'école. Quand je me regarde dans le clip, esalaka nga ba-genre ![5] Ce boulot me fait gagner de l'argent, offert par le public sur scène. Et tout enfant j'ai besoin des cadeaux. Je suis aussi fier des habits que Félix m'emmène de l'Europe. Je ne vais pas le quitter. Dans ma vie je rêve de devenir star. Toujours par la danse. Le concert de nuit me dérange. Cela m'arrange, mais des fois non, je préférerais dormir. Pour ma coiffure (une raie au milieu du front), je suis flatté que ce soit Maître Kula, le coiffeur de Wazekwa. J'aimerais bien aussi chanter, à côté de la danse. En outre, jamais je n'ai séché une séance de répétition. J'ai vraiment du souffle pour cela. Comme c'est le travail que Dieu m'a donné, je n'y puis rien ; je suis obligé de faire le travail en tant que don divin. S'il faudrait opérer un choix, je choisirais la musique et l'école, mais au final l'école.

Cas Nikia

Nikia Masumbuku Miezi, 17 ans, 7 mois (2004) et mère d'enfant, exerce la profession de danseuse depuis deux ans. Elle dévoile les travers sexuels des responsables de groupes dont sont victimes les danseuses. En rupture avec l'école, elle est arrivée à la danse par souci de meubler les temps creux des vacances scolaires, mais y est restée par passion, au grand dam principalement de son père, séparé de sa mère, qui découvre le métier de sa fille à la télévision (vidéoclips).

Récit

Ayant arrêté à 15 ans ma scolarité, j'ai embrassé la danse comme Nyonyo dans le ballet Percussion Molokaï de Papa Wemba. C'était un beau jour, en 2002, en visite chez une amie à Matonge, j'apprendrai par un communiqué télévisé qu'on recrutait des danseuses. Au sein du groupe, je deviendrai, de fil en aiguille, cheftaine des Nyonyo. Mon père a manifesté son mécontentement. Je n'ai pas intentionnellement arrêté mon instruction scolaire à cause de la danse, moins encore du manque de finance, mais c'est arrivé avec la période creuse des vacances que je voulais combler. J'ai essayé puis la danse m'a emballée. Sous prétexte d'aller à l'école, je continuais à participer aux séances de répétitions. Puis est venu le moment où l'on devait tourner des vidéoclips, papa était surpris de voir sa fille à la télévision. J'ai pris la précaution de fuir de chez lui pour me réfugier ici chez ma mère. Celle-ci à son tour manifesta sa désapprobation. Dans ce métier, la chanteuse Abeti Masikini demeure mon idole. Mais ce ne sont là que des influences lointaines.

À la veille d'un voyage pour l'Europe, il était question que douze « maîtres » (sbires)[6] de Molokaï[7] couche avec chacune des onze Nyonyo. Je me suis résolue à ne pas m'offrir en holocauste pour le bon plaisir de voir l'Europe. J'ai pris alors pour une main de Dieu la personne qui est venue me proposer le marché de travail dans Dream Team. Papa Wemba pouvait ou ne pas être au courant de cette cabale, mais la personne qui assurait l'administration directe des danseuses était bien dans le coup. Les choses touchant au sexe se font dans tous les groupes. Loin de se dévoiler par la parole, le leader qui a des liens intimes avec une danseuse se démasque par des attitudes. À Molokaï nous étions internées, pour préparer par exemple le voyage de Brazzaville. Celles qui ne le désiraient pas, comme moi, n'étaient pas contraintes.

Dans Dream Team, nous bénéficions d'une petite rémunération au prorata des fonds disponibles dans la caisse car les voyages n'existent pas encore. Après un concert, si tu téléphones en cas de maladie, le groupe est prêt à agir. Au village Molokaï, la rétribution n'existait pas. Le salaire mensuel n'existe pas en fait, mais plutôt la manière pour le chef de prendre soin des ses petits en pourvoyant à leurs besoins. Au sujet du contrat de travail, nulle part ailleurs il n'existe. La sécurité sociale n'est d'ailleurs pas assurée dans Viva-la-Musica (Percussion Molokai) où vous êtes abandonnée à votre propre sort en cas de maladie alors que Dream Team en prend soin.

Pour le concert de nuit, chacun y va de par ses propres moyens. Le transport pour le retour est assuré jusqu'au siège, en attendant que le soleil pointe pour que chacun regagne son logis Mon image à la télé me procure une autosatisfaction morale. Mais entre l'argent et la célébrité je place la seconde en première position. Avant d'aller chez une personnalité comme Papa Wemba, tu as le cœur battant la chamade. La première fois que je l'ai salué j'ai craqué, pourtant il n'est pas Dieu. Mais il faut avouer qu'ils sont nombreux à ne lui avoir jamais serré la main. Moi je l'ai fait, j'ai compté parmi ses convives : je garde un souvenir très agréable à propos. Il comptait auparavant comme mon idole à travers ses danseuses [Fioti-fioti], qui ont excité mon envie d'évoluer dans son groupe.

Nos tenues de scène sont normales : pantacourt jusque-là, pantalons ouverts mais avec un linge (« cycliste ») au-dessous, tout ce qui est sexy. Je danse sans avoir pris de la drogue. Je consomme bien sûr de la bière. Mais il n'est pas recommandé de monter sur scène après l'avoir consommée au risque de s'essouffler. Nez percé d'une vis et crayon noir au milieu du front (look indien), je suis pourtant simple. Il faut plutôt me voir dans mes plus beaux apparats vestimentaires : nabetaka ngo lokola nyama.[8] Je suis de toutes les griffes, de tous les goûts mais je n'expose pas le nombril. Je mets aussi des trucs à mi-cuisses, comme tout le monde sait que je suis danseuse. Il y a des recommandations qui nous sont données pour les soins corporels, et selon la teinte désirée pour sa peau ; mais moi je préfère garder ma peau noire.

L'argent que je gagne sert à pourvoir à mes besoins et à ceux de mon enfant. Je soutiens aussi la maison (maman), dans la mesure du possible. Je sais que ce travail finira par me récompenser. Rentrer à l'école devient difficile car la musique coule dans mes veines.

Cas Rachel

Danseuse dès l'âge de 13 ans chez Papa Wemba, Rachel Omole a une trajectoire professionnelle de quatre ans qui l'a conduite à se balader à travers trois groupes différents. Orphéline de mère, elle retrace la fortune et l'infortune de son métier grâce auquel elle prend parfois en charge la scolarité de ses frères, et sa grand-mère chez qui elle vit même au vif de l'union de ses parents. Mais son discours sur la politique de rémunération paraît trop sérieux.

Récit

C'est à 13 ans (2000), en 3e secondaire, que j'ai débuté ma carrière chez Papa Wemba. Nous y sommes allées avec Nikia, une amie du quartier [Yolo-Nord]. J'ai préféré aller chez Papa Wemba parce qu'il embauchait les petites filles (Nyonyo). Mon oncle m'a sermonnée jusqu'à me soumettre à deux alternatives : l'école ou la danse. Mon choix a été clair et reste opposable à tous les projets de la famille. J'ai opté pour la musique qui est une alternative pour assurer mon avenir. Je peux terminer ma scolarité mais où trouver de l'emploi ?

Dès mon enfance je dansais à l'église, comme majorette des cérémonies de mariage jusqu'à me retrouver chez Kester Emeneya via chez vieux Bokul.[9] La télévision a beaucoup joué dans mon choix de carrière. La chanteuse Mukangi « Déesse », que je meurs d'envie d'égaler, a constitué mon modèle. J'étais plutôt fan de Reddy Amisi, puis de Kester Emeneya par ma mère, son adulatrice qui fréquentait aussi ses concerts. J'ai gardé en mémoire beaucoup de ses chansons de par ma mère. Je ne considère pas le leader du groupe avant tout comme mon idole, mais bien comme mon patron.

La musique est un travail. Après le test, le recrutement mais assorti d'aucun contrat de travail. Le salaire était insignifiant dans le premier groupe à tel point que ça ne pouvait permettre d'acheter un linge. Dans Victoria le salaire est conséquent. On me paie de l'argent qui puisse me permettre parfois de supporter les frais de scolarité de mes petits frères. Victoria Eleison a garni ma garde-robe, m'a procuré un poste téléviseur, du mobilier, un petit congélateur. Je suis encore petite mais j'épaule la maison à la taille de ma bourse. D'un maximum de 100$, la prime est payée à la fin de chaque mois comme après chaque apparition scénique. Au bout du mois je touche plus ou moins 250 US$.

Pour un concert qui se termine tard la nuit, on nous ramène au Ranch[10] où nous avons nos couches. Le staff administratif ou les proches du patron nous ont assez rebattu les oreilles avec leur trafic d'influence. J'en suis déjà aguerrie. Je leur réponds que mes compétences professionnelles et l'avis du président vont militer pour faire partie de la délégation pour l'Europe. La tournée de Victoria en Angola m'a permis de gagner, par les congratulations des diamantaires congolais sur le podium et le salaire, 3 000$, rien que par la danse. Dans les conditions où tu as beau faire preuve de talents sans jamais être du voyage, tu es prête à boire du poison. Quand je me regarde à la télévision, j'ai des frissons émotionnels. Ma propre scène de danse en gros plan, me procure quelque chose d'inexplicable. A la maison ces passages télévisés font hurler les gens de plaisir. C'est alors que je fais passer la musique aux décibels supérieurs, les gens me laissent chanter et danser au milieu du salon. Au moindre zapping, je me fâche !

J'ai quitté Viva-la-Musica à cause du maître chorégraphe et encadreur des Nyonyo qui me harcelait, malgré mes plaintes auprès de vieux Bokul qui n'avait pourtant pas réagi à la hauteur de la gravité des faits. Et j'étais visionnaire : on danse, on fait des spectacles mais l'on ne bénéficie pas d'argent, entre-temps la peau noircissait. J'ai perdu ma riche chevelure pour répondre aux exigences du look imposé. Notre vieux-là [patron du groupe], il est chic en termes de formation professionnelle, mais ne rétribue pas. On dansait, on était soumise à des exercices physiques éprouvants, on noircissait, la somme de toutes ces souffrances non compensées m'a contrainte à plier bagages.

Dans Dream Team [faction de Victoria Eleison], au fil du temps j'ai été la première de toutes les danseuses à rendre le tablier : aucun voyage, toujours travailler pour le bon plaisir de Mambo [manager et financier de ce nouveau groupe] qui ne faisait jamais des libéralités. Je pris ainsi la résolution d'abandonner le métier de la danse qui n'avait plus d'attrait sur moi. Il était alors important que je renoue avec l'école dont l'abandon a provoqué la colère de mon père. Le pasteur de notre église prenait cette fois-ci la charge de ma scolarité. L'esprit s'étant une fois de plus révolté, j'ai renoué avec la danse en intégrant Victoria Eleison D.T.D.B., une grande formation qui élève mon statut en me faisant découvrir le monde.

Contre le tract en scène, les danseuses de Victoria consomment de la bière. Que mes collègues qui s'enivrent de chanvre se départent de cette pratique physiquement avilissante. L'opinion de la rue est telle que beaucoup de gens me déconsidèrent à cause de ce métier. Quand au look, il est de bon ton de garder la décence au lieu d'exposer son nombril. Je m'offre en contre-exemple du look des danseuses : aucune fioriture comme le piercing du corps, sauf celui du nez et cette touche de crayon.

Propos de la grand-mère et tutrice de Rachel

Mes convictions religieuses militaient pour la musique chrétienne. Mais devant sa préférence pour la danse profane, j'en suis désarmée. Après tout c'est sa vie. Tire-t-elle des dividendes de son travail ? Moi plutôt je n'en vois pas. Parce que c'est un métier sans lendemain et limité par l'âge. Quand bien même elle m'achète des habits, me donne de l'argent ou subvient à mes besoins.

Propos d'une sœur à Rachel

Nous sommes auréolés de prestige par les images télévisées de Rachel. Même quand la tante passe dans la rue, elle est reconnue comme parente de Rachel. Que son patron prenne soin d'elle, car on trouve aujourd'hui des danseuses qui disposent d'un parc automobile. Elles ont bénéficié d'une chance énorme par le voyage d'Angola. Elle est rentrée avec beaucoup d'argent qui aurait pu lui procurer une voiture Mercedes ou une demi-parcelle.

Cas Hermione

La belle Hermione a 20 ans, extasiée de danse en dépit du fouet de son père, colonel de surcroît. Son court parcours professionnel (3 ans) reste pourtant rocambolesque. Sans détours, sauf à quelques exceptions près, elle a donné l'essentiel de sa vie de danseuse à travers laquelle elle a même séjourné en prison par obstination de voir l'Europe et mourir.

Récit

J'ai commencé à l'école où j'excellais comme danseuse lors des fêtes scolaires. Pendant la récréation, on formait avec les camarades un groupe de danse dans lequel les garçons jouaient la batterie. Le venin de la danse m'a depuis lors empoisonnée jusqu'au jour où une amie, vivant près du village Molokaï, me proposa de m'emmener auprès de Lambio-Lambio.[11] J'accueillis favorablement la proposition parce que c'est de là, grâce aux Fioti-fioti, que part ma passion pour la profession. J'ai formulé la demande et réussi au test avant d'être engagée contre paiement de 30 $ au maître chorégraphe. Mais en tant que cousine à sa femme (nièce de mon père), j'ai bénéficié d'une réduction des frais. C'était en 2001, à 17 ans, en 2e année secondaire.

J'ai par la suite quitté [ce groupe de Papa Wemba], pour Dream Team où j'ai retrouvé Nikia, Rachel... toutes transfuges du village Molokaï. N'y voyant pas l'avenir en rose, j'ai plié bagage pour Empire Fondation de Boeing. Aussitôt entrée, je faisais partie du voyage du groupe le surlendemain dans le Bas-Congo, au Cabinda (Angola). Rentré à Kinshasa, le groupe traverse le fleuve pour Brazzaville, avant de s'envoler pour l'Europe via le Cameroun. C'était en 2002. À l'aéroport de Maya-Maya, nous sommes aux arrêts à cause de l'usage de faux documents, ce qui nous coûte un mois d'emprisonnement à Brazzaville. Au sortir de cette incarcération, nous avons encore tenté de partir pour l'Europe. Nous avons ensemble cette fois-ci franchi l'étape de Brazzaville jusqu'à Douala. Sur place, une partie de la délégation traverse les mailles du filet, une autre est interceptée. Nos documents sont saisis et sommes obligés de séjourner à l'aéroport jusqu'au jour de rapatriement. Entre-temps, le président du groupe se trouvait déjà en Europe, et à Kinshasa le reste du groupe était en débandade. Je suis restée « méditer » chez nous à la maison. Je vais alors me résoudre à aller tenter ma chance chez Werrason, d'autant plus que là il est hors de question de voyager dans la clandestinité. Chez Werrason, je fis encore sensation. Un mois après mon nom est aligné sur la liste pour le voyage de Pointe-Noire. De retour à Kinshasa, le groupe prépare le voyage de Londres. Mais mon état de santé ne me permet pas de faire partie de la délégation. J'attends de me requinquer pour reprendre du service.

Je vis toujours chez mes parents, scandalisés par mon option. Mais malgré les sanctions physiques très sévères qu'ils m'ont infligées, je suis restée impavide au point qu'ils se sont fatigués. À la base de mon départ de chez Papa Wemba, une calomnie des collègues qui vont rapporter à ma cousine que je sortais avec son mari [maître chorégraphe].C'était vraiment malséant au point que chacune de nous (ma cousine et moi) est montée sur ses chevaux. Je pris la décision de m'en aller. Dans Dream Team j'ai constaté beaucoup de désordre, rien de sérieux et trop d'embrouille. On vivait dans l'espoir des voyages qui ne venaient pas, aucun salaire malgré le travail acharné. Le refoulement à mi-chemin de l'Europe du personnel d'Empire Bakuba a motivé aussi mon départ comme celui de tant d'autres : « Muana na muana bendana ! ».[12] J'ai même une amie, Mamie, ensemble nous avons vécu la mésaventure de Douala. Après avoir opté pour Quartier Latin (Koffi Olomide), elle a bénéficié d'un voyage en Europe et aujourd'hui ses images défilent dans tous les clips et CD du Monde Arabe. C'est ainsi que moi aussi de mon côté je bosse dur et persévère.

Le patron Boeing payait le « salaire » chez lui, mais il reste un secret personnel. Il n'était pas mensuel mais au rythme des productions scéniques. Chez Papa Wemba, n'étaient payés que les frais de transport au retour d'une séance de répétitions. Les sollicitations sexuelles des danseuses par les encadreurs des groupes ne s'apprécient que selon le libre arbitre de chacune.

Par ailleurs le retour sur le banc de l'école me paraît impossible aujourd'hui depuis que je me suis plongée dans la danse. Aller encore m'asseoir sur le banc de l'école deviendrait trop lourd pour moi, surtout pas ici à Kinshasa. Peut-être là-haut [Europe]. Aucune envie de changer de travail. Le mariage viendra à son temps, quand je me serai lassée de la danse. Plus d'un pense que les danseuses sont des ndumba, tshel, bula,[13] c'est plutôt une autre réalité. La danse est un métier, la prostitution en est un autre. Si sur le lieu de travail nous laissons à découvert le nombril – c'est bien normal! -, à la cité nous devons nous habiller avec décence au risque d'indisposer la société. Les recommandations pour l'esthétique corporelle sont fondées sur la propreté, l'élimination des tâches sur la peau et les soins appropriés pour le maintien de son teint d'origine. L'argent gagné par mon travail me sert à couvrir mes dépenses de toilette pour mon glamour. Il m'arrive aussi, de mon gré, de dépanner la maison en nourriture. Mes voyages m'ont procuré de l'argent ; à ce jour j'ai tout dépensé.

Cas Patricia

Issue d'une union matrimoniale dissolue, Patricia Kasa est élevée par sa mère. A 14 ans, elle a abandonné l'école pour embrasser la danse chez Papa Wemba. Elle se dit, voilà 5 ans, heureuse de son métier grâce auquel elle soutient sa mère, ses frères et bénéficie de l'aura de son patron considéré avant tout comme son idole.

Récit

Tout est parti du divorce de mes parents. Papa nous a abandonnés, mais je poursuivais ma scolarité tout en étant animée d'amour pour la danse. D'abord engagée dans des mouvements de jeunesse catholiques, j'ai chanté dans la chorale, même en dehors de l'église. En tant que majorette, j'ai beaucoup dansé dans des cérémonies de mariage jusqu'au jour où je suis devenue Nyonyo, à 14 ans, parmi les premières de la série. C'était un beau jour de l'année 2000, en uniforme de classe, je me laissais aller à la danse sur la voie publique quand tout à coup un homme au volant de sa Mercedes me proposa de m'accompagner le lendemain à Molokai. Ce qui m'extasia de plaisir au point que j'ai séché l'école ce jour-là.

Le maître chorégraphe des Nyonyo (papa Seigneur) me posa les conditions d'embauche : une somme d'argent et l'autorisation parentale écrite, la condition sine qua non. Maman refusa d'écrire. Une aînée du quartier se chargea de la tâche. Le problème se posa alors au niveau de la signature, car je pressentais qu'on pouvait convoquer les parents. J'ai arrêté le stratagème de faire signer mon cahier de devoirs scolaires à maman afin de lui permettre d'imiter sa signature. La *stratégie réussie, j'étais retenue sur la base d'un test et débutai mon travail après paiement d'une somme de 30$.*

Maman n'était pas du tout d'accord, mais alertée un jour, comme toute la maisonnée, par le passage de mes images à la télévision, elle a donné son feu vert, sur foi de destin divin. Papa qui ne vivait plus avec elle était au courant de mon métier via le même média et la voix des autres jusqu'au jour où il m'appelle sur mon portable pour me fixer rendez-vous chez maman afin de me prodiguer des conseils : j'ai pris les bons et rejeté les mauvais.

Je suis aujourd'hui hébergée chez Lambio-Lambio. Je n'avais jamais arrêté mes études (troisième secondaire) à cause du manque de finance, mais par passion pour la danse. Je n'ai aucun modèle, mais la télévision m'a beaucoup influencée à travers les Fioti-fioti. Je suis donc devenue Nyonyo, effectuant des voyages et capable de me prendre en charge, d'engager des frais ne fût-ce que pour la scolarité des jeunes frères, le loyer et tous les biens meubles de notre maison familiale. Il n'est pas dit que je soutiens à 100 pour cent les frais d'études de mes frères et sœurs, mais à partir de mon salaire j'allège la tâche à maman.

Le salaire, si insignifiant soit-il, existe. Il faut alors remercier Dieu pour cette compensation à la sueur versée. Il n'y a pas de régularité dans son paiement, mais en fonction d'apparitions scéniques. Papa Wemba, je le considère d'abord comme mon idole, ensuite mon patron. Mon idole parce que c'est une célébrité internationale. Et j'ai la chance d'être à ses côtés : Elekelaka ngai ![14] Pour le premier face-à-face j'ai eu des très forts frissons. 2004, à la sortie de Papa Wemba de la prison parisienne, le groupe, dont quatre danseuses, l'a rejoint en Angola. Beaucoup de compatriotes venus au concert nous ont estampillés de billets de banque sur le visage [...], c'était chouette! Au total j'ai gagné 300$ du public, mais je me tais sur le chiffre de la rémunération mensuelle. J'ai ramené du voyage 1 000$. Les matolo[15] existent aussi dans le métier, comme, à l'opposé, ce tribut payé aux vieux et particulièrement à celui ou celle qui t'a appris la danse au sein du groupe. La télévision m'a sortie de l'anonymat, mais ce n'est pas pour autant que je préfère le succès à l'argent. En cas de voyage (pas encore pour l'Europe), s'il est annoncé que tout le monde sera de la délégation, l'esprit d'un chacun est très serein. Au cas contraire, ça donne toujours du kipelekese[16] avant la publication de la liste.

Le look de danseuse doit plutôt traduire l'humilité. Moi d'ailleurs je n'aime pas être reconnue comme telle n'eût été, peut-être, le piercing du nez. Ni l'habillement, ni la teinte de la peau me trahissent. Or dans plusieurs groupes, on se décape la peau. Néanmoins Papa Lambert [Lambio-Lambio] nous a imposé un style unique de cheveux : les dreadlocks. La rue colporte bien des ragots sur les danseuses qu'elle qualifie de putes, des tshels, moi je ne le suis pas. Aucun gêne sur ma tenue de scène ou de travail, car pour bien danser je dois porter une tenue légère. Je suis prête à faire des entailles sur les flancs du pantalon afin de laisser libre court aux mouvements des jambes. Notre danse se nomme nkila mogrosso,[17] et j'ignore les raisons qui ont motivé la puissance publique à la censurer ; mais nous, nous continuons à l'exhiber. L'État s'est fatigué. Moi j'aime bien cette danse. Mon comportement sur scène n'est pas fonction des volutes de fumée du chanvre ou de la cigarette. En plus, dès que le staff s'en aperçoit, tu es exclue parce que les deux produits coupent le souffle. Nous conditionnons le corps par l'entraînement physique. Disons tout de même que je consomme un peu de bulles euphorisantes de la bière.

Approche compréhensive et explicative des récits

Les cinq récits précédents se présentent comme des tableaux des résultats d'enquête sur un échantillon à choix raisonné à partir duquel je me suis essayé à comprendre et à expliquer l'activité infantile et juvénile de la danse au sein des groupes de musique populaire kinois. La lecture critique de ces tableaux renseigne sur la situation du métier, à savoir les trajectoires individuelles des agents, le contexte social global (national) et familial des agents, les conditions de travail et la satisfaction y relative en rapport avec les motivations individuelles et les pesanteurs sociales (familiales, professionnelles, économiques...) qui dévoilent les formes d'exploitation, parfois insoupçonnée, dont sont victimes ces agents. Entre-temps, il s'impose que, loin d'un juridisme (moralisme) pseudosociologique, la réalité sociale en cause soit objectivement critiquée ou améliorée à l'aune d'instruments juridiques internationaux et nationaux sur le travail des enfants et du contexte social et culturel spécifique.

Contexte social global du travail des enfants et des jeunes à Kinshasa

L'effilochage du tissu économique national à la suite de la faillite d'un État postcolonial prédateur, qui a aussi ouvert les vannes aux puissances étrangères et à leurs institutions financières d'appauvrissement (FMI et Banque Mondiale) en gage de la pérennité des dirigeants locaux au pouvoir, a généré une misère sociale sans précédent au Congo/Zaïre dès la seconde moitié des années 1970 (zaïrianisation) jusqu'aux années 1980 (politique d'ajustement structurel). Les tentatives de redressement économique, social et politique du pays à partir d'une transition politique dont les règles du jeu seront définies par la Conférence nationale souveraine en 1991-1992, convoquée sous le coup de la perestroïka africaine, n'ont pas produit les résultats escomptés. Non seulement parce que la transition, ouverte par le discours présidentiel du 24 avril 1990, est manquée, mais aussi parce que « l'idéal démocratique masque de plus en plus mal le détournement des aspirations populaires par une classe politique que déchire et rassemble à la fois la quête des honneurs, du pouvoir et de l'argent » (De Villers et Omasombo 1997:4e p. de la couverture). Et lorsque le 17 avril 1997, Laurent-Désiré Kabila, à la tête de l'Alliance des forces démocratiques pour la libération du Congo (AFDL) relance la transition, c'est sans compter avec les conflits internes et les guerres avec les voisins des Grands Lacs- sous l'ombre desquels se masquent les puissances étrangères- qui l'ont militairement aidé à se hisser au perron du pouvoir à Kinshasa. Sa gestion autiste et nationaliste a conduit à son assassinat le 16 janvier 2001 et à sa succession par son fils sous escorte de quatre adjoints (vice-présidents). Ce qui a privatisé et fragilisé davantage l'État et institué la précarité sociale.

À cause donc d'une crise récurrente, ayant provoqué à travers les pillages militaro-populaires (1991 et 1993) et les multiples guerres d'agression des pertes d'emploi, beaucoup de familles se sont disloquées, séparées géographiquement, déplacées de l'est à l'ouest du pays au point que Kinshasa va démultiplier le nombre d'enfants de la rue, d'enfants déscolarisés. En conséquence, nombre d'entre eux se sont engagés dans la prostitution, la mendicité forcée, la violence (armée) et le processus de travail informel ou la pratique de petits métiers. D'autres, dopés par les images musicales vertigineuses que déversent à longueur de journées et de nuits les médias en inflation numérique à Kinshasa, rêvant de célébrité, d'Europe et forts de leur talent artistique, vont se lancer dans la musique ou la danse qui semble offrir l'ascension sociale la plus rapide, c'est-à-dire un raccourci pour la vie (Manimba 2000) et pour le pouvoir dont l'accès par la voie politique et économique formelle reste verrouillé. À ce titre, il était déjà dit que

> [sur] le plan sociétal, la musique bénéficie de l'amour inconditionnel du grand public et constitue, à l'instar du football, un canal d'ascension sociale très prisé ; elle attire particulièrement des enfants issus de milieux pauvres, à peine scolarisés et décidés à conjurer la crise en misant sur leurs talents. Animés d'une rage de vaincre (et de convaincre), ces enfants sont prêts à tout pour sortir de l'anonymat, obtenir la reconnaissance du public kinois, le droit de cité et, surtout, le pouvoir (Tsambu Bulu 2004:211).

Cette conclusion est corroborée par celle d'une enquête sur l'exploitation économique et sexuelle des enfants menée en octobre 2002 à Kinshasa par la Ligue de la

Zone Afrique pour la défense des droits des enfants, des étudiants et des élèves (Lizadeel) qui notait :

> Il est (…) symptomatique de constater que dans la panoplie des métiers dont rêvent ces jeunes, avenir du pays, ils citent fréquemment : « vedette de théâtre ou de musique ». « Et la musique! N'est-ce pas devenu chez nous, le raccourci pour devenir riche, ou du moins, pour s'afficher avec de grosses limousines, des villas dans les quartiers chics et des courtisan(e)s à longueur des journées ? (Lizadeel 2003:17 et 18).

Telle est la toile de fond sur laquelle se construisent les pratiques sociales qui conduisent au processus de travail juvénile, particulièrement dans le secteur de la danse au sein des groupes de variétés.

Profil sociologique des travailleurs(ses) de la danse

Le sexe, l'âge, la scolarité, la parure, la profession, l'emploi et le revenu des parents, leur statut matrimonial… constituent des propriétés sociales qui renseignent sur la vie d'un individu en société, son comportement, ses habitus, sa position dans un champ spécifique. J'ai observé que sur l'ensemble des 5 cas de danseurs échantillonnés, 3 cas sont constitués d'enfants, c'est-à-dire des moins de 18 ans, et les 2 autres des individus qui ont atteint ou dépassé l'âge minimum de 18 ans pour ne plus porter le statut d'enfant, en vertu de la Convention Internationale des Droits de l'Enfant,[18] ratifiée par la R.D.C. Or faudra-t-il admettre une évidence selon laquelle à travers leurs trajectoires respectives, les sujets de l'enquête ont, tout enfants, commencé la danse, d'abord comme loisir, pour plus tard entrer- toujours comme enfants- et grandir dans le métier. Qu'ils soient « enfants » ou « jeunes », ils traversent tous, sauf Lomboto, la période d'adolescence : « qui se situe entre l'enfance, qu'elle continue, et l'âge adulte » ; « qui débute vers douze-treize ans et se termine vers dix-huit à vingt ans (…) selon les sexes, les conditions géographiques et les milieux socio-économiques ». Sur le plan psychologique, cette période de crise et de troubles « est marquée par la réactivation et l'épanouissement de l'instinct sexuel, l'affermissement des intérêts professionnels et sociaux, le désir de liberté et l'autonomie, la richesse de la vie affective » (Sillamy 1979:13). C'est en définitive, enfants ou jeunes, des catégories et des forces sociales aux limites d'âge, de rôle, d'ethnicité, de religion, de classe… imprécises, mais « des constructions sociales et culturelles » (De Boeck et Honwana 2000:5-6).

Je peux encore, à la lumière des données en présence, alléguer que c'est en pleine enfance et/ou adolescence (ici de 6 à 17 ans) qu'on entre dans le métier de la danse et du spectacle, en bravant l'autorité parentale, en optant pour le choix de la liberté, au détriment de l'école. Ainsi ai-je eu à noter d'abord la pratique de l'école buissonnière chez Nikia et Patricia, et finalement la rupture totale avec l'école chez tous les danseurs, excepté le petit Lomboto qui combine encore avec bonheur les deux. Pourvu que ça dure ! Mais doit-on déplorer l'enfermement qu'il endure dans le bureau de la direction de son école pendant la recréation. Il n'est pas préparé psychologiquement à supporter le poids de son vedettariat précoce. Par ailleurs, le recours au travail de la danse au détriment de l'école trouve entre autres sa justification dans la justesse des propos ci-après :

Rachel : « J'ai opté pour la musique qui est une alternative pour assurer mon avenir. Je peux terminer ma scolarité mais où trouver de l'emploi ? » (Entretien).

Hermione : « Le retour sur le banc de l'école me paraît impossible aujourd'hui depuis que je me suis plongée dans la danse. Aller encore m'asseoir sur le banc de l'école deviendrait trop lourd pour moi, surtout pas ici à Kinshasa. Peut-être là-haut [Europe] » (Entretien).

Dans la sex-ratio des danseurs, la majorité, soit 4 contre 1 est du genre féminin par rapport au genre masculin. Ce que la danse en tant que métier spécifique, sauf pour le maître chorégraphe, est féminisée à 90 pour cent, et que dans la mentalité du milieu, ce sexisme professionnel confère peu de prestige aux hommes. Il faut donc noter que les danses congolaises et d'Afrique centrale sont à forte connotation sexuelle, sollicitant à grand renfort d'énergie le roulement des hanches. De ce fait, les jeunes qui se sont lancés dans ce métier sont pour la plupart soupçonnés de perversion sexuelle, c'est-à-dire d'homosexualité.

Par ailleurs, à l'âge du début de la profession, le souci de répondre avant tout à une vocation, la quête d'honneurs, d'escapisme en Europe et de célébrité par les médias paraissent plus expressifs que la quête de capital économique qui n'intervient que dans la maturation physique et sociale des agents. Cela peut être illustré par les propos de Hermione :

> Je vis toujours chez mes parents qui ont été scandalisés par mon option. Mais malgré les sanctions physiques très sévères qui m'ont été infligées, je suis restée imperturbable au point qu'ils se sont fatigués (Entretien).

La situation socio-familiale montre que 4 danseurs sur 5, sans distinction de sexe, sont issus d'unions familiales libres, dissolues (parfois par la mort d'un parent) ou monoparentales. Cette situation matrimoniale des parents met l'enfant en totale liberté, surtout lorsqu'il n'est placé que sous la garde ou la tutelle de sa mère ou grand-mère (Lomboto, Rachel, Patricia, et Nikia qui a fui de chez son père), sous-entendant ainsi une crise d'autorité et un rabais de chance de scolarité complète justifié aussi par la faiblesse du pouvoir économique de la femme.

Le rôle du médium télévision devient central dans l'émergence de la vocation de danse et du travail, ou l'homogénéisation de trajectoires professionnelles. Ainsi tous les jeunes travailleurs sont-ils venus dans le métier à partir de la séduction suscitée par les images de danse et le pouvoir symbolique que la télévision confère d'abord aux vedettes de la chanson prises pour idoles, ensuite aux danseuses qui ont marqué l'histoire passée ou récente de la scène musicale. Même pour Patricia qui se dit sans modèle, elle reconnaît pourtant l'influence des *fioti-fioti* à partir de la télévision. Et les obstacles dressés par sa mère ont sauté devant le plaisir esthétique de voir défiler les images de sa fille à la télévision. La mère de Lomboto a aussi dit : « Déjà à 5 ans, Lomboto faisait ses premiers pas dans la danse à partir de la maison, devant l'écran de télévision, puis dans la rue (….). La télévision bien sûr l'a influencé par le fait qu'il voyait sur le petit écran les danses qu'il imitait ».

Mépris de la loi en matière du travail de la danse

L'engouement de la jeunesse kinoise vers la musique n'est pas sans susciter des interrogations sur les conditions de travail auxquelles elle reste soumise, dans un monde où les rapports de force entre l'employeur (leader-président de groupe) – en position de dominant – et le personnel – en position de dominé – n'obéissent à aucune règle du jeu écrite et officielle, mais à celle propre au champ musical et intériorisée par les agents du champ. Car, par exemple, dans ces ensembles musicaux, « la gestion est du ressort exclusif du président qui, pour ce faire, s'entoure d'un véritable état-major composé « des serviteurs attachés à sa personne… des employés qu'il a embauchés ou… des favoris et des familiers qui ne sont pas propriétaires, c'est-à-dire qui ne sont pas possesseurs de plein droit des moyens de gestion… » » (Tsambu Bulu 2004:194-195). Les patrons d'orchestre sont donc, en dernier lieu, seuls détenteurs du droit d'embauche ou de révocation, sans se plier à aucune contrainte de texte.

À l'engagement d'une danseuse, il n'y a aucun texte qui puisse sanctionner cet acte alors que l'acte de suspension ou de révocation, souvent abusif, serait notifié. Ici, à la faveur peut-être de la nature spécifique d'un travail qui s'apparente au jeu et au soutien à l'éclosion des talents, l'âge de travailler pour un enfant, élevé à 16 ans[19] n'est jamais, a priori, pris en compte. Mais au sein du groupe Viva-la-Musica, par exemple, on sollicite la présence d'un parent avant de sanctionner l'engagement tacite d'une danseuse. Ce qui n'est en fait pas une condition *sine qua non*. Or là où le bât blesse, c'est lorsque certains parents, accompagnés de leur enfant, vont jusqu'à harceler le patron de Viva-la-Musica en lui proposant de la main-d'oeuvre, misant ainsi sur les opportunités de voyage en Europe pour leur fille, et sur le profit matériel à tirer de son travail. En vertu de l'article 2 de la Commission nationale de la censure des chansons et des spectacles, celle-ci se charge, entre autres, « de veiller à la sauvegarde (…) des bonnes mœurs dans les chansons et spectacles [concerts, films vidéo, DVD, etc.] produits en public ou à l'intention du public » en RDC. Ainsi ces spectacles ne doivent-ils pas « inciter à la débauche, à la prostitution (…), à la délinquance ou à toute autre tendance nuisible à la société » (Journal Officiel 1989:21). Or, au vu de l'âge des danseuses, du caractère lascif des danses qu'elles exécutent et des tenues qu'elles arborent sur scène, on ne rechignerait pas à l'idée qu'elles sont utilisées à la pornographie.[20]

La non-signature d'un contrat de travail a trouvé malicieusement, chez les patrons de groupe, une justification d'après laquelle on se demande de quel droit faut-il embrigader des gens qui exercent un métier libéral. Pareille stratégie de lutte sur le champ musical et d'accumulation du capital économique par le leader-patron peut trouver son fondement dans la jurisprudence, car aucune des parties n'a jamais tenu à respecter les clauses d'un contrat dans ce monde-à-part musical congolais. L'absence de contrat de travail qui garantisse le salaire et la sécurité sociale de l'employé ne gênerait pas l'application *a contrario* d'un principe sacré par lequel la demandeuse d'emploi est sommée de payer un montant de 30$: ce qui ressort des récits des danseuses qui ont évolué au sein de Viva-la-Musica ou sa sous-branche Percussion Molokaï.

Dans tous les groupes kinois, en dépit des propos très aménagés, bien contrôlés et teintés d'amour-propre de Nikia, Rachel et Patricia, le salaire est une fiction face à un système où les employés vivent d'expédients à l'issue d'un concert. Patricia semble dire qu'il existe, mais se gêne de donner le montant. Pour Nikia, qui se trouve dans la situation d'un groupe qui ne voyage pas encore, le « salaire mensuel n'existe pas en fait, mais plutôt la manière pour le chef de prendre soin des ses petits (...) ». Cette auto-infantilisation traduit la complicité du dominé à sa propre domination. Et en cas d'un concert sponsorisé par une société brassicole de la place, le gros du cachet revient au président-fondateur qui se taille automatiquement la part du lion. Récapitulons en disant que la réalité est telle qu'en dépit de la boulimie financière du patron, aucun groupe n'est en mesure d'assurer un salaire mensuel à son personnel, car le système en place ne le permet pas. Ce sont les opportunités de tournées internationales, les *matolo* ou *bendaski* qui aident à soigner leur look et à entretenir l'illusion. Et lorsque les tournées internationales font défaut, elles laissent place au nomadisme artistique du personnel, particulièrement des danseuses.

Par ailleurs, le travail des enfants et adolescents à des heures indues s'entache des risques du fait que non véhiculés ou non accompagnés à leur retour de travail, ils peuvent subir viol, agressions ou extorsions. Or les variétés ont tendance à se tenir la nuit. Même s'ils se produisent en « matinée », les groupes congolais sont fichés (à l'extérieur) comme n'ayant jamais du respect pour le temps dans leurs programmations scéniques. Le travail de nuit de Lomboto peut nuire à son développement physique et mental. Et pendant ou en dehors de ces spectacles, de jour comme de nuit, la consommation d'alcool (reconnue par Nikia, Rachel et Patricia) et de drogue (j'en suis témoin oculaire) pour lutter contre le tract est une pratique qui fragilise la santé physique et mentale des enfants et des adolescents, près de devenir facilement des toxicomanes.

La consommation d'alcool et d'autres drogues accroît également le risque d'être victime de violence sexuelle. Après avoir consommé de l'alcool ou de la drogue, les femmes ont plus de mal à interpréter les signes de danger et à agir en conséquence pour se protéger. La consommation d'alcool peut aussi placer les femmes dans des endroits où elles risquent plus de rencontrer un agresseur potentiel (Krug et al. 2002:175).

Exploitation économique, sexuelle et violence symbolique sur les danseuses

L'absence de salaire supra évoquée, qui justifie le système des *matolo*, constitue une des formes d'exploitation dont sont victimes les enfants et jeunes qui besognent dans la danse au sein des groupes de variétés. Malgré l'agilité qu'ont eue Rachel et Patricia à brandir respectivement les montants de 3 000 et 1 000$ rapportés d'une tournée de leurs groupes en Angola, elles n'ont pas eu le culot d'étaler au grand jour le montant de leur salaire mensuel afin de ne pas se couvrir de ridicule. L'instinct de conservation a poussé Rachel à avancer des chiffres irréels (250 $) à titre de salaire, encensant *ipso facto* son employeur. Patricia comme Hermione n'ont pas à leur tour voulu dévoiler ce qu'elles considèrent toutes comme un « secret professionnel ». La mère du petit Lomboto, pense en aparté que son fils reste victime d'une exploitation économique, même si elle se refuse à le « vendre » aux enchères.

Le récit d'un ancien membre du staff d'un groupe de variétés kinois éclaire davantage tout ce qui vient d'être évoqué sur les conditions du métier de la danse :

> À l'issue d'une séance de répétitions, on te donne 300 à 400 FC[21] et te dit que l'orchestre est un « centre de coopération ».[22] Une fois dedans, essaie de te construire un réseau de relations, un monde à toi composé des gens de l'extérieur qui de temps en temps peuvent te soutenir financièrement : C'est ton salaire car on te répète le statut institutionnel de « centre de coopération ». Alors qu'un musicien, un chanteur, visible en permanence sur le podium, ne bénéficie pas de salaire, *a fortiori* pour une fille venue en position de faiblesse. Ce qui arrive ce que les filles sont obligées d'avoir un copain à l'extérieur et un autre à l'intérieur de l'orchestre (…) Après un concert, on donne quelque chose, mais à quelle régularité se succèdent ces spectacles par mois ? Ce qu'on donne reste vraiment insignifiant. L'une des causes, c'est la faiblesse du cachet : pour un concert à la Fikin, on peut proposer au patron du groupe 1 000 à 1 500 dollars. Si tu as du succès, on te respecte ; au cas contraire, ça devient l'affaire du service de marketing du sponsor. Parce qu'en fait dans ce domaine les sponsors sont devenus eux-mêmes des producteurs camouflés chacun derrière son homme de main : jeune Kinois, courageux, à qui on demande de créer sa maison de production de façade. Suivant le programme de sponsoring de spectacles, il lui est demandé de faire une proposition des concerts mais qui soit profitable aux agents de marketing afin qu'ils défendent le projet au sein du conseil d'administration de l'entreprise-sponsor. (…). Par voie de conséquence, ils vont soutirer leur pourcentage de l'argent libéré par l'entreprise et la solde est payée au producteur qui à son tour doit aménager la part qui revient au leader du groupe à titre de cachet, 3 à 5 000 dollars. À son tour le leader va faire ses calculs : « d'abord le droit de X ». (…) X c'est lui-même en tant que patron de l'orchestre. Vous êtes 40 personnes hormis lui-même. Il retire 50 pour cent du montant et vous laisse la moitié à vous partager entre quarante personnes, en réalité entre plus que ça puisqu'il faut compter le « staff », et si ce dernier est malhonnête, il ne rétribuera pas les gens comme il faut, parce que les membres du staff ont eux-mêmes leur famille a nourrir (entretien avec Serge Makobo).

Dans la logique d'un patron de groupe pris d'abord pour idole par ses employées danseuses (cas Patricia, Nikia vis-à-vis de Papa Wemba), et dans une vie professionnelle bâtie à l'espère d'un voyage à *lola*,[23] toutes les conditions sont réunies pour subir la domination (exploitation) économique dans cette compétition autour des intérêts spécifiques du champ musical. Mais cette forme d'exploitation, économique, ne doit pas voiler une autre qui est sa conséquence et se fonde sur la violence symbolique exercée par le patron-idole et détenteur de la clé de *lola* : c'est l'exploitation sexuelle - que seules Nikia et Hermione ont avouée – de la danseuse au sein du groupe sous forme de soumission érotico-morale à l'autorité du leader avant tout et/ou de ceux qui l'entourent. Car le refus de satisfaire à la luxure du patron, pris pour idole, de se soumettre au droit de cuissage, fait miroiter la menace de licenciement, de rater son embauche ou d'exclusion de la liste de voyage pour l'Europe où sourirait la chance d'embrasser le « bonheur », sinon de (re)démarrer une carrière dans la prostitution. Nikia a réveillé la conscience publique sur une « tentative » de viol collectif des danseuses par des sbires afin, d'après l'argument brandi, d'être alignées sur la liste de voyage dans son ancien groupe. Patricia a avoué : « En cas de voyage (…), s'il est annoncé que tout le monde sera de la délégation, l'esprit d'un chacun est très serein. (…) Ça donne toujours du *kipelekese* avant la publication de la liste ». Hermione à dû traverser trois groupes à la quête de voyage pour l'Europe en dépit de la mésaventure de Brazzaville et de Douala. Rachel a indiqué que ne pas se retrouver sur la liste de voyage se vit comme un drame : « Dans les conditions où tu as beau faire preuve de talents sans jamais être du voyage, tu es prête à boire du poison ».

L'entourage du leader, le staff et les autres membres du personnel artistique et technique (parents ou familiers du leader, chanteurs et musiciens, recruteurs de danseurs, maître chorégraphe, sbires ou portiers…) une frange de dominés dans la classe de dominants, chacune des catégories sociales joue sa carte dans ce jeu érotique auquel la rue, en traitant les danseuses de *tshels*, n'est pas dupe ; car nombreuses se recrutent à partir des milieux de vie libertins : les hôtels, les night-clubs ou les foyers dissolus aux moeurs relâchées. A fleur d'âge, servant de support de marketing, de packaging de spectacle ou des vidéoclips par leur glamour ou sex-appeal qui laisse libre cours à la concupiscence que connotent déjà leurs danses sensuelles, les danseuses exercent une violence métaphorique sur le public (Tsambu Bulu 2001:23). Par conséquent, à l'intérieur ou à l'extérieur du groupe, le harcèlement sexuel, le trafic d'influence, les grossesses (in)désirables, les avortements commandités constituent le lot quotidien de la travailleuse de la danse dans les groupes de variétés à Kinshasa. Kambilo (2004), maître chorégraphe, en témoigne :

Quand elle vient vers le groupe, la fille doit au départ s'adresser à moi après avoir franchi le portail gardé par des « maîtres ». Elle passe d'abord son test avec le maître chorégraphe, mais le dernier mot reviendra au leader-patron du groupe. Dans le groupe où il est mal payé, le sbire de sécurité placé devant le portail pourra bien se jouer de la demandeuse d'emploi sans que finalement elle soit présentée auprès des responsables. Il ira jusqu'à lui exiger des faveurs sexuelles contre des promesses fallacieuses de soutenir son dossier auprès du leader. Il y a bien sûr aussi des maîtres chorégraphes qui tombent dans les mêmes travers. Le staff qui entoure le président n'en est pas non plus excepté. Car je dis que ces choses arrivent voire par les très proches du leader qui essaient de convaincre la demandeuse qu'ils talonnent le chef et vivent dans son pré-carré. Ils promettent monts et merveilles en cas de faute de travail lourde ou de voyage. Pourtant ce sont des abus que la réalité mettra à nu.

Au chapitre des coulisses du processus de recrutement et de casting, non dévoilées par les récits de nos enquêtées par amour-propre et souci de conserver leur capital symbolique (honneur), notre enquête à révélé d'autres formes de stratégies mobilisées pour capitaliser le profit sexuel du champ musical, à savoir des pratiques d'intimidations exercées sur la candidate à l'emploi, sous prétexte de rechercher sur sa peau des vergetures ou une poitrine en faillite, afin de la déshabiller moralement. Ainsi, à en croire Serge Makobo (entretien) :

> Il y a dans la foulée des filles qui, avant même d'être recrutées, auront couché avec une série d'individus. Huit filles sur dix passent sous les fourches caudines avant de bénéficier de l'emploi. Malgré le talent, si tu brilles de beauté, tout le monde dans le

groupe se précipite pour se baigner le premier [dans ton bassin] parce qu'après ce serait trop tard dès lors que le patron lui-même se serait saisi du dossier : la danseuse deviendrait alors une chasse gardée du leader obligé de prendre régulièrement sa cure de jouvence.

En octobre 2004, le procès fortement médiatisé du chanteur Koffi Olomide, accusée par ces anciennes danseuses d'avoir abusé d'elles, ne peut que conforter l'argumentation d'abus sexuels sur les danseuses qui vivent dans l'enfermement permanent ou occasionnel.[24] Et les exemples sont légion des danseuses rendues grosses par leurs patrons (potentiels proxénètes à la fois), ou les proches du patron, même si, dans de rarissimes cas, certaines ont trouvé la voie (provisoire) du mariage. D'autres ont même été mises à contribution pour rendre malléable un producteur redoutant les risques d'insuccès financier d'un spectacle à l'Olympia par exemple. En dépit du rapport de force inégal, l'exploitation sexuelle ne fonctionne toujours pas comme des abus subis mais parfois comme des stratégies mobilisées par la danseuse afin de se maintenir dans le groupe et continuer, en restant dans les grâces d'un patron hissé sur le socle d'idole, à bénéficier des profits du champ musical tels les voyages en Occident. Mais ce point de vue paraît invraisemblable.

Exploitation économique du travail de la danse par la famille

Brisons l'amnésie sur le cas *supra* évoqué de Papa Wemba qui a argumenté d'abord devant la Commission nationale de censure des chansons et spectacles, puis devant la télévision de l'encombrement humain provoqué devant le siège de son groupe par des parents qui lui apportent leurs enfants pour un poste de danseuse au sein de son groupe. Motivés par la pauvreté économique, misant sur les opportunités de voyage de leurs enfants pour l'Europe, ces parents se livrent à un trafic symbolique de leurs progénitures afin d'en tirer des dividendes sur la sueur de leur front. L'enquête a donc prouvé que les 4 enfants et jeunes travailleuses de la danse subviennent aux besoins de leur famille. Ainsi Rachel a-t-elle déclaré qu'elle prend en charge sa grand-mère, la scolarité de ses frères ou sœurs. Sans être obligée, Hermione arrive à soutenir leur foyer en cas de disette, et Patricia, logée par l'employeur, vient en aide à sa mère sur les rubriques du loyer, de la scolarité des ses cadets, outre qu'elle a meublé leur maison. Nikia pourvoit à ses besoins personnels et aux soins de sa fillette tout en soutenant occasionnellement leur famille monoparentale. Seule la raison d'âge et/ou l'absence potentielle de rétribution matérielle font que Béni Lomboto ne soit pas un petit forçat du travail de la danse au profit de sa famille (monoparentale). Néanmoins, outre que les petites enveloppes d'argent qu'il rapporte de son lieu de travail, ou de l'audience de ses parents à la mairie de la ville et au ministère des mines sont gérées par sa mère, les projections sur sa réussite financière éventuelle font déjà de Lomboto un enfant économiquement exploité par sa famille. Car il n'y a pas deux manières de comprendre la déclaration suivante de sa mère :

> Mais dans l'éventualité d'une somme d'argent importante payée en guise de salaire par son patron, je me proposerais d'aider avec ça les frères, les grands-parents, les petits-frères, la famille de Lomboto ainsi que la personne qui a prophétisé sur son avenir.

Donc, malgré la résistance qui eût existé au début, l'on voit clairement dans la plupart des cas des jeunes gens précocement programmées, consciemment ou inconsciemment, pour servir de soutien matériel à leur famille en cas de réussite financière par le travail exercé. La pauvreté des parents devient alors un des facteurs essentiels qui envoient les enfants au travail, cautionne leur exploitation et les abus dont ils sont victimes de la part de l'employeur.

Si les employeurs n'étaient pas prêts à exploiter les enfants, le travail des enfants n'existerait pas. Les parents des enfants travailleurs sont souvent au chômage ou sous-employés, recherchant désespérément un emploi et un revenu sûrs. Pourtant c'est à leurs enfants que l'on offre des emplois. Pourquoi ? Parce qu'on peut les payer moins cher, bien sûr (Enda 1997:142).

D'où l'inversion des rôles où l'on voit les enfants et jeunes au travail de la danse soutenir les ménages et la scolarité des leurs frères et sœurs, meubler la maison, payer le loyer… en lieu et place des parents. C'est donc en priorité pour le bien-être des parents que nos jeunes travailleurs de la danse s'activent alors que, comme le recommande l'Unicef, le bien-être de l'enfant « doit l'emporter sur tous les autres intérêts, y compris ceux de la famille. Le principe qui prévaut est 'les enfants d'abord' » (Enda 1997:256), comme l'a si bien chanté Félix Wazekwa (2001).

Conclusion

La présente étude sur le métier de la danse et du spectacle au sein des groupes musicaux de variétés a démontré qu'à Kinshasa les tranches sociales appelées enfants ou jeunes constituent une catégorie sociale et culturelle très dynamique. En quête (précoce) d'autonomie, d'affirmation et d'autoréalisation face à la crise sociale totale qui sévit en RDC, les jeunes Kinois, particulièrement les filles, se sont rués vers un métier qui fonctionne en toute liberté vis-à-vis des normes éthiques et professionnelles telles que codifiées par les législations internationales et nationales en matière de travail et des droits de l'enfant. Dans cette anomie sociale, les formes d'exploitation que les jeunes travailleuses de la danse subissent sont principalement d'ordres économique et sexuel, comme l'ont démontré ou effleuré les études antérieures de Kapinga, Madibwila et Ilunga.

Mais quoique tributaires de la pauvreté matérielle des parents qui tirent en partie profit du revenu professionnel précaire de leurs progénitures, les travailleuses de la danse sont loin de tomber dans l'économisme face au besoin de répondre à une vocation (voir leurs premiers débuts ludiques à la danse) et à la quête de célébrité qui guident au départ le choix du métier, en plein cursus scolaire ou pas. D'où l'impératif de relativiser les motivations économiques et de renforcer la tendance vers la réalisation d'une vocation artistique et du rêve (endormi) de l'Eldorado occidental. C'est dans ce contexte qu'il sied de comprendre l'émotion de la *Fioti-fioti* Patricia (non comprise dans l'échantillon) qui déclarait : « L'Europe me plaît beaucoup, il y a des gens de toutes les races ici. Je remercie Papa Wemba parce qu'il m'a amené (sic) en Europe pour la danse, je ne croyais pas dans ma vie qu'un jour je poserais le pied ici. » (www.fioti. free.fr).

Aussi, dans ce métier du showbiz très fréquenté par les filles, où le corps fait partie de capital, l'utilisation du corps manipulé physiquement (piercing du nez et/ou du nombril, tatouages, maquillages) et virtuellement (effets spéciaux), du sex-appeal et du travail de la danseuse dans les vidéoclips et à la télévision, plutôt que de paraître comme une force de travail non rétribuée, est perçue comme du loisir soft par le consommateur qui oublie l'effort physique engagé et investi par la danseuse. Elle (utilisation) procure cependant un capital symbolique à l'intéressée en terme de starisation à partir de laquelle elle pourra se construire un capital économique à travers les *matolo*, si dérisoires soient-ils, ou dans une prostitution à peine camouflée. En d'autres termes, le rêve des lendemains meilleurs en termes d'opportunités de voyage pour l'Europe mythifiée, la célébrité et le prestige immédiats gagnés grâce aux médias (télévision, vidéoclips) favorisent dans la durée l'exploitation économique et sexuelle des danseuses au sein et en dehors des groupes musicaux qui les emploient. En définitive, il n'est pas loin de qualifier de pire forme de travail[25] l'inféodation des danseuses à la luxure du patron, lui-même potentiel proxénète devant un public séduit par leurs attraits physiques et performances musico-scéniques qu'il croit transposables sur d'autres scènes de la vie.

Les leurres et le caractère ambulant de ce métier sont tels qu'ils détournent les enfants et jeunes de l'école, ce qui affaiblit davantage leur position au sein du champ musical, les condamne à la pauvreté intellectuelle au point de ne pas disposer des stratégies nécessaires pour la conquête des intérêts spécifiques du champ. Ils ne disposent alors que de leur talent naturel et/ou de leur sex-appeal. À la fin de leur carrière, de surcroît très éphémère, les danseuses éprouvent alors de la peine à se resocialiser. Certaines se sont converties en serveuses de café en Europe, d'autres se sont recyclés sur les carrières de diamant à Lunda Norte (Angola), nombreuses (re)deviennent filles-mères.

Par ailleurs, il faut savoir établir les limites exactes entre travail et encadrement des jeunes talents. Les enfants danseurs qui s'engagent trop tôt à mener une vie d'adulte (travail de nuit) risquent un déséquilibre psychologique et social en l'absence d'un encadrement conséquent. Cette critique est nuancée par l'argumentation très logique de la vedette Félix Wazekwa au sujet de Béni Lomboto qui s'essaie déjà au chant en dehors de la danse :

> Dans l'art nous avons les aveugles et les infirmes. Même dans les cirques, on voit les animaux amuser le public, mais l'on ne dira pas pourtant « pourquoi exploite-t-on les animaux qui devraient rester dans leur site naturel ? ». On naît avec le talent. Et c'est vrai qu'à Kinshasa nous ne sommes pas habitués à encourager les talents. C'est un enfant qui pourra grandir avec son talent. À l'âge adulte, il fera son chemin. S'il sera musicien, il n'aura pas opéré un mauvais choix. C'est de l'art! Prenons l'exemple du chanteur Wendo [80 ans en 2005], nous devrions encore nous dire : « Pourquoi faisons-nous chanter un vieux ? » Or dans le domaine de l'art, il a sa place (...). De même dans la peinture on ne s'insurgera pas contre l'exposition d'un tableau réalisé par un enfant ou un vieux ! Beaucoup de carrières s'arrêtent à 30-35 ans comme en foot, mais en musique on arrive jusqu'à 90 ans, pourvu qu'on garde la maîtrise de son art (...) (Wazekwa 2004).

En somme, cause de déperdition scolaire, la musique joue aussi bien un rôle socialisateur. « On note le cas d'enfants de [la rue] qui se sont 'recyclés', l'espace d'un matin, dans la musique et se sont produits comme danseurs en Europe » (Tsambu Bulu 2004:208). Certaines danseuses ont réussi à se construire de la renommée et à ramener voitures et biens matériels de leurs voyages professionnels en Occident. Néanmoins, le rôle socialisateur de la musique ne doit pas nous imposer un silence sur la réalité, quand elle apparaît abjecte, du travail des enfants et jeunes dans la danse et le spectacle au sein des groupes musicaux de variétés. A ce titre, je formule quelques suggestions qui, loin de condamner en bloc ce travail, doivent plutôt penser à le repenser et à le règlementer selon les normes en vigueur et le contexte social et culturel spécifique en RDC. Pour ce faire, je propose la création des clubs et écoles de danse qui loueraient les services ou d'où l'on recruterait les danseuses (enfants, adolescentes) le temps d'un spectacle, d'un tournage de clips, et ce sous l'autorité morale du responsable du club ou de l'école. Ce dernier est censé accompagner l'équipe en cas de déplacement du groupe hors du pays. On éviterait alors de considérer la danse, la musique comme un métier de raccourci dans la vie. Le respect obligatoire d'un minimum de degré de scolarité classique (6 années primaires) avant de fréquenter l'école de danse. Je préconise en même temps la réglementation du travail en matière d'éthique et du contrat qui devrait fixer le salaire payable aux parents pour les enfants de moins de 16 ans. À la Commission nationale de censure des chansons et spectacles de veiller aux heures, au contenu et à la diffusion des spectacles où interviennent des enfants et adolescents comme chanteurs, musiciens, animateurs ou danseurs. Mais l'inefficacité partielle d'une pareille mesure se trouve dans l'hypertélédiffusion des clips internationaux qui frisent le strip-tease et dont les enfants et adolescents se comptent parmi les fidèles consommateurs. L'interdiction de la consommation d'alcool et de drogue aux jeunes artistes devrait rimer avec celle d'utiliser le spectacle d'enfants et adolescents dans les spots publicitaires sur les boissons alcoolisées et la nicotine. Je pense aussi qu'il faille appliquer les textes légaux internationaux tels que ratifiés par l'État congolais sur les droits et le travail de l'enfant. D'où le besoin immédiat pour la RDC de se doter d'un code de protection de l'enfant afin de combler le vide juridique en la matière. Mais en définitive, toutes ces mesures ne seront porteuses d'effets qu'à partir d'une lutte tous azimuts contre la pauvreté socioéconomique et intellectuelle de la population, et de l'encadrement efficient des enfants au foyer ou sans foyer, à l'école et pendant les vacances.

Notes

1. L'expression *fioti-fioti*, tirée de la langue kikongo, a pour synonyme ici *kamoke* en swahili. Littéralement elle signifie « très petite » à cause de l'âge de ces petites filles prostituées qu'elle sert à désigner. Mais il a fallu attendre que Papa Wemba popularise l'expression à travers le phénomène des filles mineures danseuses au point de faire des « Fioti-fioti » une marque déposée.
2. Les filles aux seins fermes, expression empruntée à la profession diamantaire pour identifier des gemmes très petites (De Boeck 2004:177). Cette définition est complétée

par celle de la danseuse Patricia dans son récit. Les *Nyonyo* sont plus jeunes que les *Fioti-fioti*, une génération qu'elles ont remplacée. Pour Patricia Kasa, « *Nyonyo* signifie les petits cristaux de diamant. Nous sommes de très petites filles, qui exhibent des danses simples, capables d'emballer même les patrons dans leur costume-cravate. Nous disons encore *Nyonyo* parce que jamais ces cristaux ne se vendent isolement, mais en vrac afin qu'ils gagnent en poids. Voilà pourquoi nous dansons toujours en équipe de dix » (Entretien).

3. D'après l'article 1 de la Convention Internationale des Droits de l'Enfant, par exemple, l'« enfant s'entend de tout être humain âgé de moins de dix-huit ans, sauf si la majorité est atteinte si tôt, en vertu de la législation qui lui est applicable » (http://www.droitsenfant.com/cide.htm).
4. Il avait ouvert la porte à la femme afin de lui permettre de jouer un rôle plus substantiel dans les groupes musicaux.
5. Expression argotique pour dire : ça me transporte vers un autre état.
6. Ce sont les sbires qui existent dans tous les groupes musicaux. Ils ont une formation dans les arts martiaux – d'où le qualificatif de « maître » – et sont proposés à la sécurité de la résidence du leader, du leader (garde du corps), du siège du groupe et de ses membres. Le leader peut les utiliser pour les basses besognes telles qu'aller semer le désordre dans le camp opposé, passer au tabac un dissident. Ce qui justifie aussi leur ancienne appellation de « gorilles ».
7. Siège artistique de Papa Wemba, au 42A, rue Kanda-Kanda. À l'image de la République de Kalakuta du Nigérian Fela, Papa Wemba va créer en 1977 le Village Molokaï en plein Matonge en forgeant un acronyme à partir de quelques noms de rue de son quartier : Masimanimba, Oshwe, Lokolama, Kanda-Kanda, Inzia. On est donc loin des îles Molokaï de Père Damien et ses lépreux.
8. Je suis d'une science animale dans le domaine de la mode.
9. Autre nom de scène de Papa Wemba.
10. Résidence du leader, siège du groupe et lieu où se déroulent les séances de répétitions de Victoria Eleison. C'est, par souci de globalisation, un rapprochement onirique avec le monde américain médiatisé par Hollywood à travers, notamment, la série télévisée *Dallas* qui avait connu un succès retentissant à la télévision congolaise en 1982-1983.
11. Sobriquet tiré de son prénom Lambert. Il est maître chorégraphe, créateur, formateur et encadreur des *Fioti-fioti* et des *Nyonyo* dans le groupe de Papa Wemba dont il assumait symboliquement la présidence jusqu'à sa dissidence en 2005.
12. Que chacun tire son épingle du jeu ; que chacun s'en aille là où il trouvera mieux.
13. Variété de sens ou de catégories pour désigner la prostitution féminine. Cf. le texte de José Bazonzi : « Problématique de la prostitution infanto-juvénile à Kinshasa : cas des 'tshels' ».
14. Ça dépasse toujours mon entendement.
15. Libéralités financières obtenues par voie qui frise la mendicité. Au sein du groupe Cultur'A Pays-Vie, on fait surtout usage du terme *bendaski*, du lingala *kobenda* : tirer, soutirer (de la poche d'autrui, mais pas à son insu).
16. Terme du lingala argotique pour dire : ne pas savoir à quel saint se vouer.
17. Forgé du kikongo (*nkila*) et de l'italien (*grosso*), ce terme signifie littéralement grosse queue. La gestuelle de la danse et l'état orgasmique qu'elle évoque font penser que cette queue n'est rien d'autre que le phallus.
18. Cf. note 3.

19. Cf. l'avant- projet du code de protection de l'enfant congolais (Secrétariat permanent du Conseil national de l'Enfant, Direction de la protection de l'enfance au Ministère de la condition féminine et famille, débaptisé, en 2008, Genre, enfant et famille.
20. Le protocole facultatif onusien à la Convention relative aux droits de l'enfant, concernant la vente d'enfants, la prostitution des enfants et la pornographie, du 26 juin 2000, définit à son article 2c la « pornographie mettant en scène des enfants toute représentation, par quelque moyen que ce soit, d'un enfant s'adonnant à des activités sexuelles explicites, réelles ou simulées, ou toute représentation des organes sexuels d'un enfant, à des fins principalement sexuelles » (www.droitsdel'homme-france.org).
21. ±2$US en novembre 2004, soit 1$=380FC.
22. Dans le sens où le terme « coopération », devenu « coop » en lingala argotique, signifie opération suspecte, illicite ou informelle dans le contexte de lutte pour la survie et de la débrouille au quotidien en RDC.
23. Paradis, tel quel les Kinois mythifient l'Europe.
24. Il arrive que les danseuses soient logées chez l'employeur, et vivent ainsi sous la protection de sa garde rapprochée censée se comporter en eunuques. Cette formule d'enfermement est presque d'application chez tous les leaders de groupe en cas de séjour européen pour éviter l'évasion d'une fille, ou lors du « maquis » (période de travail ardu à huis clos qui généralement précède la sortie d'un nouveau groupe ou d'un groupe reformé), et inclut alors le personnel artistique du groupe dans son ensemble.
25. la Convention sur les pires formes du travail des enfants (Genève 1999) les définit à l'article 3d comme « les travaux qui, par leur nature ou les conditions dans lesquelles ils s'exercent, sont susceptibles de nuire à la santé, à la sécurité ou à la moralité de l'enfant ». (http://www.droitsenfant.com/telecharge/pires-formes-travail-1999pdf.pdf).

Références

Biaya, T., K., 2002, *Enfant en situation de conflit armé et de violence urbaine*. Bibliographie annotée et signalétique, Série des monographies, Dakar: CODESRIA, 63 p.

De Boeck, F., 2004, « Être shege à Kinshasa : les enfants, la rue et le monde occulte », in Theodore Trefon (éd), *Ordre et désordre à Kinshasa. Réponses populaires à la faillite de l'État*, Cahiers Africains n° 61-62, Tervuren, Paris: MRAC/ L'Harmattan, pp.173-191.

De Boeck, F. et Honwana, A. (éd.), 2000, « Enfants, jeunes et politique », *Politique africaine*, n° 80, décembre, 110 p.

De Villers, G. et Omasombo Tshonda, J. (éds.), 1997, *Zaïre. La transition manquée (1990-1997)*, Tervuren/Paris: Institut Africain-CEDAF/L'Harmattan. (Cahiers Africains, n° 27-28-29), 302 p.

Enda T. M., 1997, *Emploi, travail et droit de l'enfant. « Dossier documentaire »*, Dakar: Enda-La Documentation Centrale, 332 p.

Entretien avec Kambilo Kasongo, Kinshasa, 25 décembre 2004.

Entretien avec Serge Makobo, Kinshasa, 24 novembre 2004.

Entretiens avec Rachel Omole et avec sa famille, 4 décembre 2004.

Entretien avec Nikia Masumbuku Miezi, Kinshasa, 4 décembre 2004.

Entretien avec Patricia Kasa, Kinshasa, 24 décembre 2004.

Entretiens avec Bijou et Béni Lomboto, 23 décembre 2004.

Entretien avec Hermione, 24 décembre 2004.

Focus group avec les parents de Reagan, Kinshasa, le 27 décembre 2004.

Inswan Sabakar, F., 2004, *Impact de la musique congolaise moderne sur l'éducation de la jeunesse kinoise*, Travail de fin de cycle, Faculté des Sciences Sociales, Administratives et Politiques, Département de Sociologie et Anthropologie, Université de Kinshasa, manuscrit en cours.

Journal Officiel de la République du Zaïre, « Ordonnance n° 89-091 du 12 mai 1989 portant création d'une Commission Nationale de Censure des Chansons et Spectacles », in *Journal Officiel de la République du Zaïre*, n° 10 du 15 mai 1989.

Kambilo, K., entretien à Kinshasa, 7 décembre 2004.

Krug, E. G., Dahlberg, L. L., Mercy, J. A., Zwi, A. et Lozano-Ascenscio R. (ed), 2002, *Rapport mondial sur la violence et la santé*, Genève: OMS, 376 p.

« Le travail des enfants », http://www.droitsenfant.com/travail_ampleur.htm , 7 mars 2008.

Lizadeel (ed.), 2003, *Situation des droits de l'enfant en République Démocratique du Congo*, Kinshasa: Lizadeel, 66 p.

Madibwila Itumba, P., 2003, *Étude sociologique du travail de danseuse dans la musique congolaise moderne*, Travail de fin de cycle, Faculté des Sciences Sociales, Administratives et Politiques, Département de Sociologie et Anthropologie, Université de Kinshasa, 44 p.

Manimba, N., 2000, *L'impact de la fille danseuse dans la société kinoise*, Travail de fin de cycle, Faculté de Psychologie et Sciences de l'Éducation, Département de Psychologie, Université de Kinshasa, inédit.

Sillamy, N., 1979, *Dictionnaire de la psychologie*, Paris: Librairie Larousse, coll. Les dictionnaires de l'homme du XXe siècle, 319 p.

Stewart, G., 2000, *Rumba on the River. A History of the Popular Music of the Two Congos*, London, New York: Verso, 436 p.

Tsambu Bulu, L., 2001, « Les images sociomentales de la femme dans la musique congolaise moderne », *Alternative*, n° 007, Kinshasa, pp. 19-24.

Tsambu Bulu, L., 2004, « Musique et violence à Kinshasa », in Théodore Trefon (éd), *Ordre et désordre à Kinshasa. Réponses populaires à la faillite de l'État*, Cahiers Africains n° 61-62, Tervuren, Paris: MRAC/ L'Harmattan, pp. 193-212.

Tshisekedi, I. K., 2002, *Situation des adolescentes danseuses d'orchestres modernes de Kinshasa*, Travail de fin de cycle, Faculté de Psychologie et Sciences de l'Education, Département des Sciences de l'Education, Université de Kinshasa, inédit.

Wazekwa, F., 2001, « Les enfants d'abord », CD *Signature*, JPS Productions, Paris.

Wazekwa, F., 2004, « Entretien sur Tropicana TV », Kinshasa, 7 novembre.

www.droitsenfant.com/cide.htm, *Convention Internationale des Droits de l'Enfant.*

www.droitsenfant.com/telecharge/pires-formes-travail-1999pdf.pdf.29, *Convention sur les pires formes du travail des enfants (Genève 1999).*

www.droitsdel'homme-france.org, *Protocole facultatif à la Convention relative aux droits de l'enfant, concernant la vente d'enfants, la prostitution des enfants et la pornographie mettant en scène des enfants, fait New York le 25 mai 2000.*

www.fioti. free.fr. 17 avril 2004.

12

Conclusion

Osita Agbu

The contents of this volume on children and youth in the labour process in Africa clearly indicate that though children have engaged in work activities in Africa within their communities for centuries, the mode, nature and scope of this engagement in the twenty-first century has become of great concern to many, including governments and civil society. Though the centrality of labour in life cannot be overstated and one participates in his or her society through work, the current trend in which children and youth are exploited in the labour process in Africa gives great cause for concern. The experiences from Tanzania, Kenya, Congo DRC, Nigeria, Ghana, Senegal, Morocco and other countries in Africa paint a picture of the fact that children are under pressure to work and not living out their role as children. Many children in Africa are increasingly engaged in hazardous or what the ILO defines as Worst Forms of Child Labour, and this situation could get worse unless the economic conditions and social arrangements encouraging this situation are comprehensively addressed. Worse still is the type of future that awaits children and youth!

Right from the beginning of this compendium, the authors have tried to present and expose the various facets and dimensions of child labour in Africa, especially in the present century. There is very little doubt that the nature and character of the current phase of globalization has worsened rather than constrained the transmutation from child work to child labour. The complexity of today's world, including the advancement in communications technology and travel time, means that the rate at which nefarious individuals and cartels that indulge in child labour, for instance, operate, is much widened and deepened. The present triumph of capitalism as a mode of production and the strangulation of communalism and social welfarism as organizing concepts of the collective good have served to jeopardize the situation of children and youth in Africa. Against this background, we need to re-examine the kind of education and schooling that we have today in Africa. Is it better than what we had before in terms of the collective betterment of our societies? Are we being educated to serve our societies or to serve globalization and capitalism? How does this development impact on the lives of children?

Based on the experiences and lessons from the trafficking of children, and their utilization as cheap sources of labour, several interventions have been proposed, and many are presently under implementation. For instance, there are efforts to stop the trafficking of children both within and across countries, and to improve access to basic services for children and youth, including access to health, nutrition, education and income-generating activities. These are being pursued through advocacy, partnerships with NGOs, sensitization of the public, capacity-building initiatives for field officers involved in helping these children, as well as the review of data and information about child labour, of which this book could be a good source.

In many of the cases of child exploitation in the labour process examined here, the most practical recommendation, at least in the long run, is the necessity for a strategy that will economically address the structural basis that creates the environment for child exploitation in relation to labour. This is as against recommendations that proffer legislative measures alone, and fall short in examining the underlying factors that have contributed to the problem. Beginning from the 1990s, child trafficking, for instance, was virtually treated as a new phenomenon with various legislative measures enacted. However, it was not long before it was realized that legislative measures alone, and even addressing poverty at its face value, were not enough to tackle the menace of child trafficking. Indeed, it was also realized that the causes of child labour are more complex than just poverty. While it is important to understand the economic structure and the political economy of a particular society in seeking solutions, with emphasis on production relations one should also not overlook the socio-cultural and psychological factors, some of which have proven to be obstacles to addressing the problem.

A major observation from the studies encapsulated in this book is that governments in Africa are yet to pay the kind of attention that is required in addressing the problem of child labour. These governments are yet to address the contemporary issues and conditions that affect the welfare of children and the youth. The problem is even more compounded in situations of conflict, as in Angola, Congo DRC, Liberia and Sierra Leone. From the experiences of the children, they literally became commodities to be bought and sold for diverse purposes, ranging from cheap labour to sexual toys and even providers of human spare parts. And the height of this exploitation is the fact that the transactions were not for their benefit, but to the benefit of their adult exploiters. We do indeed have a very serious problem in our hands – a development that requires a complex of innovative and practical measures to be addressed. Economic, political, socio-cultural and historical factors may all need to be invoked, depending on the geographical location and character of the child exploitation. This implies a multiplicity of actors, including governments, NGOs and community-based organizations (CBOs) as well as private individuals.

Child labour is about child rights and the rights of human beings engaged in a relationship in which they have little bargaining power. The dominant mode of production and reproduction – capitalism in its present manifestation – has stripped the child in disadvantaged parts of the world of his or her childhood. There is hence the need for legal and social protection for children and youth. There is also a need to pay greater attention to the legislation on children and their protection and how the laws could be better domesticated. African governments are enjoined to take more seriously the implementation of these laws. In Africa, efforts at addressing poverty and the push and pull factors fuelling child labour should be at the core of government's interests. Civil society, which has been much engaged around the continent, should also strive to understand the conceptual foundations and manifestations of child labour and distill appropriate strategies to address the problem in context.

Our hope is that this book would have served its purpose if it contributes to exposing the dimensions and adding to our understanding of the experiences of children and youth in the labour process in Africa. Often taken for granted or simply absent from the consciousness of Africa's leaders and civil society, the problem of child labour also indicates the extent of the development crises in Africa, and should be addressed in tandem with other major issues bedevilling the continent. The onus lies with all and sundry, especially governments that wield the instruments of legislation, the international community, international and local civil society groups, and rural communities of Africa to embark on concrete measures singly and collectively that will address the problem of children being engaged in hazardous work, and also protecting those that are already involved, whatever the reason.

www.ingramcontent.com/pod-product-compliance
Lightning Source LLC
Chambersburg PA
CBHW072120020426
42334CB00018B/1657